iOS Development at Scale

App Architecture and Design Patterns for Mobile Engineers

Eric Vennaro

Apress®

iOS Development at Scale: App Architecture and Design Patterns for Mobile Engineers

Eric Vennaro
San Francisco, CA, USA

ISBN-13 (pbk): 978-1-4842-9455-0   ISBN-13 (electronic): 978-1-4842-9456-7
https://doi.org/10.1007/978-1-4842-9456-7

Managing Director, Apress Media LLC: Welmoed Spahr
Acquisitions Editor: Miriam Haidara
Development Editor: James Markham
Editorial Assistant: Jessica Vakili

Cover image designed by eStudioCalamar

Distributed to the book trade worldwide by Springer Science+Business Media New York, 1 New York Plaza, Suite 4600, New York, NY 10004-1562, USA. Phone 1-800-SPRINGER, fax (201) 348-4505, e-mail orders-ny@springer-sbm.com, or visit www.springeronline.com. Apress Media, LLC is a California LLC and the sole member (owner) is Springer Science + Business Media Finance Inc (SSBM Finance Inc). SSBM Finance Inc is a **Delaware** corporation.

For information on translations, please e-mail booktranslations@springernature.com; for reprint, paperback, or audio rights, please e-mail bookpermissions@springernature.com.

Apress titles may be purchased in bulk for academic, corporate, or promotional use. eBook versions and licenses are also available for most titles. For more information, reference our Print and eBook Bulk Sales web page at http://www.apress.com/bulk-sales.

Any source code or other supplementary material referenced by the author in this book is available to readers on GitHub (github.com/apress). For more detailed information, please visit https://www.apress.com/gp/services/source-code.

Paper in this product is recyclable

*To Steph for her unwavering love and support.
And to Nick for his inspiration and help throughout
the process.*

Table of Contents

About the Author

 **Eric Vennaro** is a tech lead at Meta, where he has a track record of delivering high-impact, technically complex projects across mobile, web, and back-end infrastructure. He is interested in applied machine learning and privacy, especially the intersection of improving privacy using machine learning–backed integrity tooling. While working on the iOS platform and recruiting new iOS engineers, Eric noticed a gap in the existing literature for mobile engineering best practices and architectural principles at scale. To address this gap, he decided to write this book using his experience in leading mobile projects. Before working at Meta, Eric founded his own company and worked at Stitch Fix during its explosive growth phase and subsequent IPO.

About the Technical Reviewers

Mezgani Ali is a doctor in God sciences and religious studies and a Ph.D. student in transmissions, telecommunications, IoT, and artificial intelligence (National Institute of Posts and Telecommunications in Rabat). He likes technology, reading, and his little daughter Ghita. Mezgani's first program was a horoscope in BASIC in 1993, and he has done a lot of work on the infrastructure side in system engineering, software engineering, managed networks, and security.

Mezgani has worked for NIC France, Capgemini, HP, and Orange, where he was part of the Site Reliability Engineer's (SRE) team. He is also the creator of the functional and imperative programming language PASP.

Mezgani is the founder of and researcher at Native LABS, Inc., which manufactures next-generation infrastructures with a great interest in Internet protocols and security appliances.

Vishwesh Ravi Shrimali graduated from BITS Pilani in 2018, where he studied mechanical engineering. Currently, he is working at Mercedes-Benz AG as a development engineer. He has also authored multiple books on data science and AI. When he is not writing blogs or working on projects, he likes to go on long walks or play his acoustic guitar.

Introduction

This book will teach you how to build mobile applications that will scale for millions of users while growing your career to the staff and principal levels.

The book is structured to mirror an engineer's career path and maps the career stages to the tools needed for success at each one. We start with the basics of engineering covered with a Swift language focus; however, most fundamentals are applicable beyond the Swift programming language. This is by design because, over time, frameworks and languages will come and go (SwiftUI, obj-c), but the fundamental concepts underlying them will not. Understanding these basic concepts allows you to apply them to changing environments and efficiently learn new tools – an even more critical skill at scale because many large companies write custom implementations. Understanding the fundamentals marks the first stage of a software engineer's career and the first part of this book.

The book's second part will discuss building better applications using design patterns and application architecture principles. Mastering iOS application architecture and fundamental design patterns is critical for reaching the senior engineer level. At this stage, you are most likely capable of managing your own work autonomously and can help junior engineers ramp up on the fundamental aspects of application development. This is where most books stop, but this is only the career midpoint, and technical skills alone will not take you beyond senior engineer.

While technical depth is the most important and transferable aspect, engineers also need a breadth of experience, including top-notch communication skills – the focus of the book's third part. In this part, we will explore several areas of breadth for software engineers, including a focus on communication, leadership, mentorship, and experimentation. These skills will help you to understand what projects to push for and how to achieve them by working collaboratively across a large team. Here, you will leverage the engineering fundamentals and combine them with a broader skill set required for working at scale.

Parts one, two, and three of this book mirror an engineer's career path from junior to senior engineer. You need the skills from each part to reach the next level, but your career becomes more open-ended after reaching senior. You can go into management, or you can expand your breadth of knowledge and combine that with the depth you possess in mobile applications to accelerate up the individual contributor career track.

This book is tailored for individuals who want to become well-rounded developers, often called the "t-shaped" developer and illustrated in Figure 1. This model consists of the depth of knowledge (iOS fundamentals and design patterns) and breadth consisting of experimentation, software project management, testing, release cycle management, and soft skills. Soft skills such as communication and leadership techniques are given great importance, as they are crucial for driving progress and leading a team. The book concludes with Part 4 including a practical example that demonstrates how to apply the concepts learned throughout the book to advance in your career.

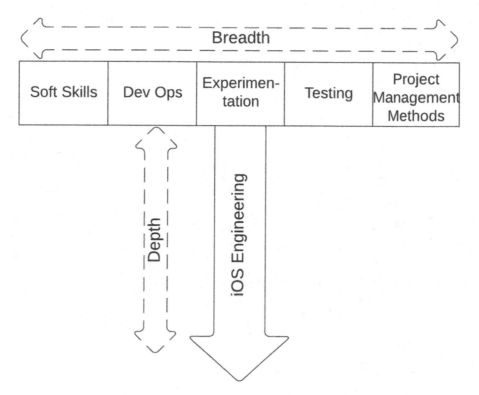

Figure 1. *Example t-shaped developer modeled through this book's chapters*

PART I

General Apple System Knowledge

CHAPTER 1

Swift Familiarization

This chapter aims to provide the reader with the tools and knowledge to architect application components and serve as a familiarization for future sections that reference the types outlined here. We will go over structs, classes, protocols, and generics. This chapter is not a detailed overview of every Swift type and language feature. For that, please refer to the official Apple documentation.

This Chapter Includes

1. A first look into evaluating engineering trade-offs. This chapter covers the most basic level of evaluating engineering trade-offs. More complex situations discussed later in the book involve product requirements, timelines, and cross-functional concerns.

2. For those less familiar with the Apple ecosystem or still primarily using Objective-C, this chapter serves as a Swift primer covering the basic types and structures referenced in later sections.

© Eric Vennaro 2023

E. Vennaro, *iOS Development at Scale*, https://doi.org/10.1007/978-1-4842-9456-7_1

Structures and Classes

We will start by reviewing structures (structs) and classes. Structs and classes are general-purpose, flexible constructs that are the building blocks for your program's code. In Swift, classes and structs are both used to construct instances; however, the class is still what is thought of when constructing an object in the traditional object-oriented sense.

Note   Object-oriented programming is a programming style where classes are created to model real-world objects with both state and behavior. An object is an instance of a class where the state is composed of the properties of the class, and the behaviors are the things that it does (the methods).

The following code sample outlines the basic structure of a class. It models a Dog, including properties that make up the state and methods that make up the behavior of our Dog object. This code sample, as well as others in this chapter, is run via a playground. The chapter's playground is also included in the associated code repository for the book.

```swift
// import foundation for usage with NSDate
import Foundation

enum DogBreed {
    case other
    case germanShepard
    case bizon
    case husky
}
class Dog {
    // parameters - part of the state.
    // the dog's name
```

```swift
var name: String
// the dog's breed, which could control barking volume
var breed: DogBreed
// when the dog was last fed, updates when the dog is fed
var lastFed: Date?

// initializer
init(name: String,
     breed: DogBreed,
     lastFed: Date? ) {
    self.name = name
    self.breed = breed
    self.lastFed = lastFed
}

// method - part of the behavior
// setting the time fed to time now
func feed() {
  lastFed = Date()
}

// method - part of the behavior
func bark() {
  switch (breed) {
    case .germanShepard:
      print("barking loud")
    default:
      print("barking moderate")
  }
}
}
```

```swift
let dog = Dog(name: "Steve",
              breed: .germanShepard,
              lastFed: nil)
dog.bark()
```

Similarly, we could model this behavior with a struct:

```swift
struct DogStruct {
  var name: String
  var breed: DogBreed
  var lastFed: Date?

  init(name: String,
       breed: DogBreed,
       lastFed: Date? ) {
    self.name = name
    self.breed = breed
    self.lastFed = lastFed
  }

  // method - part of the behavior
  // setting the time fed to time now
  func feed() {
    lastFed = Date()
  }

  // method - part of the behavior
  func bark() {
    switch (breed) {
      case .germanShepard:
        print("barking loud")
```

```
    default:
       print("barking moderate")
    }
  }
}
```

From the preceding code samples, it would appear that classes and structs are the same; however, they have many differences that stem from how they are managed in memory. Classes are reference types, while structs are value types. For value types, such as structs, each instance keeps a unique copy of its own data. Other value types include enums, arrays, strings, dictionaries, and tuples. In contrast to value types, reference types share a single copy of the data and reference that copy via a pointer. The only reference type in Swift is the class; however, everything inheriting from NSObject is a reference type, meaning that iOS engineers will interact with both value and reference types, and being familiar with them is a must.

In addition to the lower-level differences between value and reference types that are discussed in the next chapter, the two tangible changes at the application level are as follows:

1. Value types protect the programmer from unintended mutation due to the differences between reference and value semantics.

2. Classes can additionally utilize inheritance.

Exploring Reference and Value Types

To understand better how value types protect engineers from an unintended mutation in their code, the following example walks through creating both a struct and class and evaluates modifying them. The example will investigate what happens when a parameter (in this case, the name) is modified after the initial object is created.

```
var dogClass = Dog(name: "Esperanza",
                   breed: .bizon,
                   lastFed: nil)
var refDog = dogClass
refDog.name = "hope"
// False - we have a reference type
print(dogClass.name != refDog.name ?
    "True - we have a value type" :
    "False - we have a reference type")

var dogStruct = DogStruct(name: "Esperanza",
                          breed: .bizon,
                          lastFed: nil)
var valDog = dogStruct
valDog.name = "hope"
// True - we have a value type
print(dogStruct.name != valDog.name ?
    "True - we have a value type" :
    "False - we have a reference type")
```

When utilizing a class, it was possible to change the dog's name for the initial variable; however, with the struct, it was not. In practice, this extra layer of protection protects against unintended mutations. The protection from unintentional modification is especially helpful in ensuring thread safety. Even so, value types are not entirely safe because it is possible to add a reference type inside a value type. When a reference type is added inside a value type such as adding a class instance to an array (a value type), the class (reference type) is modifiable. The following example explores how this could happen:

```
var dog1 = Dog(name: "Esperanza",
               breed: .bizon,
               lastFed: nil)
```

```
var dog2 = Dog(name: "Bella",
               breed: .germanShepard,
               lastFed: nil)
let arr = [dog1, dog2]
var dTemp = arr[0]
// Esparanzabadvalue!
arr[0].name.append("badvalue!")
print(dTemp.name)
```

Apple has mentioned this in their documentation as unintended sharing. That said, it's not always unintended; sometimes, sharing is necessary to maintain shared storage for efficiency reasons. Even in this situation, best practices dictate adding some optimizations to prevent any unintended side effects from changing state. This optimization is referred to as the copy-on-write optimization (before writing, the instance is copied, and the write occurs on the copy).

So far, we have gone over reference and value types; however, the iOS ecosystem introduces some additional complexities in how values/objects express their typing. Apple refers to this as value and reference semantics. An example of this is using the let keyword. By utilizing the let keyword, we can get a reference type to express a bit of value semantics. To do this, we create an instance of our Dog class from earlier only this time with the let keyword. Now it is impossible to mutate the instance itself (dog4 = dog5); however, it is possible to change the name property.

```
let dog4 = Dog(name: "Esperanza",
               breed: .bizon,
               lastFed: nil)
dog4.name = "test"
let dog5 = dog4
dog4.name = "Max"
print("Dog4: \(dog4.name) Dog5: \(dog5.name)")
// dog4 = dog5 - error cannot assign to a let constant
```

Note   For reference types, let means the reference must remain constant. In other words, you cannot change the instance that the constant references, but you can mutate the instance itself.

For value types, let means the instance must remain constant. No properties of the instance will ever change, regardless of whether the property is declared with let or var.

Interestingly, immutable reference types can have value semantics. While they are reference types, they have value semantics when made immutable because they behave like values in that no one else can modify them. This behavior aligns with Apple's guidance and push toward using value types and semantics.

This behavior also implies that types have value semantics relative to their access level. This is because a variable exhibits value semantics if the only way to modify its value is through that variable itself. So, if a type has a file-private access modifier on something related to the type, then it is only accessible by code defined in the same file. Conversely, if the variable is not file-private, code written outside the same file could modify it.

Summarizing Value and Reference Types

Breaking down the behaviors we have seen for value and reference types:

1. If dealing with a simple struct, value semantics are guaranteed by default.

2. If dealing with a struct containing composite properties (composite value type), it is necessary to ensure they also exhibit value semantics.

3. If dealing with a class (reference type), it will have reference semantics by default. However, making the class immutable using the let keyword and constant properties will cause the class to exhibit value semantics. Again, the properties of the class and those properties themselves must have value semantic types.

In general, value types are copied, whereas reference types get new references to the same underlying object. For reference types, this means that mutations are visible to everything with a reference, whereas mutations to value types only affect the storage you're mutating. However, it is possible to make reference types immutable, which helps to insulate the program from unintended changes in state. When choosing between a value and a reference type, consider how suitable your type is for copying (value type). Consider first using a value type for copyable types, and when using reference types, consider utilizing immutability.

Inheritance for Classes

Inheritance in Swift is uniquely reserved for classes. Similar to other languages, inheritance allows classes to utilize methods, properties, and other characteristics from another class. When one class inherits from another, it is called the subclass, and the class it inherits from is the superclass. The behavior of inheriting from another class is often referred to as subclassing. A class that does not inherit from any other class is commonly referred to as a base class.

Swift inheritance supports calling and accessing methods, properties, and subscripts belonging to their superclass. It allows subclasses to provide overriding versions of those methods, properties, and subscripts to modify their behavior. In addition, Swift allows for classes to add property observers to inherited properties. Property observers enable the programmer to observe changes to the property and take action on these changes. Property observers work for both stored and computed properties.

Note   Swift does not support multi-inheritance. Multi-inheritance is when a class can inherit from multiple base classes.

We can utilize inheritance to abstract some of the state and behavior in the previously created Dog class. To abstract these common attributes, a base class Animal is created. For demonstration purposes, it is assumed that all animals have a name and breed and are required to have eaten at some point. Each new animal type we create can extend our base class and gain this functionality for free. In the following example, the new superclass, Animal, is used to also create a new subclass for dogs.

```swift
class Animal {
    // even wild animals have names (you just don't know them)
    var name: String
    var breed: DogBreed
    // changing to lastEaten since wild animals don't get fed
    var lastEaten: Date?

    init(name: String,
         breed: DogBreed,
         lastEaten: Date?) {
        self.name = name
        self.breed = breed
        self.lastEaten = lastEaten
    }
}
```

```swift
func eat() {
  self.lastEaten = Date()
}

// lions roar, cats, purr, dogs bark so subclasses will
// define this
func makeNoise() {
  fatalError("requires implementation in subclass")
}
}

// Now we can define a Dog as a subclass of an animal
class DogSubClass: Animal {
  override func makeNoise() {
    if (breed == .germanShepard) {
      print("barking loud")
    } else {
      print("barking moderate")
    }
  }
}
```

The preceding inheritance chain is fine and dandy, but what happens when we have wolves? And lions (and tigers and bears – oh my)? Should these inherit directly from the animal base class? Or should they have their own superclasses to better model the traits of their specific scientific classification suborders? For example, it may be necessary to create separate superclasses for the mammalian suborders Caniformia and Feliformia with more specific shared attributes for those suborders. Establishing separate intermediate superclasses seems like an easy way to better model animals and still reuse code; however, this approach tends to create long, tightly coupled inheritance chains. Over time these chains become brittle and difficult to maintain (especially as the development team changes).

For classes in Swift, inheritance allows for code reuse and the benefits of dynamic polymorphism through overloading and overriding functions. Luckily for value types, Swift provides protocols as a way to achieve static polymorphism.

Note   Classes can also use protocols; however, structs cannot use inheritance (although default implementations on protocols provide similar benefits).

A Brief Note on Static and Dynamic Polymorphism

Static polymorphism occurs at compile time and allows for functions to have the same name and different implementations. The decision of exactly what method implementation to utilize is determined via static dispatch.

Dynamic polymorphism occurs at runtime and allows for functions to have the same name and different implementations. The decision of exactly what method implementation to run is determined by inspecting the actual object in memory at runtime.

Inheritance vs. Polymorphism

- Inheritance allows developers to reuse existing code in a program.

- Polymorphism allows developers to dynamically decide what form of a function to invoke.

Inheritance is a mechanism we can use to achieve polymorphism in our code via the use of a class hierarchy.

Protocols

A protocol is another way for our Swift code to leverage polymorphism. Much like an interface, a protocol defines a set of methods, properties, and other requirements a class, structure, or enumeration can adopt. To implement a protocol, the struct, or other types, must provide a concrete implementation of the requirements defined by the protocol. A type that satisfies a protocol is said to conform to the protocol, and types can conform to many protocols promoting the idea of composing objects based on behaviors.

Additionally, protocols are extensible, which allows them to provide a default implementation for types that extend them (by defining behavior on the protocol itself). Protocols allow extensions to contain methods, initializers, subscripts, and computed property implementations.

A well-designed protocol suits a particular task or piece of functionality, and types can conform to multiple protocols, promoting composition. With that in mind, let us review our previous example, but this time with protocols.

Since a type can conform to multiple protocols, our example decomposes individual characteristics of mammals into separate protocols avoiding complex hierarchical chains associated with inheritance.

```swift
// Provides a default implementation for eating, if an animal
requires custom logic say always making a noise when eating
we could override the default implementation of our specific
animal struct.
extension FeedsProto {
  mutating func eat() {
    lastFed = Date()
  }
}
```

```swift
protocol ProduceSoundProto {
  func makeNoise();
}
// Now we can easily create dogs, wolves, and any number
of animals
struct Dog_ProtoExample: AnimalProto, FeedsProto,
ProduceSoundProto {
  var lastFed: Date?
  var name: String
  var breed: DogBreed

  // conforming to our protocol
  init(name: String, breed: DogBreed) {
    self.name = name
    self.breed = breed
  }

  func makeNoise() {
    print("barking...")
  }
}

struct Lion_ProtoExampe: AnimalProto, FeedsProto,
ProduceSoundProto {
  var lastFed: Date?
  var name: String
  var breed: DogBreed

  // conforming to our protocol
  init(name: String, breed: DogBreed) {
    self.name = name
    self.breed = breed
  }
```

```swift
func makeNoise() {
  print("roar...")
}

mutating func eat() {
  lastFed = Date()
  // lions always roar while eating (obviously)
  makeNoise()
 }
}
```

Our animal hierarchy is no longer modeled by a tightly coupled chain of classes. Instead, it is possible to compose different animals with different behaviors by using a subset of our defined protocols. Within the Swift community, a lot has been made about protocol-oriented programming (POP) and preferring structs to classes because they are easier to reason about. While this is all true, there are times when the additional capabilities provided by classes are required. As a senior software engineer, it is your job to critically analyze the situation and pick the best tool for the job. Don't start with a protocol just for the sake of protocol-oriented programming. Fully understand the problem and let that drive the solution, whether that solution is functional programming, object-oriented programming, protocols, or something else entirely.

For example, in our simple Dog class earlier, we modify the state every time the dog is fed. If we were using MVVM architecture and the Dog class was a view-model updated with new data either from an application action or server update, it is common to keep the model immutable. Thus, we could have our Dog class become a struct; however, the struct would no longer make sense if we wanted a mutable state. Or if our object was something more complex, say, a network socket, then it cannot be inherently copied and thus does not make sense as a struct.

Importantly, you can safely pass copies of values across threads without synchronization.

Wrapping Up Classes and Structs

So far, we've discussed some of the similarities and differences in how classes and structs are managed in memory and how they can take advantage of advanced programming concepts for applied polymorphism.

Classes and Protocols

- Define properties to store values.

- Define methods to provide functionality.

- Define subscripts to give access to their values using subscript syntax.

- Define initializers to set up their initial state.

- Extend expanding their functionality beyond a default implementation.

- Provide standard functionality.

Classes Have Capabilities That Structs Do Not Have

- Inheritance: This enables one class to inherit the characteristics of another.

- Typecasting: This allows a program to interpret the type of a class instance at runtime.

- Deinitializers: These enable an instance of a class to free up any resources it has assigned.

- Reference counting: This allows more than one reference to a class instance.

Generics in Action

In addition to structs, classes, inheritance, and protocols, there is one more important concept that is referenced throughout this book: generics.

In its most simplistic form, generic programming is a style of programming where the programmer creates functions and types containing input and/or output parameters without specifying the exact types. The concrete types of input and output parameters are left unspecified and only instantiated when needed.

The usage of generic programming allows for flexible, reusable code that works for various parameter types. Supporting multiple parameter types enables programmers to define standard functions that take different types as inputs (as long as those types meet specific requirements defined by the program). Overall, generic programming avoids duplication and aids programmers in building better abstractions. Most programming languages support generics by providing language constructs for programmers to utilize. Software engineers rely on these built-in language constructs to create generic programs; here, we will discuss how Swift implements these constructs.

Generic Functions

To better understand generics in action, let's start with an example of a basic generic function:

```swift
func swap<T>(_ a: inout T, _ b: inout T) {
  let temp = a
  a = b
  b = temp
}
//call the function as normal
var x = 0;
var y = 5;
swap(&x, &y)
```

19

In the preceding function, we *in place* swap the values of a and b. The advantage of this function is that it can swap any type. Otherwise, without generics, every type would need its own specific swap function, an enormous maintenance burden.

The first thing that sticks out about the preceding function is using the <T> as part of the method signature. The brackets denote that the character (or characters) in between them represents a placeholder type. In our example, the placeholder type, T, is used instead of an actual type name. The placeholder type name doesn't say anything about what T must be; it only means that both a and b must be of the same type, T. The actual type to use in place of T is determined each time the function (in our case, swap) is called.

Notes on Placeholder Types

1. Any character is eligible for use as a placeholder type; however, T is commonly used (other traditionally used placeholder types are U and V).

2. It is essential to use upper camel case when signifying a placeholder type to represent that they are not values.

3. It is legal to specify multiple type parameters with the syntax: <T, U>.

Generic Types

In addition to generic functions, Swift allows for creating generic types. These classes, enums, and structs are customized to work with any type. An excellent example of generics in action is the Swift collection types (array, dictionary). Creating generic types is quite similar to creating a generic function, except that the placeholder type is defined on the type itself. As an example, let's look at creating a generic Queue in Swift:

20

```
// The placeholder type is defined on the struct.
struct Queue<T> {
  var items: [T] = []

  mutating func push(_ item: T) {
    // TODO
  }

  mutating func pop() -> T {
    // TODO
  }
}
// The concrete definition of the placeholder type is required
when instantiating the struct.
var q = Queue<Int>()
```

In the preceding Queue, the placeholder type is defined with the struct and used throughout the type. In this way, the Queue works for any type. Without this behavior, programmers would need a separate Queue struct for each type.

Generics are also utilized in protocols to create richer type experiences. To express generic types in protocols, Swift utilizes *typealiases* and *associatedtypes*. An associated type is used in the protocol, while the typealias specifies the type used in the protocol's concrete implementation. In other languages, typealiases are primarily syntactic sugar to wrap a long, more complex type in an easier-to-understand way; however, in Swift, typealiases also serve as a semantic requirement on types adopting a protocol with an associated type.

Next, let's extend our animal example from earlier to include a protocol for all animals. This new protocol also specifies that each animal eats a specific food, where a food is a separate struct defined by the concrete implementation of the animal protocol.

```swift
protocol Animal_Proto { }

struct Dog: Animal_Proto { }

// now we could have
let myDog: Animal_Proto = Dog()
// and
let arr = [myDog]
// now say we add an associated type to define the type of food
that the animal is eating.
// grass versus meat.
protocol Animal_Proto {
  // declare a requirement
  associatedtype Food
  func eat(food: Food) -> ()
}
struct Grass {}
struct Meat {}
struct Dog: Animal_Proto {
  // meet the requirement
  typealias Food = Meat

  func eat(food: Food) -> () {
    print("Eating the food: ")
  }
}
struct Antelope: Animal_Proto {
  // meet the requirement
  typealias Food = Grass

  func eat(food: Food) -> () {
    print("Eating the food: ")
  }
}
```

By defining the type of food on the concrete animal implementation, Swift allows for much richer type expressions than allowed by a typical inheritance-based structure. For example, in an inheritance-based design, one animal could not eat meat and the other grass since they do not conform to a base type. However, with protocols, we can. Even though the protocols with associated types are more expressive, they cannot be added to a collection. Since the kind of food (associated type) does not converge to a common type, the dynamic dispatch for type lookup cannot ascertain the correct type. Similarly, instances conforming to a protocol with an associated type cannot be typecasted to that protocol.

```
let dogs = [DogEV2(), Antelope()]
// Heterogeneous collection literal could only be inferred to
'[Any]'; add explicit type annotation if this is intentional

let myDog2: Animal_EV_Proto2 = DogEV2() as! Animal_EV_Proto2
// error: protocol 'Animal_EV_Proto2' can only be used as a
generic constraint because it has Self or associated type
requirements
```

In previous versions of Swift, a wrapper class could be implemented to erase the type constraints and allow for protocols with associated types to appear as homogenized collections. This wrapper is illustrated here for example purposes.

Note   Type Erasure is a term for coalescing a strongly typed parameter into a more generic type. In the following, this is implemented via wrapper type for demonstration purposes.

```
struct AnyAnimal<T>: Animal_Proto {
  private let _eat: (T) -> Void

  init<U: Animal_Proto>(_ animal: U) where U.Food == T {
    _eat = animal.eat
  }

  func eat(food: T) {
    _eat(food)
  }
}
```

In previous versions of Swift, we could then box our types using the preceding wrapper. However, Swift now requires that at initialization, Antelope conforms to Animal_Proto.

```
// Error: Initializer 'init(_:)' requires that 'Antelope'
conform to 'Animal_Proto'
let y = AnyAnimal(Antelope())
let x: MyProto = Foo()
```

This makes sense since the wrapper object is merely hiding the underlying types. However, it is still a good example of generics in protocols. More practically, try altering the code architecture to avoid the issue. For example:

```
enum Food {
  case grass
  case meat
}

protocol Animal_Proto {
  func eat(food: Food) -> ()
}
```

Now the food is represented as an enum that actually allows more flexibility for omnivores. While this example is a bit contrived, it is important to think about the overall architecture of the code and not only what fits the use case but also what is supported by the language and frameworks themselves. The nexus of this represents good design.

Summary

In this chapter, we reviewed some basic types and fundamental Swift language concepts such as inheritance, polymorphism, and generics.

Three Key Takeaways from This Chapter

1. Structs and classes both have their place. As an engineer, it is essential to understand both of them and the trade-offs associated with them and choose the correct abstraction for a specific use case. Additionally, when reviewing other engineers' code, it is important to be able to read and understand the underlying implications of their changes. Are there changes thread-safe? Will they lead to unintended state changes? Could they have utilized a better abstraction? This is all high-quality feedback that will make your code reviews more valuable and position you as a leader on your team.

2. Understanding reference and value semantics is a concept that extends beyond the Apple ecosystem and can impact how you develop code in many areas. Having a good understanding of this fundamental concept will assist you in debugging and creating bug-free applications.

3. Understand how to leverage generic types in code and protocols, all with an awareness of the limits of the Swift type system.

Further Learning

1. Swift language guide:

   a. `https://docs.swift.org/swift-book/LanguageGuide/TheBasics.html`

2. WWDC Talk on protocols:

   a. `https://developer.apple.com/videos/play/wwdc2015/408/`

CHAPTER 2

Memory Management

Understanding memory management is key to developing programs that perform correctly and efficiently. This section dives into how computer memory is allocated and released for Swift programs, how the Swift memory model is structured, and best practices for memory management.

The overall quality of a software application is primarily judged by its performance and reliability, which are highly correlated with good memory management. Memory management becomes crucial in large-scale multinational applications where older devices are prevalent.

This Chapter Includes

1. An overview of the Swift memory model, how this applies to different Swift types, and how to leverage this to improve code quality

2. A deep dive into automatic reference counting and how memory management works in Swift

© Eric Vennaro 2023
E. Vennaro, *iOS Development at Scale*, https://doi.org/10.1007/978-1-4842-9456-7_2

Swift Program Memory Usage

When a program is running, it takes up memory. This memory includes many segments:

1. The stack: Static memory

2. The heap: Dynamic memory

3. Program data: For storing global variables

4. Executable binary: The code being executed

Each memory location is assigned an address (a byte of memory) in the program. The addresses go from zero to the largest address allowable for the machine's architecture. Figure 2-1 shows the executable binary, program data, and heap segments have low address numbers, while the stack memory has higher addresses. In this chapter, we will focus on the stack and the heap.

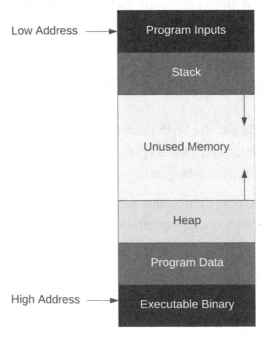

Figure 2-1. *Program memory layout; unused memory represents the memory that the heap or stack could use as they grow*

The Stack

At its core, a stack is a simple last-in, first-out (LIFO) data structure. Stacks must support at least two operations: push and pop. Inserting or removing from the middle of a stack is not allowed. The data items pushed on the runtime stack may be any size. Stacks are somewhat rigid in that they only allow access at the top. Nevertheless, this rigidity makes stacks easy to implement with efficient push and pop operations.

Inside a program, when calling a function, all local instances in that function are pushed onto the current stack. Furthermore, all instances are removed from the stack once the function has returned.

Characteristics of Stack Memory

- Static in memory where allocation happens only during compile time.

- The stack is a LIFO (last in, first out) data structure.

- Fast access through push and pop operations.

- The stack does not allow objects that change in size.

- Each thread has its own stack.

- Stacks store value types, such as structs and enums.

- The stack tracks memory allocation via a stack pointer, decrements the stack pointer to allocate memory, and increments the stack pointer to deallocate memory. These operations are outlined in Figure 2-2.

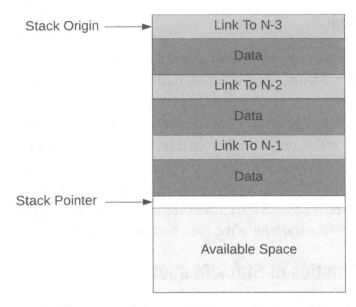

Figure 2-2. *Stack memory; this stack grows downward. Push copies data to stack and moves pointer down; pop copies data from the stack and moves pointer up*

Note   LIFO is an abbreviation for **last in, first out**. This is when the first element is processed last, and the last element is processed first. Conversely to LIFO, we can process data in a **first in, first out** manner commonly abbreviated as FIFO. With FIFO, the first element is processed first, and the newest element is processed last.

The Heap

In contrast, the heap is more flexible than the stack. The stack only allows allocation and deallocation at the top, while the heap programs can allocate or deallocate memory anywhere. The heap allocates memory by finding and returning the first memory block large enough to satisfy the request. Memory is returned or freed in any order. When the program deallocates or releases two adjacent memory blocks, the heap merges them to form a single block. Doing this allows the heap to flexibly meet demands for large memory blocks and is documented in Figure 2-3.

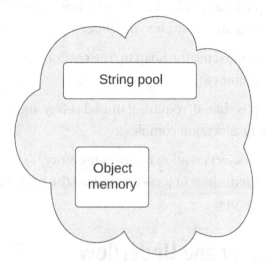

Figure 2-3. *The heap. Currently stored on the heap are the string pool and an object*

The heap's increased flexibility comes at a performance cost for two reasons:

1. The program must scan the heap to find a large enough memory block.

2. Adjacent freed memory blocks are combined to form a single block.

Characteristics of Heap Memory

- Allocation happens during runtime (dynamic memory).

- Values are referenceable at any time through a memory address.

- No limit on memory size.

- Slower access.

- When a process requests a certain amount of memory, the heap will search for a memory address that fulfills this request and return it to the process.

- A process must tell the heap to free sections of unused memory.

- The heap is shared, requiring thread safety and increasing allocation complexity.

- Dynamic object creation requires memory management since objects created on the heap never go out of scope.

Buffer Overflow and Underflow

Buffer underflow and overflow can affect both the stack and the heap. These occur when memory is accessed beyond the buffer limits and can lead to crashes or the execution of unauthorized code. This is a major security concern as it goes beyond a program's security policy. Heap-based overflows can even overwrite function pointers stored in memory, redirecting them to the attacker's code. This can result in the loss of critical user data.

Apple has taken measures to prevent memory-related issues by making Swift a memory-safe language. The compiler ensures that everything is initialized before use, and direct memory access is limited. However, Swift also offers unsafe API with no automated memory management or alignment guarantees.[1] To assist developers in detecting memory access errors, Xcode 7 and later include a thread analyzer in instruments.

---

[1] https://developer.apple.com/documentation/swift/unsafepointer

This check reports overflow if the accessed memory is beyond the end of the buffer and underflow if the accessed memory is before the beginning of a buffer. Additionally, Xcode sanitizes heap and stack buffers, as well as global variables.[2]

Swift Memory Model

Now that we have looked at a general overview of the stack and the heap and how they help manage a program's memory, we are ready to look at some Swift specifics.

Swift Stack Allocation

As a general rule of thumb, Swift value types are stored on the stack, meaning that they will not increase the program's retain count (more about this in the next section). Now, let us walk through an example (outlined in Figure 2-4) of stack allocation utilizing the dog struct from the previous chapter. When the dog struct is instantiated, the compiler allocates space on the stack for the instance. If the dog instance is copied to a new instance, space is allocated for both instances. Since both instances point to different locations in memory, changing a value in one will not affect the other – value semantics at work.

```
struct Dog {
  var age: Int
  func bark() {
    print("barking")
  }
}
```

---

[2] https://developer.apple.com/documentation/xcode/overflow-and-underflow-of-buffers

```
// creating the instance
let dog1 = Dog(age: 2)
let dog2 = dog1
```

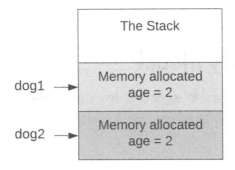

Figure 2-4. *Stack allocation for value types*

One caveat to this is that if the size of a value type cannot be determined at compile time, it will be allocated on the heap. This is typically because the value type contains a reference type (or is contained by a reference type).

Note   Value types do not increase the retain count. However, copying a value type with inner references requires increasing the reference count of its children.

Swift Heap Allocation

In addition to classes, if the size of a value type cannot be determined during compile time (because of a protocol/generic requirement) or if your value type recursively contains/is contained by a reference type (remember that closures are also reference types), then it will require heap allocation.

To explore heap allocation, let us look at a Dog class similar to the preceding struct.

```
class Dog {
  var age: Int
  func bark() {
    print("barking")
  }
}
// creating the instance
let dog1 = Dog(age: 2)
let dog2 = dog1
```

For the Dog class, memory is first allocated on the stack. This memory references memory allocated on the heap (a pointer from the stack to the heap). The heap allocation occurs on initialization (the heap is searched for an appropriate block of memory), and the instance is copied so both dog1 and dog2 point to the same memory on the heap, so a change to dog1 will affect dog2 – reference semantics at work. Figure 2-5 outlines the interaction.

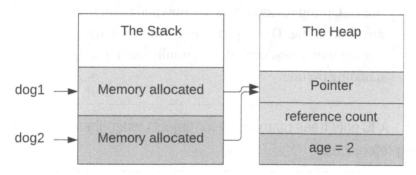

Figure 2-5. *Heap allocation for reference types*

Note   Strings store their characters on the heap. If a struct (stack storage) contains a string, the string will still incur reference counting overhead and heap storage.

Automatic Reference Counting

Automatic reference counting is a form of automated memory management. The compiler automatically inserts the necessary retain and release operations for the program and deallocates memory when the retain count reaches zero. In Swift, a retain count is implemented every time a strong reference is made to an instance. ARC exposes the following lifetime qualifiers to help developers manage memory properly:

1. Strong: Any property labeled strong will increment a reference count. As long as something references a strong object, it will not be deallocated.

2. Weak: Any property labeled weak will not increment the reference count and does not protect the object from being deallocated.

3. Unowned: Similar to a weak reference, unowned references do not increase the retain count of the referred object. However, an unowned reference is not an Optional. Additionally, unowned references are nonzeroing. The object does not zero out the pointer when deallocated, potentially leading to a dangling pointer.

Note   ARC only frees up memory for objects when there are zero strong references.

Having a form of memory management such as ARC is important for managing objects created dynamically by the program. Without ARC, programmers would be forced to perform memory management manually, leading to errors. In general, poor memory management can lead to the following:

1. Memory leaks: Memory leaks occur when memory is not freed, but there is no longer a pointer to it, resulting in no way to access (or free it) now. Memory leaks can cause crashes for long-running processes and generally degrade program efficiency.

2. Dangling pointers: A dangling pointer is when a pointer points to memory that has already been freed (meaning the storage is no longer allocated). Trying to access it might cause undefined behavior and/or a segmentation fault.

Memory leaks and dangling pointers lead to app crashes and poor user experiences.

Reference Counting in Action

Here is an example of ARC where we reference and assign it to another variable, thus incrementing the reference count. Note how both strong references are broken before memory deallocation occurs.

```
var reference1: Car?
var reference2: Car?
class Car {
  let name: String
  var engine: Engine?

  init(name: String) {
    self.name = name
    print("\(name) is being initialized")
  }
```

```
  deinit {
    print("\(name) is being deinitialized")
  }
}

reference1 = Car(name: "Herby")
// Prints "Herby is being initialized"
reference2 = reference1
// retain called
// Now there are two strong references to the single Car instance
reference1 = nil
// release called
reference2 = nil
// release called
// Prints "Herby is being deinitialized"
// Note how both strong references had to be broken before
memory deallocation occurred
```

In the following example (Figure 2-6), we explore what happens when creating a strong reference cycle. A strong reference cycle happens when two class instances hold a strong reference to each other, such that each instance keeps the other alive.

```
class Engine {
  let type: String
  init(type: String) {
    self.type = type
  }
  var car: Car?
  deinit {
    print("Engine \(type) is being deinitialized")
  }
}
```

```
var herby: Car?
var inlineSix: Engine?

herby = Car(name: "Herby_V2")
inlineSix = Engine(type: "Inline Six Cylinder")

herby?.engine = inlineSix
inlineSix?.car = herby

herby = nil
inlineSix = nil
//Note neither deinitializer is called
```

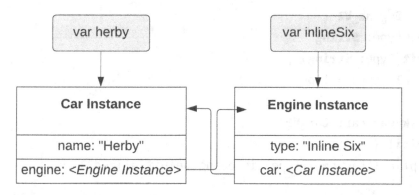

Figure 2-6. *The two initialized variables; the solid line denotes the strong reference cycle between the engine in the car*

As illustrated in Figure 2-7, ARC still maintains a reference for the car and the engine. Neither is deallocated even after assigning each variable to nil. To fix this, use a weak reference (visually depicted in Figure 2-8).

```swift
class Car_V2 {
  let name: String
  var engine: Engine_V2?
  init(name: String) {
    self.name = name
    print("\(name) is being initialized")
  }
  deinit {
    print("\(name) is being deinitialized")
  }
}

class Engine_V2 {
  let type: String
  init(type: String) {
    self.type = type
  }
  weak var car: Car_V2?
  deinit {
    print("Engine \(type) is being deinitialized")
  }
}

var ford: Car_V2?
var inlineFour: Engine_V2?

ford = Car_V2(name: "Ford")
inlineFour = Engine_V2(type: "Inline Four Cylinder")

ford?.engine = inlineFour
inlineFour?.car = ford
```

```
ford = nil
inlineFour = nil
// Prints:
// "Engine Inline Four Cylinder is being deinitialized"
// "Ford is being deinitialized"
```

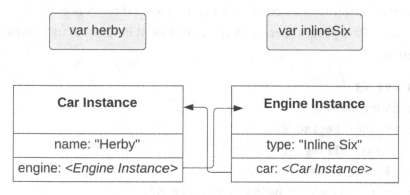

Figure 2-7. *A strong reference cycle still exists between the engine and the car even after the variables are deallocated*

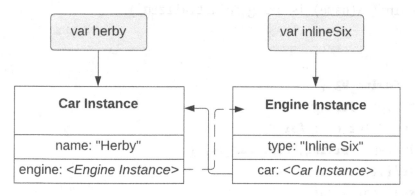

Figure 2-8. *The two initialized variables and the references between them. The weak reference is denoted by the dotted line*

Pretty cool, right? Now we can avoid memory leaks; however, we could slightly improve this. Since we know a car must always have an engine, we could also set the property as an unowned reference. Using an unowned reference will remove the need to unwrap the optional and mirrors our hypothetical product requirement of a car always having an engine. When using an unowned reference, one must be careful to fully understand the software requirements since accessing an unowned reference when it is nil causes a fatal program error. When in doubt, it is safest to use a weak reference.

```swift
class Car_V3 {
  let name: String
  var engine: Engine_V3?
  init(name: String) {
    self.name = name
    print("\(name) is being initialized")
  }
  deinit {
    print("\(name) is being deinitialized")
  }
}

class Engine_V3 {
  let type: String
  unowned let car: Car_V3
  init(type: String, car: Car_V3) {
    self.type = type
    self.car = car
  }
  deinit {
    print("Engine \(type) is being deinitialized")
  }
}
```

```swift
var chevy: Car_V3? = Car_V3(name: "Chevy")
chevy!.engine = Engine_V3(type: "V8 Super", car: chevy!)
// Prints:
// "Chevy is being deinitialized"
// "Engine V8 Super is being deinitialized"
```

A very common scenario to see a retain cycle is when implementing the delegate pattern, such as

```swift
class ViewController: ViewModelDelegate {
  let model = ViewModel()
  init() {
    model.delegate = self
  }

  func willLoadData() {
    // do something
  }
}

protocol ViewModelDelegate {
  func willLoadData()
}

class ViewModel: ViewModelType {
  // if this is a not labeled weak it will lead to a
retain cycle
  weak var delegate: ViewModelDelegate?

  func bootstrap() {
    delegate?.willLoadData()
  }
}
```

Another common use case for this is within capture lists for closures.

```
let closure = { [weak self] in
  // Remember, all weak variables are Optionals
  self?.doSomething()
}

let closure = { [weak self, unowned person] in
  // Weak variables are Optionals
  self?.doSomething()
  // Unowned variables are not.
  person.eat()
}
```

ARC Observed Lifetime Bugs

In Swift, it is possible to observe these object life cycles. In fact, we did this throughout the preceding code. In practice, this is widely considered bad practice because relying on observed object lifetime relies on the Swift compiler. The observed life cycle may change if the compiler changes, causing complex bugs.

Some Potential Solutions

1. Use the extended lifetime modifier. This modifier can extend the scope of weak references; however, it would need to be sprinkled across the code base (increasing maintenance) and puts the additional burden of correctness and maintenance on individual engineers and code reviewers.

2. Think critically about the API design and encapsulating logic to avoid unintended access.

3. Think critically when using weak and unowned modifiers. Can a different class design avoid any potential of a reference cycle and/or deinitializer side effects? This could eliminate the class of bugs but may not be possible depending on the code.

None of these potential solutions is a silver bullet, but when reviewing code, writing code, and bug-fixing, it is important to think through these trade-offs and thoroughly understand ARC so that code is well written, designed, and bug-free.

Method Dispatch

The last area of the Swift memory model we will touch on here is method dispatch. Swift needs to execute the correct method implementation when called at runtime. The way that the programming language, Swift, ascertains the correct method to call occurs at either compile time (statically) or runtime (dynamically). Objective-C heavily utilized runtime dispatch, giving the language immense flexibility; however, Swift leans heavily on static dispatch, allowing the compiler to optimize the code. With runtime dispatch, dispatches cannot be determined at compile time and are looked up at runtime blocking compile-time visibility and optimizations.

One such compiler optimization is inlining. Inlining is when the compiler replaces method dispatches with the actual implementation of the function, removing the overhead of static dispatch and associated setup and teardown of the call stack. This optimization becomes more of a performance enhancement when an entire chain of dispatches can be inlined.

Direct Static Dispatch

This type of method dispatch is simplistic and fast. Static dispatch owes its speed to the fact that there is only one implementation of the method that will be stored somewhere in memory during runtime. The runtime can directly jump to that memory address and execute it. Since direct static dispatch does not support multiple implementations of the same method, it does not support polymorphism.

Dynamic Dispatch

In contrast to static dispatch, dynamic dispatch provides a great deal of flexibility. It provides polymorphism and inheritance for reference types and is implemented via a virtual-table (V-table) lookup. A V-table lookup is created at compile time during SIL (Swift Intermediate Language) generation, which specifies the actual implementation of the method that should be called at runtime. During runtime, this lookup table is held as an array of addresses to the actual location in memory where the implementation resides (virtual pointer). V-tables help inherited classes to generate the correct calls to overridden and non-overridden methods. If the class is marked as final, Swift also provides an optimization to remove the dynamic dispatches for the class and statically dispatch those methods.

To better understand V-tables, it is helpful to visualize what is going on. In Figure 2-9, we have an array of Animal objects. The array has no specific type information, only that each entry points to an object of type Animal. Dogs, cats, and tigers all fit into this category because they are derived from the Animal base class and can respond to the same messages. With dynamic dispatch, the compiler does not know that the elements of the array are anything more than Animal objects. When a function is called through the base class address (our Animal array), the compiler generates a lookup through the type to the virtual method table, which contains the virtual pointer to the proper method implementation.

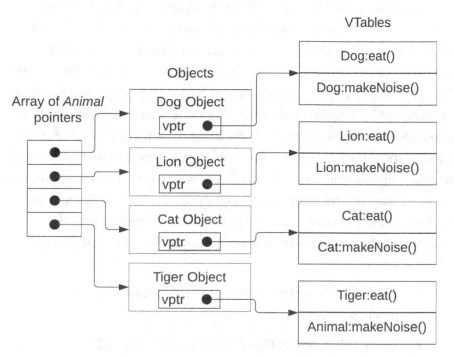

Figure 2-9. *V-table dispatch with animal objects*

If the subclasses of Animal override a function declared on the base class, the compiler creates a unique V-table for that class, seen on the right of Figure 2-9. That table places the addresses of all the functions that are declared in this class or the base class. If a function is not overridden, the compiler uses the address of the base-class version in the derived class. (You can see this in the adjusted entry in the tiger V-table.) Then the compiler places the virtual pointer (VPTR) in the class. Once the VPTR is initialized to the proper V-table, the object "knows" what type it is.

Supporting Polymorphism for Value Types

As stated earlier, static dispatch, in its simplistic sense, does not support polymorphism, and value types utilize static dispatch. So how do value types support polymorphism in Swift? We cannot use V-table dispatch due to the lack of a common object chain (meaning the types do not share a standard memory layout), so a new system using a Protocol Witness Table (PWT) is used. The PWT allows protocol-backed types to take advantage of polymorphic behavior while still using value semantics and avoiding heap allocation where possible. By avoiding dynamic allocations on the heap, protocol-backed value types allow for faster code while still getting the power of dynamic dispatch. The PWT lookup is more complex than the V-table lookup and requires multiple components to work because value types have different sizes in memory. This section breaks down the various components that make polymorphism possible for value types. In all, we will cover the following:

1. Existential Container: Wraps different protocol types to allow for array-based storage.

2. Inline Value Buffer: This allows for the storage of larger types.

3. Protocol Witness Table: Similar to a V-table.

4. Value Witness Table: Handles a value's life cycle.

Note   Using protocols for polymorphic relationships can improve performance by allowing the compiler to optimize the code.

The Existential Container

The Existential Container solves the problem of storing protocol value
types in an array by wrapping the different protocol types in a container
(the Existential Container). Since the Existential Container has a consistent
memory layout, it can be stored in an array even though the protocol types
cannot. As illustrated in Figure 2-10, the Existential Container contains

1. Inline Value Buffer

2. Pointer to the Value Witness Table

3. Pointer to the Protocol Witness Table

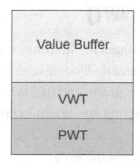

Figure 2-10. *The Existential Container with a three-word value
buffer and a pointer to the VWT and PWT*

Inline Value Buffer

The Inline Value Buffer is three words long. If the type is too large to fit in
the Inline Value Buffer, the value buffer will instead contain a pointer to the
heap where the value is stored in memory (depicted in Figure 2-11).

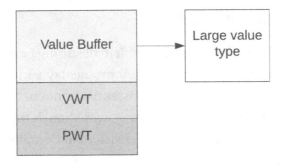

Figure 2-11. *The Existential Container with a pointer to a "large" value type is stored on the heap. If this were a "large" reference type, it would also be stored on the heap and include a reference count*

Value Witness Table (VWT)

The Value Witness Table manages the lifetime of a value type. It handles the allocate, copy, destruct, and deallocate operations for a value. There is one VWT per type in the program, and this is linked to the Existential Container. The VWT's operations are shown in Figure 2-12.

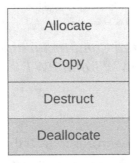

Figure 2-12. *The VWT with its associated operations*

Protocol Witness Table (PWT)

Lastly, the Existential Container includes a reference to the PWT. A separate Protocol Witness Table is created for each type that implements a protocol. Each entry in the table links to the implementation of the type, allowing for the correct implementation of the method to be used when referenced via a protocol dispatch. In Figure 2-13, each concrete animal implementation is wrapped in a PWT because they conform to the animal protocol.

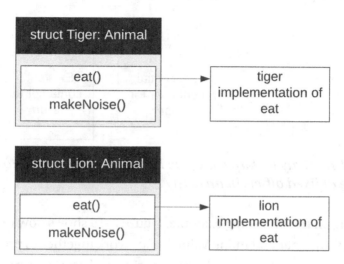

Figure 2-13. *The PWT for two structs conforming to the animal protocol*

The PWT does not provide a uniform memory size for each type; for that, we need the Existential Container. Using the Existential Container, which refers to a specific PWT, we can add our value types to an array and then reference the concrete implementations through the PWTs. Figure 2-14 shows how this storage mechanism would function for an array of Animal objects.

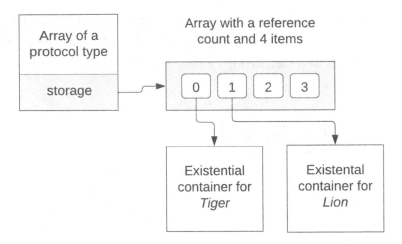

Figure 2-14. *Array lookup using the Existential Container to allow for storage at fixed offsets in an array*

Building on the preceding example, Figure 2-15 shows how the Existential Container and Inline Value Buffer work together to provide a fully functioning system for uniformly storing and accessing protocol-backed value types.

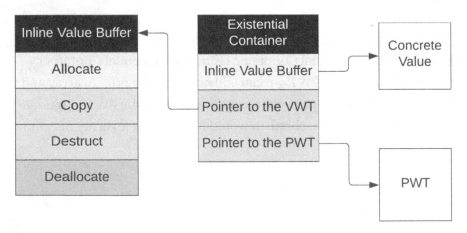

Figure 2-15. *Linking between the VWT, Existential Container, and PWT*

In the figure, the VWT table tracks the allocation of the value types and tracks the pointer to the Existential Container. When allocate is called on the type, the VWT allocates memory on the heap and stores a pointer to that memory in the value buffer of the Existential Container.

Suppose the value type is copied in code. In that case, the copy function is called to copy the value from the source of the assignment (where the local variable was initialized) to the Existential Container's value buffer. Note that since the type is large, it is not stored directly in the value buffer.

When the object is deallocated, the VWT will call the destruct entry to decrement any reference counts if they exist. Lastly, the memory on the heap is deallocated for the value. If any references exist, the deallocate operation also removes any references in the Existential Container.

Handling Nested Reference Types

In some cases, a value type may contain a reference type. In this situation, the references will still utilize the value buffer as shown in Figure 2-16. Storing the references in the value buffer can lead to unintended state sharing if you are creating a copy of the value type since the underlying reference will stay the same (just increasing the reference count). To avoid this, Swift implements copy-on-write (before writing to the class, we check if the reference count is greater than one. If so, we copy the instance and then write to the copy).

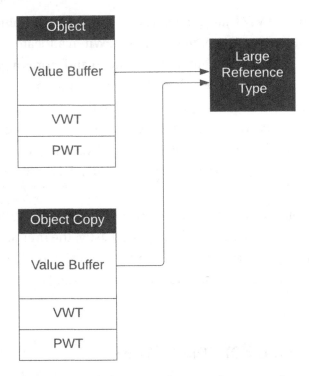

Figure 2-16. *Unintended sharing of state when copying a large reference type*

Pseudocode for copy-on-write:

```
class CatStorage {
  // implement all attributes of an Animal
}

struct Cat: Animal {
  var storage: CatStorage
  init() {
    storage = AnimalStorage()
  }
  // implement any functions
  mutating func move() {
```

```
  // check reference count >= 1
  if !uniquelyReferenced(&storage) {
    storage = CatStorage(storage)
   }
 }
}
```

By implementing this optimization, the heap storage needs are decreased.

Handling Generics

Generics in Swift is a form of static parametric polymorphism, and Swift Generics leverages this to optimize code at compile time further. Swift creates a type-specific version of the generic function for each type used in code. This allows for the compiler to inline the method calls and only create specific functions for types used in code. In addition, to optimize the code via inlining, the compiler can also utilize whole module optimization to optimize the code based on what types are used in the module. In practice, using generic types (where applicable) allows for additional performance enhancements and code architecture improvements.

Note   The whole module optimization removes this limit for Swift code, allowing the optimizer to analyze all the source files in a module.

The Implications of Different Sized Types on PWT Memory Management

Small Types

For both protocol types and generic types:

1. Small types will fit in the value buffer (avoiding heap allocation).

2. Incur a reference counting overhead only if the type is a class (reference type).

3. Utilize the Protocol Witness Table for dynamic dispatch.

Large Types

For both protocol types and generic types:

1. Large types will still incur heap allocation (use indirect storage as a workaround for value types).

2. Incur a reference counting overhead only if the value contains reference types.

3. Utilize the Protocol Witness Table for dynamic dispatch.

Applied Memory Management

Choosing a fitting memory abstraction with the least dynamic runtime requirements by leveraging value types will enable static type checking, additional compiler optimizations, and less state sharing. One example of providing a better fitting memory abstraction is to replace a String type with a value type UID, which would avoid heap allocation, providing better performance and type safety.

When evaluating design decisions, consider what we have discussed:

1. Stack vs. heap allocation:

   a. Is heap storage opening the program to unintended sharing?

   b. Is unnecessary heap allocation causing a performance overhead?

2. Dynamic vs. static dispatch:

   a. Is too much dynamic dispatch not allowing the program to take advantage of compiler optimizations associated with static dispatching?

3. Reference counting overhead?

   a. Are reference types causing many reference counting calls? Can these be modified to use value types?

Bug Fixing

Engineers are not only tasked with writing quality code but also with fixing bugs. Especially as a mobile engineer, some of these bugs will be related to mismanaged memory. For debugging these issues, it is essential to understand them and what tools Xcode and the iOS ecosystem provide to help fix them.

1. Instruments: Do not forget to profile on an iOS device. The runtime architecture of the simulator is different and may not be helpful when debugging.

2. Memory graph: An excellent tool to look through features.

Beyond using the provided tools in Xcode, it is important to think about what tools your company has for improved debugging. Is there anything that could be added? It is also important to think about bug reports from users. Do they have accurate stack traces and the necessary information to debug and replicate issues?

For example, let's say your notification service extension is running out of memory and causing crashes for certain users who are receiving a large volume of background push notifications. Does your team have the tooling to detect this from bug reports? Are there detailed stack traces? And once detected, do you have the tools to replicate the bug and fix it? We will talk more about this in Part 3 of this book.

Summary

This chapter walked through the Swift memory model, how automatic reference counting works, and how to avoid common memory management pitfalls. While most of this chapter was more theoretical in discussing how things work, this applies to day-to-day software engineering as it

1. Improves debugging ability. By better understanding how Swift functions as well as how to best leverage existing tooling for identifying memory issues, you are better equipped to debug issues and understand stack traces.

2. Improves feature architecture. Understanding how to fit your feature architecture to best utilize the systems underlying memory management system helps develop performant features and narrow the design space. This generally assists in building things right the first time, speeding up long-term development, and reducing bugs.

3. Depending on your specific team, this may directly impact your work as a performance reliability engineer or potentially if you work on a lower-level mobile library where performance optimizations are crucial.

Further Learning

1. Performance tuning:

   a. `https://developer.apple.com/library/archive/`
      `documentation/Performance/Conceptual/`
      `PerformanceOverview/Introduction/Introduction.`
      `html#//apple_ref/doc/uid/TP40001410`

2. Instruments user guide:

   a. `https://help.apple.com/instruments/mac/current/`

CHAPTER 3

iOS Persistence Options

Overview

Persistent storage is a crucial component of any software system; sometimes, iOS applications use only the server as the persistent store; however, more complex apps require persistent in-app storage. Persisting data between application cold starts on the device is essential for

1. Storing application and user preferences

2. Providing an offline mode

3. Caching

4. Storing authentication/authorization data

5. Providing the user with a performant experience on cold start

Picking the correct storage format is critical for security and providing a consistent, accurate user experience. Determining the proper storage system requires critical thinking and understanding of the underlying storage implementation because the underlying storage implementation will largely dictate the level of persistence, performance, and security.

© Eric Vennaro 2023
E. Vennaro, *iOS Development at Scale*, https://doi.org/10.1007/978-1-4842-9456-7_3

This Chapter Includes

This chapter includes an overview of the most common iOS persistence options and presents important trade-offs to consider when choosing. This chapter does not detail specific implementation APIs. Instead, it provides approaches to the subject from a system design perspective, weighing the pros and cons of different techniques and how they can affect large-scale applications. While additional third-party options exist, this chapter focuses on the default Apple implementations and the underlying storage formats. Understanding the underlying storage formats is essential because even if your company uses a custom wrapper or custom implementation, they will still utilize the same underlying storage solutions, allowing you to reason quickly about any bespoke persistence libraries or frameworks. We will cover

1. Saving directly to a file on the device

2. NSUserDefaults

3. The keychain

4. Core Data

5. SQLite

6. A practical example centered on caching

We will not cover third-party storage options such as Realm (NoSQL) and Firebase as they are not native to the ecosystem.

iOS Persistence Options
Saving to a File

At the most basic level, Apple allows iOS applications to save data to a file. While serializing data and storing it in a file is relatively simple, it is also a powerful tool allowing for the persistent storage of data and objects via serialization and deserialization. Apple only allows an application to access the file system within the application's container for security reasons. There are three folders within the app container:

1. Documents: This is an excellent place to save user-generated content. It's also backed up to iCloud automatically. The documents directory can be made available to the user through file sharing, so it should only contain files that users should see.

2. Library: This is used for storing application-specific data that should persist between launches. Files are deleted from the device if the device does not have enough free space. Some important purpose-specific subfolders within the library folder are as follows:

    a. Application Support: Files that the application uses to run. These files should also remain hidden from the user. This directory is also backed up by default.

    b. Caches: Cache data is, as it sounds, data that, if stored, would improve application performance but is not required for the application to function. This is temporary data for which it is beneficial to persist it longer than data in the tmp directory, but not as long as an Application Support file.

    c. Preferences: This directory contains app-specific preference files. The preferences directory is used through the provided NSUserDefaults API. You should not create files in the preferences directory yourself! Instead, use the NSUserDefaults API, discussed in the next section. In iOS, the contents of this directory are backed up to iCloud.

3. Tmp: In this folder, you can save files that the application needs temporarily. They can be deleted by the operating system when the app is not running.

It is important to think critically about where to place files since the directory can change the level of persistence, potentially expose the file to users, and slow the syncing and backup processes on iOS devices if the files are large. Additionally, storing large files can consume a large amount of a user's available storage, which can cause them to delete your application.

File System Security

With any modern application, security is paramount. Apple provides a variety of tools to this end. For files, the iOS ecosystem includes three main security features:

1. Sandboxing: Sandboxing prevents applications from writing to parts of the file system that they should not have access to. Each sandboxed application receives one or more containers that it can write into. An application cannot write to other applications' containers (or to most directories outside of the sandbox). These restrictions limit the potential damage caused by a security breach.

2. Access control: Access to files and directories is governed by access control lists (ACLs). Access control lists are a set of fine-grained controls that define what exactly can and cannot be done to a file or directory and by whom. With access control lists, you can grant individual users different access levels to a given file or directory.

3. Encryption: When saving data to a file, it is possible to encrypt the data using the foundation API's options.

```
// Set data protection for file
try data.write(to: fileURL, options: .completeFileProtection)
// change the data protection level for a file
try (fileURL as NSURL).setResourceValue(
                URLFileProtection.complete,
                forKey: .fileProtectionKey)
```

Some of the concerns related to writing directly to the file system are ameliorated when utilizing one of the higher-level frameworks discussed in the rest of the chapter.

NSUserDefaults

NSUserDefaults is an Apple-provided interface for interacting with the underlying user defaults system. The defaults "database" is a property-list-backed file store intended to store application-level preference data. A property list (plist) is an XML file. At runtime, the UserDefaults class keeps the contents of the property list in memory to improve performance, and changes are made synchronously within your application's process. NSUserDefaults is intended for use with data that is not scoped to a specific user inside the context of the application because NSUserDefaults does not consider your application's user model.

Note   Apple provides caching and thread safety for NSUserDefaults, making it a good option for storing application-level preference data.

NSUserDefaults also provides a set of domains that denote different levels of persistence and form a search hierarchy for the order in which values are returned. When requesting a value for a key, the domain hierarchy is searched from top to bottom, and the first value found is returned. The domains are searched in the same order as in Table 3-1. For domains listed as volatile, the values are only valid for the lifetime of the NSUserDefaults instance.

Table 3-1. *NSUserDefaults domains and persistence values*

Domain	Persistence Value
NSArgument	Volatile
Application	Persistent
NSGlobal	Persistent
Languages	Volatile
NSRegistration	Volatile

In addition to choosing an appropriate domain when considering NSUserDefaults, it is also important to consider

1. How your application will handle potential data loss

2. How your application handles the account setup and login experience for different users since NSUserDefaults is scoped at an application level and not to a specific user

While several persistent domains are used with NSUserDefaults, there is a slight chance of unexplained data loss.[1,2] Due to the slight possibility of data loss, it is not recommended to store data in NSUserDefaults where

---

[1] https://developer.apple.com/forums/thread/15685
[2] https://openradar.appspot.com/16761393

persistence is absolutely critical (which would cause a critical application failure or unacceptable user experience).

Potentially more common and more impactful to your usage of NSUserDefaults is that NSUserDefaults is not scoped to a specific user inside of your application. The lack of user-specific scoping can cause additional complications; for example, say your child shares your iPhone and has a separate child account on YouTube. If your child adjusts the video playback speed while signed in, and this is stored in NSUserDefaults, the change will also apply to your YouTube account. To scope user defaults to a specific user, many companies create a custom wrapper providing this behavior for engineers.

Another shortcoming of NSUserDefaults is that the preferences do not sync across devices since they are stored on the device. If YouTube video playback speed was stored using NSUserDefaults, then adjusting your YouTube video playback on your iPhone would not sync to your iPad or computer.

Let us walk through an example to better understand the system as a whole and expose the values stored in plain text. First, let's add some values to NSUserDefaults:

```
UserDefaults.standard.set("bar", forKey: "foo")
UserDefaults.standard.set(false, forKey: "enabled")
```

Now we can run our application in the simulator and view the underlying plist in the finder tool. To view the plist file, we can output the file path to the console like so:

```
print(NSHomeDirectory())
```

You will get a directory path like this:

```
/Users/myMac/Library/Developer/CoreSimulator/Devices/0F7B40
DB-67ED-43DD-B387-CD4E30FD7B45/data/Containers/Data/Application
/A5EB65F7-6192-4F7A-8A5F-620CB137DD96
```

When inspecting that folder, the plist is inside the *Library* ➤ *Preferences* folder. Figure 3-1 shows the results of navigating to the directory path in Finder.

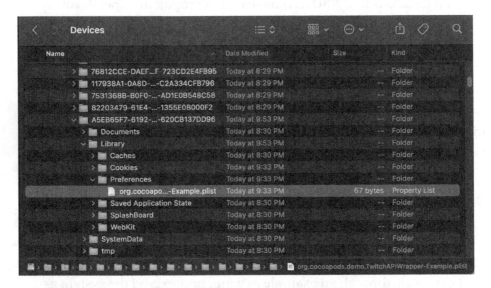

Figure 3-1. *Folder hierarchy containing the NSUserDefaults plist*

Opening the plist (Figure 3-2) displays the values in plain text, presenting a security flaw; for example, if the plist included a user setting for enabling paid features or an authentication token, the values could be viewed and easily modified, potentially for nefarious means.

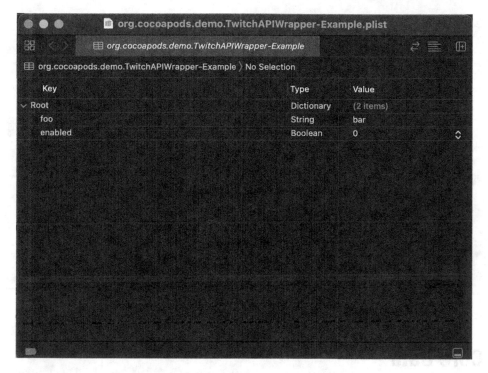

Figure 3-2. NSUserDefaults plist opened via finder

Keychain

The keychain services API provides a mechanism to store small amounts of data, such as an authentication token, in an encrypted database. The keychain solves the problem presented by NSUserDefaults storing data in plain text. The keychain API is a bit low level and older, which can require some boilerplate code, especially with Swift. To avoid this, most companies utilize keychain wrappers, either built in-house or by using a third-party library.

Some key concepts to keep in mind are as follows:

1. The keychain provides secure and encrypted storage for sensitive data.

2. A keychain item is a registry in the keychain.

3. A keychain item class is a template of information you want to store. The keychain offers classes for different standard credentials, such as username/password pairs, a certificate, a generic password, and more.

4. Keychain information retrieval is linked to the developer provisioning profile used to sign the application and its bundle ID. If either of these changes, the data becomes inaccessible.

Core Data

The Core Data framework is similar to an object-relational mapper (ORM). Core Data is an object graph management framework. It maintains a graph of object instances, allowing an application to work with a graph that does not fit entirely into memory by faulting objects in and out of memory. Core Data also manages constraints on properties and relationships and maintains referential integrity. Core Data is thus an ideal framework for building the "model" component of a small MVC-based iOS application (support also exists for Swift UI). IOS Core Data supports the following storage formats as an underlying persistence layer:

1. SQLite

2. In Memory

3. Binary

Note   Referential integrity is a data property stating that all of its references are valid. For relational databases, if a value of one table's column references another table, then the referenced value must exist.

Managed Objects

Core Data provides an NSManagedObject class that allows the user to define Core Data–backed properties to support populating the model objects from the persistent store. The NSManagedObject class serves as the base class for all Core Data–backed entities. The managed object is associated with NSEntityDescription, which provides metadata related to the object, such as the name of the entity that the object represents and the names of its attributes and relationships. A managed object is also associated with a managed object context that tracks changes to the object graph. Figure 3-3 outlines this interaction with SQLite as the underlying data store.

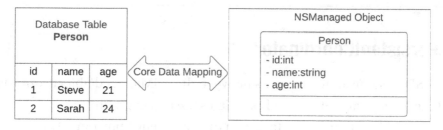

Figure 3-3. *Mapping database table to NSManagedObject*

NSManagedObjectContext

The NSManagedObjectContext encapsulates model objects and sends a notification when the managed object has changed (when an operation such as a create, read, update, or delete occurs) and is used to manipulate and track changes to managed objects. Each managed object knows which context it's in, and each context knows which objects it is managing. Together with the NSManagedObjects, this part of the Core Data stack is known as the object graph management and is also where the application's model layer logic lives.

NSPersistentStore

The NSPersistentStore manages the actual persistent operations, that is, where Core Data reads and writes to the file system. The persistent store is connected to the NSPersistentCoordinator. Each persistent store has its own characteristics; it can be read-only, stored as binary or SQLite, or in memory. If additional flexibility is required, it is possible to store different parts of your model in different persistent stores.

Note   Core Data makes no guarantee regarding the security of persistent stores, and no store should by default be considered inherently secure.

NSPersistentCoordinator

The NSPersistentCoordinator sits between the NSManagedObjectContexts and the NSPersistentStores and associates the object graph management portion of the stack with the persistence portion. The NSPersistentCoordinator utilizes the facade design pattern to manage object contexts such that a group of persistent stores appears as a single aggregate store and maintains a reference to a managed object model that describes the entities in the store or stores it manages. In this way, the NSPersistentContainer encapsulates all interactions with the persistent stores.

In most cases, the persistent store coordinator has one persistent store attached to it, and this store interacts with the file system (commonly via SQLite). For more advanced setups, Core Data supports using multiple stores attached to the same persistent store coordinator. Figure 3-4 outlines this interaction using the Core Data stack components.

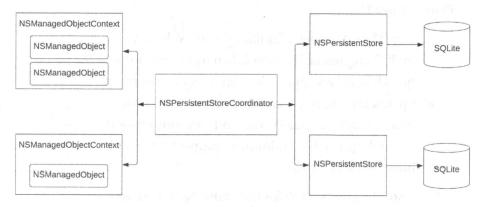

Figure 3-4. *Example of the Core Data stack*

Considering When to Use Core Data

While many iOS developers have strong opinions about the Core Data framework, it provides a valuable service by abstracting away details about the underlying storage type and providing a relatively easy-to-use set of APIs. For example, say you directly use SQLite for data storage in your iOS application. Without Core Data or a similar alternative, you would need to interface directly with the SQLite DB in code and write SQL statements, which can be fine if it is a small application. However, suppose this application has a large team of developers. In that case, this can result in each developer writing SQL statements sprinkled throughout the application, leading to a lot of one-off value objects and sprinkled SQL code of varying quality and consistency. To avoid this spaghetti code, engineers typically add different layers, commonly called a repository or data object layer, which begin to look similar to the services provided by Core Data. Instead of going through all of these steps manually, Core Data provides a well-understood out-of-the-box alternative to a custom solution. Writing your own system is often not worth the time and effort unless there is a clear use case and business need.

Pros of Core Data

1. Core Data provides a familiar default solution for iOS engineers. If you build an iOS team and quickly scale an application, engineers must ramp up quickly and be productive in your team's code base. Utilizing a well-known and well-understood technology can help minimize ramp-up time and increase productivity.

2. Core Data works well for the majority of use cases. By starting with an easy-to-implement solution like Core Data, you can quickly iterate on your application and identify issues that a more complex, custom solution could fix.

3. Core Data provides an easy-to-implement framework that can act as the "model" component of your application's architecture, including mechanisms for versioning your data model and migrating user data as your application evolves. The features already built into Core Data, while not perfect, help remove the need for writing complex custom APIs.

Cons of Core Data

1. Some engineers find the managed objects unwieldy to work with and can introduce some complexities for concurrent applications.

2. Potential performance issues when dealing with large data sets. Performance issues are more common when using an in-memory backing store because the entire object graph must fit in memory.

3. Not inherently thread-safe. While Core Data is designed to work in a multithreaded environment, not every object under the Core Data framework is thread-safe, which requires the usage of managed objects.

Another benefit of Core Data is that it does not require managing query plans. While Core Data is not guaranteed to optimize your query or provide good performance (in fact, a common criticism of Core Data is that it does not have good performance for large queries), it does provide some opportunities for optimization and a strict framework to prevent mistakes. When implementing a custom SQLite solution, you as the engineer will have to perform these optimizations and ensure all queries are performant. Static query analysis can help catch bad queries at the code review level by statistically analyzing the queries, which is key to maintaining good performance and lessening the burden of manual inspection. Implementing static analysis is additional development work and must be balanced with other trade-offs, such as is a custom solution needed? What happens if we poorly perform SQL queries? Do we risk regressing our performance further?

While Core Data is far from perfect, it does provide a starting point for providing persistence and connecting the persistent storage to easy-to-use objects. As your application continues to scale and a performance bottleneck is detected at the Core Data level, or if the functionality provided is insufficient, you will have a specific use case and performance goals to guide the scoping and implementation of a tailored custom solution. Without defining a particular use case and purpose, it is easy to write a custom solution that solves the wrong problem and is not helpful long term.

Diving into SQLite

Whether you use Core Data or an alternative, you will most likely still be using SQLite underneath because SQLite provides the best way to persistently store and retrieve data that does not fit in memory, has a complex structure, or requires powerful query capabilities without writing your own database or using a third-party library like Realm. SQLite is the only database option provided natively for iOS devices. Understanding SQLite well allows you to understand the basis for any custom framework written on top of SQLite.

We won't discuss Realm here. While it is a viable alternative, it presents its own challenges since it is a third-party library including maintenance risk, potential for security vulnerabilities, increased application binary size, and difficulty with complex dependencies.

Note   Realm is a custom NoSQL database for mobile that does not use SQLite. Realm is a third-party dependency, so we do not discuss it much here; it is a viable alternative to SQLite.

What Is SQLite

SQLite is a library that provides a lightweight, fully featured, relational database management system (RDBMS). The *lite* in SQLite stands for lightweight and is related to the ease of setup, administration, and the small number of required resources for SQLite.

SQLite transactions are fully ACID compliant (**A**tomic, **C**onsistent, **I**solated, and **D**urable). In other words, all changes within a transaction take place entirely or not at all, even when an unexpected situation like an application crash, power failure, or operating system crash occurs.

In addition to transactions, SQLite has the following features that make it well suited for use in a mobile application:

1. Self-contained

2. Serverless

3. Zero configuration

We will discuss these features in depth.

Serverless

Typically, a relational database management system (RDBMS) like MySQL or PostgreSQL needs a distinct server process to run. To interact with the database server, applications utilize interprocess communication to send and receive requests. This approach, known as client-server architecture, is illustrated in Figure 3-5.

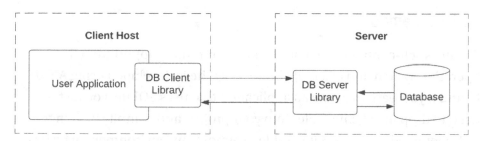

Figure 3-5. *Client-server architecture of most RDBMS*

SQLite does not use the client-server architecture. The serverless architecture allows SQLite to operate without a separate server process, which means that any program able to access the disk can use an SQLite database. Since the SQLite database engine runs within the same process as the application, no message passing or network activity is required. Figure 3-6 illustrates the SQLite serverless architecture.

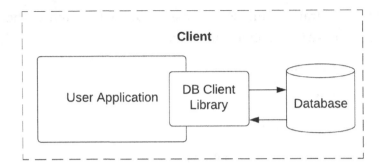

Figure 3-6. *SQLite serverless architecture*

However, without a separate server process, the database has less protection from bugs in the client application. For example, a stray pointer in a client cannot corrupt memory on the server. Additionally, with the server as a single persistent process, the database can have finer-grained locking and better concurrency unachievable with the SQLite model.

Self-Contained

SQLite is self-contained in that it requires minimal support from the operating system and external libraries. SQLite is developed using ANSI C, and if you want to create an application that uses SQLite, you just need to drop the SQLite C files into your project and compile it. Being self-contained makes SQLite usable in almost any environment, which is especially useful for embedded devices like iPhones.

Zero Configuration

Because of the serverless architecture, you don't need to "install" SQLite before using it. No server process needs to be configured, started, and stopped. Additionally, SQLite does not require complex configuration files.

SQLite Architecture

The SQLite library contains four core components (Figure 3-7):

1. Core

2. Backend

3. SQL compiler

4. Accessories

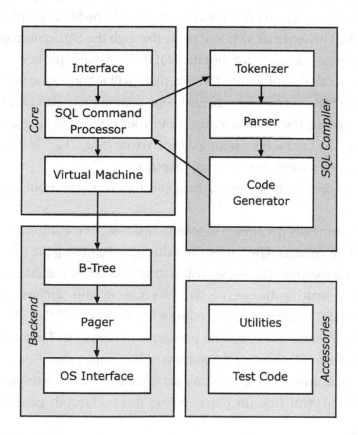

Figure 3-7. SQLite architecture diagram as shown on www.sqlite.org/

The accessories module is mainly utils and tests, so we will skip that component and discuss the core, backend, and SQL compiler in more detail. Let's start with the SQL compiler, commonly known as the front end, and walk through the components in the order that they execute for a SQL query.

SQL Compiler: The Front End

As the name would suggest, the SQL compiler will take our SQL query as input; however, we do not directly interact with the SQL compiler. We utilize the SQLite external APIs that route through the SQL command processor. Once our query reaches the SQLite command processor, the first step is to call the tokenizer. The tokenizer will tokenize the SQL query breaking the SQL text into tokens. Each SQL statement is also checked for correct syntax. If you made a mistake in your query, the tokenizer would reject the query. For example, if you wrote "SLECT ..." instead of "SELECT ...", the tokenizer will return an error.

After this process is complete, the resulting tokenized input is passed to the parser.

The parser reads the stream of tokens and assigns meaning to them based on their context. The parser does this by assembling the tokenized input into a parse tree. The parser will also help validate the information, for example, ensuring the query is written correctly and catches errors such as a WHERE statement proceeding a SELECT (WHERE id SELECT table...). SQLite utilizes the Lemon parser for parsing. The Lemon parser generates relevant C code from given sets of language rules; Figure 3-8 illustrates an example of the resulting parse tree. Once the parse tree is assembled and error-free, the parser passes this to the code generator.

```
SELECT name
FROM animals
WHERE species = "dog"
```

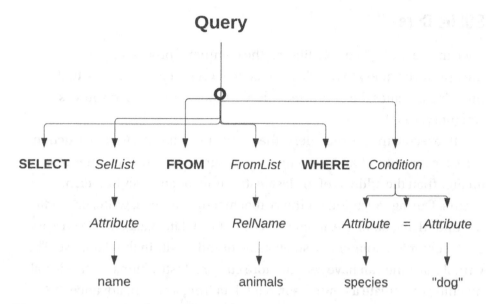

Figure 3-8. *Example parse tree for our query*

The code generator runs to analyze the parse tree and generates an SQLite virtual machine bytecode representation of the initial SQL statement. This step also includes the query planner, which algorithmically strives to optimize the initial SQL query. There are innumerable potential query paths for performing the SQL query for any SQL statement. These paths will return the correct result; however, some will execute faster than others. The query planner strives to optimize for this and pick the fastest, most efficient algorithm for each SQL statement. To assist the query planner, engineers can provide indexes that help the query planner understand the organization of the data and better create the most efficient query. Once the code generator has optimized the query, the parsed input is passed back into the core library.

SQLite Core

Back inside the SQLite core library, the command processor passes
the optimized query to the virtual machine for execution. The virtual
machine executes the optimized query if there are enough resources
(memory, CPU).

To execute the parsed query, the virtual machine starts at instruction
zero. It runs until a halt instruction, the program counter becomes one
greater than the address of the last instruction, or an execution error
occurs. During execution for the virtual machine to read, write, or modify
the underlying database, it interacts with the SQLite back end via cursors.
Each cursor is a pointer to a single table or index within the database. The
virtual machine can have zero or more cursors. Instructions in the virtual
machine can create a new cursor, read data from a cursor, advance the
cursor to the next entry in the table or index, and many other operations
outlined in the SQLite documentation.

When the virtual machine halts, all allocated memory is released, and
all open database cursors are closed. If the execution stops due to an error,
the virtual machine terminates any pending transactions and reverses
changes made to the database.

SQLite Back End

Without the SQLite back end, the virtual machine would be unable to read
and write database data from the disk. The SQLite back end is responsible
for returning the query results from the disk for query operations. It
accomplishes this by utilizing the three modules it contains: the B-tree
module, pager cache, and OS interface.

The virtual machine communicates with the B-tree module to query
and modify the SQLite database, which provides an API to interact with an
SQLite database stored using the database image format (particular format
provided and understood by SQLite). The B-tree module is aptly named

and stands for the data structure used to maintain the SQLite database on disk. The B-tree data structure provides a performant way to query structured data. SQLite uses separate B-trees for each table and each index in the database.

Deep Dive: B+ Tree Implementation

SQLite utilizes a B+ tree, a self-balancing tree with all the values at the leaf level to provide performant data access. This is especially important for databases since getting information requires disk access since it is not possible for all information to be stored in memory. For illustration purposes, let us assume

1. We have ten million items in our data set.

2. Each name is unique and represents a 4-byte key.

3. 4 bytes total for the two left and right pointers (two 32-bit integers).

4. Each user's data record is about 50 bytes.

5. An average disk sector is 512 bytes and can be accessed (read or written) in roughly 15 milliseconds (the disk speed depends on hardware, so this is purely for example purposes).

If we naively tried to utilize an unbalanced binary search tree in the worst case, we could have a linear depth and require ten million disk accesses! On average, a binary search tree's expected depth would be $Log_2 N$, with N equal to ten million, meaning about 23 disk accesses.

To avoid this, we need a more complex special-purpose data structure, such as a B-tree,[3] as it eliminates the depth of a binary tree by creating more branching with less depth. A B-tree guarantees

---

[3] What we describe as a B-tree is interchangeable for B+ tree.

1. Data items are stored at the leaves.

2. The non-leaf nodes (internal nodes) store up to M-1 keys (where M is the number of children[4]), where key i represents the smallest key in the subtree i + 1.

3. The root is either a leaf or has between two and M children.

4. All non-leaf nodes have between M/2 and M children (except the root).

5. All leaves are at the same depth and have between L/2 and L data items, where L is the number of data records that can be stored in each leaf.[5]

Now we can contrast our performance example from earlier with a B-tree where we can take advantage of the records that fit into one 512-byte sector. Let m=4. Then each node can have up to eight children and seven keys. With 50*7 bytes of information, 4*7 bytes of keys, and 4*8 bytes of children pointers, we have 410 bytes of information that fits comfortably into a 512-byte sector. With ten million records, we would have log410,000,000 = 11 disk accesses, reducing our disk accesses by half.

Figure 3-9 outlines a sample B-tree of order five. Here, all non-leaf nodes have between three and five children and two and four keys.

---

[4] An M-ary tree is where within each level every node has either 0 or M children.
[5] Mark Allen Weiss. 2012. Data Structures and Algorithm Analysis in Java. Pearson Education.

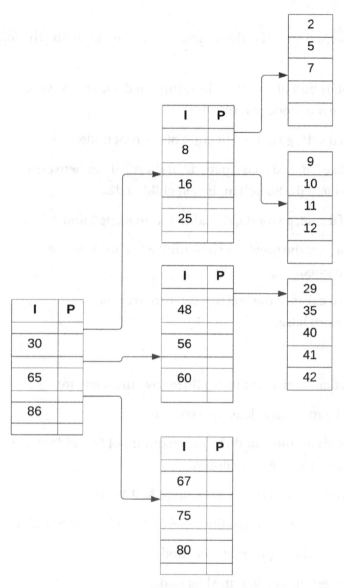

Figure 3-9. *B-tree with index (i) and pointer (p)*

Search

For searching a B-tree of order m and data d, we can define the following algorithm:

1. Start from the root node. Compare d with the keys at the root node [d1, d2...dm - 1].

2. If d < d1, go to the left child of the root node.

3. Else if d == d1, compare d2. If d < d2, d lies between d1 and d2. Search in the left child of d2.

4. If d > d2, go for d3, d4,...dm-1 as in steps 2 and 3.

5. Repeat the previous steps until a leaf node is reached.

6. If d exists in the leaf node, return true, else return false.

Insert

When inserting an element into a B-tree, we must ensure

1. The root has at least two children.

2. Each non-leaf node has a maximum of M children and at least M/2 children.

3. The non-leaf nodes store up to M-1 keys.

Algorithmically we can define inserting an element as follows:

1. Go to the appropriate leaf node.

2. Insert the key into the leaf node.

3. If the leaf is not full, insert the key into the leaf node in increasing order.

4. If the leaf is full, insert the key into the leaf node
    in increasing order and balance the tree in the
    following way:

    a. Break the node at M/2 position.

    b. Add M/2 key to the parent node as well.

    c. If the parent node is already full, recurse on steps 2 to 3.

Figure 3-10 outlines the insertion strategy.

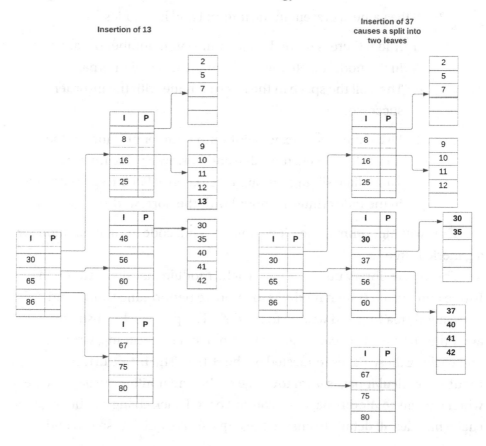

Figure 3-10. *B-tree insertion with adding a leaf and rebalancing*

Delete

We can algorithmically define deletion from a B-tree as follows:

1. If the value to be deleted is present only at the leaf node, and there is more than the minimum number of values in the node, then delete the value. Otherwise, delete the value and borrow one from the immediate sibling. Add the median value of the sibling node to the parent.

2. If the value is present in the internal and leaf nodes

   a. And if there is more than the minimum number of values in the node, delete the key from the leaf and internal nodes. Then fill the space in the internal node with the in-order successor.

   b. Else if there is an exact minimum number of values in the node, then delete the value and borrow a value from its immediate sibling (through the parent). Fill the space created in the index (internal node) with the borrowed key.

The Swift Algorithm Collection contains a full code implementation for a generic B-tree.[6]

The SQLite library utilizes a page cache module that sits between the B-tree and the file system modules to improve performance and avoid consistently reading and writing to the disk. The page cache abstracts away the complexity of caching and is responsible for reading, writing, and caching these pages requested by the B-tree. The B-tree driver requests particular pages from the page cache and notifies the page cache when it wants to modify pages or commit or roll back changes. The page cache handles all details to ensure the requests are quickly, safely, and

---

[6]https://github.com/kodecocodes/swift-algorithm-club/blob/master/
B-Tree/BTree.playground/Sources/BTree.swift

efficiently executed. In addition to caching, the page cache also provides the functionality for rollbacks, atomic commits, and locking of the database file.

Underlying the page cache module is the OS interface module that provides a way to interact with the file system uniformly and performantly across operating systems, commonly called the VFS. When SQLite needs to communicate with the file system, it invokes methods in a VFS (instead of directly on the file system itself). The VFS then invokes the operating-specific code needed to satisfy the request. The VFS provides methods for opening, reading, writing, and closing files on disk and other OS-specific tasks such as finding the current time or obtaining randomness to initialize the built-in pseudorandom number generator. The VFS serves as a helpful abstraction since adding a new OS for SQLite support involves simply adding to the VFS.

Figure 3-11 illustrates how the SQLite back-end components work in concert to performantly and reliably handle SQL operations.

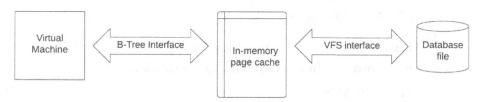

Figure 3-11. *SQLite back-end components and the interaction with the virtual machine*

Practical Example: Caching a Photo Stream

Taking a step back, let's look at a practical example using some of the persistence options discussed in this chapter. The goal of the practical example is to think through and document the solution as if you were the tech lead for the team. For this example, we will discuss the persistence layer for a Photo Stream application where a Photo Stream is a series of images a user can look through by swiping right or left. Our example project constraints:

1. We will receive images from the server to display based on the most recent timestamp.

2. After looking at all the available photos, the UI will return to the initial image.

3. We have a fantastic back-end team that has defined all the required APIs. We even get a perfectly paginated request with metadata for the user and the images.

4. Design with scaling in mind. While we are only dealing with a small amount of metadata now and only images, we want to ensure our solution can handle large amounts of user data and many different media types.

5. Users should not see images they have already seen; however, they can go back to see previous un-expired images.

6. Assume the server has a concept of seen state and won't show images seen on other devices. We also don't have to cover sending seen state to the server here.

7. Images expire after 24 hours.

8. Using GraphQL, we define the payload as

```
{
  "medias": [{
    "image_url": String
    "time_posted": String
    "id": String
  }],
  "cursor": String
}
```

Before reading ahead to the solution, stop and think about how you would architect a solution. What trade-offs would you consider?

We have two types of data for caching: text-based data associated with the media and the media (just images for now) themselves. If we were adding this to our engineering design document, we would also want to include a list of some of the trade-offs we considered when coming to the aforementioned solutions. An excerpt from a design document would look like the following.

Example Document

This document focuses specifically on the caching portion of the Photo Stream application. To properly support the broader product requirements, our caching solution must evict expired images (after 24 hours). Additionally, when necessary, we will use the cursor-based pagination method to request more data from the server. The broader design document will outline how and when we request more data from the server.

We must support text-based caching to meet the outlined product requirements and provide a performant user experience. To do so, we can

1. [Recommended] Utilize Core Data and SQLite as the backing store

   a. Quickly understood solution for most engineers.

   b. Relatively quick to implement.

    c. Well supported by Apple and does not involve pulling in any additional dependencies.

    d. It may not scale well if we have a very complex data mapping and heavy utilization across our application. If these problems occur later, we may consider switching to a custom SQLite implementation.

2. Custom SQLite implementation

    a. Similar to the aforementioned but requires additional development setup and maintenance.

    b. If we reach performance constraints with our current solution, this would be an excellent next step.

    c. Provides greater flexibility and potential for application-specific optimizations. As the application continues to scale, we may revisit this option.

3. Use the third-party library Realm

    a. App binary size increase from including the Realm library.

    b. No actual use case that Realm solves here – this may change in the future.

    c. Additional maintenance burden from Realm as a third-party library.

4. Serialize and deserialize objects from files stored on the device

    a. Storing the data in a serialized format (maybe JSON or a plist) in a file. While this would work, this would leave us to write serialization and deserialization code to our objects and may not scale as well depending on the future use cases for the application.

b. This will work now since our current data do not utilize any relationships. However, our feature plans for the application involve expanding to include relationships and a more complex data model, so we believe going with this option is short-sighted.

While Core Data is not perfect and can be somewhat tricky in multithreading situations, issues around performance will only manifest themselves later as we scale the application, and which point we can assess our biggest bottlenecks to performance and fix those in order of importance. If we want, we could switch to a more robust solution leveraging direct access to SQLite, acknowledging the additional time that would take.

Assuming we've decided to move forward with Core Data, we can start to make a preliminary architecture diagram (Figure 3-12).

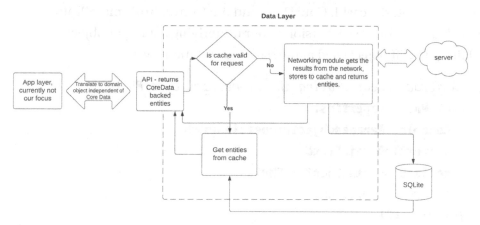

Figure 3-12. *Data layer for caching*

We must define our networking layers, model objects, and repository wrapper to translate our proposed solution into Swift code. To illustrate our model objects, we can first define our application-level plain Swift object for usage in data presentation.

```swift
struct Photo: ModelProto {
  let albumID: Int
  let id: Int
  let title: String
  let url: URL
  let thumbnailURL: URL
}
```

Now we must define our managed object for interacting with Core Data and a codable struct for decoding from JSON. For simplicity, the codable struct will also double here as the properties object for batch loading data in Core Data. For this, we implement the PhotoProperties struct and conform to the codable protocol to support decoding and encoding from JSON.

We also conform to the ManagedObjectPropertiesProto, which is utilized to interface with Core Data, and the ConvertToDomainProto, which allows for the conversion of our underlying data layer object to the plain old Swift object used in the data presentation layer.

```swift
// A struct encapsulating the properties of a Photo.
struct PhotoProperties:
    Codable, ManagedObjectPropertiesProto,
    ConvertToDomainProto {
  typealias DomainObject = Photo
  let thumbnailUrl: URL
  let url: URL
  let title: String
  let albumId: Int
  let id: Int

  // The keys must have the same name as the attributes of
  the entity.
  func getDictionaryValue() -> [String: Any] {
```

```
    return [
        "thumbnailUrl": thumbnailUrl,
        "url": url,
        "title": title,
        "albumId": albumId,
        "id": id
    ]
  }
}
```

Here, we define the Core Data required data layer object. Within the Core Data object, we also define typealiases for the DomainObject and PropertiesObject. This allows us to convert our networking and Core Data objects to the required data presentation layer struct in our repository.

```
import Foundation
import CoreData

// Managed object subclass for user
final class PhotoMO: NSManagedObject {
  typealias DomainObject = Photo
  typealias PropertiesObject = PhotoProperties

  @NSManaged var albumId: Int
  @NSManaged var title: String
  @NSManaged var url: URL
  @NSManaged var thumbnailUrl: URL

  // A unique identifier used to avoid duplicates in the
  persistent store.
  @NSManaged var id: Int
}
```

```
extension PhotoMO: ManagedObjectProto {
  static var coreDataEntityRepresentation:
  NSEntityDescription {
  return PhotoMO.entity()
  }
}
```

Lastly, we can add a protocol to convert to domain objects and add the appropriate extension code for our Core Data–managed object and network object:

```
protocol ConvertToDomainProto {
    associatedtype DomainObject
    func convertToDomain() -> DomainObject
}
```

and func implementation:

```
func convertToDomain() -> Photo {
  Photo(
    albumID: albumId,
    id: id,
    title: title,
    url: url,
    thumbnailURL: thumbnailUrl
  )
}
```

Now that our data objects are defined, we can express our repository, networking, and Core Data caching layers to complete the implementation. Here, we utilize URLSession API and wrap it in a custom protocol to support dependency injection (we will discuss it in depth in Chapter 6). The networking and Core Data layers are generic to be usable with any objects with the correct properties defined.

```swift
// Protocol to wrap URLSession for DI
protocol NetworkingProto {
  func dataTaskPublisher(
    for request: URLRequest
  ) -> URLSession.DataTaskPublisher
}
extension URLSession: NetworkingProto {}
final class NetworkManager: NetworkManagerProto {
  private let networking: NetworkingProto

  init(networking: NetworkingProto = URLSession.shared) {
    self.networking = networking
  }

  // This code is light on error handling and logging for
  // illustration purposes these cases should be handled in
  // production code
  public func send<T>(
    request: URLRequest,
    withResponseBodyType responseBodyType: T.Type
  ) -> AnyPublisher<T, Error> where T: Decodable {

    return networking.dataTaskPublisher(for: request)
      .tryMap() { element -> Data in
        guard let httpResponse = element.response as?
        HTTPURLResponse,
          httpResponse.statusCode == 200 else {
            throw URLError(.badServerResponse)
          }
          return element.data
      }
```

```
      .decode(type: responseBodyType.self, decoder:
      JSONDecoder())
      .eraseToAnyPublisher()
  }
}
```

We also need to define our caching layer utilizing Core Data.

```
import CoreData
import Combine
final class CoreDataManager: LocalStorageManagerProto {
  private let inMemory: Bool
  private let container: NSPersistentContainer
  private var notificationToken: NSObjectProtocol?
  // A peristent history token used for fetching transactions
  // from the store.
  private var lastToken: NSPersistentHistoryToken?

  init(
      persistentContainer: NSPersistentContainer,
      inMemory: Bool = false
  ) {
    self.inMemory = inMemory
    self.container = persistentContainer
    // Observe Core Data remote change notifications on the
    queue where the changes were made.
    notificationToken = NotificationCenter.default.addObserver(
        forName: .NSPersistentStoreRemoteChange,
        object: nil,
        queue: nil) { note in
          print("Received a persistent store remote change
          notification.")
```

```swift
        Task {
            await self.fetchPersistentHistory()
        }
    }
}
deinit {
    if let observer = notificationToken {
        NotificationCenter.default.removeObserver(observer)
    }
}

func getAllEntities<T>(
    for entityName: String,
    _type: T.Type) throws -> AnyPublisher<[T], Error> {
    let taskContext = newTaskContext()
    return taskContext.performAndWait {
        let request = NSFetchRequest<NSFetchRequestResult>(
            entityName: entityName)
        guard let fetchResult = try? taskContext.
        execute(request),
            let getResult = fetchResult as? NSAsynchronous
            FetchResult<NSFetchRequestResult>,
            let mos = getResult.finalResult as? [T] else {
            return Fail(error: CoreDataError.fetchError)
                    .eraseToAnyPublisher()
            }

        return CurrentValueSubject(mos).eraseToAnyPublisher()
    }
}
// skip methods for deleting and importing data...
}
```

To combine our underlying network and Core Data stacks, we can finally implement the repository itself. Here, we inject both the network and Core Data manager as dependencies and utilize a contrived cache timer to decide if we should load data from the Web or cache.

Notice how the repository itself is designated for a specific object type. This allows us to follow Swift's type-safe system and provide the necessary classes to the underlying network and local storage managers. Additionally, we have made our application framework agnostic by using dependency injection and generic types at the network and storage manager levels. If we changed from Core Data to Realm, we would not need to modify the repository. This is preferred as it keeps changes localized in the code base. For example, if we replaced Combine with a different framework, we would require changes at each code level, making for a more complex and time-consuming migration.

```swift
import Foundation
import Combine

class PhotoRepository: RepositoryProto {
  // For this example we load from the cache if < 5 minutes has
  // gone by.
  // when to use the cache vs. refresh would need to be defined
  as  a product requirement
  private var lastFetchTime: Date
  private var cancellables: Set<AnyCancellable> = []
  private let localStorageManager: LocalStorageManagerProto
  private let networkManager: NetworkManagerProto

  init(
    localStorageManager: LocalStorageManagerProto,
    networkManager: NetworkManagerProto
  ) {
    self.localStorageManager = localStorageManager
```

```
self.networkManager = networkManager
// for usage in the example, we are setting to an old time
// interval to ensure first network fetch
self.lastFetchTime = Date(timeIntervalSince1970: 0)
}

func getAll() -> AnyPublisher<[ModelProto], Error> {
  if (NSDateInterval(start: lastFetchTime, end: Date.now).
  duration <
  (5*60)) {
        return try! localStorageManager.getAllEntities(
            for: String(describing: PhotoMO.self),
            _type: PhotoMO.self)
            .compactMap { photos in
                let objs = photos.compactMap { photo in
                    photo.convertToDomain()
                }
                return objs
            }
            .eraseToAnyPublisher()
  } else {
        let sharedPublisher = networkManager.send(
            request: getURLRequest(),
            withResponseBodyType: [PhotoMO.Properties
            Object].self)
        sharedPublisher.sink { [weak self] result in
            switch result {
                case .finished:
                    self?.lastFetchTime = Date.now
```

```swift
                        case .failure(let error):
                            print("Error: \(error)")
                        }
                    } receiveValue: { [weak self] photoProperties in
                        let lsm = self?.localStorageManager
                        Task { [lsm] in
                            try? await lsm?.importEntities(
                                from: photoProperties, for:
                                PhotoMO.self)
                        }
                    }
                    .store(in: &cancellables)

            return sharedPublisher
                .compactMap { photos in
                    let objs = photos.compactMap { photo in
                        photo.convertToDomain()
                    }
                    return objs
                }
                .eraseToAnyPublisher()
        }
    }

    private func getURLRequest() -> URLRequest {
        // sample data for the example project
        return URLRequest(url:
            URL(string: "https://jsonplaceholder.typicode.com/
            photos")!)
    }
}
```

So far, we have discussed text-based caching, but what about the images themselves? Media caching comes with unique considerations; we need our caching solution to

1. Performantly fetch the images we need first

2. Persist cached images across application launches performantly and with respect to the available memory

3. Encapsulate the caching solution

We will discuss each area and combine them into our final architecture diagram in Figure 3-13.

Performantly Fetch the Images

Our image caching solution must understand the priority of the images to prioritize the download and storage of the most important images. Understanding the image priority is important because we need to prioritize images that are about to be shown to the user. We can do this by utilizing two queues: one for high-priority images and the other for low-priority images. The high-priority queue gives urgently required images exclusive access to the network. We can implement this in the form of an image pre-fetcher. We can take this a step forward and implement a pre-loader to load images that we know we will want later (potentially using the low-priority queue) in the background.

Persist Cached Images Across Application Launches

The cache is stored on the disk to ensure media asset caching persists across application launches. A cache eviction strategy is required to manage the cache's memory and ensure that users' devices do not run out of space. While NSCache provides its own cache eviction strategies, a custom class eviction strategy is also required to ensure that expired posts are purged from the cache. To avoid unnecessary disk access, it is also helpful to have an in-memory cache. By default, UIImage provides an in-memory cache, and we will utilize that here.

Encapsulate the Caching Solution

As engineers, we want to seamlessly utilize our caching solution in lockstep with our network request system. Additionally, we want minimal overhead for engineers who wish to use the cache. Minimal overhead also helps streamline the process and ensure adoption. One way to do that is to extend the existing media types to include our custom methods (obj-c category or a Swift extension), something like

```
imageView.setImageWithURL(imageURL,
    { (image, error?, cacheType, imageURL) in {
      // completion code here ...
    }
)
```

Additionally, we can provide a manager object capable of requesting media outside of our extension.

```
imageManager.loadImageWithURL(imageURL
                progress:{ (receivedSize, expectedSize) in {
                    // progress tracking code here ...
                }
                completed:{
                  (image, error?, cacheType, finished,
                  imageURL) {
```

```
if (image) {
    // completion code here ...
}
})
```

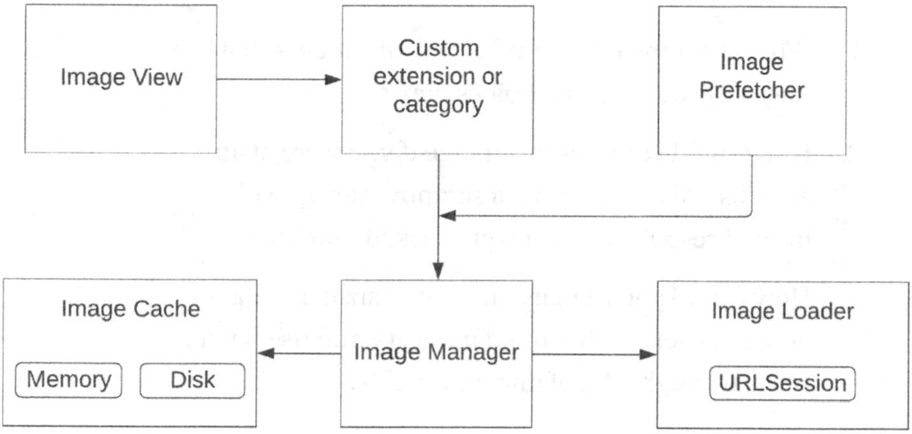

Figure 3-13. *Image cache*

Wrapping Up

The preceding example illustrates the thought process and trade-offs that ultimately result in the finished engineering design document. The solution outlined earlier is typically already implemented at most large companies either via a custom solution or utilizing a well-known third-party library (such as SDWebImage for media caching). As an engineer, it is helpful to truly understand the service these libraries provide and where the data is stored. It is easy to overlook certain aspects without truly understanding the underlying fundamentals, such as if the current solution uses an in-memory cache or is it always reaching out to the disk? Is it possible that the most important images aren't cached? Without first understanding the current cache eviction strategy, it is impossible to reason about the solution. Additionally, your application may have unique constraints that cause third-party solutions to be suboptimal; it is important to first understand the default solution so that these suboptimal scenarios become obvious.

Questions for the Reader

1. What are some other product requirements that may sway our design choices here?

2. How would your design change if you were at an established company vs. a scrappy startup with limited resources and a compressed timeline?

3. How would you manage the cache size? Taking into account users with limited memory and users who scroll through a lot of images quickly.

Summary

Deep-diving into SQLite is an exciting look at a well-designed piece of software. Also, it provides valuable insights into why databases work the way they do and how we can ensure our code uses them optimally. For example, we saw the concept of well-placed indices came up multiple times. Beyond SQLite, we looked at Core Data as a common API abstraction and other storage APIs with specific uses (NSUserDefaults and the keychain). We then looked at a practical example of building a caching solution. This example illustrated some of the trade-offs and common usages of the different storage options we discussed in the chapter. Whether you use a different wrapper over SQLite, NSUserDefaults, or the keychain, the core concepts around how these solutions best serve you still apply. The security risks presented by NSUserDefaults are also an excellent example of how we as engineers must carefully weigh different solutions and fully understand dependencies in our code base lest we risk introducing bugs and/or security vulnerabilities.

Key Takeaways from This Chapter

1. Security and privacy are essential. Ensure you understand the level of security required and act accordingly (utilize the keychain).

2. Beyond security, understanding storage solutions is critical for application performance, reliability, and ultimately delivering a quality user experience. While not glamorous, utilizing the wrong storage solution can lead to bugs and poor performance.

3. Understanding the underlying storage frameworks. NSUserDefaults is an excellent example of this; it becomes more difficult to reason about the security implications without understanding how the data is stored.

4. SQLite is essential as it is the main database available for iOS applications and is realistically the most used data storage system. Even if the internals are abstracted away by a framework (Core Data), understanding the underlying implementation assists in optimizing the solution.

Further Learning

1. Preferences and settings guide:

   a. `https://developer.apple.com/library/archive/documentation/Cocoa/Conceptual/UserDefaults/Introduction/Introduction.html#//apple_ref/doc/uid/10000059i`

2. SQLite documentation:

   a. `www.sqlite.org/`

3. SQLite and Core Data implementation:

   a. `www.objc.io/issues/4-core-data/SQLite-instead-of-core-data/`

4. Apple file system:

   a. `https://developer.apple.com/library/archive/documentation/FileManagement/Conceptual/FileSystemProgrammingGuide/FileSystemOverview/FileSystemOverview.html#//apple_ref/doc/uid/TP40010672-CH2-SW1`

5. Core Data guide:

   a. `https://developer.apple.com/documentation/coredata`

CHAPTER 4

Concurrent Programming

Overview

Concurrent programming is essential to application development; it allows your iOS application to perform multiple operations simultaneously while allowing the user to interact with the application seemlessly. However, with great power comes great responsibility, as concurrent programming presents some of the most challenging aspects of application development. To mitigate some of the challenges when using concurrent programming, it is crucial to have a well-designed system that considers the fundamental concepts of concurrent programming and the capabilities of the iOS ecosystem.

This Chapter Includes

This chapter includes an overview of the different types of concurrent programming and briefly discusses how they are expressed in the iOS ecosystem; however, understanding how to use the tools provided by Apple is only half the battle. Understanding the underlying concurrency paradigms and system design principles is more critical when architecting

© Eric Vennaro 2023
E. Vennaro, *iOS Development at Scale*, https://doi.org/10.1007/978-1-4842-9456-7_4

large-scale libraries and complex iOS applications. A correct architecture can help mitigate unnecessary code complexity and nondeterministic bugs. To address these topics, the second half of the chapter covers

1. Common pitfalls

2. Concurrent systems design based on real-world examples

Throughout the chapter, we will refer to several terms that, to avoid confusion, I would like to define here.

1. *Thread* refers to a separate path of execution for code for performing sequential computation. The underlying implementation is based on the POSIX threads API.

2. *Process* refers to a running executable, which can encompass multiple threads.

3. *Task* refers to the abstract concept of work that needs to be performed.

4. Signal is a form of interprocess communication mechanism used to notify or interrupt other processes or threads about a particular event or condition. It allows processes or threads to communicate with each other asynchronously and coordinate their actions.

5. Mutex, short for "mutual exclusion," is a synchronization primitive used in concurrent programming to protect shared resources from simultaneous access by multiple threads or processes. It ensures that only one thread or process can access the protected resource at any given time,

preventing data races and inconsistencies that could occur when multiple threads try to modify the same resource concurrently.

Concurrent Parallel or Async?

The terms "concurrency," "parallelism," and "asynchronous programming" are commonly thrown around and are surprisingly often confused with one another. In this first section, we will strive to define them.

Concurrency

In its most simplistic sense, concurrency is interleaving the execution of multiple tasks instead of executing each task sequentially. In programming, the "multiple tasks" are synonymous with having multiple logical threads of control. These threads may or may not run in parallel.

Multithreading

Multithreading specifically refers to computing with multiple threads of control. Once created, a thread performs a computation by executing a sequence of instructions, as specified by the program, until it terminates. A program starts a main thread that can then create or spawn other threads and synchronize with other threads using a variety of synchronization constructs, including locks, synchronization variables, mutexes, and semaphores.

Figure 4-1 represents multithreaded computation as a directed acyclic graph (DAG). Each vertex represents the execution of an instruction (an addition operation, a memory operation, a thread spawn operation, etc.).

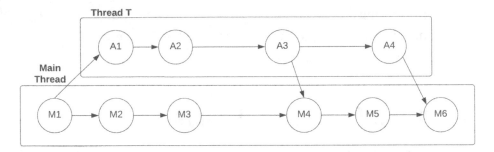

Figure 4-1. *DAG of multithreaded execution*

Parallelism

Parallelism is when multiple tasks are performed in parallel. A parallel program may or may not have multiple threads. Parallelism could take the form of using multiple cores on a processor or multiple servers. In this way, we can write parallel software by utilizing structured multithreading constructs. Figure 4-2 compares concurrent execution to parallel execution. In this example, the parallel execution can be considered two separate processes.

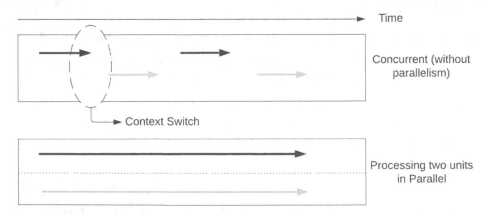

Figure 4-2. *Concurrent and parallel execution*

Parallelism and concurrency are orthogonal to each other. Some applications are concurrent, others are not, and many concurrent applications utilize parallelism. For example, an iOS application that is a concurrent application may use a parallel algorithm to perform specific tasks at the system or user level. One way we can implement parallelism in our code is via a fork-join system.

To implement fork-join parallelism, we must designate specific points to fork into multiple logical processes or threads of execution (a branch point). When all branches are complete, the program joins the branches back to the main execution point. Figure 4-3 represents a potential parallel execution utilizing fork-join methodology.

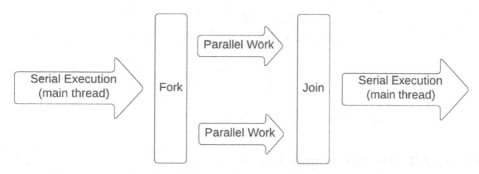

Figure 4-3. *Fork-join method parallelism*

Asynchronous Programming

Asynchronous programming is a separate, often related concept referring to the fact that two events may occur at different times. Figure 4-4 illustrates the difference between a synchronous and an asynchronous execution. The actors correspond to threads in the following example; however, they could also be processes or servers. The most common use case of asynchronous programming in iOS is using GCD (Grand Central Dispatch) to dispatch a networking call to a background thread while allowing the main thread to stay unblocked for UI updates.

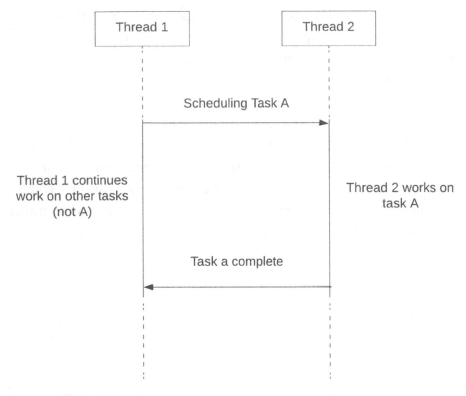

Figure 4-4. *Asynchronous execution*

Where Is This Going?

The biggest sea change in software development since the OO revolution is knocking at the door, and its name is Concurrency.

—Herb Sutter[1]

Concurrency and parallelism are now firmly at the core of everything we do as iOS developers. In iOS development, it is almost an implicit requirement to prioritize application performance by performing

---

[1]*www.gotw.ca/publications/concurrency-ddj.htm*

computational work in parallel. In practice, developers typically use GCD for concurrent programming because GCD provides an easy-to-use wrapper. To fully understand GCD, a baseline understanding of concurrency, parallelism, and its implementation is required. A deeper understanding of the underlying components allows for the architecture of concurrent software that can go beyond just using GCD to build better software, whether the result is a new application or an underlying library for application development.

Cost of Concurrency

Before diving into implementing concurrency in iOS, we will look at some of the trade-offs involved. Even though concurrency is a must for modern iOS applications as it allows them to process tasks in the background while unblocking the main thread for user interaction, it does have some drawbacks and performance considerations that we must account for.

Thread Cost

Creating threads costs your program in both memory use and performance. Each thread requires memory allocation in both the kernel memory space (core structures for thread management and scheduling) and your program's memory space (thread-specific data). The kernel memory requirement is 1 KB. Additional threads, other than the main thread, have an added in-memory cost, with the minimum stack size for a secondary thread being 16 KB; however, the actual stack size could change depending on the use case, as illustrated in the following code sample:

```
let current = Thread.current
print("current thread", current, current.stackSize)

let newThread = Thread()
```

```
newThread.name = "secondary"
print("second thread with default size",
      newThread,
      newThread.stackSize)

let newThreadTwo = Thread()
newThreadTwo.name = "tertiary"
// stack size must be a multiple of 4kb
newThreadTwo.stackSize = 4096 * 512
print("third thread",
      newThreadTwo,
      newThreadTwo.stackSize)
```

In addition, some of the extra work involved in multithreading is
due to the operating system and how it manages memory. For memory
management, most operating systems utilize memory pagination, also known
as memory paging or virtual memory paging, as a technique to manipulate
the memory resources of a computer system. It allows the system to allocate
physical memory efficiently by dividing it into fixed-size blocks called pages
and storing them in disk-based storage called a page file or swap space.

When using concurrent programming, memory pagination can have
a significant impact on performance, particularly when it comes to page
faults. A page fault happens when a process or thread attempts to access
a page that is not currently in physical memory. This can cause execution
delays as the operating system must retrieve the needed page from the
page file, which results in additional disk I/O operations. In parallel
execution situations, page faults can disrupt the execution of multiple
tasks, creating synchronization overhead and decreasing the overall
advantages of parallelism.

Overall, memory pagination is a net positive as it enables systems
to have a larger effective memory capacity than the physical memory
available. This can be advantageous for parallel execution as it allows

multiple processes or threads to execute concurrently, each with its own virtual memory space. Additionally, by dividing memory into pages, each process or thread can have its own dedicated virtual memory space. This isolation prevents interference between parallel tasks, enhancing the stability and security of the system. The specific impact will depend on factors such as the nature of the parallel tasks, memory access patterns, and the efficiency of the operating system's memory management algorithms.

The last impact from thread creation we will mention here is the startup cost at creation time due to the required context switches. The exact startup timing can vary by iOS device and is worth tracking in your application (covered in Chapter 14).

Managing State Sharing

Utilizing threads creates the need to manage shared resources and shared state. No matter what mechanism you use to manage the sharing of resources, some inherent context switching must occur. This context switching and the potential for deadlocks and race conditions produce memory and latency overhead that must be balanced and accounted for when planning.

Difficult to Debug

Writing and testing concurrent programming can be difficult, especially because many of the bugs are due to the nondeterministic execution of the code. Luckily Xcode provides tools to help identify threading issues, including the Thread Sanitizer (which detects race conditions between threads) and the Main Thread Checker (which verifies that system APIs that must run on the main thread actually do run on that thread). However, even when using these tools, debugging concurrency-related bugs can still require long periods of time spent reading stack traces and adding additional logging.

Implementing Concurrency

In this section, we will cover a few different concurrency models starting with the most basic implementation of threads and locks. In each section, we will tie the implementation to architectural best practices.

Threads and Locks

Anytime implementing concurrency is discussed, the conversation begins with threads and locks. Utilizing threads and locks is the most well-known implementation of concurrency. The concepts here underlie GCD and many other, more abstracted concurrency models. In this model, threads are created by the user, and the user must

1. Create and deallocate threads and adjust the number dynamically to reflect changing system conditions

2. Leverage synchronization mechanisms like mutexes, locks, and semaphores to orchestrate resource access between threads, adding more overhead to application code

Brief Aside on Locks

Locks provide a way to synchronize access to threads and protect access to a given region of code. Different locks exist:

1. Semaphore: Allows up to N threads to simultaneously access a given region of code.

2. Mutex: Ensures that only one thread is active in a given region of code at a time.

3. Spinlock: Causes a thread trying to acquire a lock to wait in a loop while checking if the lock is available. It is efficient if waiting is rare but wasteful if waiting is common.

4. Read-write lock: Provides concurrent access for read-only operations but exclusive access for write operations. Efficient when reading is common and writing is rare.

5. Recursive lock: A mutex that can be acquired by the same thread many times.

Directly utilizing threads provides the maximum amount of control to the programmer and consequently provides the largest surface area for bugs. It is common to run into race conditions and deadlocks if the approach is not planned out well from the beginning. Let's look at an example of programming a banking application that accepts withdrawals on a predefined balance. We can naively program the Bank to have a name and a balance for withdrawals.

```
class Bank {
  let name: String
  var balance: Int

  init(name: String, balance: Int) {
    self.name = name
    self.balance = balance
  }

  func withdraw(value: Int) {
    print("\(self.name): Checking balance")
    if balance > value {
      print("\(self.name): Processing withdrawal")
      // sleeping for some random time, simulating a
```

```
    // long process
    Thread.sleep(
      forTimeInterval: Double.random(in: 0...2))
    balance -= value
    print("\(self.name): Done: \(value) withdrawn")
    print("\(self.name): Current balance: \(balance)")
  } else {
    print("\(self.name): Insufficient balance")
  }
 }
}
```

When we have one bank teller executing all transactions synchronously, our program works fantastically. However, at any large-scale bank, we will have multiple tellers making multiple transactions, so let us test how our program handles this situation.

To model having multiple tellers using threads, we can create a class to drive the program's execution and then two threads to simulate two tellers executing transactions.

```
class ProgramDriver {
  let bank = Bank(name: "PNC", balance: 1200)

  func executeTransactions() {
    let thread = Thread(target: self,
                        selector: #selector(t1),
                        object: nil)
    let thread2 = Thread(target: self,
                         selector: #selector(t2),
                         object: nil)
    thread.start()
    thread2.start()
  }
```

```swift
@objc func t1() {
  bank.withdraw(value: 1000)
}

@objc func t2() {
  bank.withdraw(value: 400)
}
}
```

ProgramDriver().executeTransactions()

Now as we execute the transactions, we immediately uncover an issue; we have allowed the balance to go negative!

```
PNC: checking balance
PNC: checking balance
PNC: Processing withdrawal
PNC: Processing withdrawal
PNC: Done: 1000 withdrawn
PNC: Current balance: 200
PNC: Done: 400 withdrawn
PNC: Current balance: -200
```

How did this happen? In our current implementation, we have no way to synchronize the balance between transactions, meaning that when our multiple threads try to perform the withdrawal operation simultaneously, they can execute out of order and lead to a negative balance. This is an example of a race condition.

How to handle the situation when multiple people try to access the same resource simultaneously?

To combat this, we want to synchronize access to the shared resource, thus enforcing *mutual exclusion*. We can do this naively by implementing an NSLock, which only a single thread can hold at a time. In the following code sample, we modified our Bank to include a lock around the contentious withdrawal function.

121

```swift
let lock = NSLock()
class Bank {
  let name: String
  var balance: Int

  init(name: String, balance: Int) {
    self.name = name
    self.balance = balance
  }

  func withdraw(value: Int) {
    lock.lock()
    print("\(self.name): checking balance")
    if balance > value {
      print("\(self.name): Processing withdrawal")
      // sleeping for some random time, simulating a
      // long process
      Thread.sleep(
        forTimeInterval: Double.random(in: 0...2))
      balance -= value
      print("\(self.name): Done: \(value) withdrawn")
      print("\(self.name): Current balance: \(balance)")
    } else {
      print("\(self.name): Insufficient balance")
    }
    lock.unlock()
  }
}
```

Now, when we run our code, we see

PNC: checking balance
PNC: **Processing** withdrawal
PNC: **Done**: 1000 withdrawn
PNC: **Current** balance: 200
PNC: checking balance
PNC: **Insufficient** balance

While adding the lock has seemingly solved the race condition at a larger scale, this would involve adding in locks across the code base and in general requires precise unlock location. Using GCD typically provides a more robust, easy-to-use alternative.

Using GCD and Dispatch Queues

Luckily for us, Apple has introduced GCD, which acts as a system-level wrapper for the thread management code to provide a robust solution for applications like our Bank application discussed previously. GCD provides a queue structure, a thread pool, and concurrency controls (semaphores) to manage concurrent code and provide asynchronous execution of tasks (represented as closures – blocks in obj-c).

GCD Key Concepts

Instead of interacting with threads, using GCD allows you to add blocks of code to queues and reason about work items as tasks in queues rather than threads. Behind the scenes, GCD manages a thread pool and decides which thread to execute your code on based on available system resources. This alleviates the problem of creating expensive threads by providing a way to centrally manage thread creation and abstract it away from the application developer.

GCD exposes five different queues:

1. The main queue running on the main thread

2. Three background queues with different priorities

3. One background queue with an even lower priority,
    which is I/O throttled

In addition to the provided queues, you can create custom queues,
which can be serial or concurrent. While custom queues are a powerful
abstraction, all blocks you schedule on them will ultimately trickle down to
one of the system's global queues and its thread pool.

There are many more options available to GCD to customize the
priority of the queue and execution order, all of which make GCD a very
robust and flexible solution for concurrency. Figure 4-5 outlines the basic
GCD system. For more details on the GCD API, see the "Further Learning"
section.

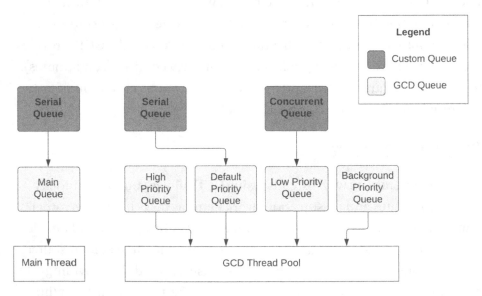

Figure 4-5. *GCD overview*

Applying GCD to Our Example

Now, GCD does not solve all our concurrency problems immediately. However, it does help structure our code and provides easy-to-use constructs for serial and asynchronous execution. To illustrate this, we can easily improve our concurrency approach for our banking application by removing the lock and replacing it with a serial queue.

```
// custom dispatch queues are serial by default
let serialQueue = DispatchQueue(label: "Serial Queue")
class Bank {
  let name: String
  var balance: Int

  init(name: String, balance: Int) {
    self.name = name
    self.balance = balance
  }

  func withdraw(value: Int) {
    serialQueue.async {
      print("\(self.name): checking balance")
      if self.balance > value {
        print("\(self.name): Processing withdrawal")
        // sleeping for some random time,
        // simulating a long process
        Thread.sleep(
          forTimeInterval: Double.random(in: 0...2))
        self.balance -= value
        print(
          "\(self.name): Done: \(value) withdrawn")
        print(
          "\(self.name): Current balance: \(self.balance)")
```

```
    } else {
    print("\(self.name): Insufficient balance")
    }
  }
 }
}
```

Now replacing lock-based code with queues eliminates many of the penalties associated with locks and also simplifies your remaining code by reducing the risk for deadlocks and more easily protecting shared resources. Lastly, queues make code more readable and easier to reason about; however, using queues does not prevent deadlocks. For example, synchronously dispatching a task from a serial queue to the same serial queue will immediately cause a deadlock because the caller thread is waiting for the dispatched block to execute, but the dispatched block will never execute because the serial queue is blocked from executing the caller code. Additionally, using a lock or serial queue only allows access to one thread at a time, potentially slowing down the application.

This can be a performance bottleneck if the state is shared across various components and requires access from multiple threads. An example of this is a value that can change periodically and requires network access for updates, for example, a cache or network access token.

Going back to our example, let us say we want to add a function to read our bank account balances. This creates a scenario similar to a cache, where we would want to allow concurrent operations for reads but exclusive writes. This scenario is an example of a reader-writer lock.

To implement this in iOS, we can use a concurrent queue, a concurrent queue allows us to perform multiple tasks at the same time. Even though tasks are added in a specific order, they may finish in a different order as they can be executed simultaneously. The dispatch queue manages separate threads for each task, and the number of tasks running at once depends on the system's conditions.

Along with our concurrent queue, we will need to use a GCD barrier flag. A GCD barrier creates a synchronization point within a concurrent dispatch queue. A barrier flag is used to make access to a certain resource or value thread-safe. This allows our concurrent queue to synchronize write access while we keep the benefit of reading concurrently. Figure 4-6 highlights the differences in execution between the serial, concurrent, and concurrent plus barrier flag queues we discussed.

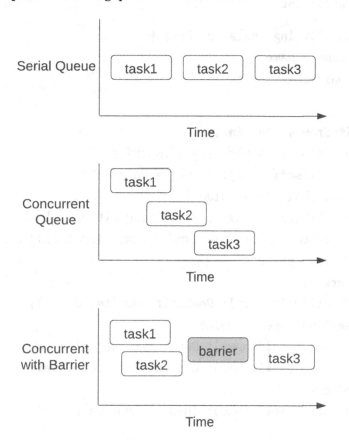

Figure 4-6. *Serial, concurrent, and concurrent with barrier flag queue execution*

Let us modify our previous example to include the concurrent queue and barrier flag.

```
let concurrentQueue = DispatchQueue(label: "Concurrent Queue",
attributes: .concurrent)
class Bank {
  let name: String
  var balance: Int

  init(name: String, balance: Int) {
    self.name = name
    self.balance = balance
  }

  func withdraw(value: Int) {
    concurrentQueue.async(flags: .barrier) {
      print("\(self.name): checking balance")
      if self.balance > value {
        print("\(self.name): Processing withdrawal")
        // sleeping for some random time, simulating a
        // long process
        Thread.sleep(
          forTimeInterval: Double.random(in: 0...2))
        self.balance -= value
        print("\(self.name): Done: \(value) withdrawn")
        print("\(self.name): Current balance: \(self.balance)")
      } else {
        print("\(self.name): Insufficient balance")
      }
    }
  }
}
```

```
func getBalance() -> Int {
  var tempBalance = 0
  concurrentQueue.sync {
    tempBalance = balance
  }
  return tempBalance
  }
}
```

One additional concept that is worth noting about all of our concurrent approaches is that we have encapsulated the concurrent code so that a caller does not need to worry about how to manage the concurrent operations. In our toy example, this is trivial; however, in more complex applications, understanding at what level of abstraction you choose to handle concurrent code in your application is an important design decision when developing a library. Typically, it is best practice to manage it at the library level instead of leaving it up to users of your API to manage the concurrent states. It is also essential to annotate the thread-safety level of your code clearly.

Operation Queues

Operation queues are a high-level abstraction on top of GCD. Instead of starting the operation yourself, you give the operation to the queue, which then handles the scheduling and execution.

An operation queue executes its queued objects based on their priority and in FIFO order and performs its operations either directly by running them on secondary threads or indirectly using GCD.

Benefits of Operation Queues

1. The Operation API provides support for dependencies. You can create complex dependencies between tasks more easily than in GCD.

2. By using Key-Value Observing (KVO), you can track various properties of NSOperation and NSOperationQueue classes.

3. You can monitor the state of an operation or operation queue.

4. Operations can be paused, resumed, and canceled, providing greater control over the operation life cycle. With Grand Central Dispatch, you have less control and visibility into the execution of that task.

5. With operational queues, you can set a limit on the number of queued operations that can run at the same time. This feature allows you to easily manage the number of simultaneous operations or create a queue for sequential execution.

6. Unlike GCD, they do not conform to the first in, first out order.

Swift Concurrency

Swift introduced actors and support for asynchronous functions via the async and await keywords as part of a new way to interact with concurrent code. The async and await keywords are relatively straightforward and allow for the restructuring of code to avoid completion blocks. Swift actors are class-like and protect their internal state through data isolation, ensuring that only a single thread can access the underlying data structure at a given time.

In this section, we will dive into the different building blocks that make up Swift concurrency (starting with async functions and actors) and then discuss the architectural considerations and the benefits of Swift concurrency when compared to GCD.

Async Functions

Asynchronous function annotations help structure concurrent code in a readable and maintainable manner compared to completion blocks associated with dispatch queues. While the asynchronous function syntax is straightforward, the actual execution is a bit more complex. Before diving in, let us review how synchronous functions execute. In a synchronous function, every thread in a running program has one stack, which it uses to store state for function calls. When the thread executes a function call, a new frame is pushed onto its stack (as outlined in Chapter 2). Now for asynchronous functions, we have a slightly more complex layout where calls to an asynchronous function (annotated by the await keyword) are stored on the heap with a pointer from the stack.

For asynchronous threads, there is no guarantee that the thread that started executing the async function (before the await keyword) is the same as the function that will pick up the continuation (breaking atomicity). In fact, await is an explicit point in code that indicates that atomicity is broken since the task may be voluntarily de-scheduled. Because of this, you should be careful not to hold locks across an await that, as we will discuss in more detail later, breaks the Swift runtime contract of making forward progress.

Actors

The actor model is a versatile and reliable programming model used for concurrent tasks. It is commonly used in distributed systems like Erlang and Elixir. In this model, actors are the core element of concurrent computation. When an actor receives a message, it can make local decisions, create other actors, and send messages. Actors can modify their own private state but can only interact indirectly with each other through messaging, which eliminates the need for lock-based concurrency.

Actors are a new fundamental type in Swift that has many benefits for concurrent programming:

1. Actors guarantee mutually exclusive access to their state.

2. Unlike serial queues that execute in FIFO order, the Actor runtime allows for re-ordering items based on priority and helps avoid priority inversion. This behavior is known as actor re-entrance.

3. Calls within an Actor are synchronous and always run uninterrupted until completion.

Swift Tasks

As mentioned earlier, Swift structured concurrency utilizes async and await statements to provide a readable and more intuitive way to architect your concurrent code. However, we still need a way to support concurrent execution. To support this, Swift includes the concept of a task, where multiple tasks can execute in parallel to, for example, download many images at once to your cache.

In order to run asynchronous code concurrently, a task creates a new execution context. These tasks are incorporated into the Swift runtime, which helps prevent concurrency bugs and schedules tasks efficiently. It's important to note that calling an async function does not automatically create a new task – tasks must be explicitly created within the code.

Structured Tasks

Swift structured tasks have built-in features that allow for cancellation of tasks and handling of abnormal task exits caused by errors or failures. If a task exits abnormally, Swift will automatically mark it as canceled and wait for it to finish before exiting the function. Canceling a task does not stop it but rather informs the task that its results are no longer needed. Additionally, Swift maintains a mapping of structured task execution, so when a task is canceled, all its descendants are also canceled automatically.

For example, if we implement URLSession with structured tasks to download data and an error occurs, the individual structured tasks will be marked for cancellation. The asynchronous function containing our URLSession will exit by throwing an error once all structured tasks created directly or indirectly have finished. Once a task is canceled, it is up to your code to appropriately wind down execution and stop. This is important for specific situations, such as if a task is in the middle of an important transaction where immediately stopping the task is inappropriate.

Unstructured Tasks

So far, we have discussed Swift structured tasks that provide many great benefits; however, they are constraining as the system maintains the lifetime of the task and the priority (based on the contextual execution context). Sometimes, more custom implementations are needed, which is where unstructured tasks come in. They provide the ability to create tasks where the lifetime is not confined to any scope. Because of this, they can be launched from anywhere (even non-async functions) and require manual cancellation, life cycle management, and the developer to explicitly await the task (all things that Swift structured tasks would handle for you).

The final type of unstructured tasks is detached tasks. Detached tasks provide even more flexibility and are completely independent of the originating context, which allows them to control the priority further.

What is unique about Swift concurrency is that we can utilize all three types of tasks concurrently to take advantage of the benefits of each while limiting their faults. For example, say we are on the main Actor (main thread) and want to utilize a task to store items in our cache. We could use a detached task to add items to a cache at a lower priority (only available as a detached task since an unstructured task would take the priority and context from the surrounding code). Additionally, say we want to do logging to annotate when cache writes occur. To do this, we could create a bunch of detached or independent tasks, but this would mean we have to handle the cancellation of all tasks and priorities. This makes a Swift structured task a better choice; however, even with a structured task, we still need to account for each child task individually. To account for this, we could use a task group and spawn each background job as a child task into that group. Using a task group means we can cancel all child tasks just by canceling the top-level detached task.

Furthermore, child tasks automatically inherit their parent's priority, allowing us to easily keep all work on the background queue without worrying about forgetting to set background priority and accidentally blocking UI work.

```
let objs = fetchObjs(for: ids)
Task.detached(priority: .background) {
 withTaskGroup(of: Void.self) { group in
   group.async { writeToCache(objs) }
   group.async { logResult() }
}
```

This creates the easily cancellable task hierarchy illustrated in Figure 4-7.

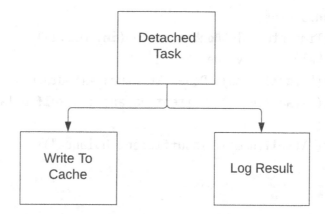

Figure 4-7. *Detached task hierarchy*

Applying Swift Concurrency

Now that we've discussed the basics of Swift concurrency, let us take our previous bank example and turn it into an actor:

```
actor Bank {
  let name: String
  var balance: Int

  init(name: String, balance: Int) {
    self.name = name
    self.balance = balance
  }

  func withdraw(value: Int) {
    print("\(self.name): checking balance")
    if self.balance > value {
      print("\(self.name): Processing withdrawal")
      // sleeping for some random time, simulating a
      // long process
```

```
    Thread.sleep(
      forTimeInterval: Double.random(in: 0...2))
    self.balance -= value
    print("\(self.name): Done: \(value) withdrawn")
    print("\(self.name): Current balance: \(self.balance)")
  } else {
    print("\(self.name): Insufficient balance")
  }
}

func getBalance() -> Int {
  return balance
}
}
```

Now we also have to change the way we trigger our balance to conform to the new framework.

```
class ProgramDriver {
  let bank = Bank(name: "PNC", balance: 1200)

  func executeTransactions() async {
    let thread = Thread(target: self,
                        selector: #selector(t1),
                        object: nil)
    let thread2 = Thread(target: self,
                         selector: #selector(t2),
                         object: nil)
    thread.start()
    thread2.start()
  }
```

```
@objc func t1() {
  Task.detached {
    await self.bank.withdraw(value: 1000)
  }
}

@objc func t2() {
  Task.detached {
    await self.bank.withdraw(value: 400)
  }
 }
}

Task{
    await ProgramDriver().executeTransactions()
}
```

Contrasting with GCD

Let us take a step back to compare architecting a system with GCD and compare that to Swift concurrency. To do so, we will revisit our application from the last chapter, where we discussed a caching layer and overall architecture for a Photo Stream. In that example, we had a UI layer, cache, database, and a networking module to fetch context and write to the feed. Using GCD, we could create the following concurrent setup outlined in Figure 4-8:

1. Dispatch serial queue async to database cache:

   a. Dispatch queue leaves the main thread free.

   b. DB access is protected as a serial queue guarantees mutual exclusion for DB writes.

2. Networking module:

a. URL session callback is a concurrent queue.

b. Synchronously update the database cache with any updates.

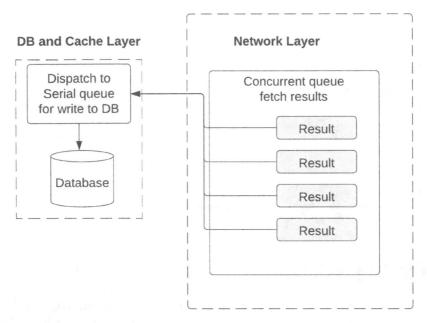

Figure 4-8. *GCD queue structure*

Note   Mutual exclusion refers to ensuring that only one process or thread can access a shared resource or critical section at a given time. It is a technique used to prevent concurrent access and potential conflicts that may arise when multiple processes or threads attempt to modify a shared resource simultaneously.

The purpose of mutual exclusion is to maintain data integrity and prevent race conditions, where the outcome of operations depends on the specific timing and interleaving of concurrent executions.

By enforcing mutual exclusion, conflicting or inconsistent states of shared resources can be avoided, ensuring that each process or thread can access the critical section exclusively and in a serialized manner.

Now we can sketch out the pseudocode for this using mostly standard iOS libraries:

```
let urlS = URLSession(configuration: .default,
                      delegate: self,
                      delegateQueue: concurrentQueue)
// later
for item in downloads {
  let dataTaks = urlS.dataTask(with: item.url) {
    data, response, err in
  guard let data = data else { return }
  do {
    let deserializedItem = try deserialize(from: data)
    databaseQueue.sync {
      updateDB(with: deserializedItem)
    }
  } catch { }
  dataTask.resume()
}
```

With the GCD-based model outlined previously, threads will block access to the DB queue, causing more threads to be spun up in the networking layer. As this happens, more context switching will occur, slowing the application down and potentially leading to crashes. This problem is called thread explosion and is further discussed in the concurrency pitfalls section on thread explosion. Now to address this in

GCD, we can limit the number of threads created through something as simple as a dispatch semaphore. While this may seem simple, it can be more complex in a real application, and however we choose to manage thread explosion, we have to do it manually.

In the following code sample, we transition our GCD code to using Swift concurrency. To do this, we will use a task group to get our data from the server and change our updateDB method to an async method.

```
await withThrowingTaskGroup(of: [Item].self { g in
  for item in downloads {
    g.async {
      let (data, response) =
        try await URLSession.shared.data(from: item.url)
      let items = try deserialize(from: data)
      await updateDB(with: items)
      return items
    }
  }
}
```

Now with Swift concurrency, we do not have to manually implement a solution for thread explosion; the runtime handles this. The Swift concurrency runtime environment limits the number of threads to the number of CPU cores because in the Swift concurrency environment, threads only switch between continuations (not performing a full context switch), and there is less overhead.

Rough Edges

Despite all the shiny new features, Swift concurrency still has some inherent costs, including additional memory allocation and management overhead. Just because Swift concurrency has easier-to-use syntax does not mean it cannot be overused.

Lastly, be cautious when using unsafe primitives such as NSLock, DispatchSemaphore, and NSCondition because they hide dependencies from the Swift runtime and consequently prevent the runtime scheduler from making correct decisions. For example, the following code sample could block indefinitely until another thread unblocks it – violating the forward progress contract of Swift concurrency.

```swift
func updateFoo() {
  let semaphore = DispatchSemaphore(value: 0)
  Task {
    await asyncUpdateFoo()
    semaphore.signal()
  }
  semaphore.wait()
}
```

Conclusion on Swift Concurrency

Swift concurrency has several primary benefits:

1. Cooperative thread pool – Swift underlying infra limits thread width to the number of CPU cores and performs other optimizations to prevent thread explosion.

2. Transparently controlled concurrency in the default runtime.

3. Compile-time safety.

4. Preserves runtime contracts for threads to always make forward progress.

5. Actor reentrancy helps address priority inversion.

The suite of Swift concurrency features includes

1. Async and await keywords to support asynchronous functions that provide a structured basis for writing concurrent code

2. Actors that provide data isolation to create concurrent systems that are safe from data races

3. AsyncSequence, which includes the task groups and other features that make a standard interface for working with asynchronous data streams

In totality, these features combine to make writing concurrent code in Swift easy and safe while removing some of the challenges associated with GCD. However, it is worth keeping in mind that Swift concurrency is still very new and may not be introduced in all applications or cover all use cases. This is a good example of the difference between starting a zero-to-one project where you can drive all technical decisions from the ground up (typically using the latest and greatest features) and an existing application where it may be best to continue with the status quo or require a solid data-driven reason to perform a costly migration.

Deep Dive: Challenges of Implementing Concurrency

Race Condition

A race condition occurs when one thread is creating a data resource or reading data while another thread is accessing it or writing on it. Anything you share between multiple threads is a potential point of conflict, and you have to take safety measures to prevent these conflicts. We have already demonstrated this problem in our implementing concurrency example involving our bank account.

Let us say we have thread A and thread B both reading the balance from memory; let's say it is 1000. Then thread A deposits money into the account, increments the counter by 200, and writes the resulting 1200 back to memory. At the same time, thread B also increments the counter by 400 and writes 1400 back to memory, just after thread A. The data has become corrupted at this point because the counter holds 1400 after it was incremented twice from 1000 (see illustration in Figure 4-9).

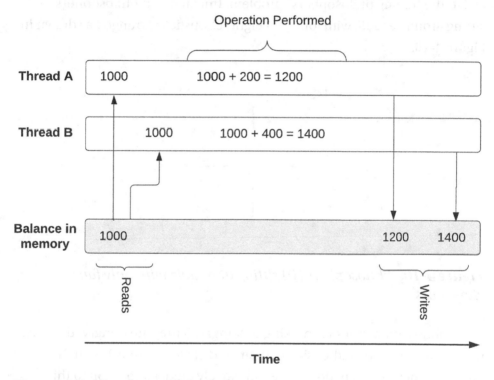

Figure 4-9. A race condition

To limit the threat of a race condition, we can utilize locks, dispatch semaphores, and/or GCD queues to design our concurrent operations. Avoiding a race condition can open the door for deadlocks.

Deadlock

Following along with our banking example, to solve a race condition, we can introduce locks. However, locks introduce the potential for a deadlock. A deadlock occurs when multiple threads are waiting on each other to finish and get stuck.

To demonstrate deadlock, we will use a common academic example called the "dining philosophers" problem. Imagine four philosophers sitting around a table with four (not eight) chopsticks arranged as drawn in Figure 4-10.

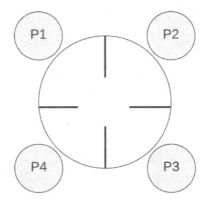

Figure 4-10. *Philosophers (P) sitting at a table with only four chopsticks*

A philosopher is either thinking or hungry. If they are hungry, they pick up the chopsticks on either side of them and eat for a while. When they are done, they put them down. We can naively model a solution to this problem utilizing dispatch semaphores.

```
struct Philosophers {
  let left: DispatchSemaphore
  let right: DispatchSemaphore
```

```
var leftIndex = -1
var rightIndex = -1

init(left: DispatchSemaphore,
     right: DispatchSemaphore) {
    self.left = left
    self.right = right
}

func run() {
  while true {
    left.wait()
    right.wait()
    print("Start Eating…")
    sleep(100)
    print("Stop eating, release lock…")
    left.signal()
    right.signal()
  }
}
}
```

Now, we could run this on our computer, and it will run successfully for a while. However, it will eventually stop working. This is because if all the philosophers decide to eat at the same time, they all grab their left chopstick and then find themselves stuck in a situation where each has one chopstick and each is blocked, waiting for the philosopher on their right.

A simple rule guarantees you will never experience a deadlock again when you acquire locks in a fixed, global order. However, as simple as that sounds, it is considerably harder to implement in a large-scale application where it is nearly impossible to understand its global state. For a more robust deadlock-free solution, see the Ray Wenderlich algorithm club solution:

```
https://github.com/raywenderlich/swift-algorithm-club/blob/
master/DiningPhilosophers/Sources/main.swift
```

Priority Inversion

Priority inversion occurs when a lower-priority task blocks a higher-priority task from executing, effectively inverting task priorities. More specifically, priority inversion can occur when you have a high-priority and a low-priority task sharing a common resource and the low-priority task takes a lock to the common resource. The low-priority task is supposed to finish quickly and release its lock, allowing the high-priority task to execute. However, after the low-priority task executes, there is a small amount of time for the medium-priority task to take priority and run because the medium-priority task is now the highest priority of all currently runnable tasks. At this moment, the medium-priority task stops the high-priority task from acquiring the lock, further blocking the high-priority task from running. GCD exposes applications to this risk because the different background queues can have different priorities (one is even I/O throttled). As iOS engineers, we need to be aware of priority inversion. Priority inversion is graphically illustrated in Figure 4-11.

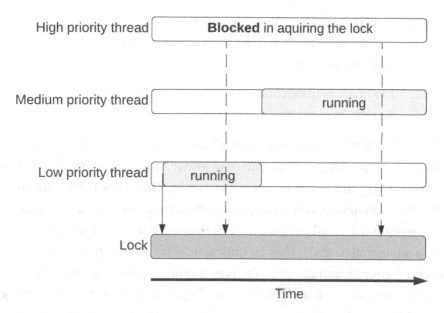

Figure 4-11. *Priority inversions, with the dotted lines representing attempts to acquire the lock*

Priority inversion can be hard to avoid. Depending on the situation, we can avoid blocking by using async. Alternatively, although not always ideal, you can minimize priority inversions by sticking to the default quality of service classes when creating private queues or dispatching to the global concurrent queue.

Thread Explosion

After reading the section on GCD queues, it might be tempting to make numerous queues to gain better performance in your application without worrying about creating too many threads. Unfortunately, this can lead to excessive thread creation. Excessive thread creation can occur when

1. Too many blocking tasks are added to
    concurrent queues forcing the system to create
    additional threads

2. Too many private concurrent dispatch queues exist
    that all consume thread resources

Thread explosion can lead to a deadlock where the main thread is waiting for a thread from the thread pool and all the threads from the thread pool are waiting on a resource, the main thread. They're both waiting on each other, and neither will give up that resource, so we have a deadlock.

One potential solution is to use global async queues; however, this is not a silver bullet, and it may be impractical for your application to execute entirely asynchronously. When synchronous execution is required, you can use a small number of dispatch queues and avoid using DispatchQueue.global(). In any performance optimization situation, measuring the change and choosing the best option for your specific problem are always advisable.

One prudent approach is to start with a serial queue. Then you can profile your application, see what, if any, portions require faster performance and could benefit from executing work in parallel, and specifically design those pieces of work in ways that are well managed to avoid thread explosion.

Another alternative here could be to use NSOperation queues that have concurrency limits.

Considerations for Real-World Applications

So far, we have covered the lower-level details of concurrent systems and walked through a toy example to get familiar with the building blocks and principles of concurrent programming. However, a toy example is not good enough to understand how to architect a real-world application with concurrency. To cover this portion, we will review two real-world examples and key takeaways based on their design decisions.

Example 1: Scaling Meta's Newsfeed

Working on a large-scale existing application means that there are already going to be set ways of handling common concurrent components, including caching, making network requests, and performantly updating the UI. Understanding the underlying concurrency constructs is essential to successfully work within the given system and hopefully work to improve it. The system may use less commonly seen tools like spin locks to optimize performance in niche situations. By familiarizing yourself with the deep concepts, you will quickly understand these limiting ramp-up times and increase the potential for you to suggest improvements.

An example of this is how Meta (then Facebook) improved its newsfeed performance. In 2012, Meta migrated its News Feed from HTML5 to a native iOS application to optimize performance. But over time, as other sections such as Groups and Pages were moved to native, the performance of News Feed degraded. Meta engineers leveraged performance logging to help debug and identify the root cause of the issue. For News Feed performance, engineers determined that the root cause was the data layer, specifically due to huge Core Data entities.

To address the large Core Data entities, the model layer was rewritten utilizing three principles:

1. Immutability: In the new data layer, models are entirely immutable after creation. A developer must create a new model object to modify even a single field. Since you cannot change the object, there's no need for locks, and thread-safety becomes trivial. This also allows for writing functional reactive code, reducing programmer error and making the code clearer.

2. Denormalized storage: To serialize these models to disk, Meta chose to use NSCoding. With each part of the app assigned its own cache, there was no longer contention for the single Core Data store shared by the entire app. It also ensures that products that do not want to cache to disk do not have to.

3. Asynchronous, opt-in consistency: By default, there are no consistency guarantees. By making consistency opt-in instead of opt-out, Meta ensured that database indexes were not used in situations where consistency was unnecessary. To opt in, a developer passes a model to a consistency controller; when it detects that a consistent field has changed inside the model, it hands the developer a new model with those updates. Behind the scenes, this consistency controller uses a GCD background queue to compute these updates, ensuring the main thread is never blocked.[2]

This also meant moving away from the Core Data framework, which guarantees strong data consistency but comes at the cost of performance. The discussion and outcome of Meta's engineering challenge are especially relevant for two reasons:

1. It demonstrates the importance of the immutability principle and asynchronous programming.

2. It demonstrates the move away from Core Data discussed in the previous chapter. We mentioned that Core Data is a great starting point; however,

---

[2] https://engineering.fb.com/2014/10/31/ios/making-news-feed-nearly-50-faster-on-ios/

it has some performance trade-offs. In the linked paper, Meta engineers outline how they saw degraded performance due to a bottleneck in Core Data and then used the same trade-offs we've discussed along with good monitoring and decided to move off of Core Data to a custom denormalized solution. The thought process and moving away from Core Data are a perfect example of excellent engineering leadership, and the goal of this book aims to teach you how to get, analyze, and act on data to make these decisions for your application.

Key Takeaway: Design for Scaling

When designing for scale, create best practices for application-wide patterns and abstract core components to a separate library (or libraries). This allows for specific optimization and better ease of use. You will be responsible for defining concurrency patterns for the application and ensuring that these create a consistent state. For example, if your application has underlying libraries that directly interact with the database and/or large C libraries that may implement their own concurrency, it may be your responsibility to ensure they mesh together performantly. Even though they have different concurrency implementation libraries, the principles of mutual exclusion, limit locking, and separating shared states still apply. Additionally, for ideas on how to implement this, it is always good to look at what the iOS standard library does for inspiration.

Lastly, when building a library, the concurrency paradigm must be standardized; otherwise, your library users might not organize their calls on the correct threads and may cause deadlocks (or other threading issues). Having org-wide standards and practices can help as well as invariants to check if the application is on the main thread. This help to ensure that best practices are maintained in high churn environments where it is not guaranteed users have a good context on past design decisions.

Example 2: Building Swift Concurrency

In Lattner's proposal for Swift concurrency, he outlines the proposal for what became Swift structured concurrency and the importance of a first-class concurrency model in Swift, specifically for asynchronous operations, which he states is the *next fundamental abstraction that must be tackled in Swift*.[3] Lattner outlines the goals of the proposal:

1. Design

2. Maintenance

3. Safety

4. Scalability

5. Performance (stretch goal)

6. Excellence (offering a better solution than other languages do)

Throughout the proposal, Lattner outlines core principles and why the actor model proposed satisfies them. He mentions explicitly how a shared mutable state is bad and how the actor model prevents this. Overall, Lattner touches on the same principles outlined in this chapter:

1. Avoid shared mutable state.

2. Reliability.

3. Scalability.

---

[3] https://gist.github.com/lattner/31ed37682ef1576b16bca1432ea9f782#overall-vision

Key Takeaway: Principles Transcend the Implementation Details

In the first part of this chapter, we mainly discussed implementation details and some trade-offs to consider. While the implementation details and specific APIs are important to understand for the technically competent team lead it is critical to understand the overall concurrency paradigms and architectural tradeoffs to set the overall project direction. At a higher level, a tech lead sets the overall direction for the project and outlines the key milestones, deliverables, and principles for building a scalable maintainable solution. In the aforementioned proposal, Lattner does an excellent job outlining the overall vision of the system.

Summary

Many higher-level abstractions can be added to improve application developers' use of concurrent programming. Different companies may even have more custom abstractions over GCD or custom C-level frameworks with their own APIs and way of managing concurrency. As an engineer, it is important to understand the basics of concurrent programming and how to best leverage the provided abstractions, and where potential issues may occur. Some of the most complex and inconsistent bugs are related to bugs in concurrent programming. By understanding the fundamentals and the iOS abstractions, you can help limit bugs in your own code and that of those you review.

Additionally, as you begin to design more complex systems that may interact with peripherals or custom client-infrastructure stacks outside of the iOS framework, managing concurrency will be more important and more challenging and will require relying on the fundamental principles and potentially dipping into the lower-level land of locks.

Three Key Takeaways from This Chapter

1. Almost all operations in an iOS application require multitasking, even something as simple as a network request, and with this chapter's in-depth analysis of the different concurrency options available, you should be able to select the one that works best for your needs. Whether that is a simple network request using NSURLSession or a complex, custom, multilayer networking library.

2. Concurrency fundamentals are key not only for ensuring the application's performance but also its correctness. Not following these principles can lead to complex nondeterministic bugs.

3. Familiarizing oneself with the optimization techniques for concurrent programming will allow you to optimize your application's model and business logic layers and suggest the best solutions for new features.

Further Learning

1. Apple documentation on dispatch queues:

   a. `https://developer.apple.com/documentation/DISPATCH`

2. Master GCD:

   a. `https://cocoacasts.com/series/mastering-grand-central-dispatch`

3. Not iOS based but an excellent overview at a systems level:

   a. `https://go.dev/blog/waza-talk`

   b. `www.youtube.com/watch?v=cNICGEwmXLU`

4. Swift concurrency:

   a. `https://developer.apple.com/videos/play/wwdc2021/10134/`

   b. `https://developer.apple.com/videos/play/wwdc2021/10254/`

PART II

Application Architecture and Design Patterns

## CHAPTER 5

The Importance of Good Architecture

Overview

This chapter marks the start of Part 2 of this book. In the previous chapters, we discussed Swift and iOS ecosystem concepts critical for correct coding. Without those fundamentals, programs will not execute correctly. However, as a senior engineer working on a production application, it is not just about the code; there is also a need for a well-defined architecture. A well-defined architecture promotes easier modification, ease of testing, and better developer experience. In Part 2, we will discuss application architecture, starting with the components and building up to the overall application.

As software engineers, we aim to implement functional architecture for our applications and enforce best practices within our code bases. We can achieve good architecture in many ways (as we will see in the modularity case studies); however, there are several fundamental principles that almost all quality architectures follow. Using these principles provides a template for creating well-architected applications.

This chapter will define

1. What an excellent practical architecture is

2. Why it is essential

3. The fundamental principle for achieving this

4. Case studies on how large-scale companies have leveraged this

In subsequent chapters, we will deep dive into different industry best practice design patterns and how these patterns, combined with coding best practices, feed into the behaviors of staff and principal-level engineers.

Defining Good Architecture

Good architecture can be defined in many ways. We will define it here as modular and testable. A modular application promotes the idea of single responsibility – where each object has only one responsibility. Modularity extends beyond that to enforce that distinct application segments, such as the onboarding flow, are self-contained units. This modularity also promotes flexibility since it becomes straightforward to substitute components at different application levels – whether that is a new onboarding flow or a new logging dependency. Lastly, we want our application to be testable; this allows us to be confident in our changes and quickly iterate.

The preceding mental model follows the common SOLID acronym for software design. The SOLID concepts are as follows:

1. The single-responsibility principle: Every class should have only one responsibility.

2. The open-closed principle: Software entities should be open for extension but closed for modification.

3.   The Liskov substitution principle: Functions that use pointers or references to base classes must be able to use objects of derived classes without knowing it.

4.   The interface segregation principle: Clients should not be forced to depend upon interfaces they do not use.

5.   The dependency inversion principle: Depend upon abstractions, not concretions.[1]

Applying Our Modular and Testable Framework to SOLID

The SOLID principles have long been the gold standard for software architecture. Let us see how the modular and testable mindset fits into these principles.

Single Responsibility Principle

By creating a situation where every class only has one responsibility, we are decoupling our components and preventing massive view controllers (and classes in general). We can think about this as modularizing our code at a micro level. Every class is a module that does only one thing.

This also applies to how we test our code. By making every class have a single responsibility, it is easy to define the class's behavior for testing and then write the tests. Writing the unit tests also helps us visually enforce we are following the single responsibility principle.

---

[1] Martin, R. C. (2003). Agile software development: principles, patterns, and practices. Prentice Hall PTR.

The Open-Closed Principle

To suit new requirements changes, modules should be extendable; however, the resulting changes should not cause any modifications to the module's source code. Consider a method that does one thing. Let's say it calls a specific API endpoint, the name of which is hard-coded into the method. If the requirements change and the endpoint changes in different situations, we must open up the method to change the endpoint. If the endpoint were passed in as a parameter, the behavior of this method would be modifiable without changing its source, keeping it closed to modification. To support a more complex module design like this, we can use protocols.

When creating modular code, it is important to consider what and how the code could change in the future and what downstream effects this could have. It is very frustrating to work in a code base where what seems like a small change can take weeks because it has unintended effects on other parts of the code, requiring building and rigorous testing of unrelated modules.

By following the open-closed principle, we can limit unintended changes for unrelated modules. For example, when writing tests for a change, we should only need to create unit tests to test and capture the behavior of the new feature. We do not need to add any new tests to other classes whose behavior is not changed.

Liskov Substitution Principle (LSP)

At its heart, LSP is about the behavior of a superclass and its subtypes. The goal of the LSP is for objects of a superclass to be able to be replaced by objects of its subclasses without breaking the application. This requires the objects of your subclasses to behave the same way as those of your superclass, meaning that subclasses need to follow these rules:

1. Don't implement any stricter validation rules on input parameters than enforced by the parent class.

2. Apply at the least the same rules to all output parameters as applied by the parent class.

To follow these rules in practice, we must utilize object composition strategies (think protocol-oriented programming) or inheritance. To illustrate the LSP principle, we can return to our animal's example from earlier. Say we have our canines class; some canines bark, while others howl (wolves). We could create a design where

```
public class Canine{
    public void bark(){}
}
public class GoldenRetriever extends Canine{}
```

The Golden Retriever can bark because it is a canine, but what about this:

```
public class Wolf extends Canine{}
```

The problem with the preceding model is that while a wolf is a canine, it howls and does not bark. The Wolf class is a subtype of the class Canine, but it should not be able to use the bark method, which means we are breaking the LSP principle. We could define a better model for this relationship by

```
protocol Canine{}
class BarkingCanines: Canine {
    public void bark(){}
}
class GoldenRetriever: BarkingCanines {}
class Wolf: Canine{}
```

In this new example, we have decomposed our Canine into additional subtypes to allow for more flexibility in how they make noise. In this way, we have made our design more modular; we have decomposed what it means to be a canine into bit-sized pieces of code and can then compose complex canines from our modular pieces.

From a unit testing perspective, the implications are similar to the open-closed principle implication. Unit tests need to be written for only the new feature, as other parts of the application should not be touched.

Interface Segregation Principle

The interface segregation principle is easy to understand and aims to prevent clients from being forced to rely on interfaces they don't need. By breaking software into separate independent parts, this principle, like the single responsibility principle, helps reduce side effects and the need for frequent changes. However, it's important to keep in mind as software evolves and new features are added to properly determine where new methods and features belong and how to segregate them into modules.

Dependency Inversion

The principle is straightforward: ensure that high-level modules, which contain intricate logic, can be reused without being affected by changes in low-level modules that provide utility features. Dependency inversion is used to achieve this by introducing an abstraction that separates the high-level and low-level modules. To enforce this, we should ensure that

1. High-level modules should not depend on low-level modules. Both should depend on abstractions.

2. Abstractions should not depend on details. Details should depend on abstractions.

With dependency inversion, we do not change the direction of the dependency. The dependency inversion principle helps us to create abstractions and handle the interaction between different modules.

From a testing perspective, following dependency inversions makes our code significantly easier to test. We can inject the mock-dependent objects to ensure that the class under test behaves as expected. Furthermore, for testing more complex behavior or integration tests, we can inject our test dependencies at higher levels and test the interactions.

Instead of injecting the dependencies for testing, utilizing mocks at the individual class level or a mocking framework that creates mock objects is possible. While a mocking approach is fast and easy, it becomes technical debt as dependency usage increases and changes, which is why dependency inversion is a preferred means of promoting testability.

Rather than remembering the individual principles of the SOLID acronym, I prefer to define good application architecture as modular and testable because no matter what design patterns, architecture paradigms, or release strategies we use or could use, given what is invented in the future, we always want to adhere to these base principles. We can easily frame design decisions around how to abstract the application components into modular units and how we will test everything, both in isolation (unit tests), together (integration tests), and on actual users (dogfooding or some type of alpha/beta testing). Once we have framed our design decisions, we can look to apply proven design patterns tailored to accomplish our goals in a scalable manner. Lastly, to ensure testability and application correctness, we will want to include the necessary development operations infrastructure to distribute the builds and gather actionable data from the tests (logging and bug reporting) into our overall plan.

Modularity

The tenet of modularity transcends the SOLID design principles and encompasses design patterns like the facade or builder pattern from the Gang of Four. Whenever you are designing a component or broader application, it is vital to consider how modularity applies at each level (design patterns, distinct frameworks, and the overall application architecture).

Even with the best design patterns in place, an application can become unwieldy if everything is coupled into a single framework or library. This coupling leads to slow build times, complex merge conflicts, and a complicated ownership model for large software teams. To best illustrate the pitfalls of a tightly coupled application, let's explore a case study of how Uber split their ride application.

Modularity Case Studies

Uber Redesign for Scale

In 2009, Uber decided to redesign their rider application completely. At the time, Uber faced problems scaling their code base related to previous design decisions and felt that a redesign would give them more freedom to build architecturally correct new features vs. continuing to make compromises. Specifically, Uber stated that *our trip module grew large, becoming hard to test. Incorporating small changes ran the chance of breaking other parts of the app, making experimentation fraught with collateral debugging, inhibiting our pace for future growth.*[2]

To shrink their module size, Uber moved away from traditional application architecture patterns and created RIBLETS. Each RIBLET comprises one router, interactor, builder, and optional presenters and views. Inside of the RIBLET, the router and interactor handle the business

---

[2] https://eng.uber.com/new-rider-app-architecture/

logic, while the presenter and view handle the view logic. In this way, RIBLETS are modular; however, they also need to interact with one another. To accomplish this, the interactor component of the RIBLET makes service calls to fetch data. The data flow is unidirectional from the service to the model stream and from the model stream to the interactor. The model stream produces immutable models, thus enforcing the requirement that the interactor classes use the service layer to change the application's state.

In this way, at a feature level, an individual engineer writing a driver rating module using RIBLETS will, by default, separate the business logic, view logic, data flow, and routing, making a modular component. At an application-wide level (a team of engineers working on a logging library), this framework provides a clear separation of concerns of the different flows in the Uber application (made up of RIBLETS) and helps prevent the application from increasing in complexity in the future.

While RIBLET is not a traditional iOS application architecture (although it does follow functional reactive programming data flow), it does enforce modularity by clearly separating concerns and thus providing a scalable foundation for Uber engineers across the company. Even if Uber engineers had been using Gang of Four design patterns perfectly, they still would have encountered the same issues around growing complexity due to large modules and would need a better way to enforce modularity.

Creating Component Kit

Meta (then Facebook) shows another example of the importance of modularity by creating ComponentKit for reusable iOS views. ComponentKit takes a functional, declarative approach to building UI and emphasizes a one-way data flow from immutable models to immutable components that describe how views should be configured. ComponentKit was created to solve the problem of building user interfaces that require a lot of imperative code.[3]

Initially, ComponentKit was rolled out on Facebook and provided numerous benefits, including the following:

1. Reduce the size of our rendering code by 70% by removing manual and intricate layout code.

2. Significantly improve scroll performance by creating a flatter, more optimal view hierarchy for components.

3. Improve test coverage by making it easy to build a modular UI that is testable in isolation.

While the initial goal of ComponentKit was to lessen the burden of imperative code by providing a declarative way to build view hierarchies, the end result of abstracting ComponentKit into a reusable module provided a great way to optimize performance. Now the ComponentKit website[4] boasts a declarative layout framework that is very performant, having the following:

1. Asynchronous Layout lays out your UI ahead of time without blocking the UI thread.

2. Flatter view hierarchies reduce the number of UIViews your UI contains and improve memory and scroll performance.

3. Fine-grained view recycling reduces the need for multiple view types and improves memory usage and scroll performance.

---

[3]https://engineering.fb.com/2015/03/25/ios/introducing-componentkit-functional-and-declarative-ui-on-ios/
[4]https://componentkit.org/

Splitting ComponentKit into its own module allowed a dedicated team of engineers to optimize its performance. It also allowed engineers across the company to take advantage of the provided features. Another win for modularity!

Airbnb Designing for Productivity

As Airbnb's iOS application grew, Airbnb's mobile engineers faced many challenges. Since most of their code was organized into modules within a flat directory, it was hard for engineers to find the existing implementations of general-purpose capabilities. Additionally, the application itself was becoming larger as increasing numbers of engineers iterated on complex features. The increase in the size of the code base led to a whole host of Xcode-related problems. For Airbnb, as the Xcode project files grew in size, they became challenging to review, resulting in merge conflicts and race conditions inhibiting teams from moving at a high velocity. Xcode took between one and two minutes to become interactive when loading a workspace with all of their source code. iOS engineers were beginning to spend most of their day waiting for code to compile and build instead of building features.[5]

To address these issues, Airbnb further modularized its code by

1.   Adopting buck as a modern build system. Buck provided; network caches of build artifacts, a query interface for the build graph, and a seamless way to add custom steps as dependencies leading to considerably faster build times.

---

[5] https://medium.com/airbnb-engineering/designing-for-productivity-in-a-large-scale-ios-application-9376a430a0bf

2. Moving code from a flat folder to a hierarchy with module types (a semantically meaningful group of modules). Each module type has a strict set of visibility rules defining allowed dependencies, including that feature modules cannot depend on each other. The strict visibility rules enforce encapsulation and further modularize the Airbnb application.

3. Creating Dev Apps. Airbnb's usage of buck and strong modularity enabled Dev Apps. A Dev App is an on-demand, ephemeral Xcode workspace for a single module and its dependencies. Minimizing the IDE scope to only the files that need editing dramatically reduces the friction in developing large-scale applications by limiting build and compile times.

Adopting module types allowed Airbnb to break costly dependencies between functional units. Now modules have minimal dependencies, ensuring that building a single feature module and all of its dependencies is much cheaper than building the entire Airbnb application. Since feature modules cannot depend on other feature modules, there is no chance of a mega feature that transitively builds the entire application. Layering on a modern build system further allowed Airbnb to create Dev Apps, which increased code ownership and developer productivity – freeing engineers from the constraints of large application development.

Wrapping Up Modularity

When designing an entire application, the design is the sum of the individual subsystems. While the individual subsystems should utilize design patterns and sound architecture principles, this isn't enough if the individual subsystems are simply mushed together. Avoiding this mush is the overall goal of modularity because that allows for the easy construction of applications from subsystems, faster build times, and better code reuse (think shared UI libraries or optimized networking stacks).

Testability

A good practical architecture is easy to iterate on, expand upon, and quickly build and iterate on features to achieve business goals. A large portion of building and iterating on features comes down to the ease of making changes and testing their correctness. A well-architected app with no testing leads to slow progress since all changes require a good deal of manual testing. In an ideal world, engineers make succinct code changes without side effects; however, to be sure, we still need to verify this.

By having a high-quality suite of automated unit and integration tests, developers can be reasonably certain of the correctness of their changes. But testability does not stop here; no matter what change we make, we need to verify that it is not regressing overall application experience. Additionally, UI-based changes must meet design specifications for all areas (which can require manual inspection). To help expedite this process and ensure good coverage, teams can utilize QA resources, UI snapshot testing, and dogfooding to gather user feedback. Performing all three functions succinctly requires additional developer operations infrastructure for automated build/distribution pipelines and high-fidelity logging. These considerations are also required for high-quality architecture and firmly fall under the banner of testability.

Testing Case Studies
Large-Scale Testing and Sapienz at Meta

Meta has placed a lot of effort and attention on integration tests for mobile applications. They have heavily invested in frameworks for regression detection, including Sapienz. To support these efforts, Meta has created a large-scale distributed testing framework allowing engineers to run tests by accessing thousands of mobile devices available in their data centers.

Additionally, Meta built a new, unified resource management system, code-named One World, to host these devices and other runtimes such as web browsers and emulators. Engineers at Facebook can use a single API to communicate with these remote resources within their tests and other automated systems. One World aims to support any application that an engineer might want to use with a remote runtime and minimal modifications to their code or environment, providing the illusion that remote devices are connected locally. To support this, Meta built a system consisting of four main components:

1. Runtime worker service: Each resource type has its own runtime worker service that runs on machines managing the resource. The worker service manages the resource's life cycle and responds to clients' requests to use its resources.

2. One World daemon: This lightweight service runs on machines that will connect to remote resources and creates the environment to allow local processes to communicate with remote resources.

3. Scheduler: The scheduler matches clients with available workers matching their specified requirements.

4. Satellite: A minimal deployment of the worker service that allows engineers to connect local resources to the global One World deployment.[6]

Additionally, Facebook invested in Sapienz, which leverages automated test design to make the testing process faster, more comprehensive, and more effective. Sapienz originated as a research paper and utilizes machine learning to understand and design the best integration tests to run continuously. Sapienz has dramatically sped up the testing process and has an extremely low false positive rate. Seventy-five percent of Sapienz reports are actionable and result in fixes.[7]

Meta has put a lot of time and effort into designing an iOS application ecosystem to support automated integration testing with low friction and a high success rate. This has allowed their engineers to have high confidence in their code changes. When designing an iOS application, it is also essential to keep testability in mind. As illustrated by Meta, investments in testability can become gigantic projects all on their own.

Ziggurat Square's Testable Architecture

Ziggurat is a layered, testable architecture pattern incorporating immutable view-models and one-way data flow developed by Square to improve testability and avoid massive view controllers.

To achieve this, Ziggurat introduced a series of components:

1. **A Service** contains most of the app's business logic and is the only layer that mutates the underlying state. This separation guarantees immutability at all subsequent layers.

---

[6] https://engineering.fb.com/2017/05/24/android/managing-resources-for-large-scale-testing/

[7] https://engineering.fb.com/2018/05/02/developer-tools/sapienz-intelligent-automated-software-testing-at-scale/

2.   **A Repository** abstracts the I/O details.

3.   **A Presenter** queries the Service objects to generate a ViewModel. It has no state.

4.   **A ViewModel** is passed into a ViewController to update it. It is an immutable struct that contains simple types.

5.   **A ViewController** manages a view hierarchy and responds to user actions. Following a one-way data flow, ViewControllers cannot query other objects. Instead, they are updated with new data when it is available.

6.   **A View** is appearance centric and owned and managed by a ViewController.

7.   **A Renderer** listens to signals that the state has changed and coordinates the app update.

8.   **The Context** is a lazy object graph used for dependency.

Incorporating the context as a first-party design principle makes it clear that Square is focused on utilizing dependency injection and following the dependency inversion principle. Because of this, Square engineers were able to find flaws in their initial design by discovering circular dependencies in their dependency graph. Secondly, the Ziggurat pattern combined with dependency injection made it easy to add tests. For example, we use the view-model layer to compare structs as expected output. This wouldn't be feasible in MVC.[8]

---

[8] https://developer.squareup.com/blog/ziggurat-ios-app-architecture/

Wrapping Up Testability

While testing is not the most glamorous software engineering task, it is very important. Not only can testing help influence our architecture as it did with Square's development of Ziggurat, but it can also expose additional opportunities, as shown in Meta's case, where better testability became a large investment area, including distributed systems and research-backed ML tooling to ensure application correctness.

Choosing an Architecture

While we have discussed the principles of good architecture, we have not discussed how to choose the right architecture. In truth, choosing an architectural pattern is not as crucial as understanding the problems you wish to solve and following architectural best practices to reach the ideal state. By taking the time to understand the issues you want to tackle, you can concentrate on the most impactful aspects of the application's architecture. Many of these problems will be unique to your use case just like how Square developed Ziggurat. However, by understanding the principles of systems design, you can apply them to any use case.

Before applying system design principles, we still do have to evaluate the architectural decisions. To do so, we need to identify the key pain points we are trying to solve by listening to those around us and their problems and actively thinking about how we can do better. For example:

1. Do what should be small refactors often take much longer than estimates?

2. Do engineers tend to step on each other's toes and find themselves editing similar software?

3. Do simple changes often break unrelated areas of production code?

4.   Do engineers feel efficient working in the code base?

5.   Is the code base difficult to understand?

Additionally, utilizing project retrospectives is a helpful tool to help suss out this information.

Summary

Once we have gathered the necessary information for our application architecture, we can leverage the knowledge of best practices and the system design principles discussed here to craft the best solution. This chapter is our first foray into application architecture. In the rest of Part 2, we will further review design patterns to provide a solid foundation for defining and enforcing good architecture.

The subsequent chapters in Part 2 will further break down our architecture discussion to include covering specific design patterns and common application architecture patterns. Design patterns and architecture patterns make up significant portions of the overall application development and serve as the building blocks for module applications.

Three Key Takeaways from This Chapter

1.   Good architecture can take many forms. Whether using a common iOS pattern like MVVM or VIPER or something more bespoke like Uber's RIBLETS or Square's Ziggurat.

2.   No matter the architecture pattern, it is always important to follow the key tenets of modularity and testability. By following these tenets, whatever application you build will be done scalably, flexibly, and with maximum testability.

3. While often overlooked when reviewing application architecture, it is essential to think about the broader testing and developer ecosystems so the application can continue to scale.

Further Learning

1. Design Patterns: Elements of Reusable Object-Oriented Software

2. Clean Architecture: A Craftsman's Guide to Software Structure and Design

CHAPTER 6

Common Design Patterns

Overview

Now that we have discussed the importance of good architecture and defined it (modular and testable), we need to achieve it. To do so, we need to start with the right building blocks, and the basic building blocks for good architecture are design patterns. Design patterns provide a base for developing scalable, readable, and maintainable software. Design patterns leverage proven best practices to ensure your code is easily understood and help to prevent your code from degrading into the proverbial ball of spaghetti. Once we know design patterns, we can expand our scope to application-wide architecture patterns.

This Chapter Includes

This chapter includes aiding in the quest for the perfectly designed application; this chapter covers some of the most common and important design patterns specifically geared toward iOS. The following chapters build on this chapter and discuss broader application-level design

E. Vennaro, *iOS Development at Scale*, https://doi.org/10.1007/978-1-4842-9456-7_6

patterns – we will call that application architecture patterns. In this chapter, we will cover types of design patterns and specific design patterns themselves. The design patterns we will cover are as follows:

1. Delegate pattern

2. Facade pattern (pseudocode only)

3. Factory pattern

4. Singleton

5. Dependency injection (pseudocode only)

6. Builder pattern

7. Coordinators (pseudocode only)

8. Observer

To help understand the preceding design patterns, Swift code is included in the associated GitHub repository. For some of the design patterns, the associated code is written as pseudocode here for ease of understanding. The pseudocode is not expected to compile and run.

The pseudocode is specifically for patterns whose value comes from looking more holistically at the system. These patterns are implemented in other book chapters as part of fully functioning application examples. These chapters are noted for reference.

Why Design Patterns Are the Building Blocks for Design

As we discussed in the previous chapter, we want our iOS application to be modular and testable. This allows us to split out our code into reusable objects and split out a large application into modules (libraries and frameworks) that can be built independently to reduce build times, build size, and promote faster development and code reuse. Achieving this requires a great deal of skill and knowledge from past experience and, in many cases, multiple redesigns. While redesigning software is a fact of life for software engineers, it is helpful to understand best practices to limit redesigns. By leveraging design patterns, we can leverage the past experiences of the broader engineering community to avoid common causes of redesign.

Specific Needs of Mobile Engineers

While the majority of our work as iOS engineers is focused on developing user-focused applications which we will define as application-level development (the layer of iOS development focused on user interaction – model view controller layer), at the application layer, we care most about code reuse, maintainability, and extensibility to promote quick iteration. Design patterns provide this by promoting code reusability, ease of development, and separation from underlying libraries and frameworks.

However, it is hard to solely classify iOS development as application-level development as it is important to abstract components into libraries and frameworks to keep compile times manageable and take advantage of shared or existing frameworks to speed development time. At scale, iOS development is very much about understanding how to manage many frameworks at different levels of the stack and ensure they cooperate in a structured manner.

To produce well-architected applications that utilize frameworks, we need to ensure the frameworks themselves are well architected, which is possible by decomposing our frameworks into multiple design patterns. In fact, proper framework design is almost more important than user-facing application design since the framework needs to work for all applications that want to use it while also interacting well with other frameworks and the common iOS application architectures.

181

Note   A framework is a set of classes or libraries that constitute a reusable design for a specific class of software, such as UIKit, which provides the core objects required for building applications.

Design Patterns

Overarching Themes

Design patterns are typically divided into having either creational, structural, or behavioral purposes, where

1. Creational patterns focus on the process of object creation

2. Structural patterns focus on the composition of classes or objects

3. Behavioral patterns focus on how classes or objects interact and distribute responsibility

In addition to the classical representation of design patterns, we have included delegation, coordinators, and dependency injection. We feel that while these are not included in the seminal work *Design Patterns: Elements of Reusable Object-Oriented Software,* they are every bit deserving of a place next to these patterns due to their wide utilization in iOS development and applicability to designing modular and testable iOS applications.

Creational

Creational design patterns help create a system independent of how objects are created and composed. Typical object-oriented creational patterns delegate instantiation to a different object. As a mobile application grows, creational patterns become important as a way to manage the system's complexity and increase modularity.

Creational patterns help enforce a more modular system because they emphasize defining objects with a smaller set of behaviors that can be composed into more complex ones (as opposed to a hard-coded fixed set of behaviors). It is worth noting that creational design patterns do add additional overhead because creating objects with certain behaviors starts to require more boilerplate code than simply instantiating a class.

All creational patterns encapsulate knowledge about the concrete classes they use. The broader application is only aware of the objects by their interfaces as defined by a Swift protocol (or base class). This allows for a lot of flexibility and configuration in what behavior exists behind the interface. The object behavior can be determined statically at compile time (if using a struct) or dynamically at runtime (if using a class). See Chapter 2 for more details on Swift memory management.

Structural

Structural design patterns describe ways to compose objects to create larger structures and new functionality while keeping these structures flexible and efficient. Object-based structural design patterns rely on object composition, while class-based patterns rely on inheritance. We will focus mostly on object composition patterns here.

Behavioral

Behavioral patterns describe the communication between objects and characterize complex control flow based on how objects are interconnected. One behavioral pattern used throughout iOS development is the Chain of Responsibility pattern, which backs the iOS responder chain (UI interactions such as tap). The Chain of Responsibility pattern provides loose coupling by sending a request to an object through a set (chain) of candidate objects where any candidate may fulfill the request at runtime.

Delegate Pattern

An alternative to inheritance that prompts object composition

The Problem

Suppose there is an existing class **Oracle** that implements a whatIsTheMeaningOfLife method. Now in our program, we want a custom version of this method that adds the capability of answering with 42 if we are playing on hitchhikers guide to the galaxy mode. To solve this, we implement inheritance by creating a special subclass of **Oracle** called **HitchhikersOracle,** and in our subclass, we will override the whatIsTheMeaningOfLife method to customize its behavior.

This is problematic because it introduces a complex relationship between our class and the **Oracle** base class. We respond to all messages that **Oracle** responds to, and we must mesh our methods with the methods in **Oracle**, which requires a detailed understanding of **Oracle** and tightly couples the two entities, making changes difficult and subject to potential unintended consequences.

The Solution

Enter the delegate pattern. The purpose of the delegate pattern is to allow an object to communicate back to its owner in a decoupled way. By not requiring an object to know the concrete type of its owner, we can write code that is much easier to reuse and maintain. Delegation is analogous to inheritance, where a subclass defers behavior to a parent class while providing looser coupling.

Architecture

In our delegate diagram, Figure 6-1, we outline the following:

1. The object oracle that needs a delegate (the delegating object). The delegate is usually held as a weak property to avoid a retain cycle where the delegating object retains the delegate, which retains the delegating object.

2. A delegate protocol defines the methods a delegate may or should implement.

3. A delegate is the helper object that implements the delegate protocol.

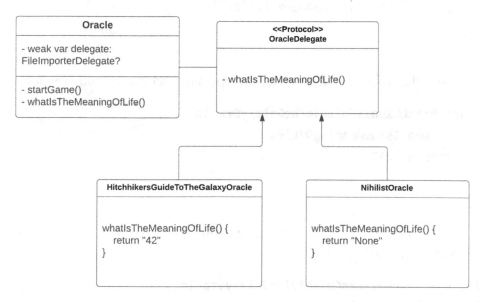

Figure 6-1. *Delegate pattern architecture*

The code becomes more flexible when using the delegate protocol instead of a concrete object or subclassing.

Code

To implement our code utilizing the delegate pattern, we must first create a delegate protocol and then have the object that requires the delegate to hold a weak reference to it.

```
protocol OracleDelegate: AnyObject {
  func whatIsTheMeaningOfLife() -> String
}

class Oracle {
  weak var delegate: OracleDelegate?

  func whatIsTheMeaningOfLife() {
    guard let d = delegate else { return }
    print(d.whatIsTheMeaningOfLife())
  }
}
```

We will also use our delegate for our special HitchhikersGuide version.

```
class HitchhikersGuideToTheGalaxyOracle {
  func whatIsTheMeaningOfLife() {
    return "42"
  }
}
```

Lastly, we can connect our delegate to our oracle so that the oracle can properly delegate behavior.

```
let h = HitchhikersGuideToTheGalaxyOracle()
let oracle = Oracle()
oracle.delegate = h
oracle.whatIsTheMeaningOfLife()
// 42
```

Another way we could achieve similar delegating behavior is by using closures. The following is a code sample for implementing the oracle using a closure:

```
class OracleClosure {
  private let meaningOfLife: () -> Void

  init(predicate: @escaping () -> Void) {
    self.meaningOfLife = predicate
  }

  func whatIsTheMeaningOfLife() {
    meaningOfLife()
  }
}
// playing on nihilist mode
let meaningOfLife = {
  print("there is none")
}
let newOracle = OracleClosure(predicate: meaningOfLife)
newOracle.whatIsTheMeaningOfLife()
// there is none
```

Trade-Offs

The delegate pattern is a huge part of the Apple ecosystem. It is necessary for using many built-in functions, such as UITableViewControllers, making them a great choice for many situations.

1. Delegation makes it easy to compose behaviors and change the way they're composed.

2. Delegates via protocols can cause ambiguous state decisions if the delegate is absent.

3. While delegation is less coupled than inheritance, it still creates some coupling between objects that can be avoided by using closures.

4. Using the protocol-based delegate is a well-established pattern that most iOS developers are familiar with.

Facade Pattern (Structural)

The Problem

You are an engineer working on adding a new feature for displaying friends' photos in a new component view. In addition to creating the component and linking it to the broader application navigation, you need to create a new network request. You realize that the existing networking library is sophisticated and requires the initialization of many objects necessary for caching and other bespoke parts of the network request library that must be executed in a specific order.

The next day during standup, you report slower-than-expected progress and push the deadline for completion to the next sprint. You further explain the delay is because you need to understand the inner workings of the network library and cannot just focus on the business logic of your component.

The Solution

Enter the facade pattern. A facade is an object that provides a simple interface to a complex subsystem. A facade wraps the functionality of a complex subsystem in an easily usable external API. While this provides less flexibility compared to working with the subsystem directly, it should include only those features that clients really care about and greatly enhance developer speed and overall maintainability.

Using a facade for our networking library would allow us to integrate the new image component with the sophisticated networking library without needing to understand its inner workings.

Architecture

The facade provides convenient access to a subsystem's functionality. Underneath the facade, the underlying library knows how to direct the client's request and utilize its own classes and subsystems to achieve the desired functionality.

The client uses the facade directly to avoid having to utilize the subsystem libraries. In this situation, the complex subsystem is a networking library consisting of dozens of objects related to caching and network requests. Behind the facade, the objects are correctly orchestrated, allowing you, as the user of the networking library, to call a method instead of directly orchestrating all the objects for the network request. As illustrated in Figure 6-2, our client only needs to care about making a request. The other details on executing the request are abstracted into the complex subsystem.

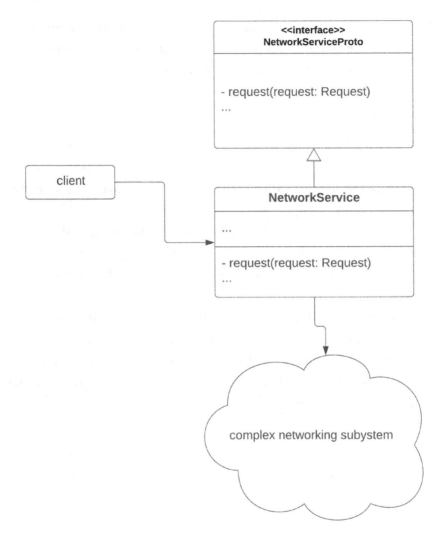

Figure 6-2. *Facade pattern*

Pseudocode

Because this pattern mostly deals with linking to subsystems, there is not a specific code sample in this chapter. However, in Chapter 3, the practical example implements a repository pattern, which is an example of a facade. Additionally, Chapter 7 implements the model view controller (MVC) architecture pattern utilizing the facade. Please reference those for working code samples. Here, we outline the pattern without all implementation details starting with a NetworkFacade class that encompasses many complex dependencies.

```
class NetworkFacade {
  // local vars required for the Facade
  //potential examples
  let cache: CacheProto
  let socket: SocketProto
  let mediaUploader: MediaUploaderProto

 //skip init, could use dependency injection here
  func request(request: Request) -> RequestCompletion {
    // fulfill network request
  }
}
```

From the client call site:

```
networkFacade.request(request: myNetworkRequest)
```

Trade-Offs

In general, the facade pattern does an excellent job of isolating your code from the complexity of a subsystem promoting weak coupling. This can speed development and assist in separating concerns as the components of the subsystem can be changed without affecting users of the facade.

In addition to speeding development, the weak coupling gained by using the facade pattern helps create layers in the system. A common example in iOS is using the facade pattern to create a data repository separating the data layer from the application layer. A by-product of this is reduced dependencies between objects and the ability to compile the application layer separately from the subsystem. This reduction in compilation dependencies reduces recompilation time for localized changes in the broader system.

An additional benefit of the facade pattern is that it does not inherently block access to the classes in the subsystem, so the user can choose between the ease of use and customizability.

One common pitfall of the facade pattern is that if not carefully managed, a facade can become an all-encompassing object coupled to all classes of an application. In this way, the facade loses its link to a specific subsystem and tends to manage all subsystems. To prevent this, it is important to define the responsibilities of the facade.

Note   A common usage of a facade in iOS programs is the repository pattern. A repository pattern is a specific name for a facade pattern that is specifically designed to deal with the data layer.

The Builder Pattern

Creational Pattern

The Problem

You are working for a mobile gaming startup building a new, never-before-seen expansion pack for Monopoly atop their existing game engine. The game engine consists of many complex objects and requires step-by-step initialization of many fields and nested objects since they are used for many different types of games. The initialization code is buried inside a monstrous constructor with many parameters, making it difficult to reason about as you try to construct and subclass the correct objects for your turn-based game.

With the expansion pack, the Monopoly board will still have a theme, a starting balance, and many other shared properties of the existing game board class. However, they will also feature increased properties, new property colors, and a higher starting balance. To solve this, you consider extending the base game board class and creating a set of subclasses to cover your combination of the required parameters. While investigating the merits of this approach, developers on some other games have already started doing this, and the application is becoming bloated with these subclasses as any new parameter further grows this hierarchy.

Brainstorming other approaches, you consider simply creating a giant constructor right in the base class with all possible parameters that control the object. While this approach eliminates the need for subclasses, it creates another potentially more harmful problem. A constructor with many potentially unused parameters, for example, none of the expansion pack options, will be included in the standard Monopoly game.

The Solution

Enter the builder pattern. The builder pattern is a creational design pattern that allows for the construction of complex objects in a step-by-step manner and allows for the creation of different types and representations of an object with the same underlying construction code. This reduces the need to keep mutable states, resulting in simpler and generally more predictable objects. Additionally, by enabling objects to become stateless and allowing the creation of different representations of an object, the builder pattern promotes easier testing.

Note   While the explicit builder pattern is not common with Apple's platforms, it is more common at the application level.

Architecture

The builder pattern consists of three core entities:

1. The product class, which is the type of complex object that is generated by the builder pattern. In our example, this is the Monopoly game board.

2. The builder protocol defines an abstract representation of all the required steps to create an object. The included build() method is used to return the final product.

3. The concrete builder implementation. The associated concrete subclass implements the behavior defined in the protocol. Any number of concrete builder classes can implement the builder protocol. These classes contain the necessary functionality to create a particularly complex product.

There is also an optional fourth entity that is not very common in iOS. The fourth entity is the director. The director class controls the order in which to call construction steps so that you can create and reuse specific configurations of builders. A director object includes a parameter to capture the concrete builder object used for generation. The benefit of the director is that it works with any builder instance that the client code passes to it, allowing for the construction of several product variations using the same build steps. Figure 6-3 outlines all four entities.

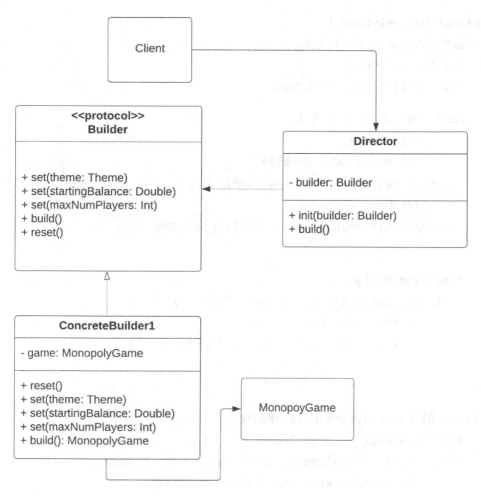

Figure 6-3. *Builder pattern with director*

Code

```
enum Theme: String {
  case `default`, darkMode, monopoly
}
// Monopoly does not share a common protocol with other games
```

```swift
struct MonopolyGame {
  let maxNumPlayers: Int
  let theme: Theme
  let startingBalance: Double

  init(maxNumPlayers: Int,
      theme: Theme,
      startingBalance: Double) {
      self.maxNumPlayers = maxNumPlayers
      self.theme = theme
      self.startingBalance = startingBalance
  }

  func printObj() {
    print("maxNumPlayers: \(maxNumPlayers), " +
          "theme: \(theme), " +
          "startingBalance: \(startingBalance)")
  }
}

protocol MonopolyGameBuilderProto {
  func setTheme(_ theme: Theme)
  func setStartingBalance(_ startingBalance: Double)
  func setMaxNumPlayers(_ maxNumPlayers: Int)
  func reset()
  func build() -> MonopolyGame
}

class MonopolyGameBuilder: MonopolyGameBuilderProto {
    public private(set) var maxNumPlayers: Int = 0
    public private(set) var theme: Theme = .default
    public private(set) var startingBalance: Double = 200
```

```swift
    func setTheme(_ theme: Theme) {
        self.theme = theme
    }

    func setStartingBalance(_ startingBalance: Double) {
        self.startingBalance = startingBalance
    }

    func setMaxNumPlayers(_ maxNumPlayers: Int) {
        self.maxNumPlayers = maxNumPlayers
    }

    func reset() {
        self.theme = .default
        self.maxNumPlayers = 0
        self.startingBalance = 200
    }

    func build() -> MonopolyGame {
        return MonopolyGame(
          maxNumPlayers:maxNumPlayers,
          theme: theme,
          startingBalance: startingBalance
        );
    }
}

// The director which is responsible for executing the building
steps in sequence.
class MonopolyGameDirector {
    let builder: MonopolyGameBuilderProto
    init(builder: MonopolyGameBuilderProto) {
     self.builder = builder
    }
```

```
  func buildStandardMonopolyGame() {
    // separate enum not documented here that
    //contains UI theme information
    builder.reset()
    builder.setTheme(.monopoly)
    builder.setStartingBalance(200)
    builder.setMaxNumPlayers(8)
  }

  // the director allows for the building of
  // product variations such as the expansion pack
}
// client code creates the builder object,
// passes it to the director and initiates
// the construction process.
class GameManager {
  func makeMonopolyGame() {
    let monopolyBuilder = MonopolyGameBuilder();
    let gameBuilder = MonopolyGameDirector(
        builder: monopolyBuilder);

    gameBuilder.buildStandardMonopolyGame();
    // Here final object is retrieved from the builder
    // object directly since the director isn't
    // aware of and not dependent on concrete
    // builders and products.
    let game = monopolyBuilder.build()
    game.printObj()
  }
}
GameManager().makeMonopolyGame()
// maxNumPlayers: 8, theme: monopoly, startingBalance: 200.0
```

Note: A Simpler Builder

While the traditional builder pattern does provide more layers of abstraction and structure, it is also common to see a more stripped-down builder. This version removes some of the boilerplate while keeping with the core tenets of the pattern. However, without the director, every client needs to know exactly how the building works, which can lead to problems, especially in large code bases with many engineers. The Swift standard library has examples of the following builder pattern throughout the URL and Regex library and is documented in proposal 56607.[1]

```
enum Theme: String {
  case `default`, darkMode, monopoly
}

struct MonopolyGame {
  var maxNumPlayers: Int = 0
  var theme: Theme = .default
  var startingBalance: Double = 200

  func printObj() {
    print("maxNumPlayers: \(maxNumPlayers), " +
          "theme: \(theme), " +
          "startingBalance: \(startingBalance)")
  }
}

class MonopolyGameBuilder {
  private var maxNumPlayers: Int = 0
  // separate enum not documented here that contains
  // UI theme information
  private var theme: Theme = .default
```

---

[1] https://forums.swift.org/t/url-formatstyle-and-parsestrategy/56607

199

```swift
  private var startingBalance: Double = 200

  func set(maxNumPlayers: Int) -> Self {
    self.maxNumPlayers = maxNumPlayers
    return self
  }

  func set(theme: Theme) -> Self {
    self.theme = theme
    return self
  }

  func set(startingBalance: Double) -> Self {
    self.startingBalance = startingBalance
    return self
  }

  func reset() {
      // reset builder values
  }

  func build() -> MonopolyGame {
    return MonopolyGame(
      maxNumPlayers:maxNumPlayers,
      theme: theme,
      startingBalance: startingBalance
    );
  }
}

let monopolyGame = MonopolyGameBuilder()
      .set(maxNumPlayers: 10)
      .set(theme: Theme.default)
      .set(startingBalance: 100)
      .build()
```

```
monopolyGame.printObj()
// maxNumPlayers: 10, theme: default, startingBalance: 100.0
```

Trade-Offs

The builder pattern is a creational pattern and is generally a good choice when objects have a large number of fields in the constructor.

Pros

1. The size of the constructor is reduced, and parameters are provided in highly readable method calls.

2. The builder pattern removes the need to have a lot of optional parameters and to pass in nil to the constructor.

3. The object being built is always instantiated in a complete state.

4. The builder pattern creates an easy way to build immutable objects.

5. Flexibility and readability are improved.

Cons

1. It increases the amount of boilerplate code for creating objects by requiring a separate ConcreteBuilder for each different type.

The Factory Pattern

Creational Pattern

The Problem

You are a new engineer on a legacy application. Your first project is to utilize the newly developed in-house logging framework for replacing an older third-party framework that was no longer viable. Both loggers implement the majority of the same methods; however, the old third-party framework has additional functionality for attribution tracking from advertising campaigns, so it cannot be completely removed until the new logger also supports this functionality.

Currently, the logging is sprinkled throughout the code and sometimes initialized slightly differently, tightly coupling the existing code to the logger framework's usage. You must sprinkle if statements throughout the code to implement the needed functionality. To make your life easier, you wrap both logger frameworks in a shared protocol that defines the functionality of both. This way, when the third-party framework is deprecated, you can easily remove it. But you notice that you have to instantiate each logger multiple times throughout the code base and that the initialization itself is somewhat long and repetitive with a few minute changes. Sighing, you start thinking about how to abstract some of this logic.

The Solution

Enter the factory pattern. The factory pattern is a creational design pattern that allows us to decouple the creation of an object from its usage and encapsulate complex instantiation logic in a single place. This allows for the abstraction of our code, so when modifications are made to a class, the client can continue to use it without further modification. There are multiple factory patterns, including the factory method and abstract factory, which we will cover in detail. Each factory pattern aims to isolate object creation logic within its own constructor. The abstract factory pattern is a good choice here because we can encapsulate the logging behavior behind a shared protocol and keep our instantiation logic in one shared location.

202

For the Factory Method

If we chose to implement our solution using the factory method, we could declare a method on our loggers that handles creation in a specific way for each logger (illustrated in Figure 6-4). Once created, the logger will have different implementation details for the same method, which is abstracted from the caller.

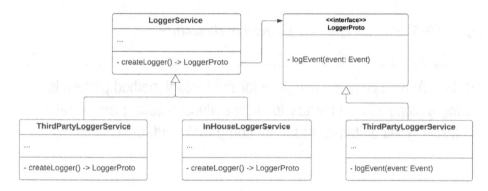

Figure 6-4. *Factory method architecture*

For the Abstract Factory

With the factory method, we have successfully abstracted away the specific details of our logger implementations. However, we still have to deal with instantiation logic. To help with this, we can utilize an abstract factory. With the abstract factory, we have a specific class designated to initialize the correct concrete implementation to avoid call-site-specific if statements (illustrated in Figure 6-5).

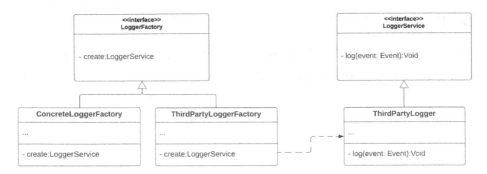

Figure 6-5. *Abstract factory pattern architecture*

Note   A more common use case for the factory method pattern is using it along with an iterator to allow collection subclasses to return different types of iterators that are compatible with the collections.

Architecture

For the factory pattern, we have a factory that handles our object creation and creates concrete implementations of our objects that conform to a common interface.

For the factory method, the creation logic lives in a specific create method defined in a common interface.

For the abstract factory pattern, we abstract the creation logic to its own entity, and both the factories and entities the factories create subscribe to specific common protocols. The creation logic occurs in a specific class that handles which concrete implementation to instantiate; in Swift, it is common to use a switch statement at the factory level.

Code

Factory Method

Our factory method implementation is relatively straightforward. We will declare a static method in our class that knows how to create itself. We have also defined a protocol for our service and included an ID as a way to identify the different services.

```
protocol LoggerService {
  var id: String { get }
}

// MARK: Factory Method
class ThirdPartyLogger: LoggerService {
  var id: String = "ThirdParty"
  // implement class methods ...

  // factory method
  public static func create() -> LoggerService {
    return ThirdPartyLogger()
  }
}

class InHouseLogger: LoggerService {
  var id: String = "InHouse"
  // implement class methods ...

  // factory method
  public static func create() -> LoggerService {
    return InHouseLogger()
  }
}
```

Abstract Factory

To transform our previous code into an abstract factory, we will no longer directly utilize our static methods in the client code. Instead, we will utilize our intermediate factory object. To enable this, first, we must create our individual factories.

```
protocol LoggerFactory {
  func create() -> LoggerService
}

class InHouseLoggerFactory: LoggerFactory {
  func create() -> LoggerService {
    return InHouseLogger()
  }
}

class ThirdPartyLoggerFactory: LoggerFactory {
  func create() -> LoggerService {
    return ThirdPartyLogger()
  }
}
```

Now we can connect our individual factories to the abstract factory intermediate object. We have also defined an enum here to differentiate which factory to build in a type-safe manner.

```
// abstract factory
class AppLoggerFactory: LoggerFactory {

  enum Logger {
    case thirdParty
    case inHouse
  }
```

```swift
var logger: Logger

init(logger: Logger) {
  self.logger = logger
}

func create() -> LoggerService {
  switch self.logger {
    case .thirdParty:
      return ThirdPartyLoggerFactory().create()
    case .inHouse:
      return InHouseLoggerFactory().create()
  }
}
}
```

Lastly, we can instantiate our factory, utilize it to create our service, and inspect the resulting service ID.

```swift
let factory = AppLoggerFactory(logger: .thirdParty)
let service = factory.create()
print(service.id)
// ThirdParty
```

Trade-Offs

1. More boilerplate – by abstracting our factories, we do create more boilerplate code for each new model.

2. You may want to consider other creational patterns to see which best fits your situation. For example, the builder pattern is a better option if you need to create objects with complex or lengthy initialization

patterns. In contrast, the factory pattern is more useful when objects share a common interface and pairs well with dependency injection.

3. When comparing the abstract factory to the factory method, consider that the abstract factory pattern influences the entire application's logic, while the factory method only affects the local portion.

Note   Keep in mind that the builder and factory patterns are different. The factory pattern is used to create different implementations conforming to the same interface, while the builder pattern ties the built object to the associated builder class (no common interfaces).

Singleton

Creational Pattern

The Problem

You are working for a large bank on their internal tools team. As part of the office modernization, you are working to connect each employee to the printer on their floor. Digging into the code, you see that each employee object needs an instance of a printer to print. We want to avoid providing each employee with their own instance of the printer for two reasons:

1. This would not model real-world behavior.

2. This could create a situation where one could not easily understand the status of all the jobs sitting in the physical printer's queue (each instance of a printer in code would have an incomplete view).

A more optimal solution is to limit the number of printer instances to one that is contained in the main context of the system.

```
void steve = Employee("Steve", "CTO")
Printer printer = new Printer()
steve.printCurrentAssignment(printer)
```

While this solves the immediate problem, it also allows for the initialization of the class from anywhere. Additionally, the public constructor becomes a dangerous opportunity for the system. What if a developer sits in another part of the code and does not have the printer object available? Well, they could just initialize it and use it to create two printer objects in the code. Having multiple printer objects in code does not model the real-world situation. It leads to the earlier problem where we start to lose the ability to track the global printer status (such as tracking all pages in the last hour or all current jobs in the queue).

The Solution

Enter the singleton pattern. The singleton solves this problem by ensuring that there is only ever one global instance of the class. The singleton does this by providing a unified access point for resources or services shared across the application.

We can utilize the singleton pattern to simplify our design since having only one instance of our printer object will better model the real-world situation and provide us with easier insight into data, such as how many jobs are in the printer's queue.

> **Note**   The singleton is a controversial design pattern; however, it is also very common and is used extensively by Apple (UIApplication, NSURLSessionManager, etc.).

The Architecture

The singleton class declares a static property shared that returns the same instance of the singleton class. This static property is the only way of accessing the singleton object. The singleton's constructor is private and hidden from the client code. Figure 6-6 describes the basic singleton pattern visually.

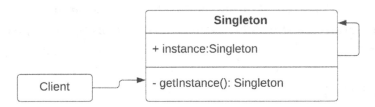

Figure 6-6. *Singleton design pattern*

Code

In Swift, we can create singletons using a static-type property. The statically typed property is lazily initialized only once, even when accessed simultaneously across multiple threads.

```
class Printer {
  static let shared = Printer()
}
```

Suppose your object requires a more complex setup (beyond simple initialization). In that case, we can utilize the same static property but utilize a closure to encapsulate the complex initialization logic and then assign the result of the closure to the global constant.

```
class Printer {
  static let shared: Printer = {
      let instance = Printer()
      // setup code
      return instance
  }()

  func printAssignment(text: String) {
    print(text)
  }
}
```

Then we can access our shared instance throughout the code base.

```
let printer = Printer.shared;
printer.printAssignment(text: "assignment");
// assignment
```

Trade-Offs

The singleton is a controversial design pattern and requires special consideration when using.

Pros

1. The singleton provides an easy way to ensure that there is only ever a single instance of your class.

2. The singleton provides a global access point to a single instance of the class.

3. The singleton efficiently controls access to shared resources.

Cons

1. The singleton pattern requires careful consideration in multithreaded environments to ensure that multiple threads do not create or access a singleton object simultaneously.

2. Testing a singleton typically requires a creative mocking solution because the singleton constructor is private.

3. The singleton pattern can lead to hidden dependencies as it is easy to access the singleton anywhere.

Dependency Injection (DI)

The Problem

Let us revisit our logging example from earlier. Here, we had a logger instance being used and instantiated throughout our code base. This approach made it difficult for us to substitute a new logger. It also would make testing more complex as well since we would need to use mocks. Our logging code sprinkled in different classes looked like the following:

```
class ModuleA { // High Level
    let foo: Logger // Low Level
}
```

The dependency inversion principle that DI is based on states that a module should not directly depend on another. Direct dependency leads to tight coupling between high-level and low-level modules. With tightly coupled modules, high-level modules need to reflect every alteration in a low-level module, just as we see in our logging example.

The Solution

Enter dependency injection. Dependency injection provides a way
to separate our concerns around constructing and using objects.
Dependency injection is one way we can ensure inversion of control in
our programs, making it easy to substitute new concrete implementations
without having to modify client code and improving testability by
providing a way to inject fully testable classes.

The Architecture

In our example, we will have the Authenticator require a logger service.
Our logger service can be created in the application delegate (or a similar
spot during application startup). Figure 6-7 depicts our new dependency
injection based architecture.

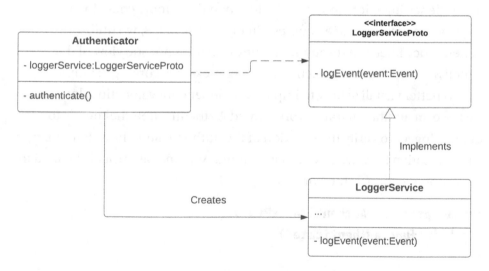

Figure 6-7. *Dependency injection of the LoggerService*

To achieve this hierarchical dependency mapping across the
application, we pull our dependencies up to our top-level module and
inject them down, so any class that needs access to the logger can add

that in its constructor and pull it in from the higher-level module. With much larger applications, this becomes a bit cumbersome to do in the constructor. To address this, we can utilize a dependency injection container.

A dependency injection (DI) container is a framework that helps manage our application dependencies, so we do not have to create and manage objects manually. The framework manages dependency creation and lifetime and injects dependencies into specific classes. The DI container creates an object of the specified type and injects the dependency objects through a constructor, property, or method at runtime. Additionally, the container can dispose of the dependent objects at the appropriate time.

Pseudocode

The following code is meant as a walkthrough of implementing dependency injection and is not included in the sample code. In our application architecture examples, Chapters 7, 8, and 9, we utilize dependency injection throughout. They provide a holistic view of the benefits of dependency injection in the context of a working example.

To better visualize how to implement dependency injection, let's say we have an additional framework named Authentication that needs to use our logger to verify the function of the authentication flow. For our authentication flow, we have a class named Authenticator that is located in the Authentication framework for authenticating users.

```
public protocol AuthenticatorProto {
  public func authenticate()
}

public class Authenticator: AuthenticatorProto {
  public init() { }
  public func authenticate() { }
}
```

Inside the authenticate method, we also want to utilize our logger for error logging something like

```
public class LogggerService {
  func logEvent(event: Event) {
    // log event
  }
}
```

So far, so good. Still, we should not use a concrete type when injecting our LoggerService dependency since this would make switching logging frameworks complex and require direct code change. To model this in code, we can create a LoggerServiceProto that defines a contract that all logger services will follow.

```
public protocol LoggerServiceProto {
  func logEvent(event: Event)
}
```

Now we can use that protocol to inject our LoggerService into the Authenticator class.

```
public class Authenticator: AuthenticatorProto {
  private let loggerService: LoggerServiceProto

  public init(loggerService: LoggerServiceProto) {
    self.loggerService = loggerService
  }

  func authenticate() {
    // authentication code ...
    // log associated event
    loggerService.log(event: event)
  }
}
```

So dependencies are inverted to a new protocol called LoggerServiceProto, and it's safe to import our LoggerService to any module. To use this properly in our application, we would need to instantiate our loggerService at the top level it is needed. For this example, we could do this in the ApplicationDelegate. This would allow us to pass our logger framework down a potentially complex dependency tree to where it is needed (since this is a logging framework, it is safe to assume it is needed in many places).

```
let loggerService = ThirdPartyLoggerService()
let authenticator = Authenticator(loggerService: loggerService)
```

In our preceding example, we only add our logging framework to the constructor; however, it is easy to imagine a more complex app that requires a multitude of dependencies where the init statements could become quite large. Instead of adding to each init statement, we can utilize a framework to containerize our injection behavior (commonly referred to as a dependency injection framework).

Dependency injection frameworks come in a multitude of flavors and potential methods of instantiation; here, we present an option using property observers.

```
@Injected(.loggerService)
var loggerService: LoggerService
```

```
@InjectedSafe(.by(type: FetchService.self, key: "network"))
var networkService: FetchService?
```

```
@Injected
var printerService: ExternalService
```

Trade-Offs

1. Dependency injection via constructors can lead to complex constructors and can cause one small change to require changes in many other classes.

2. Utilizing a dependency container framework can help alleviate this; however, it means your application must now include another framework. This can contribute to the maintenance burden of the application.

3. While dependency injection does increase testability, it also increases boilerplate code and potentially increases the number of overall dependencies your application has (via a DI framework).

Coordinators

Structural Design Pattern

The Problem

Imagine you are developing the Facebook application. You start with a simple newsfeed and code mainly in a view controller. Navigation is simple; the user enters the application, scrolls through some posts, and clicks to enter a basic details view. Besides the main flow, there is a simple authentication flow and profile page. Thinking to yourself, wow, this is easy. You quickly code the additional routing logic as part of the view controller. Since there are only a few screens and distinct flows, you tell yourself this is fine, and with the tight deadline, it is best this way.

Everything works perfectly until your project manager tells you that groups are being added to the application. Groups are basically the same as feed, but for a specific group of people, and from the group's page, you will have access to the profile flow, authentication flow, and details view for posts. Looking at your application, you realize everything needs to change. All the navigation logic will need additional if-else statements to handle the new flows. After completion, you realize your code is starting to resemble a big ball of spaghetti with classically massive view controllers, as illustrated in Figure 6-8. You look at your routing function and think to yourself, there has to be a better way.

```swift
private func routingUtil(param: String) {
  if param == "group" {
    router.groupController()
  } else if param == "auth" {
    router.openAuthController()
  } else if param == "newsfeed"  {
    router.openNewsfeedController()
  }
  // and it goes on and on...
}
```

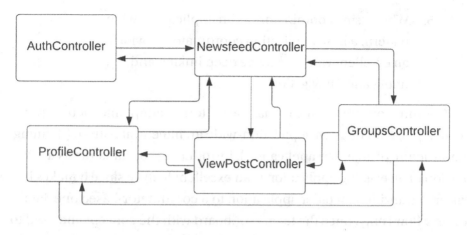

Figure 6-8. Big growing ball of spaghetti

The Solution

Enter the coordinator pattern. The coordinator pattern is a common structural iOS design pattern that helps encapsulate different flows in an application. The pattern was initially adapted from the application command pattern and popularized in the iOS community as the coordinator pattern. Coordinators help to

1. Modularize an application by breaking it into distinct application segments.

2. Provide greater control over application navigation since the navigation logic passes from the view controller to the coordinator.

3. Promote view control reuse since the coordinator controls the navigation logic.

4. When combined with dependency, injection coordinators can improve testability.

5.   When using coordinators as an application-wide pattern, a base application coordinator provides an excellent way to manage deep linking and notification navigation.

Coordinators are unique in that the pattern is adoptable for only part of an application or as an application-wide architectural pattern (defining the structure of an entire application). Introducing coordinators as a portion of an existing application is an excellent feature since it makes it easier to transition an older application to a coordinator-based one. First, for new flows only, once the team is onboard with the concept and used to the flow, older portions of the application can be refactored until the entire application utilizes coordinators.

To apply coordinators in our preceding example, we could have started out by simply adding a GroupsCoordinator for the group's flow without needing to change much about the existing application. Next, once familiar with the pattern, the base application and existing newsfeed flow can be refactored to include coordinators.

Architecture

Basic Coordinator

At the most basic level, a coordinator is a class that references a view controller and controls its navigation flow. Typically, it can also instantiate subcoordinators for other flows in the application. Figure 6-9 applies this to our example using the newsfeed and posts detail view as an example.

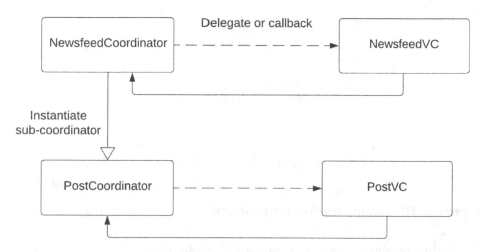

Figure 6-9. *Coordinator flow. Strong references are solid lines, while weak references are dotted*

To improve the testability of coordinators, it is common practice to utilize dependency injection via protocols. By utilizing dependency injection, the concrete implementations of the coordinators, router (potentially), and view controllers are decoupled. Dependency injection has another added benefit of allowing a parent coordinator to hold onto various concrete child coordinators in a single property (thanks to generics and protocol conformance). Figure 6-10 outlines this for a common coordinator protocol.

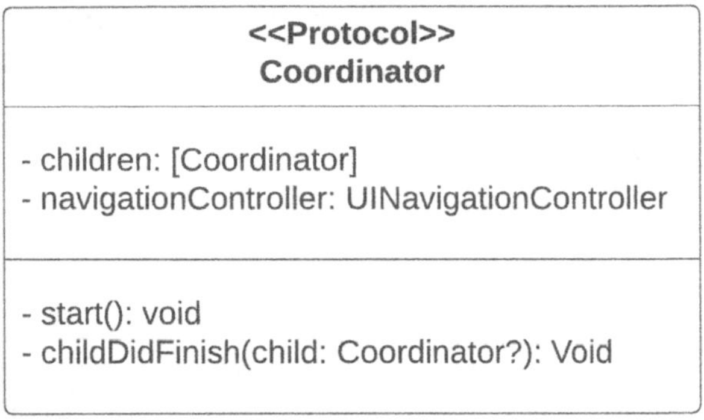

<<Protocol>> Coordinator
- children: [Coordinator] - navigationController: UINavigationController
- start(): void - childDidFinish(child: Coordinator?): Void

Figure 6-10. *Basic coordinator protocol*

In the coordinator protocol, we have the following:

1. The child view controllers. The view controllers do not know about each other; instead, they delegate to the coordinator to handle transitions.

2. The navigation controller. This handles the routing for the coordinator flow.

3. Start method that kicks off the flow the coordinator manages.

4. childDidFinish method to perform specific actions when the flow is completed.

While this basic coordinator can work well, we are making the coordinator control the presentation of the view controllers and navigation. We are also limiting our ability to test by not injecting our dependencies. To fix this, we can utilize factories to abstract our dependencies further and better follow the single responsibility principle. This is outlined in Figure 6-11.

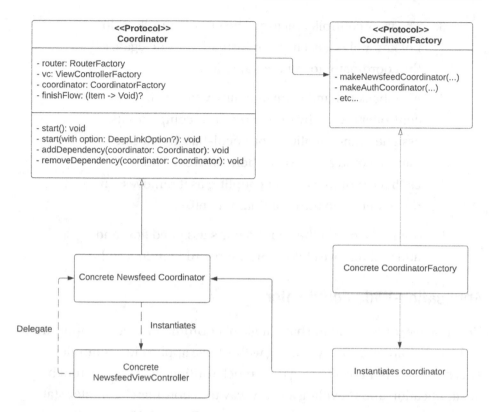

Figure 6-11. *Application coordinator with child coordinators*

Now we have the following:

1. The coordinator factory. It knows how to create view controllers and the order in which view controllers should be displayed.

2. The router factory. The router controls the navigation flow of the application and knows when to present and dismiss view controllers. The coordinator tells the router which view controller to present.

223

3. The view controller factory. The view controllers do not know about each other; instead, they delegate to the coordinator to handle transitions.

4. A callback to handle functionality when a view controller owned by the coordinator completes its assigned functionality. A protocol-based delegate pattern could also be used here; however, the callback promotes looser coupling as it removes any dependency on the coordinator itself.

5. Methods to start the coordinator's assigned flow and add and remove child coordinators (dependencies).

Application-Wide Coordinator

Now that we understand the basic logic of coordinators, we can apply them to the entire application by starting with a base application controller. This has the benefit of allowing us to mock routing all the way through the application and providing an easy way to "coordinate" complex state changes from notifications and deep links. In Figure 6-12, we outline what that might look like in our newsfeed application.

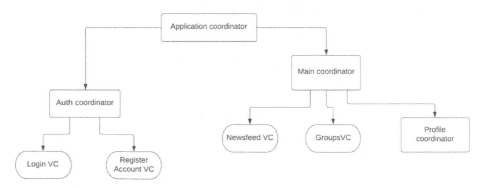

Figure 6-12. *Application coordinator with child coordinators*

Pseudocode

Now that we understand the overall flow for the coordinator pattern, let us explore a pseudocode implementation. In Chapters 7 and 8, we include a fully working application architecture example with coordinators.

Before creating our coordinator, let us set up our dependencies. For the factories we inject, we will follow a standard pattern. For brevity, we only show the CoordinatorFactory; however, all factories follow the same pattern.

```
protocol CoordinatorFactoryProtocol {
  func makeAuthCoordinator(
    router: RouterProto,
    coordinatorFactory: CoordinatorFactoryProto,
    vcFactory: VCFactoryProto) -> AuthCoordinator

  func makeMainCoordinator(
    router: RouterProto,
    coordinatorFactory: CoordinatorFactoryProto,
    vcFactory: VCFactoryProto) -> MainCoordinator

  func makeNewsfeedCoordinator(
    router: RouterProto,
    coordinatorFactory: CoordinatorFactoryProto,
    vcFactory: VCFactoryProto) -> NewsfeedCoordinator
}

final class CoordinatorFactory:
  CoordinatorFactoryProtocol {

    func makeAuthCoordinator(
      router: RouterProto,
      coordinatorFactory: CoordinatorFactoryProto,
      vcFactory: VCFactoryProto
    ) -> AuthCoordinator {
```

```
    return AuthCoordinator(
        router: router,
        coordinatorFactory: coordinatorFactory,
        vcFactory: vcFactory)
}
// cont for other coordinators...
```

Now we can get to our actual implementation.

```
protocol Coordinator: class {
  var vcFactory: VCFactoryProto { get set }
  var router: RouterProto { get set }
  var coordinatorFactory: CoordinatorFactoryProto { get set}
  var finishFlow: (Item -> Void)?

  func start()
  func start(with option: DeepLinkOption?)
}
```

To simplify some of the boilerplate, we can also implement a base class called our **BaseCoordinator**. The **BaseCoordinator** has the logic for adding and removing coordinators. The children array stores active coordinators. A strong reference is required; otherwise, they will be removed from memory.

```
// using a base class to provide some sensible defaults
class BaseCoordinator: Coordinator {
  var children: [CoordinatorProto]
  // skipping initialization

  func add(_ coordinator: Coordinator) {
    for element in childCoordinators {
      if element === coordinator { return }
    }
    childCoordinators.append(coordinator)
  }
```

```swift
func remove(_ coordinator: Coordinator?) {
  guard childCoordinators.isEmpty == false,
    let coordinator = coordinator else { return }

  for (index, element) in
    childCoordinators.enumerated() {
      if element === coordinator {
        childCoordinators.remove(at: index)
        break
      }
    }
}

func start() {
  start(with: nil)
}

// optional for deep link functionality
func start(with option: DeepLinkOption?) {}
}
```

To complete the coordinator flow, we need to define our applicationCoordinator and start it in the application delegate.

```swift
class AppDelegate: UIResponder, UIApplicationDelegate {
  // instantiate coordinator and other vars
  func application(_ application: UIApplication,
    didFinishLaunchingWithOptions launchOptions:
    [UIApplicationLaunchOptionsKey: Any]?) -> Bool {
    // start with could include deeplink
    // or notif options we pass to our coordinator
    self.applicationCoordinator.start(with: nil)
    return true
  }
}
```

```swift
final class ApplicationCoordinator: BaseCoordinator {
  private let coordinatorFactory: CoordinatorFactoryProto
  private let router: RouterProto
  private let vcFactory: VCFactoryProto

  override func start(with option: DeepLinkOption?) {
    if option != nil {
      // utilize deeplink or notif options
    } else {
      switch launchInstructor {
        case .auth: runAuthFlow()
        case .main: runMainFlow()
      }
    }
  }

  // methods to instantiate flows
  private func runMainFlow() {
    let coordinator =
      self.coordinatorFactory.makeMainCoordinator(
        router: self.router,
        coordinatorFactory: CoordinatorFactory(),
        vcFactory: VCFactory())
    coordinator.finishFlow = {
      [unowned self, unowned coordinator] in
        self.removeDependency(coordinator)
        self.launchInstructor =
            LaunchInstructor.configure()
        self.start()
    }
    self.addDependency(coordinator)
    coordinator.start()
  }
```

```
private func runAuthFlow() {
  // instantiate auth flow...
}

init(router: Router,
     coordinatorFactory: CoordinatorFactory) {
  self.router = router
  self.coordinatorFactory = coordinatorFactory
}
}
```

With the preceding code, we can launch our application and navigate to the main flows of our application using coordinators. Now, when we want to add the group's tab with access to the profile, we can simply create a new instance of the selected coordinator.

```
final class GroupsCoordinator:
  BaseCoordinator,
  CoordinatorFinishOutput {

  private func showProfile(module: GroupsVC) {
    // instantiate coordinator and start the flow
  }
}
```

Trade-Offs

While the coordinator pattern is widely accepted, there are some potential trade-offs to consider when attempting to introduce the coordinator pattern to an existing application:

1. Introducing the development team requires time and potential convincing.

2. Transitioning existing application code to coordinator-backed flows can be ambiguous and time-consuming with little business benefit – refactors are always hard to prioritize.

In general, the coordinator pattern provides a way to abstract the role of navigation out of our view controllers while supporting dependency injection. This provides a better separation of concerns and encapsulation of the navigation logic.

Observer

Behavioral Pattern

The Problem

You are working on an established iOS application that uses the model view controller architecture pattern. Recently due to an ongoing push for monetization, your team has introduced a new shopping feature. For this feature, when an item is added to the cart, the associated count of that item in the shopping list view must be incremented in the cart badge icon and any other view that tracks the cart item count. This change will require updating multiple view controller hierarchies.

The Solution

Enter the observer pattern. The observer pattern allows for dependent objects to be notified automatically of changes. The observer pattern accomplishes this by defining a one-to-many dependency between objects. We can think about this as a publisher and many subscribers where the subscribers are notified of changes to the publisher's state.

Utilizing the observer pattern allows us to update one object, our item, and have the change propagate to all views that track item changes. Through the observer pattern, we can do this without knowing the details of what objects need updating. Additionally, we do not need to make any assumptions or understand the implementation details of the changed objects, promoting loose coupling.

Architecture

Our implementation of the observer pattern, illustrated in Figure 6-13, has two objects:

1. The subscriber is the observer object and receives updates.

2. The publisher is the observable object and sends updates.

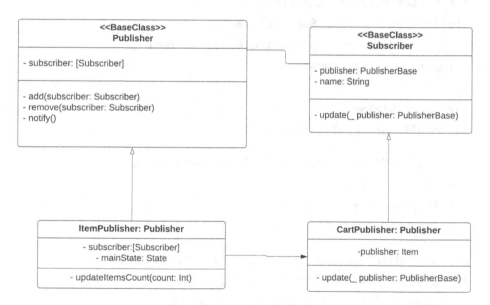

Figure 6-13. *Observer pattern architecture*

Additionally, for the observer value, we care about the specific value that is changed, the value we are observing. In our concrete implementation, we are monitoring the updateItemsCount and notifying the shopping cart when the number of items changes.

Example Code

This is the only pattern where we will leverage inheritance. Because we are storing a reference to an array of subscribers and a reference to the publisher, it is impossible to implement a pure protocol-oriented approach due to generic type constraints containing self.

First, let us define our Subscriber base class. Here, we have implemented the Equatable method to utilize our class within an array collection.

```swift
// Base class for the Subscriber (also called observer)
class SubscriberBase: Equatable {
  static func == (lhs: SubscriberBase,
                  rhs: SubscriberBase) -> Bool {
    lhs.name == rhs.name
  }
  var name: String
  var publisher: PublisherBase

  init(name: String, publisher: PublisherBase) {
    self.name = name
    self.publisher = publisher
  }

  // The subject passed to the Update operation
  // lets the observer determine which subject
  // changed when it observes more than one
```

```
public func update(
  _ changedPublisher: PublisherBase) {
    // update based on item count
    // updateUIForItemCount(context.itemCount)
    fatalError("must implement in subclass")
  }
}
```

Next, let us define our base publisher that will publish updates to subscribers. Here, we have implemented add and remove to update the subscriber list and to notify all subscribers of an update.

```
// Base class for the Publisher (also called subject)
class PublisherBase {
  private var subscribers: [SubscriberBase] = []

  func add(subscriber: SubscriberBase) {
    subscribers.append(subscriber)
  }

  func remove(subscriber: SubscriberBase) {
    guard let i = subscribers.firstIndex(of: subscriber)
    else { return }
    subscribers.remove(at: i)
  }

  func notify() {
    for s in subscribers {
      s.update(self)
    }
  }
}
```

Now we can implement our observer pattern for our item shopping cart relationship.

```swift
// Item is a concrete subscriber for our shopping cart
class Cart: SubscriberBase {
  let _publisher: Item

  init(name: String,
      publisher: Item) {
        _publisher = publisher
        super.init(name: name, publisher: publisher)
  }

  override func update(
     _ changedPublisher: PublisherBase) {
      if type(of: changedPublisher) ==
         type(of: _publisher) {
           print("Updated item count: " +
               "\(_publisher.itemsCount)")
      }
  }
}

// Cart is our concrete publisher or subject
class Item: PublisherBase {
  var subscribers: [SubscriberBase] = []
  var itemsCount = 0

  func updateItemsCount(_ count: Int) {
    itemsCount = count
    notify()
  }
}
```

Here, we instantiate our item publisher and our cart that subscribes to updates on the item's count.

```
var item = Item()
var cart = Cart(name: "cart", publisher: item)

item.add(subscriber: cart)
item.updateItemsCount(5)
// Updated item count: 5
```

Now we have completed a sample implementation of the observer pattern. However, we do not have to implement this pattern from scratch. Apple provides the Key-Value Observing (KVO) and the Combine framework, both of which can be used to model the same behavior.

To monitor changes with KVO, we can utilize the observe(_:options:c hangeHandler:) method to set up a closure that handles any change to a property. The closure receives an NSKeyValueObservedChange object that describes the change event and retrieves the changed property.[2]

```
class Item: NSObject {
    @objc dynamic var count: Int = 0
}
@objc var item = Item()
var observation: NSKeyValueObservation?
// later in code
observation = observe(\.item.count, options: [.new]) {
    object, change in
        print ("updated item count")
}
```

---

[2]https://developer.apple.com/documentation/combine/performing-key-value-observing-with-combine

We can also utilize KVO with Combine by replacing the observe(_:opt ions:changeHandler:) method with a KVO Combine publisher (NSObject. KeyValueObservingPublisher), which we can get by calling publisher(for:) on the publisher object, our item.

```
//...everything stays the same, but we add a
// cancellable var for Combine usage
var cancellable: Cancellable?
//...later on in our code we can use combine
cancellable = item
        .publisher(for: \.count)
      .sink() {
count in print ("updated item count")
        }
```

One key difference here is that the Combine KVO publisher produces the element of the observed type, whereas the KVO closure returns a wrapped type (NSKeyValueObservedChange), which requires unwrapping to access the underlying changed value. We will cover Combine further in Chapter 8, when we discuss the reactive programming paradigm.

Trade-Offs

Runtime Behavior

With the observer pattern, behavior changes are distributed across multiple objects, making it difficult to track state changes in a consistent way (one object often affects many others).

Moreover, the observer pattern requires runtime checking of the notification object, which means we cannot fully take advantage of the Swift compiler and static type checking.

Memory Management

We must be aware of the potential for dangling references if publishers are deleted. We can avoid dangling references by having the publisher notify its subscribers as it is deleted so that they can adjust their reference counts appropriately. Deleting the observers is not recommended since other objects may reference them.

Complex State Management

Due to the nature of the observer pattern, subscribers are not guaranteed to be notified in the same order and could be notified of a change more than once. This can occur when there exists a complex relationship between publishers and subscribers. To combat this, we can utilize an intermediate object called a ChangeManager. Figure 6-14 outlines a potential observer architecture that leverages a change manager. The ChangeManager serves to encapsulate complex update logic by

1. Creating and maintaining a mapping from a publisher to its subscribers, eliminating the need for publishers to directly maintain references to their subjects and vice versa

2. Defining an update strategy

3. Updating all dependent observers at the request of a subject

With the ChangeManager in place, the publisher calls the ChangeManager to register, unregister, and notify methods from its own add, remove, and notify methods.

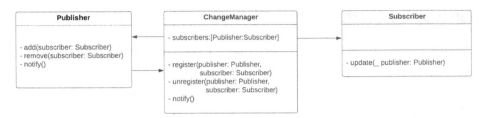

Figure 6-14. Observer pattern with a ChangeManager object

Summary

There are many documented design patterns, and in this chapter, we
have covered some of the most commonly used design patterns in
iOS applications. When reviewing these patterns, we focused on four
key points:

1. The problem they solve

2. How the design pattern solves this problem

3. The architecture of the design pattern

4. The trade-offs associated with the design pattern

When considering your application architecture and evaluating
architectural trade-offs, it is helpful to frame your decisions according to
these principles. The principles help to lay out clearly what problem you
are trying to solve and why that specific design pattern helps. While we can
never exhaustively cover all design patterns, we can provide a framework
(these four points) to evaluate future design patterns and architectural
decisions.

Two Key Takeaways from This Chapter

1. Utilizing tried and true design patterns can help solve many common software engineering problems and improve application quality.

2. Framing architectural decisions around the problem, how your solution addresses the problem, the technical details of this, and the associated trade-offs of the decision can help clarify architecture decisions and keep a bar for high code quality.

Further Learning

1. Design Patterns: Elements of Reusable Object-Oriented Software

CHAPTER 7

Model View Controller (MVC)

Overview

In Chapter 6, we discussed common foundational design patterns in iOS and how they help form the foundation of good architecture by helping you to structure your code and improve modularity and testability. In addition to the previously mentioned design patterns, there is a class of design patterns geared toward the iOS application layer design, *application-wide* design patterns. Application-wide design patterns address the application layer structure, how it is modularized, the control flow, and the data flow. This is the first chapter where we will address application-wide architecture patterns, and we will start with the most basic of them all, the model view controller (MVC) pattern.

This Chapter Includes

This chapter focuses on the MVC pattern and is the first deep dive into this type of application-wide architecture pattern. It includes an in-depth look at the MVC pattern, trade-offs and considerations for its usage, and when we could best use it in real-life applications.

© Eric Vennaro 2023
E. Vennaro, *iOS Development at Scale*, https://doi.org/10.1007/978-1-4842-9456-7_7

A Detailed Look at MVC

The MVC architecture consists of three main components:

1. The model manages data and the associated business logic.

2. The view handles the UI layout and display.

3. The controller is the glue between the model and the view by routing commands to the view, updating the model, and observing model changes.

The MVC design pattern is also the default pattern provided by Apple. The goal of the MVC pattern is to *separate our concerns* by assigning clear responsibilities between the model, view controller, and view. This division of labor also improves maintenance. Additionally, the MVC pattern forms the basis of other design patterns, including the MVP (Model, View, Presenter) pattern and the MVVM (Model, View, View-Model) pattern, discussed in the subsequent chapter.

Figure 7-1 outlines how the MVC components act in concert to create a fully functioning application.

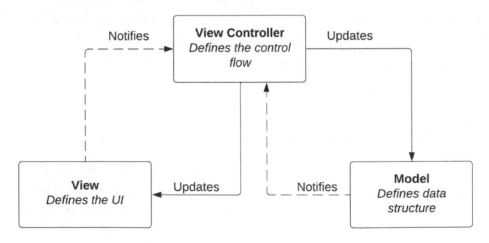

Figure 7-1. *General MVC architecture*

Figure 7-2 outlines an MVC hierarchy for our Photo Stream application which we will apply our MVC architecture to in the "Practical Example" section of the chapter. In this diagram, we assume we only want to display the basic photo information in our photo model to the UI.

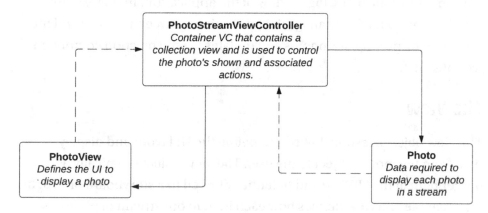

Figure 7-2. *MVC architecture applied to the Photo Stream application*

MVC Components

Now that we have reviewed the overall pattern, let's dive into the individual components and how they relate to our Photo Stream application.

The Model

The model object is a Swift class encapsulating the data and associated business logic specific to the application. In our Photo Stream application, the model specifies what information each item in our list consists of (caption, title, description).

The View Controller

The view controller object is an intermediary between the view and the model. The controller is typically a descendant of a UIViewController and serves to control the logical flow of the application. In our example, the view controller will manage the interaction between the view and the model for displaying our photos and updates via the reaction component we construct.

The View

The view object's responsibility is to define the UI layout and display data from the model object to the user. The view object is typically a descendant of the UIView and potentially linked to a storyboard or XIB. In our example, the view defines how each item in our stream of photos is presented to the user and what other UI components are available for interaction.

Component Interactions

Now that we have defined our components, we need to describe how they interact and are constructed.

Object Construction

There are different ways to approach object construction; in general, construction should start at a high-level controller that loads and configures views with the pertinent information from the model. A controller can explicitly create and own the model layer or access the model via an injected dependency.

Updates to the Model

The controller receives view events (the dotted line in Figure 7-2) mainly via the target action mechanism and delegates. In our example, we construct all views programmatically (using storyboards or SwiftUI makes little difference to the architecture pattern, only the in-code implementation). Regardless of the setup, the controller knows what kind of views it's connected to, but the view has no static knowledge of the controller's interface. When a view event arrives, the controller can then change the model.

Updates to the View

For our implementation of MVC, we would like a unidirectional data model. A unidirectional data model's primary benefits are simplicity, better data flow control, and less object coupling. Applying this to our MVC pattern means view actions get turned into model changes, and the model sends messages reflected as view changes.

Furthermore, the controller should not directly change the view hierarchy when a model change view action occurs. Instead, the controller is subscribed to model messages and changes the view hierarchy once a model message arrives.

The View Controller's Role

Revisiting our Photo Stream example, we will allow users to like or dislike photos via a *reactions component*. These actions require the model to be updated. When user interaction in the view triggers an update, the result is sent to the ViewController, which completes the update by appropriately manipulating the model and sending the model update to the view.

Alternatively, your controller could update the view to display the data in a different format, for example, changing the photo order from friends to discovering new content. In this case, the controller could handle the state change directly without updating the model.

The View State Storage and Updates

The view state is typically stored as properties on the view and controller as needed.

Updating the application's view state typically requires Internet connectivity and network-specific code to handle the network connection. In MVC, networking responsibilities are not defined in a precise location, leaving both the view controller and the model as popular locations. While it is possible to achieve similar results either way, our implementation utilizes a network service and model-owned networking.

Figure 7-3 outlines the MVC pattern with details on component interactions.

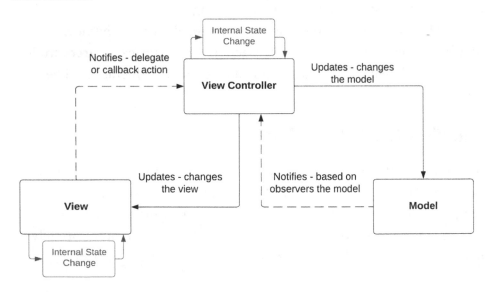

Figure 7-3. *MVC architecture with component interaction*

Practical Example

The practical examples here use Combine to create a one-way data pipeline. We could have used either delegates, callbacks, or the NSNotification framework. Here, we chose Combine as it provides an observable structure (as opposed to utilizing delegates or callbacks) and more control than notifications.

Key Architectural Decision   Using Combine to control the one-way data flow of our application. We chose Combine as it provides an observable framework with more control than NSNotification.

Our previous iOS application example from Chapter 3 implemented a form of controller-based networking. In that example, we trigger the network request explicitly in the view controller by calling the underlying network method in the repository.

```
// MobileDevAtScale/Chapter 3/NetworkingLayer
photoRepository.getAll()
  .receive(on: DispatchQueue.main)
  .sink { result in
    // potential area to handle errors and edge cases
    switch result {
    case .finished:
      break
    case .failure(let error):
      print("Error: \(error)")
      break
    }
```

```
} receiveValue: { [weak self] photos in
  guard let sSelf = self else {
    return
  }
  sSelf.photos = photos.compactMap{ $0 as? Photo }
  self?.tableView.reloadData()
}
.store(in: &cancellables)
```

By using controller-based networking, we cut down on overall code and, in the short term, speed development; however, we lose flexibility, limit code reuse, and contribute to massive view controllers.

The model-based networking presented in this chapter helps us further abstract our concerns and isolate networking logic from the controller. Additionally, model-based networking allows for easy state updates for other pages or components that may be listening for model changes.

To move this to model-based networking, we implement our networking code in the model itself. To ensure that our model publishes updates our controller can respond to, we will utilize Combine and make the *allPhotos* property observable via the *@Published* keyword.

Key Architectural Decision   Using model-based networking. This is a principle we define here and would enforce throughout our application as it provides greater flexibility and abstracts logic from the *ViewController*.

```
// Protocol for usage with dependency injection

protocol PhotoModelProto {
  // Cannot use the @Published annotation in a
  // protocol so we expose the type
```

```
  var allPhotosPublished:
  Published<[PhotoModel.Photo]>.Publisher { get }
  func getAllPhotos()
}
class PhotoModel: PhotoModelProto, ObservableObject {
  // nested struct representing the model properties
  struct Photo: ModelProto {
    let albumID: Int
    let id: Int
    let title: String
    let url: URL
    let thumbnailURL: URL
  }

  var allPhotosPublished:
  Published<[Photo]>.Publisher { $allPhotos }
  @Published private var allPhotos:
  [PhotoModel.Photo] = []
  private var cancellables: Set<AnyCancellable> = []

  private let photoRepository: RepositoryProto

  // dependency injection is used to inject the photos
  // repository which handles networking
  init(photoRepository: RepositoryProto) {
    self.photoRepository = photoRepository
  }

  // Method exposed by the model to get all photos for
  // display
  func getAllPhotos() {
    photoRepository
      .getAll()
```

```
    .receive(on: DispatchQueue.main)
    .sink { result in
      // potential area to handle errors
      // and edge cases
      switch result {
      case .finished:
        break
      case .failure(let error):
        print("Error: \(error)")
      }
    } receiveValue: { [weak self] photos in
      guard let sSelf = self else {
        return
      }
      sSelf.allPhotos = photos
        .compactMap{ $0 as? PhotoModel.Photo }
    }.store(in: &cancellables)
  }
}
```

Now, in our controller, we can perform an initial get request on *viewDidLoad* and then subscribe to the *allPhotos* variable to receive model updates when the *allPhotos* request returns. This code sample also includes a rudimentary collection view to display the data similar to our previous UI specifications for the Photo Stream application. The provided UI is by no means a production-ready UI. It only serves to illustrate the component orchestration and interaction.

```
import UIKit
import Combine

class PhotoStreamViewController: UIViewController {
  private let photoModel: PhotoModelProto
```

```swift
private var photos: [PhotoModel.Photo] = []
private var cancellables: Set<AnyCancellable> = []

private lazy var collectionView: UICollectionView = {
  let collectionView = UICollectionView(
    frame: .zero,
    collectionViewLayout: flowLayout)
  collectionView.register(
    PhotoStreamCollectionViewCell.self,
    forCellWithReuseIdentifier: "cell")
  collectionView.dataSource = self
  collectionView.delegate = self
  return collectionView
}()

private lazy var flowLayout:
UICollectionViewFlowLayout = {
  let layout = UICollectionViewFlowLayout()
  layout.minimumInteritemSpacing = 5
  layout.minimumLineSpacing = 5
  layout.sectionInset = UIEdgeInsets(
    top: 5,
    left: 5,
    bottom: 5,
    right: 5)
  layout.scrollDirection = .horizontal
  return layout
}()

// The photo model is injected
init(photoModel: PhotoModelProto) {
  self.photoModel = photoModel
  super.init(nibName: nil, bundle: .main)
}
```

251

```swift
required init?(coder: NSCoder) {
  fatalError("init(coder:) has not been implemented")
}

override func viewDidLoad() {
  super.viewDidLoad()
  // subscribe to updates
  photoModel
    .allPhotosPublished
    .sink { [weak self] ret in
      self?.photos = ret
      self?.collectionView.reloadData()
    }
    .store(in: &cancellables)

  photoModel.getAllPhotos()
}

override func loadView() {
  view = collectionView
}
}
```

Notice how we have used dependency injection via initializer override in both of these examples. Each variable is backed by a protocol and injected via the initializer. This allows us to easily substitute our dependencies for testing or if a third-party dependency changes. Here, we initialize our top-level dependencies in the scene delegate.

Key Architectural Decision   Using dependency injection to
promote testability and we have chosen to utilize initializer overrides
to achieve this due to their simplicity. We define this principle here
and would enforce it throughout our application.

```swift
func scene(
    _ scene: UIScene,
    willConnectTo session: UISceneSession,
    options connectionOptions: UIScene.ConnectionOptions
) {
    guard let _ = (scene as? UIWindowScene)
        else { return }
    guard let windowScene = scene as? UIWindowScene
    else { return }
    let window = UIWindow(windowScene: windowScene)
    // setup dependencies for injection here
    let coreDataManager = CoreDataManager(
        persistentContainer: container,
        inMemory: false)
    let networkManager = NetworkManager(
        networking: URLSession.shared)
    let repository = PhotoRepository(
        localStorageManager: coreDataManager,
        networkManager: networkManager)
    let photoModel = PhotoModel(
        photoRepository: repository)
    let vc = PhotoStreamViewController(
        photoModel: photoModel)
    window.rootViewController = UINavigationController(
        rootViewController: vc)
```

```
self.window = window
window.makeKeyAndVisible()
}
```

One issue with the MVC pattern is that the view controller's ability to display data is tightly coupled to the model's definition. To demonstrate this, we will add reactions to our example.

To add reactions, we first need to add a *Reaction* object to our model. Since reactions are tied to specific photos, let us assume we have a rockstar team of back-end engineers who have added reactions following the JSON API Standard[1] for us to consume as a subresource in the *included* section.

```
"included": [{
    "type": "reactions",
    "id": "9",
    "attributes": {
      "thumbsUpCount": "0",
      "thumbsDownCount": "0"
    },
}]
```

Now we can add reactions to our *PhotoModel*. We will add this to our model and create a fake update method that modifies the reaction count on an update to imitate a server request (since we do not have reactions in our sample API).

First, we create our reactions model with the data we want to capture from the network request.

```
class ReactionModel {
  var thumbsUpCount: Int
  var thumbsDownCount: Int
```

---

[1] https://jsonapi.org/

```
init(
    thumbsUpCount: Int = 0,
    thumbsDownCount: Int = 0
) {
    self.thumbsUpCount = thumbsUpCount
    self.thumbsDownCount = thumbsDownCount
}

// creates a mutable function so we can mock updates,
// ideally models are immutable
func update(upCount: Int, downCount: Int) {
    thumbsUpCount = thumbsUpCount + upCount
    thumbsDownCount = thumbsDownCount + downCount
}
}
```

Now we can attach our reaction to our *PhotoModel*, including our update method to fake a server update for reactions.

```
struct Photo: ModelProto {
    // skip other params...
    let reactions: ReactionModel

    init(
        albumID: Int,
        id: Int,
        title: String,
        url: URL,
        thumbnailURL: URL,
        // Default value to allow fake results
        reactions: ReactionModel = ReactionModel()
    ) {
        self.albumID = albumID
```

```
    self.id = id
    self.title = title
    self.url = url
    self.thumbnailURL = thumbnailURL
    self.reactions = reactions
  }
}
  // ...
  // fake update reactions on photo, just updates all
  // photos uniformly
  func updateReactionCount(
    upCount: Int, downCount: Int) {
      // we would send an update to our network layer,
      // instead loop through and
      // update all reactions. This is purely for
      // illustration purposes
      for photo in allPhotos {
        photo.reactions.update(
          upCount: upCount, downCount: downCount)
      }
      allPhotos = allPhotos
  }
```

Lastly, we are ready to display our reactions to the UI. Here, we want to allow the user to thumbs up or thumbs down a photo and track the overall number of reactions. Monitoring and displaying the number of reactions in each category bring up a problem. Our server does not have a representation of how we want to show the reaction count to our users, meaning we need to create this in the iOS application.

We can format this string in our model and expose the property for displaying to the user, or we could format the string in the view. Either solution is problematic. Changing the model means our model no longer represents our server data. And making the change in the view makes our change more difficult to test. It violates the principle that the view should describe a controller-agnostic container free of complex formatting (other reaction components may not want to display this value the same way).

To increase the testability of our change, we will add the formatted string as a property on the model; however, if we continue to do this for a complex view hierarchy, we may end up with a very large model object that is now handling multiple responsibilities (server data representation and view formatting logic – not very modular).

Key Architectural Decision   Moving formatting code from views to models to promote testability and remove dependencies from views. We define this principle here and would enforce it throughout our application.

```
// added to our reactions model
var reactionsLabelText: String {
  return "\(thumbsUpCount) 👍 and \(thumbsDownCount) 👎"
}
```

In the next chapter, we will discuss a more view-centric approach to solving this type of problem by utilizing the MVVM architecture. A more view-centric architecture is well suited for complex applications with many UI components and interactions, such as if we added additional features such as comments and sharing. By switching to a view-centric approach and avoiding massive model files, we also allow our application to scale more easily. We can accommodate more engineers working across the application with fewer conflicts from editing shared files and an easier-to-understand code base.

To finish our reactions implementation, we must connect our reactions view to our collection view cell.

```
// PhotoStreamCollectionViewCell.swift
func configureCell(
  title: String,
  reactionsLabelText: String,
  thumbsUpCount: Int,
  thumbsDownCount: Int,
  target: Any?,
  sel: Selector
) {
  self.title = title
  reactionsView.thumbsUp = thumbsUpCount
  reactionsView.thumbsDown = thumbsDownCount
  reactionsView.reactionsLabelText = reactionsLabelText
  reactionsView.thumbsUpButton.addTarget(
    target,
    action: sel,
    for: .touchUpInside)
  reactionsView.thumbsDownButton.addTarget(
    target,
    action: sel,
    for: .touchUpInside)
}
```

Lastly, we need to connect our view to the view controller for display. Notice we have used a helper method to abstract away some of the view configuration logic.

```
// PhotoStreamViewController.swift
func collectionView(
  _ collectionView: UICollectionView,
```

```
   cellForItemAt indexPath: IndexPath
) -> UICollectionViewCell {
  guard let cell = collectionView.dequeueReusableCell(
           withReuseIdentifier: "cell",
           for: indexPath
     ) as? PhotoStreamCollectionViewCell else {
           return UICollectionViewCell()
     }
  cell.configureCell(
    title: photos[indexPath.row].title,
    reactionsLabelText: photos[indexPath.row]
           .reactions
           .reactionsLabelText,
    thumbsUpCount: photos[indexPath.row]
           .reactions
           .thumbsUpCount,
    thumbsDownCount: photos[indexPath.row]
           .reactions
           .thumbsDownCount,
    target: self,
    sel: #selector(updateReactionCount))
  return cell
}
```

Another architectural decision we made is to utilize a view hierarchy and helper method to configure the complex view. Given the complexity of the collection view cell implementation, we could implement it as a separate view controller. For example, if our main *PhotoStreamViewController* starts to become full of other responsibilities, directly managing the cell's implementation may start to bloat the controller. This is addressable by creating a specific *ViewController* to manage the *CollectionViewCell*.

However, this comes with its own complications. We would then need to manage the *ViewController*'s state and ensure we implement this performantly by recycling *ViewControllers* (similar to how Apple does this for *CollectionView* cells). Another factor in deciding whether to create a separate *ViewController* is the number of engineers working on the component. If there are a lot of engineers, further modularizing the feature will make it easier to avoid merge conflicts and overlapping changes.

Key Architectural Decision   We chose a simple design where the view configures itself via a helper method promoting abstraction and ease of development. We feel it is premature to use a separate view controller for this change. We are making this design decision here and would want to document it for future maintainers and use it as a precedent for future decisions.

The last architectural decision of abstracting view controllers is a perfect example of working in an application at scale. As a senior engineer, you will need the ability to identify pain points and potential solutions. Most day-to-day work is not creating a new application or a complete architecture rewrite but instead optimizing the existing design based on the best practices and needs of the company.

While it is rare to design the application ourselves from scratch, we still need to understand the existing base architecture and design patterns to produce new features. If problems arise, you can suggest new design patterns or architectural changes that fix them, such as suggesting moving away from the MVC pattern if the models representing network data are not matching the view state, causing complex logic, fat models, and slower development.

Discussion

In the "Practical Example" section, we walked through building our Photo Stream application utilizing the MVC architecture for our application layer. We also included some of the critical decisions we faced during our application design and example construction. This section will discuss some of the trade-offs associated with MVC, potential effects on testability and modularity, and the reality at scale.

Trade-Offs

We have already started discussing the potential trade-offs earlier as we added our reactions component to our sample application. There are several other areas that the MVC pattern does not cover particularly well, including the following:

1. How to modularize complex application interactions

   a. Where to add routing logic?

   b. Where and how should data manipulation occur? Should model data be immutable?

   c. How do we interact with the network and other complex libraries?

2. How do we test our components? Can we test our controllers?

   This is not to say that the MVC pattern is not valid; overall, the MVC pattern allows applications to separate their main concerns and encapsulate object functionality. Like any other application design pattern, it will have some shortcomings. This section will address the preceding drawbacks in our Photo Stream application.

Addressing the first point, *modularizing complex application interactions*, MVC can lead our application into a state where we have combined routing, complex library interaction, and data model updates into one or two central locations, such as the view controller. Figure 7-4 outlines this potential issue across all three components.

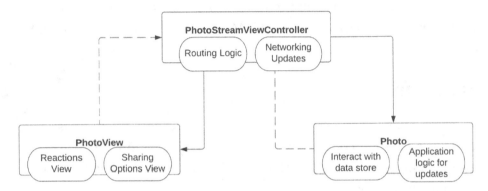

Figure 7-4. *Photo Stream application with each component taking on too many responsibilities*

While it is nearly impossible for one pattern to cover all of these concerns without explicitly calling them out, there is a tendency to miss them when designing the overall application. With this in mind, we will review the pitfalls in depth and present some potential solutions to promote modularity.

Modularity

We would expect a modular application to respect the single responsibility principle by design. However, by strictly following MVC and only using models, views, and controllers, it is typical for the code associated with networking and routing to end up in the model or controller class. Also, models end up mutable with inconsistent state updates because the associated model data manipulation is in the same class as the model. This can lead to tight coupling between components and large complex files, commonly categorized as the *massive view controller* problem.

The *massive view controller* can quickly appear in the MVC pattern because there are no clearly designated places to put business logic for applications. This situation causes many developers to place code related to data modification in the controllers. While this is an example of a *ViewController* going beyond its core purpose, this is very common due to the lack of structure with the MVC pattern. In the end, this can lead to the following:

1. Tricky bugs from shared data. Who is modifying this data and when? Without a careful design, the answer could be almost anyone, at virtually any time, with unknown, cascading side effects.

2. Hard to test code where one object has too much responsibility, making it hard to isolate behavior.

3. Complex merge conflicts for large teams. Due to the size of the files and MVCs' limiting nature, there could be a large number of developers all trying to touch the same files.

The problem of oversized view controllers is pervasive. It can affect large-scale applications in particular due to the number of engineers collaborating and the age of the application. For example, the Firefox BrowserViewController is over 2000 lines long! The Firefox application's massive view controllers are in contrast to Kickstarter's iOS application, where dependencies are abstracted from the *ViewControllers* to avoid *ViewControllers* growing over time. Enforcing the level of abstraction demonstrated in the Kickstarter application requires senior engineers to hold a high bar during code reviews and ensure engineers take the time to abstract their changes and that new features undergo architecture reviews.

No application-wide design pattern will address all possible concerns. We must actively question any application's architecture to find and address potential flaws. We can utilize some of the design patterns outlined in the previous chapter to address the aforementioned concerns.

1. We can utilize the facade pattern to abstract away complex business concerns into their underlying libraries, such as a networking library.

2. We can utilize dependency injection to avoid singletons and create a testable environment for our code.

3. We can include coordinators to manage the overall routing.

4. We can diligently break out logical components to include delegates and data sources to their own files to avoid bloat.

These patterns can allow us to extend our MVC application to suit the needs of our application further and are outlined in Figure 7-5; however, MVC is still not well suited for large-scale applications with complex user interfaces and business logic.

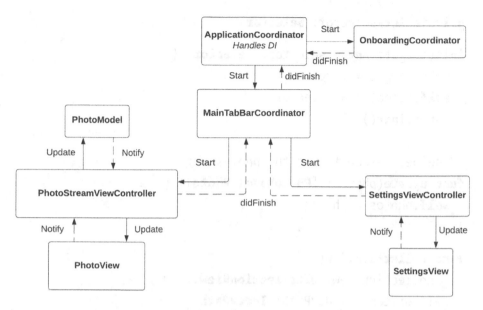

Figure 7-5. *Photo Stream application utilizing a coordinator with dependency injection (DI) for the networking library and PhotoModel*

For illustration purposes, we will abstract the data source and delegate classes from our *PhotoStreamViewController* and implement the coordinator pattern.

To abstract our *CollectionViewDataSource,* we can create a new class that implements our data source functionality from the *PhotoStreamViewController.* To do so, we must pass in the photos array and some of the values we used in our view controller.

```
final class PhotoStreamUICollectionViewDataSource:
  NSObject, UICollectionViewDataSource {
  // array we need for processing the results
  private var photos: [PhotoModel.Photo] = []
  // properties for instantiating our reactions
  // button component
  private let target: Any?
```

265

```
private let selector: Selector

init(target: Any?, selector: Selector) {
  self.target = target
  self.selector = selector
  super.init()
}
// helper method to set the photos var
func update(photos: [PhotoModel.Photo]) {
  self.photos = photos
}

func collectionView(
  _ collectionView: UICollectionView,
  cellForItemAt indexPath: IndexPath
) -> UICollectionViewCell {
  guard let cell = collectionView.dequeueReusableCell(
    withReuseIdentifier: "cell",
    for: indexPath
  ) as? PhotoStreamCollectionViewCell else {
    return UICollectionViewCell()
  }
  cell.configureCell(
    title: photos[indexPath.row].title,
    reactionsLabelText: photos[indexPath.row]
      .reactions
      .reactionsLabelText,
    thumbsUpCount: photos[indexPath.row]
      .reactions
      .thumbsUpCount,
    thumbsDownCount: photos[indexPath.row]
      .reactions
```

```
      .thumbsDownCount,
    target: target,
    sel: selector
  )
  return cell
}

func collectionView(
  _ collectionView: UICollectionView,
  numberOfItemsInSection section: Int
) -> Int {
  return photos.count
}
}
```

Now we can instantiate our object and register it as our *Collection View* data source.

```
private lazy var collectionViewDataSource:
  PhotoStreamUICollectionViewDataSource = {
    return PhotoStreamUICollectionViewDataSource(
      target: self,
      selector: #selector(updateReactionCount))
}()
```

We can follow a similar approach for the *DelegateFlowLayout*. Here, we copy over the delegate method from our *PhotoStreamViewController* and pass in the *instance of the UICollectionViewFlowLayout* so that we can utilize it in both our view controller and delegate class.

// final directive used to show the class is closed
// to extension. Also reduces dynamic dispatch.

```swift
final class PhotoStreamCollectionViewDelegateFlowLayout:
NSObject, UICollectionViewDelegateFlowLayout {
  private let flowLayout: UICollectionViewFlowLayout

  init(flowLayout: UICollectionViewFlowLayout) {
    self.flowLayout = flowLayout
    super.init()
  }

  func collectionView(
    _ collectionView: UICollectionView,
    layout collectionViewLayout: UICollectionViewLayout,
    sizeForItemAt indexPath: IndexPath
  ) -> CGSize {
    let width = collectionView.bounds.width
    let numberOfItemsPerRow: CGFloat = 1
    let spacing: CGFloat =
      flowLayout.minimumInteritemSpacing
    let availableWidth = width - spacing *
      (numberOfItemsPerRow + 1)
    let itemDimension = floor(
      availableWidth / numberOfItemsPerRow)
    return CGSize(
      width: itemDimension,
      height: itemDimension)
  }
}
```

To add coordinators, we will build on the example from Chapter 6 and have the Photo Stream display inside the *MainTabBarViewController*. In addition, to show the benefit of coordinators, we have copied over the onboarding flow and settings screen from the coordinator example in Chapter 6.

To enable our *PhotoStreamViewController* in the example in Chapter 6, we first need to create a *PhotoStreamCoordinator*. The coordinator will also include the *PhotoModel* as a dependency. This way, we can inject it into our *PhotoStreamViewController* and get our photos from the network.

```
final class PhotoStreamCoordinator: BaseCoordinator {
  // save our dependency for injection
  private let photoModel: PhotoModelProto

  init(
    router: RouterProto,
    photoModel: PhotoModelProto
  ) {
    self.photoModel = photoModel
    super.init(router: router)
  }
}
```

Next, we implement our start function, where we instantiate our view controller utilizing the factory and utilize our router to set the view controller as the root module for the tab.

```
override func start() {
  let photoStreamVC = PhotoStreamViewController(
      photoModel: photoModel)
    router.setRootModule(photoStreamVC, hideBar: false)
}
```

By setting our view controller as the root module, we are configuring the tab for navigation via a *UINavigationController*. Configuring a navigation controller allows the different items attached to the tab bar to utilize the features of the *UINavigationController* for stack-based navigation.

Now we need to wire our coordinator into the existing coordinator hierarchy; however, we need to modify the dependencies required to accommodate the *PhotoStreamViewController*'s use of the *PhotoModel*. To do so, we change the current application coordinator setup in the scene delegate and instantiate our dependencies to support injecting the *PhotoModel*.

```
func scene(
  _ scene: UIScene,
  willConnectTo session: UISceneSession,
  options connectionOptions: UIScene.ConnectionOptions
) {
  // skip some setup code...
  // setup dependencies for injection here
  let coreDataManager = CoreDataManager(
    persistentContainer: container,
    inMemory: false)
  let networkManager = NetworkManager(
    networking: URLSession.shared)
  let repository = PhotoRepository(
    localStorageManager: coreDataManager,
    networkManager: networkManager)
  let photoModel = PhotoModel(
    photoRepository: repository)
  let vc = UINavigationController()
  window.rootViewController = vc
  self.window = window
  window.makeKeyAndVisible()

  applicationCoordinator = ApplicationCoordinator(
    router: Router(rootController: vc),
    // force to onboarding to show coordinators action
    launchState: .onboarding,
```

```
  childCoordinators: [],
  photoModel: photoModel)
 // no deeplink support
 applicationCoordinator?.start()
}
```

Lastly in the MainTabCoordinator start function, we need to modify the functionality to display our updated *PhotoStreamViewController*. To do so, we create two navigation controllers and a new router instance for each tab (allowing us to utilize navigation inside our tabs).

```
override func start() {
  let tabBar = MainTabBarViewController()
  let photoStreamNavController = setupPhotoStreamNav()
  let settingsNavController = setupSettingsNav()

  tabBar.viewControllers = [
    photoStreamNavController,
    settingsNavController]
  router.setRootModule(tabBar, hideBar: true)
}
```

A Note on Avoiding Premature Optimization

Adding coordinators is an excellent way to abstract our concerns and further modularize our application. However, since we initially only had one screen, the *PhotoStreamViewController*, we realized little benefit from all the work required for our coordinator implementation. What this means is that our coordinator implementation represents a premature optimization.

The coordinators were not solving anything unique for our application, so adding them for the sake of adding them represents a common pitfall in application architecture. It is easy to theorize about future unknown problems and spend too much time attempting to architect a solution for these problems instead of finishing the initial required work. The balance of designing a scalable system and not over-optimizing is an art and takes careful thought. A general rule of thumb is

1. Follow modular and testable design principles for every feature to make future changes easier.

2. If there is no clear business use case requiring this architecture change in the next six to twelve months, then do not make the change.

If we over-optimize for non-existing use cases, we risk building the wrong system and pushing deadlines for business-critical features due to the extra development work required.

Testability

As mentioned previously, we can improve our basic MVC application by incorporating dependency injection, the facade pattern, and the coordinator pattern. All of these patterns further abstract concerns to their own modules, enhancing our ability to test individual components of our application. Additionally, we can more easily mock logic in our controllers for integration tests by abstracting our dependencies via dependency injection. While some of our testing concerns are addressed via dependency injection, MVC still makes testing difficult because MVC does not provide a clear place for manipulating data from the server-based representation to the view state representation. Commonly in MVC, the required logic for these changes ends up in the views themselves or the controllers, both of which are difficult to unit test.

To address the difficulty in unit testing the application, we can rely more heavily on integration tests; however, integration tests can be complex to set up and time-consuming to run. With an extensive application where automated tests before landing code may only run a subset of tests to avoid taking too much time, unit tests become a more effective way to get faster feedback on changes. Both MVVM and VIPER, discussed in subsequent chapters, help pull more interactions out of the view control to provide a more testable setup.

MVC at Scale

Before continuing, can you think of any additional concerns you would want to address?

We will not see MVC very much at scale as it does not provide a clear separation of concerns and often leads to massive files (not just view controllers). Additionally, we will likely not be defining the application architecture from scratch. Instead, we will work on an existing application with an existing architecture. Many of these applications will have undergone multiple architectural revisions and follow a more complex architecture pattern, such as MVVM or VIPER. However, you may also find yourself at a high-growth company rapidly scaling where the current architecture is no longer functioning well.

In this situation, if the set architecture is MVC, it is your responsibility to follow best practices to ensure the application continues to scale. If the architecture must change, you must make a valid case based on recorded pain points that the application architecture must transform to continue scaling and meeting business goals. We can quantify this process into the following steps:

1. Understand the existing architecture and hold a high bar for its current implementation.

2. Concretely identify the pain points.

3. Construct a formal proposal that evaluates different architectural solutions and the preferred solution.

4. After making changes, continue to iterate and evolve the architecture and continuously review its effectiveness to ensure it solves the intended challenges.

Application architecture patterns should not be taken as fixed rules but combined with other design patterns to form a fully functioning modular and testable application. While application design patterns attempt to cover the entire application structure, it is rare for them to do so truly. Instead, for your application, it is helpful also to combine an application design pattern with others to complete the architecture of your application. This section illustrated a potential design process for an organically growing application. We started with the core functionality (display photo and react), identified potential issues (too many concerns in the view controller), and adapted our architecture to solve the problems (abstracted delegates/data sources and added coordinators). With any growing application, it is necessary to continuously evaluate the architecture and modify it as required, allowing for continuous scaling.

Summary

Throughout this chapter, we explored the MVC application design pattern. We started by defining the architecture, components, and state interactions. Next, we used our Photo Stream example to examine the MVC architecture and some of its shortcomings critically. Finally, we discussed potential solutions to address the problems we encountered. We have attempted to present this architecture pattern in a similar format of thinking critically through the architecture design process.

Overall we have discerned that MVC is a simple pattern that requires little overhead, making it ideal for new applications, proof of concepts, and any application that requires fast iteration, leaving room for significant changes in the business use cases. As your application continually grows, you may find flaws with the initial MVC pattern that can be refactored or rebuilt utilizing a more complex or niche design pattern. In this way, even though MVC is not suited for large-scale applications, we can still use the MVC pattern to help us make progress quickly and avoid overengineering around potential problems we are unlikely to face.

There is no single solution for architecture design; every application is unique and requires fitting together multiple design patterns to accomplish your individual goals. This makes the MVC pattern perfectly suitable for some cases. You must determine when these situations occur and appropriately document them for discussion, implementation, and retrospectives. With the practical example, we discussed our ongoing MVC application and how we can apply architectural best practices to resolve problems as they occur in line with the application scaling. While some of these decisions may seem small due to the nature of the toy application in a large-scale company, adding in coordinators and moving toward model-based networking are enormous changes that can affect how hundreds of engineers work. The scale makes the change require careful planning and execution. Part 3 of this book discusses how to navigate these challenges effectively.

Three Key Takeaways from This Chapter

1. There is no single architectural solution; thus, following patterns dogmatically can lead to problems. Every situation must be assessed for its unique challenges.

2. MVC is acceptable, but it does not scale well and at minimum requires combined with other principles; however, it can serve as a good starting point.

3. Application design patterns are a misnomer since
    one pattern typically cannot encompass everything
    required for an application. Instead, we should look
    at how to break down our application holistically
    and manage the complexity at each level (keeping
    things modular).

Further Learning

1. Pinterest usage of NSNotificationCenter for model
    updates: `https://academy.realm.io/posts/slug-wendy-lu-data-consistency/`

2. Advanced iOS App Architecture: Real-World App
    Architecture in Swift by the Ray Wenderlich team

CHAPTER 8

Model View View-Model (MVVM)

Overview

We discussed the MVC design in the previous chapter and applied it to our Photo Stream example. To illustrate potential scaling challenges, we discussed adding a reactions component. To show navigation challenges, we linked our application to our coordinator example from earlier. In this chapter, we will apply a similar format to explain the MVVM pattern and apply it to our Photo Stream application while considering our architecture decisions from the previous chapter.

This Chapter Includes

The MVVM pattern includes an in-depth look at the pattern, trade-offs, considerations for its usage, and when we could best use it in our applications. In the "Practical Example" section, we will simulate the scaling of our Photo Stream example to highlight the benefits of MVVM and potential usage over MVC and other architecture patterns.

A Detailed Look at MVVM

The MVVM pattern utilizes the same components as the MVC pattern with the addition of the view-model. The view-model serves to model the view state of the application and describes the presentation and interaction logic of the scene.

The view-model derives its values from the underlying model object and applies transformations to the data so that it can be displayed directly to the views. The view-model utilizes reactive programming via properties exposed on the view-model to communicate with the view controller. While reactive programming is not strictly required for MVVM, it is a widespread implementation and is what we will utilize in this chapter. Figure 8-1 outlines how the MVVM components act in concert to create a fully functioning application.

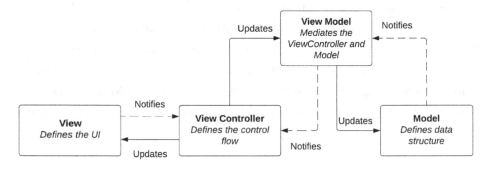

Figure 8-1. *General MVVM architecture*

While the overall design is similar to MVC, the view-model is a crucial difference as it handles a portion of the work previously in the view controller or model of the MVC application, including the view state. Suppose the view state transformations are in the view controller. In that case, testability is increased by moving the view state to the view-model, which decouples the view state from the view controller, which is tied to the iOS application framework. Suppose the view transformations were

278

placed in the model as we did in the previous chapter. In that case, MVVM serves to lessen the functions of the model and provides a centralized location for transforming model values to view-centric ones.

The MVVM pattern is most useful for applications with complex state interactions. Since applications with complex UI state interactions typically also have complicated navigation, the coordinator pattern also pairs well with MVVM since the view-model is coupled to the scene, and the coordinator can orchestrate the application flow. This leaves the view controller solely responsible for managing the view hierarchy. This combination of design patterns nicely follows the single responsibility principle and serves to modularize our application. Figure 8-2 outlines the MVVM pattern combined with the coordinators for navigation. Utilizing coordinators with MVVM does introduce another level of indirection in the application and adds additional code necessary for feature engineering.

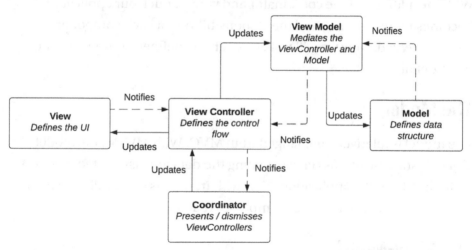

Figure 8-2. *General MVVM architecture with coordinators*

We apply these components in Figure 8-3 to our Photo Stream application. In this diagram, we focus on displaying our Photo Stream portion of the application and the navigation coordinator for that flow.

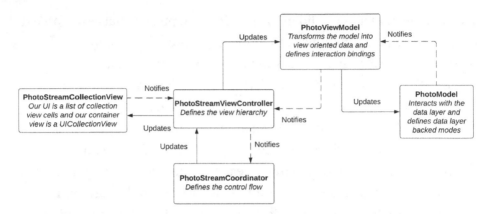

Figure 8-3. *General MVVM architecture with coordinators*

MVVM Components

With the addition of the coordinator and view-model, our application becomes more modular, and the responsibilities of each component have decreased. Now we will walk through the defined components in more detail.

The Model

The model is relatively unchanged from MVC. With MVVM, the model object is still a Swift class encapsulating the data and associated business logic specific to the application. Now with iterations on our Photo Stream application, the model also encompasses reactions.

The View-Model

The view-model is the primary change between MVC and MVVM. Traditionally, the view-model is a Swift object containing a view's state, methods for handling user interaction, and bindings to different user interface elements. In our example, we decouple the view's state to a separate immutable view-model struct; this allows us to keep our view-model object immutable. We could apply our state directly as parameters on the view-model; however, by enforcing immutability and creating immutable view-models, we help ensure application and state correctness.

One of the most critical aspects of designing a scalable application is minimizing complex state interactions to avoid potential bugs. In iOS applications, consistently handling state updates is one of the most challenging aspects of state interaction. If the UI does not match the model or has outdated data, it can lead to unexpected behavior, including application crashes and displaying or saving erroneous data.

By applying immutable view-models to the MVVM pattern, we minimize the mutable state in the application. One source of necessary state mutation is in the UI since the UI must stay updated to accurately reflect changes the user has made. With a traditional two-way-bound view-model, we would mutably update our UI state, increasing the surface area for unexpected bugs. However, by passing an immutable view-model that gets refreshed at every model change, we eliminate this type of duplicate state. After the updated view state applies itself to the UI, we can no longer modify that object.

Note   State is any place where we store a representation of a particular data type.

To further modularize our view-model, while utilizing Combine for reactive bindings, we segment our state interaction into separate input and output structs. This way, our view-model serves as immutable data and other values the view requires to reflect the model's state, and we have separate structures to model our state transformations.

The View Controller

In MVVM, the view controller object is an intermediary between the view and the view-model. The controller is typically a descendant of a UIViewController and controls the logical flow and view hierarchy. In our example, the view controller will manage the interaction between the view and the view-model for displaying our photos and establish the bindings between itself and the view-model for state updates.

Additionally, in our example, because we are utilizing coordinators for navigation, we are taking that responsibility away from the view controller, leaving the view controller solely responsible for managing the view hierarchy. Now, state updates are bound to the view-model, and navigation is bound to the coordinator.

The View

The view is unchanged from MVC.

Component Interactions

Object Construction

Similar to MVC and other design patterns, there are different ways to approach object construction. Our MVVM sample project follows a similar practice to our MVC example, where a high-level controller will load and configure views. However, with MVVM, pertinent view information will come from the view-model instead of directly from the model. We will also continue to utilize dependency injection for all our resources.

Updates to the Model

In MVVM, the model is updated via the view-model. The view-model directly updates the model based on change events received from the ViewController. The view-model knows what kind of events it can respond to and what appropriate action to take, which it utilizes to change the model.

The View-Model

The view-model knows how to handle user interactions, like button taps. User interactions map to methods or closures in the view-model. The methods do some work, like telling the model to update and then triggering state changes that result in view changes. In our example, we abstract the state changes the view-model is responsible for to separate structs and configure them in the view-model. Lastly, the view controller binds to the view-model to configure the state change interaction.

The View Controller

In contrast to MVC, where the view controller receives view events and changes the model or its internal view state, in MVVM, when a view event arrives, the view controller notifies the view-model instead. The view-model is then responsible for updating its internal state or the model.

Unlike with MVC, the view controller doesn't observe the model. Instead, the view-model observes the model and transforms the model updates in a way that the view controller understands. The view controller subscribes to the view-model's changes, typically using bindings from a reactive programming framework (Combine in our example), but any observation mechanism will work. When a view-model event arrives, the view controller changes the view hierarchy. The view-model always sends model-changing view actions through the model and only notifies the relevant observers after the model change has taken place, enforcing a unidirectional data flow.

Updates to the View

In MVVM, the view layer reacts to state changes through bindings to view-model properties. It also notifies the view-model of user interaction, like button taps or text input updates. All of these bindings are established in the controller.

In our MVVM example, we use one-way data binding to bind the UI elements from the view to the view-model. This means the view-model is the single source of truth – the view updates once the view-model changes its state.

The View State

In MVVM, the view state is stored in the view-model. Our example utilizes Combine, so the state consists of *@Published* properties. Using Combine, the view controller subscribes to the publishers.

Practical Example

Building on our previous example, we can create our view-model for our Photo Stream application. In our example, our view-model serves two usages. The overall view-model for our component

1. Handles state change interactions

2. Contains the full view state as immutable data matching the UI view state (instead of mirroring the network response)

Let us start by constructing the view state. To do so, we can take the necessary properties from the UI and create a separate struct. For later usage, we also implement the Equatable protocol.

```swift
struct PhotoViewModel {
  let title: String
  let id: Int
  let reactionsLabelText: String
  let thumbsUpCount: Int
  let thumbsDownCount: Int
}

extension PhotoViewModel: Equatable {
  static func == (
    lhs: PhotoViewModel,
    rhs: PhotoViewModel
  ) -> Bool {
    return lhs.id == rhs.id
    && lhs.title == rhs.title
    && lhs.reactionsLabelText == rhs.reactionsLabelText
    && lhs.thumbsUpCount == rhs.thumbsUpCount
    && lhs.thumbsDownCount == rhs.thumbsDownCount
  }
}
```

To populate the photo view-model, we will utilize a static builder. Since our *reactionsLabelText* is not directly available from the network model, we will construct it in the builder. Note how this code is taken from the model to the view-model builder. While our example is a bit simple, a more complex application may have a lot of transformations from the network to the view-model requiring a more robust builder. We may have to utilize results from multiple network requests to create the view-model.

Key Architectural Decision   Utilize a separate static builder function for our view-models, allowing us to easily construct complex view-models in a testable, modular way.

```swift
final class PhotoViewModelBuilder {
  static func buildPhotoStreamViewModel(
    photo: PhotoModel.Photo
  ) -> PhotoViewModel {
    let downCount = photo.reactions.thumbsDownCount
    let upCount = photo.reactions.thumbsUpCount
    let label = buildReactionsLabelText(
      thumbsUpCount: upCount,
      thumbsDownCount: downCount)
    return PhotoViewModel(
      title: photo.title,
      id: photo.id,
      reactionsLabelText: label,
      thumbsUpCount: upCount,
      thumbsDownCount: downCount
    )
  }

  private static func buildReactionsLabelText(
    thumbsUpCount: Int,
    thumbsDownCount: Int
  ) -> String {
    return "\(thumbsUpCount) 👍 and" +
    \(thumbsDownCount) 👎"
  }
}
```

Now let us define the state transformations we want to allow for our scene. To do so, we can think about this in terms of a reactive data transformation pipeline with inputs, a transformation, and outputs. Our input object defines UI events used by the model and triggers state transformation, and the output struct represents the view's state resulting from the change.

For inputs, we want to handle when the view appears and when a user taps on a reaction. To do so, we will define the allowable state input and map them to combine bindings.

```
import Combine

// struct to wrap view-model input
struct ReactionSelection {
  let id: Int
  let reactionType: ReactionType
}

struct PhotoStreamViewModelInput {
  // called when a screen becomes visible
  let appear: AnyPublisher<Void, Never>
  // called when the user reactions to a photo
  let reaction: AnyPublisher<ReactionSelection, Never>
}
```

For outputs, we want the view controller to know when the call to the model to fetch data is loading, when it has completed with the constructed view-model, and when a failure has occurred. Similar to the input struct, we will bind our transformations to Combine.

```
import Combine

typealias PhotoStreamViewModelOuput = AnyPublisher<PhotoStream
State, Never>

enum PhotoStreamState {
  case loading
  case success([PhotoViewModel])
  case failure(Error)
}
```

```swift
extension PhotoStreamState: Equatable {
  static func == (
    lhs: PhotoStreamState,
    rhs: PhotoStreamState
  ) -> Bool {
    switch (lhs, rhs) {
      case (.loading, .loading): return true
      case (.success(let lhsPhotos),
            .success(let rhsPhotos)):
          return lhsPhotos == rhsPhotos
      case (.failure, .failure): return true
      default: return false
    }
  }
}
```

Now that we have defined our allowable data transformation and immutable view state, we can connect these to our overall scene view-model. The main portion of this code is the transform function, where we take our input and apply the required transformation to make the necessary output.

Here, we have moved our call to the *PhotoModel* out of the controller and into the view-model. We have also made a minor modification to update the photo's reaction. We have done this and added the loading state to illustrate how seamless MVVM makes these changes.

```swift
final class PhotoStreamViewModel: PhotoStreamViewModelProto {
  let vcTitle: String = "Photo Stream"
  private let photos: [PhotoViewModel] = []
  private let photoModel: PhotoModelProto
  private var cancellables: [AnyCancellable] = []

  init(photoModel: PhotoModelProto) {
    self.photoModel = photoModel
  }
```

```swift
func transform(
  input: PhotoStreamViewModelInput
) -> PhotoStreamViewModelOuput {
  input
      .reaction
      .sink { [unowned self] selection in
        let upCount =
            selection.reactionType ==
                .thumbsUp ? 1 : 0
        let downCount =
            selection.reactionType ==
                .thumbsDown ? 1 : 0
        self.photoModel.updateReactionCount(
            id: selection.id,
            upCount: upCount,
            downCount: downCount)
  }.store(in: &cancellables)
  let loading: PhotoStreamViewModelOuput = input
      .appear
      .map({_ in .loading })
      .eraseToAnyPublisher()
  let v = photoModel.allPhotosPublished.map {
    photos in
    let t = photos.map {
        PhotoViewModelBuilder
        .buildPhotoStreamViewModel(photo: $0)
    }
    return t.isEmpty ? .loading : .success(t)
  }
    .merge(with: loading)
    .removeDuplicates()
    .eraseToAnyPublisher()
```

```
    photoModel.getAllPhotos()
    return v
  }
}

extension PhotoStreamViewModel: Equatable {
        static func == (
          lhs: PhotoStreamViewModel,
          rhs: PhotoStreamViewModel
        ) -> Bool {
        return lhs.photos == rhs.photos
        }
}
```

Key Architectural Decision   The separation of the input and output states to separate objects differs from the classical MVVM approach, allowing us to enforce immutability best.

Lastly, we can wire our new Combine bindings to our existing view controller utilizing pass-through subjects. Here, we have removed our model references to the *PhotoModel* and instead connect our view-model bindings.

PassthroughSubject   As a concrete implementation of Subject, the PassthroughSubject provides a convenient way to adapt the existing imperative code to the Combine framework and reactive programming model. A PassthroughSubject doesn't have an

initial value or a buffer of the most recently published element. A
PassthroughSubject drops values if there are no subscribers or its
current demand is zero.[1]

```
private let photoStreamVM: PhotoStreamViewModelProto
private var cancellables: Set<AnyCancellable> = []

private let reaction =
PassthroughSubject<ReactionSelection, Never>()
private let appear = PassthroughSubject<Void, Never>()

init(photoStreamVM: PhotoStreamViewModelProto) {
  self.photoStreamVM = photoStreamVM
  super.init(nibName: nil, bundle: .main)
}

override func viewDidLoad() {
  super.viewDidLoad()
  navigationController?.tabBarItem.title =
  photoStreamVM.vcTitle
  let input = PhotoStreamViewModelInput(
    appear: appear.eraseToAnyPublisher(),
    reaction: reaction.eraseToAnyPublisher())

  let output = photoStreamVM.transform(input: input)
  output.sink { [unowned self] state in
    self.render(state)
  }
  .store(in: &cancellables)
}
```

---

[1] https://developer.apple.com/documentation/combine/passthroughsubject

In addition, we have defined a render state function to show how we could implement a more complex loading state. Lastly, we must update the reaction count to utilize our new view-model bindings.

```swift
private func render(_ state: PhotoStreamState) {
  switch state {
  case .loading:
    print("loading...")
  case .failure:
    print("failed...")
  case .success(let photoStream):
    collectionViewDataSource.update(photos: photoStream)
    collectionView.reloadData()
  }
}

@objc func updateReactionCount(_ sender: UIButton) {
  guard let btn = sender as? ReactionsButton,
        let reactionType = btn.reactionType,
        let photoId = btn.id
      else { return }
      let reactionSelection = ReactionSelection(
        id: photoId, reactionType: reactionType)
        reaction.send(reactionSelection)
}
```

Now that we have created our view-model and added the necessary bindings to our controller, we need to update our coordinator to reflect our new dependency.

```swift
final class PhotoStreamCoordinator: BaseCoordinator {
  private let photoModel: PhotoModelProto

  init(
```

```
    router: RouterProto,
    photoModel: PhotoModelProto
) {
    self.photoModel = photoModel
    super.init(router: router)
  }

  override func start() {
    let photoStreamVM: PhotoStreamViewModelProto =
    PhotoStreamViewModel(photoModel: photoModel)
    let photoStreamVC = PhotoStreamViewController(
      photoStreamVM: photoStreamVM)
    router.setRootModule(photoStreamVC, hideBar: false)
  }
}
```

Discussion

In the practical example, we modified our MVC application to support MVVM. We did this by abstracting some of the logic from the model and view controller, adding a more realistic loading state, updating our reaction mechanism, and passing in the VC title as a param. While abstracting the view controller title as a param is a small change, it shows a more realistic situation where all strings are passed via params and are potentially configured on the server for interaction with a more extensive i18n translation system.

More significant changes included moving view state-specific logic into the view-model and moving the necessary logic to transform our server-driven data into the required UI representation. Given that our example is relatively small, these changes are relatively small in magnitude. However, the benefits are more realized in a larger-scale application with complex data interactions and state transformations.

By using a static MVVM implementation with coordinators, we have managed to separate the different layers of our application better.

Benefits

1. View and view controller implementations are smaller.

2. Classes are more modularized.

3. Enforces a one-way predictable data flow through the system.

4. Views receive view-specific view-models that are separated from the network-backed models.

5. MVVM is a well-known and understood pattern by iOS engineers.

Downsides

1. A complete view-model is created and sent every time the UI needs to update, often overwriting unchanged portions of the UI.

2. Requires some boilerplate to wire reactive bindings.

3. Requires an additional framework to support reactive bindings.

Trade-Offs

Overhead

The main trade-off of MVVM is the increased overhead compared to MVC, which is well illustrated in our toy example where we created four additional files:

1. PhotoViewModel

2. PhotoViewModelBuilder

3.   PhotoStreamState

4.   PhotoStreamViewModelInput

There are many extra classes for enabling the relatively small benefit of more easily implementing a loading state and reaction update. In addition to the extra classes, we have also introduced the need for a specific reactive programming framework.

Reactive Programming

The reactive programming style is a good choice for large-scale applications because it enforces a predictable data model. We have chosen to use Combine as our reactive framework in our application since Apple provides it. Regardless of the framework selected for reactive programming, an extra framework is required, and some application code becomes geared explicitly toward that framework. Requiring developers to understand the framework also makes your code more difficult to port to a different framework.

Modularity

With the addition of the coordinator and view-model, we remove further responsibilities held by the view controller, increasing the modularity of our application compared to the MVC architecture. The view-model helps us manage changes in response to a state change and how we transform data for our UI (our reaction string).

The main advantage of the view-model is that it provides a modular location for us to transform our model data into the view state. In MVC, we need to decide where to place our logic to transform data for the UI and typically choose between the existing three components (model, view, and controller). Previously, we achieved this by modifying the data at the model level and then passing the entire model to the view controller, where we picked what we needed by our views.

Additionally, with MVVM, we are not forced to keep a one-to-one mapping between a view-model, view controller, and view. In fact, other view-models can manage parts of the view, especially when update rates vary. For example, if we have a Google document with a chat pane open so multiple people can edit the document and collaborate via comments, we would not want to refresh the document each time a chat message arrives.

Another example is a typeahead search implementation. For typeahead search, we want a search box that gets updated with more accurate results as we enter more text. In this situation, the whole screen can be served by one view-model (say for saved photos from our Photo Stream), but the search text box can specifically listen to a specific autocomplete view-model instead. Figure 8-4 outlines a potential nested view-model setup for typeahead search.

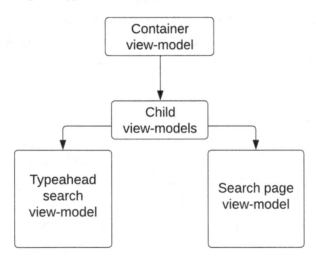

Figure 8-4. *Nested view-models for typeahead search*

Testability

By removing references to the view and view controller, the view-model is testable in isolation, increasing the testability of the entire application. The MVVM pattern increases testability by allowing independent testing of the view-model transformations separate from the application framework. Kickstarter's iOS application heavily relies on view-models for their application's testability, stating they see view-models as a lightweight way to isolate side effects and embrace a functional core and that they write them "as a pure mapping of input signals to output signals, and test them heavily, including tests for localization, accessibility, and event tracking."[2]

Summary

MVVM is an excellent design pattern to increase the modularity of our application and is easily extendable from a basic MVC application. By adding additional design patterns, such as dependency injection and coordinators, we can build an application able to scale to a large developer and user base. Due to the increased ability to create modular and testable code, MVVM is a much better choice for scaling an application.

In a traditional MVVM application, most of the view controller code is replaced with a view-model that is a regular class and can be tested more easily in isolation. To support a bidirectional bridge between the view and the model, traditional MVVM typically implements some form of Observables or a framework for reactive programming. Here, we have further built on the MVVM pattern to include immutable view-models and further modularize our code with coordinators. By further separating our concerns, we promote ease of use for large development teams.

There are other approaches to achieve a similar separation of concerns, including MVP and VIPER patterns. MVP is a common pattern in Android where the presenter modifies the model and sends it to the view layer. Here, both the

---

[2] https://github.com/kickstarter/ios-oss

view controller and the view are considered part of the view layer. The VIPER is a more detailed and decoupled form of MVP, where, in addition to the presenter from MVP, a separate "interactor" for business logic, entity (model), and router (for navigation) are added. We will discuss VIPER in the following chapter as the final application design pattern to further show another architecture option.

Three Key Takeaways from This Chapter

1. MVVM adds abstraction and increases modularity.

2. Pairs well with reactive programming to manage application state.

3. MVVM is a good architecture choice to build further on MVC as it requires only small modifications, is well known by most engineers, and enables further application scaling.

Further Learning

1. Advanced iOS App Architecture: Real-World App Architecture in Swift by the Ray Wenderlich team

2. Kouraklis, John (2016). MVVM as Design Pattern. 10.1007/978-1-4842-2214-0_1

CHAPTER 9

VIPER

Overview

So far, we have discussed MVC and MVVM architecture in our architecture chapters. We started with MVC, the basic iOS architecture paradigm promoted in Apple's documentation. Then we provided examples of modifying the pattern to become more modular and testable (better fitting our architecture principles defined in Chapter 5). Next, we moved on to MVVM to better address some of the scalability concerns presented by MVC. To further scale our MVVM application, we added the coordinator pattern, which provided an architecture that abstracted our UI business logic, routing, and data layer, making our application more modular, testable, and better equipped to scale.

Endless other architecture patterns strive to make applications more modular and scalable and are less coupled to the MVC architecture. While it is impossible to discuss every derivative found on the Internet here, we can discuss VIPER, which encompasses the basic tenets of these patterns. VIPER serves as a vehicle to summarize the ideas of creating an architecture that separates all concerns from the start. Many companies have created custom derivatives of VIPER, such as RIBLETs and Ziggurat. To summarize the ideas of these patterns and trade-offs, we will utilize VIPER. There is no set architecture, and VIPER and its derivatives perfectly represent this. However, the overall concepts are similar.

© Eric Vennaro 2023
E. Vennaro, *iOS Development at Scale*, https://doi.org/10.1007/978-1-4842-9456-7_9

This Chapter Includes

This chapter includes an in-depth look at the VIPER design pattern, trade-offs, and considerations for use. In the "Practical Example" section, we will rewrite our Photo Stream example from MVC to VIPER to highlight the benefits of the VIPER pattern and potential usage over MVC and other architecture patterns.

A Detailed Look at VIPER

The core of the VIPER architecture is the single responsibility principle. While VIPER is often discussed with MVC and MVVM, VIPER is very different in how it approaches application architecture. By breaking down each application module into five components (the View, Interactor, Presenter, Entity, and Router), VIPER creates a self-contained module for each scene orchestrated by the router. Figure 9-1 outlines the VIPER components and their interactions.

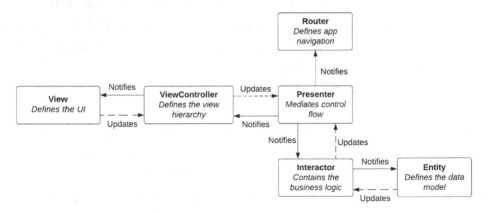

Figure 9-1. *General VIPER architecture*

There is still a significant similarity between VIPER and the MVVM architectural pattern we have discussed. They both strive to make applications more modular and testable, mainly by taking control away from UIViewController. Even when logic is separated from the view controller, we still need to be concerned with separating the navigational elements, which is why we added coordinators in MVVM. VIPER meets both of these concerns without adding coordinators or other patterns.

VIPER Components

The View

The view is unchanged from MVC and MVVM. The view presents the overall UI to the user and sends events from user interaction to the controller.

The View Controller

While sometimes lumped into the view aspect of VIPER, the view controller is separated here as it knows how to construct the view hierarchy and interact with the presenter. The view controller handles no business logic; it only lays out the view and acts as an event-forwarding layer the presenter uses.

The Interactor

The interactor contains business logic responsible for getting data from the data layer or directly making API calls. In our implementation, the interactor utilizes our existing repository and data layer pattern to get domain objects. The interactor should also be completely independent of the user interface.

The interactor can prepare or transform data from the service layer. For example, it can sort or filter before asking for the proper network service implementation to request or save the data. Because the interactor does not know the view, it has no idea how the data should be prepared for the view; that is the role of the presenter.

The Presenter

The presenter is the heart of the VIPER module and is the only layer in the module that communicates with all other layers. The presenter orchestrates all the decision-making for the module. As the central layer, it controls reactions to user-triggered events from the view, delegates navigation concerns to the router, and sends messages to the business layer. Since the presenter knows of the view, it is also responsible for preparing the data for presentation by the view.

The Entity

The entity is another name for the model, and it remains unchanged from MVVM and MVC. In VIPER, the entity is a plain class (Swift, for our example) and is used by the interactor. In our example, the model classes are defined outside the VIPER module structure because these entities are shared across the system.

The Router

The router is responsible for the navigation of the app. It has access to the navigation controllers and windows, using them to instantiate other controllers to push into them. The router communicates only with the presenter and is responsible for instantiating other VIPER modules, making it an excellent place to pass data between modules.

Component Interactions

Typically, for VIPER, the delegate pattern is utilized for communication between components inside of the module; however, since our practical example uses Combine for the Photo Stream module, we will utilize Combine reactive bindings instead of delegates.

Object Construction

Our VIPER sample project follows a similar practice to our other examples, where a high-level object will load and configure views. With VIPER, this object is not a controller but a router. The router understands pertinent information for module construction and is configured to use dependency injection for all our resources.

Updates to the Model: The Interactor

In VIPER, the model is updated via changes to the interactor. The interactor directly triggers model updates based on changes received from the presenter. The interactor weakly references the presenter to support notifying the presenter of updates.

The Presenter

The presenter acts as an event handler. UI events from the view controller are forwarded to the presenter for handling. Based on the results, the presenter can call the interactor for data model updates or the router for presenting or dismissing a module. It's the only class that communicates with almost all the other components. To handle the communication in a memory-safe way, the presenter holds a strong reference to the interactor, a weak reference to the view controller, and a strong reference to the router.

The View Controller

The view controller component interaction in VIPER is similar to that in MVVM. In VIPER, the controller receives updates from the presenter and triggers associated view hierarchy changes. Following the delegate pattern, our view controller strongly references the presenter.

Updates to the View

Updates to the view are triggered by the presenter and orchestrated via the view controller. When the user initiates a view change event, the view notifies the controller, informing the presenter. The presenter then knows how to handle the event and take appropriate action.

The View State

In VIPER, the presenter manages the view state. Our example utilizes Combine, so the state consists of *@Published* properties. Using Combine, the view controller subscribes to the publishers. Since this is an uncommon approach with VIPER, we have also included the *Settings* scene, which utilizes delegates, a more common approach for VIPER.

Practical Example

For the practical example, we will review our MVC example from the previous chapter and rewrite it to use VIPER. We will rewrite two of our modules to demonstrate the VIPER architecture pattern's use of protocols and a way to utilize Combine with VIPER. The settings module will use delegates, and the Photo Stream module will utilize Combine bindings.

The first step in transitioning our existing application to utilize VIPER is to outline our application flow. In Figure 9-2, we define our module hierarchy similar to MVVM with coordinators we have:

1. High-level application module that, based on application startup input, defines which submodules and navigation stack to load

2. Main application tab bar, which starts both our Photo Stream module and settings module

In addition to these components, we include the hypothetical onboarding flow and authentication flow, two necessary flows for most applications that we do not fully implement in this chapter.

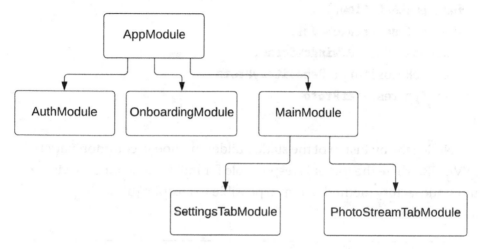

Figure 9-2. *VIPER modular architecture*

We can modify the existing code in the SceneDelegate.swift to implement our application-level module. To do so, we will create

1. AppPresenter to handle presentation logic

2. AppRouter to handle navigation logic for application startup

Since we do not have any network calls on application start, we do not need an AppInteractor here. However, if your application requires a network request on application startups, say to gather experiment settings or user login information, this could be an excellent place to do so.

First, let us define our application navigation logic outlined in Figure 9-1 as a protocol for our application router.

```swift
protocol AppRouterProto: AnyObject {
  func pushMainApp(_ view: UIViewController)
  func pushOnboardingFlow()
  func pushAuthFlow()
  static func createModule(
    windowScene: UIWindowScene,
    photoRepository: RepositoryProto
  ) -> AppPresenterProto
}
```

Notice the inclusion of the static builder method, a common pattern in VIPER, where the router is responsible for building the module via the static factory method. It is also possible to abstract this logic into a separate class.

Key Architectural Decision   Utilize a static builder method on the router to construct each VIPER module.

Concretely we can define our router to push the correct application module onto the navigation stack starting from the UIWindow.

```swift
final class AppRouter: AppRouterProto {
  private let window: UIWindow
  private var navigationController:
  UINavigationController?

  private init(window: UIWindow) {
    self.window = window
  }

  func pushMainApp(_ view: UIViewController) {
    let navigationController = UINavigationController(
      rootViewController: view)
```

```
  window.rootViewController = navigationController
  window.makeKeyAndVisible()
}

func pushOnboardingFlow() {
  // no - op
}

func pushAuthFlow() {
  // no - op
}

static func createModule(
  windowScene: UIWindowScene,
  photoRepository: RepositoryProto
) -> AppPresenterProto {
  let router = AppRouter(
    window: UIWindow(windowScene: windowScene))
  let presenter = AppPresenter(
    router: router,
    photoRepository: photoRepository)

  return presenter
  }
}
```

Next, let us define the presentation logic. To determine which launch path to take on application start, we will utilize the LaunchState enum we defined earlier.

```
protocol AppPresenterProto {
  func present(for launchState: LaunchState)
}
```

For the concrete implementation, we will utilize a switch statement to enumerate the launch options and call the correct method on the router to instantiate the flow.

```
final class AppPresenter: AppPresenterProto {
  private let router: AppRouterProto
  private let photoRepository: RepositoryProto

  init (
    router: AppRouterProto,
    photoRepository: RepositoryProto
  ) {
    self.router = router
    self.photoRepository = photoRepository
  }

  func present(for launchState: LaunchState) {
    switch launchState {
    case .auth:
      // no-op
      break
    case .main:
      let view = MainRouter.createModule(
        photoRepository: photoRepository)
      router.pushMainApp(view)
      break
    case .onboarding:
      // no-op
      break
    }
  }
}
```

Now we can connect our VIPER module to the SceneDelegate to control application loading. Here, we hard-code the launch option to load the main application flow.

```swift
var presenter: AppPresenterProto?

func scene(
  _ scene: UIScene,
  willConnectTo session: UISceneSession,
  options connectionOptions: UIScene.ConnectionOptions
) {
  guard let _ = (scene as? UIWindowScene)
  else { return }
  guard let windowScene = scene as? UIWindowScene
  else { return }

  let coreDataManager = CoreDataManager(
    persistentContainer: container,
    inMemory: false)
  let networkManager = NetworkManager(
    networking: URLSession.shared)
  let repository = PhotoRepository(
    localStorageManager: coreDataManager,
    networkManager: networkManager)
  presenter = AppRouter.createModule(
    windowScene: windowScene,
    photoRepository: repository)
  presenter?.present(for: .main)
}
```

With the application start implementation complete, we must create the subsequent VIPER modules to display the correct main application flow. Before wiring the main application flow, let us first create our Photo Stream VIPER module, as outlined in Figure 9-3. All subsequent VIPER modules will mirror the structure of the Photo Stream module.

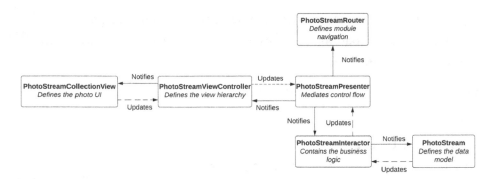

Figure 9-3. *Photo Stream VIPER module*

While other modules will mirror the structure of our Photo Stream module for demonstration purposes, we will utilize Combine for the Photo Stream module and the delegate pattern for additional modules to illustrate a more standard approach to VIPER. We are staying with Combine for the Photo Stream module because our networking logic still utilizes Combine publishers at the data layer.

Key Architectural Note   Pick a binding pattern and utilize it consistently. We should not have modules interacting utilizing different patterns. This leads to confusion. In a real application, we should pick and consistently use one pattern.

To start building our VIPER module, we will first create our interactor. The interactor will replace the networking logic in our model so we can copy over the code from the PhotoModel and create a new protocol for our interactor specifying our getAllPhotos and updateReactionCount methods.

```
import Combine

protocol PhotoStreamInteractorProto: AnyObject {
  func getAllPhotos(
  ) -> AnyPublisher<[ModelProto], Error>
```

```
func updateReactionCount(
    upCount: Int, downCount: Int)
}

final class PhotoStreamInteractor:
PhotoStreamInteractorProto {

    private let photoRepository: RepositoryProto

    init(photoRepository: RepositoryProto) {
        self.photoRepository = photoRepository
    }

    func getAllPhotos(
    ) -> AnyPublisher<[ModelProto], Error> {
        return photoRepository
            .getAll()
            .eraseToAnyPublisher()
    }

    func updateReactionCount(
        upCount: Int, downCount: Int) {
        // presenter should call this method to
        // handle the update, but we mock the logic
        //in the presenter for demonstration purposes
    }
}
```

With the interactor completed, we can move on to the presenter. Our presenter is the central hub of the VIPER module and will also have references to the router and view controller. To start, we can define a protocol encapsulating the function we want our presenter to conform to. For this, we will mirror the functionality from the MVVM application and specify a loading state and the allPhotos variable representing the Photo Stream. Lastly, we want the ability to trigger updates from the view controller.

```
protocol PhotoStreamPresenterProto: AnyObject {
  // Cannot use the @Published annotation in a protocol
  // so we expose the type
  var allPhotosPublished:
  Published<[PhotoModel.Photo]>.Publisher { get }
  var loadingStatePublished:
  Published<LoadingState>.Publisher { get }

  func getAllPhotos()
  func updateReactionCount(
    upCount: Int, downCount: Int)
}
```

Now we can define our concrete implementation for these methods in our presenter. We will use similar published properties as before, but instead of calling the model or the repository, we will call the interactor.

```
final class PhotoStreamPresenter:
PhotoStreamPresenterProto {
  var allPhotosPublished:
  Published<[PhotoModel.Photo]>.Publisher { $allPhotos }
  @Published private var allPhotos:
  [PhotoModel.Photo] = []

  var loadingStatePublished:
  Published<LoadingState>.Publisher { $loadingState }
  @Published private var loadingState:
  LoadingState = .none

  private var cancellables: Set<AnyCancellable> = []
  private let router: PhotoStreamRouterProto
  private let interactor: PhotoStreamInteractorProto
```

```
init(
  interactor: PhotoStreamInteractorProto,
  router: PhotoStreamRouterProto
) {
  self.interactor = interactor
  self.router = router
}

func getAllPhotos() {
  loadingState = .loading
  interactor.getAllPhotos()
    .receive(on: DispatchQueue.main)
    .sink { [weak self] result in
      switch result {
      case .finished:
        self?.loadingState = .finished
        break
      case .failure(let error):
        self?.loadingState = .finishedWithError(error)
        break
      }
    } receiveValue: { [weak self] photos in
      guard let sSelf = self else { return }
      sSelf.allPhotos = photos
        .compactMap{ $0 as? PhotoModel.Photo }
    }.store(in: &cancellables)
}

func updateReactionCount(
  upCount: Int,
  downCount: Int
) {
```

```
    // we would send an update to our network layer,
    //instead loop through and
    // update all reactions. This is purely for
    // illustration purposes
    for photo in allPhotos {
      photo.reactions.update(
        upCount: upCount, downCount: downCount)
    }
    allPhotos = allPhotos
  }
}
```

With the presenter and interactor defined, we can connect them to our router. The router's responsibility is to handle module navigation and creation. For this module, we have no navigation, so the router's only job is to construct the module.

```
protocol PhotoStreamRouterProto: AnyObject {
  static func createModule(
    photoRepository: RepositoryProto
  )-> PhotoStreamViewController
}

final class PhotoStreamRouter: PhotoStreamRouterProto {
  private weak var viewController: UIViewController?

  static func createModule(
    photoRepository: RepositoryProto
  ) -> PhotoStreamViewController {
    let router = PhotoStreamRouter()
    let interactor = PhotoStreamInteractor(
      photoRepository: photoRepository)
    let presenter = PhotoStreamPresenter(
      interactor: interactor,
```

```
    router: router)
  let view = PhotoStreamViewController(
    presenter: presenter)
  router.viewController = view

  return view
  }
}
```

Lastly, for our VIPER module, we need to modify our ViewController to reference the presenter instead of the PhotoModel. To do so, we change our constructor, viewDidLoad method, and reactionUpdate. We have also connected the loading state similar to the MVVM example code.

```
// .. skip other declarations
private let presenter: PhotoStreamPresenterProto

init(presenter: PhotoStreamPresenterProto) {
  self.presenter = presenter
  super.init(nibName: nil, bundle: .main)
}
override func viewDidLoad() {
  super.viewDidLoad()
  navigationController?.tabBarItem.title =
  "Photo Stream"
  presenter
    .allPhotosPublished
    .sink { [weak self] ret in
      self?.photos = ret
      self?.collectionView.reloadData()
    }
    .store(in: &cancellables)
  presenter
    .loadingStatePublished
```

```swift
  .sink { state in
    switch(state) {
    case .none:
      break
    case .loading:
      print("loading results...")
    case .finished:
      print("finished succesfully")
    case .finishedWithError(let error):
      print("Finished with error: \(error)")
    }
  }
  .store(in: &cancellables)
  presenter.getAllPhotos()
}

@objc func updateReactionCount(_ sender: UIButton) {
  guard let btn = sender as? ReactionsButton,
        let reactionType = btn.reactionType else {
          return
  }
  let upCount = reactionType == .thumbsUp ? 1 : 0
  let downCount = reactionType == .thumbsDown ? 1 : 0

  presenter.updateReactionCount(
    upCount: upCount, downCount: downCount)
}
```

With the Photo Stream module created, we need to wire it into the
main application flow for display. We must also construct the main tab bar
module, which makes the main application layout. Since the main layout
is just a tab bar controller, this module only requires the router component
over the VIPER acronym.

```
protocol MainRouterProto {
  static func createModule(
    photoRepository: RepositoryProto
  ) -> UIViewController
}

final class MainRouter: MainRouterProto {

  static func createModule(
    photoRepository: RepositoryProto
  ) -> UIViewController {
    let tabBar = MainTabBarController()
    let photoStreamNavController =
    UINavigationController(
      rootViewController:
        PhotoStreamRouter.createModule(
          photoRepository: photoRepository
        )
    )

    tabBar.viewControllers = [photoStreamNavController]

    return tabBar
  }
}
```

With the Photo Stream module complete, we can move on to our final module, the settings module. For the settings module, we will again start by defining our interactor. Here, the interactor is simple, and we will utilize it to simulate a network request getting the list of items we want to display in the settings view.

```
protocol SettingsInteractorProto: AnyObject {
  func getSettingsListItems()
}
```

Since, for this module, we will use delegates instead of Combine bindings before we implement our concrete interactor, we also need to define our presenter-interactor relationship via a protocol. Here, we define two methods. One is the happy path, where we notify the presenter that the interactor fetched the settings list. The other is the error case telling the presenter that the interactor failed to get the settings values correctly.

```
protocol SettingsInteractorToPresenterProto: AnyObject {
  func didFetchSettings(with settings:[String])
  func fetchFailed(with errorMessage:String)
}
```

Using these protocols, we construct the concrete implementations of our interactor.

```
final class SettingsInteractor: SettingsInteractorProto
{
  weak var presenter:
  SettingsInteractorToPresenterProto?

  func getSettingsListItems() {
    // mock network request
    presenter?.didFetchSettings(
      with: ["Account", "Privacy", "Logout"]
    )
  }
}
```

Since the presenter will use the interactor, router, and view controller before writing the concrete implementation, we should define the relationship via a series of protocols (in addition to the already-defined SettingsInteractorToPresenterProto).

1. SettingsPresenterToViewProto: Specifies the events the presenter triggers that the view controller processes

2. SettingsViewToPresenterProto: Specifies the events that the view triggers that the presenter is responsible for handling

Here, the SettingsPresenterToViewProto triggers when to set up the UI and when to display a data loading state and forwards the data returned from the interactor to the view controller.

```
protocol SettingsPresenterToViewProto: AnyObject {
  func setupUI()
  func showLoading()
  func settingsDidLoad(with settings: [String])
}
```

And the SettingsViewToPresenterProto is set up to handle view events. Specifically when the view did load and when a row was selected:

```
protocol SettingsViewToPresenterProto: AnyObject {
  func viewDidLoad()
  func didSelectRow(
    _ view: UIViewController,
    with item: String)
}
```

With the necessary protocols defined, we can implement the concrete presenter.

```
final class SettingsPresenter {
  weak var view: SettingsPresenterToViewProto?
  var interactor: SettingsInteractorProto?
  var router: SettingsRouterProto?
}
```

```swift
extension SettingsPresenter: SettingsViewToPresenterProto {
  func viewDidLoad() {
    view?.setupUI()
    view?.showLoading()
    interactor?.getSettingsListItems()
  }

  func didSelectRow(
    _ view: UIViewController,
    with item: String
  ) {
    router?.pushDetail()
  }
}

extension SettingsPresenter:
SettingsInteractorToPresenterProto {
  func didFetchSettings(with settings: [String]) {
    view?.settingsDidLoad(with: settings)
  }

  func fetchFailed(with errorMessage: String) {
    print("error message")
  }
}
```

Lastly, we need to modify our view controller to consume events from the presenter and send view events to the presenter.

```swift
final class SettingsViewController: UIViewController {

  var presenter: SettingsViewToPresenterProto?

  override func viewDidLoad() {
    super.viewDidLoad()
```

```
    presenter?.viewDidLoad()
  }
}

extension SettingsViewController:
SettingsPresenterToViewProto {
  func showLoading() {
    print("is loading")
  }

  func setupUI() {
    title = "Settings"
  }

  func settingsDidLoad(with settings: [String]) {
    items = settings
    tableView.reloadData()
  }
}
```

With these changes, our VIPER settings module is complete, and we can connect it to our main tab bar for display.

```
// MainRouter.swift
let settingsVC = SettingsRouter.createModule()

tabBar.viewControllers = [photoStreamNavController, settingsVC]
```

Discussion

We have officially finished our VIPER sample application, marking the end of our deep dive into iOS application design patterns. Recall we started with MVC, the pattern most people associate with iOS application architecture. With MVC, the controller modifies the view, accepts user input, and interacts directly with the model. Commonly as the application scales, the controller bloats with view logic and business logic.

To counteract the massive view controller, we introduced MVVM, a popular architecture that separates the view from the business logic in a view-model. The view-model interacts with the model and the view controller, making the change from MVC to MVVM simple. Unlike a view controller, the big difference is that a view-model only has a one-way reference to the view and the model. We additionally added coordinators to our MVVM pattern, further separating our concerns and removing the coordination and routing responsibility from the view controller, providing a modular application.

On the other hand, VIPER takes a different approach to build a modular application by starting with a series of separate components for each concern. Instead of iteratively adding to our existing application to separate our concerns, VIPER proactively begins with a modular approach. Because VIPER takes such a different approach, a larger refactor is required to switch from MVC or MVVM to VIPER seen in our sample application. In contrast, a much smaller refactor is needed when transitioning from MVC to MVVM. However, much of this depends on the application's initial state. A large refactor is required regardless if the initial application is not well architected. However, MVC to MVVM to MVVM plus coordinators represents an iterative process where we can continue to iterate on our architecture as we scale, somewhat in contrast to VIPER, which skips these iterations. So what if we started with VIPER?

Starting with VIPER means that if we have a small application, we must incorporate a lot of boilerplate code to wire our modules. So why would we start with VIPER? We may be already rewriting our application or building an iOS application based on an already-successful web application, so we know we need a lot of developers to scale quickly to meet the existing functionality of the web application.

Trade-Offs

VIPER is a more mature architecture path requiring many components working in concert, which can cause additional overhead and come with a steeper learning curve requiring engineers to think critically before choosing. While some of the drawbacks in verbosity can be handled by code generation tools for modules, the fact remains that VIPER, and similar architectures, requires more code changes to build simple components, meaning that utilizing VIPER while trying to scale quickly and deliver business value in a fast-paced environment may put you at odds with your architecture.

While VIPER does require additional overhead, neither MVVM nor MVC provides the level of modularity that VIPER does by default. By utilizing MVVM plus the coordinator pattern, we can produce a modular application we could model similar to Figure 9-2. We can either iteratively scale our application based on the need for a modular, scalable point or jump into deep waters with VIPER. Of course, as illustrated in the practical example, we do not need to utilize all VIPER components for all modules (the main tab bar only has a router component). While there is no perfect answer here, the choice will come down to determining the best architecture based on its current needs, which are primarily related to the application's size and trajectory in terms of users, engineers working on it, and the new features required.

Lastly, VIPER does not, by default, include a view-centric data model. However, it can be easily adapted to provide this instead of directly using the network-backed models. By doing so, VIPER can also account for one of the main advantages of the MVVM pattern.

Advantages

1. Scalability: For large teams on complex projects, VIPER provides a straightforward way to separate work within modules and the modules themselves, something that for MVC or MVVM-based architectures requires different patterns, such as coordinators, to achieve.

2. Source control: Due to the separation of concerns by default and modular design, VIPER allows large teams to work simultaneously on projects while avoiding merge conflicts.

3. Consistency: The ability to create module skeletons means that once developers adapt to VIPER, they understand exactly what components are required, and the scaffolding of the component can even be automated.

4. Clarity: Each component follows the single responsibility principle.

5. Testability: Separate small classes and use protocols by default to create a highly testable environment.

Drawbacks

1. Verbosity: With many files per module and modules, VIPER can cause a lot of extra code not required for certain applications.

2. Complexity: The number of required protocols and delegates can make the code base hard to understand for new team members and those unfamiliar with VIPER.

Modularity

VIPER enforces modularity at a granular level by following the single responsibility principle. At an architecture level, VIPER enforces modularity by packaging each series of components into a self-contained module. Because VIPER enforces modularity well, it can scale exceedingly well by allowing large teams to work on the application seamlessly. Additionally, we can use the self-contained modules and advanced build systems such as Buck or Swift Package Manager only to build a subset of a much larger application consisting of only the strictly necessary modules, decreasing long build times and increasing developer productivity.

Testability

VIPER's modular approach and rigid enforcement of the single responsibility principle make it ideal for testing. We can quickly test the VIPER modules' individual components with unit tests and orchestrate several modules for integration testing.

Summary

VIPER excels in stable large applications where development focuses on adding features on top of existing ones. However, VIPER requires substantially more code and component interactions, which can create a lot of boilerplate and mostly unnecessary files for smaller applications.

VIPER represents a series of architectures that diverge from the typical MVC framework to create a more modular application and has been adapted into multiple different architectures that are often necessary for companies at scale. While not necessarily the best architecture to start with, VIPER represents an actual modular separation of concerns and is applied multiple times in slightly different flavors by large tech companies such as Uber. By understanding the fundamental components and trade-offs, you can better advise your team or company if moving to this type of architecture will solve the pain points you are facing.

Three Key Takeaways from This Chapter

1. VIPER represents a genuinely modular architecture but requires additional boilerplate and setup, which makes it less ideal for applications changing quickly or with small teams.

2. The principles of clean architecture and the single responsibility principle underlie VIPER, which is also seen in many similar architectures used by big tech companies, making it a pivotal architecture to understand.

3. Ultimately the choice of what architecture to use comes down to the individual application's requirements, and VIPER and its derivatives present a mature, well-designed architecture pattern for creating a modular, testable application that scales well.

Further Learning

1. Clean Architecture: A Craftsman's Guide to Software Structure and Design (Robert C. Martin Series)

2. Soundcloud Clean Architecture with VIPER

   a. `https://developers.soundcloud.com/blog/how-we-develop-new-features-using-offsites-and-clean-architecture`

CHAPTER 10

The Reactive Programming Paradigm

Overview

In Chapter 9, we completed our tour of the data presentation layer (UI) architecture design patterns for iOS. In addition to data presentation design patterns, we covered broader iOS architecture design, including how to abstract our networking and local database code to a separate module and common design patterns to abstract code within modules. This chapter will cover a common approach for data flow across the entire application. In each architecture chapter (MVC, MVVM, and VIPER), we covered data flow at a high level and how to utilize it to manage the application's state more efficiently. One pattern we used to format and display our data was reactive programming. This chapter will cover the reactive data flow in more detail and explain how and why we have applied functional reactive programming in our applications using Combine.

© Eric Vennaro 2023   327
E. Vennaro, *iOS Development at Scale*, https://doi.org/10.1007/978-1-4842-9456-7_10

This Chapter Includes

This chapter is broken down into several sections where we will

1. Explain fundamentally what reactive programming is by breaking down the reactive programming runtime and approach to handling state change

2. Explain the benefits of reactive programming for UI-based applications such as iOS

3. Review functional reactive programming concepts and how we can apply functional programming concepts to reason about our data flow in iOS

4. Apply functional concepts to Combine

5. Apply reactive programming to architecting an iOS data flow

6. Summarize the trade-offs and benefits of a reactive data flow in a large-scale application

Reactive Programming

Reactive programming is a declarative programming paradigm utilizing data streams and change propagation throughout an application. Reactive programming allows for the expression of static (such as arrays) or dynamic (such as event emitters) data streams easily and facilitates the automatic propagation of the changed data flow.

Reactive programming is a popular data flow model used heavily for systems with complex UIs, such as mobile applications, games, and VR applications, because

1. It promotes faster UI updates by avoiding costly
    layout changes.

2. It provides a structured approach for data
    flow throughout the application, promoting
    parallelization.

A graph identifying the dependencies among the involved values
(nodes on the graph) represents the runtime model used by reactive
programming language runtimes. In the graph, nodes represent the act of
computing, and edges model dependency relationships. Such a runtime
employs the graph to help it keep track of the various previously executed
computations, which must be executed again once an involved input
changes value. In more traditional computer science terminology, we
can represent these states graphically, such as in Figure 10-1, as a marble
diagram or a directed acyclic graph (DAG).

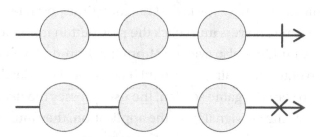

Figure 10-1. *Marble diagram*

A DAG is a directed graph that consists of vertices and edges, with
each edge directed from one vertex to another, such that following those
directions will never form a closed loop (a direct cycle). A directed graph
is a DAG if and only if it can be topologically ordered by arranging the
vertices as a linear ordering consistent with all edge directions.[1]

---

[1] Hulasiraman, K.; Swamy, M. N. S. (1992), "5.7 Acyclic Directed Graphs," *Graphs: Theory and Algorithms*, John Wiley and Sons, p. 118, ISBN 978-0-471-51356-8.

Typically software architecture state diagrams for data flows are relatively more straightforward than theoretical DAGs and are more akin to the marble diagram in Figure 10-1, where each diagram is shown as an arrow. In our diagram, each arrow represents a publisher (think Combine publisher). The circles, or marbles, on each line represent the values that the publisher emits. The top arrow has a line at the end representing a completion event. The publisher will not publish any new values after this line. The bottom diagram ends with a cross representing an error event. Errors end the stream of values, similar to a completion event.

To better understand reactive programming, we will take a step back and illustrate an example using a simple iOS game geared toward testing reaction time.

The Rules of the Game

Goal: Our game aims to have the fastest reaction time possible.

To play the game, players must click the play button from the home screen (the play button is also available from the drop-down menu). After clicking play to enter the main game, our UI consists of the Ready and Stop buttons. To start the game session, the user presses the Ready button. Once they receive the Go signal from the application, they must press the Stop button as quickly as possible. The game times the response and displays the result. After clicking the play button, users get several trials, and their reaction time across these trials is calculated for their final score, which is represented by the average response time.

Like every good game, there are ways to cheat the system, and our machine attempts to account for several of these.

1. If the user presses the ready button twice the system will alert the user via a warning dialogue but will not stop the game.

2. If the user presses the Stop button before the Go dialogue is displayed on the screen, the game is terminated for cheating. The user must press play again to try again.

To model these rules in the context of our game, we need our system to react to events for each button and a restart if users press the play button from the drop-down menu. Additionally, we need to track time. To do this, we need the ability to track the system clock time inside predetermined intervals. For reactive programming, we will need to map these input signals and game rules into states; with this in mind, we can create five-game states:

1. Idle when no game is in progress.

2. Start when awaiting a Ready event to start a trial.

3. Wait when the player waits for a Go signal from the machine.

4. React when the machine is waiting for a Stop event.

5. End, when the trial has ended, and the machine displays the response time to the user.

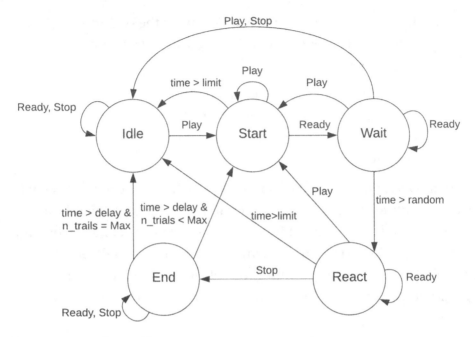

Figure 10-2. *State diagram*

Figure 10-2 encompasses how we think about reactive programming state. We outline all possible state transformations and create a system to respond and transition states via events. To take this theoretical implementation of our diagram, we need a runtime capable of handling these events (data propagation) and managing mutable state.

Data Propagation Techniques

Reactive programming runtimes typically support push or pull models to propagate data and react to state changes.

1. Pull: This technique is commonly called polling and involves the subscriber proactively querying the observed source for values and reacting whenever a relevant value is detected.

2. Push: The subscriber receives a value from the source whenever the value becomes available. These values are self-contained (containing all the necessary information) and must be queried by the consumer.

While both push and pull models work with the pull approach, achieving total data coherence with a high publish rate is difficult. Often data misses will occur if the pull interval exceeds the publish interval. If the pull interval is lower, performance will suffer. Pull performs well only if the pull interval equals the publish interval, which requires knowing the exact publish interval beforehand. However, knowing the publish interval ahead of time is problematic because it is rarely static and predictable. For example, in our reflex game, we do not know when the user will tap the screen in response. By implementing a pull-based model, we may not accurately record when the user pressed the button, thus capturing inaccurate reaction time data. A push method is employed for most modern implementations.

To implement data propagation, the reactive programming framework must maintain a dependency graph enumerating the allowable state transformations. To model this behavior at the runtime level, we can keep a graph of dependencies and control there execution within an event loop. By registering explicit callbacks, the runtime creates implicit dependencies, enforcing inversion of control. One drawback of this approach is that making the callbacks functional (i.e., returning state value instead of unit value) requires that the callbacks are compositional. Figure 10-3 represents an event loop system where the UI-level application sends tasks and the associated callback for processing. A typical example is pushing network tasks to a background thread via the event loop to avoid blocking main thread execution.

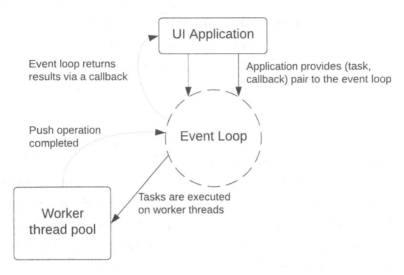

Figure 10-3. *Example event loop*

Not only does the reactive programming runtime need to know how to propagate events, but it also needs to know what data to propagate on event change. When data is changed upstream, downstream nodes affected by such changes are outdated, flagged for reexecution, and then propagated to the subscribers. To achieve this, the entire state can be computed each time to handle information propagation on state change, and the previous output is ignored. Figure 10-4 outlines how a change in the object-oriented (Swift) environment can trigger recomputation and propagation in a reactive runtime. The Swift runtime environment (bottom left) submits changes to reactive runtime via the propagation algorithm (bottom right), which instructs dependent nodes (circles) in the dependency graph (top right) to recompute by reevaluating their defining user computations (top left).[2]

---

[2] Drechsler, J. (2018). Distributing Thread-Safety for Reactive Programming In-Progress Paper.

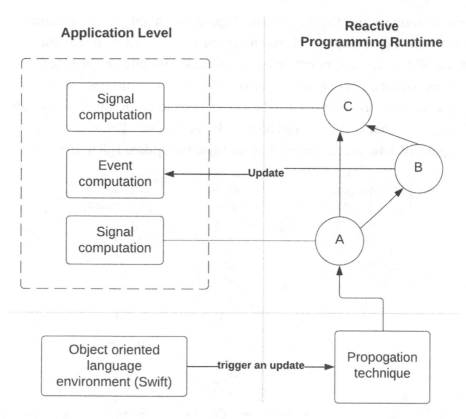

Figure 10-4. *Reactive runtime update and event propagation*

In Figure 10-4, we have implemented a naive propagation technique where the entire reactive state graph is updated on change. However, if the computational burden of recomputing the state is high, the program can implement incremental computing in the form of deltas. Each delta is a unit of information requiring an update. Delta propagation is the process of enforcing that the specified change set represented by a delta is pushed to the proper subscribers. A program using incremental computation can perform an incremental update to accommodate changes in input data without recomputing the entire state.[3] Figure 10-5 highlights an example of a theoretical network, local, and image processors. These processors would all start at the application level and trigger updates in the reactive runtime. Given an update in the network pipeline, we may not need to update both the image and local data processors to accommodate the state change; thus, nodes A2, A3, and A5 remain unchanged. This is in contrast to Figure 10-4, where in our reactive runtime, we updated all nodes.

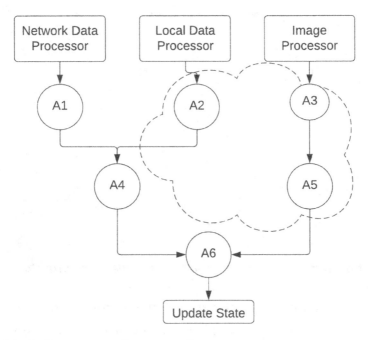

Figure 10-5. *Incremental state update*

This approach is essential when the state data is expensive to recompute due to the nodes holding large amounts of state data. It is a crucial tenet of responsive UIs as it avoids the costly recomputation of the entire UI. Regarding UI changes, an easy parallel is with a complex

---

[3] Magnus Carlsson. 2002. Monads for incremental computing. SIGPLAN Not. 37, 9 (September 2002), 26–35. https://doi.org/10.1145/583852.581482

collection view or table view layout. In this situation, it may be too costly to lay out the entire view for a small state change, and instead, we will want to ensure only an update to the affected area of the UI is updated.

Implementing incremental state updates requires that the runtime understands the structure of the dependency graph. Specifically, the runtime needs the ability to answer the following questions:

1. What nodes require updates if an input changes?

2. In what order should the nodes be updated?

Answering these questions by looking at the graph is easy enough. However, writing a program to perform the logic is more complex. One known solution to this problem is topological sorting.

Topological Sorting

With topological sorting, the program gives each node a height and uses this height and a minimum heap to answer our questions. It works as follows:

1. The program gives a node with no inputs a height of 0.

2. If a node has inputs, its height is max(height of inputs) + 1, which guarantees that a node will always have a greater height than its inputs' heights.

3. When a node's value or formula changes, the program adds the node to the minimum heap.

4. To bring the graph up to date, the program removes the node with the smallest height from the heap and recomputes it. If the node's value has changed after recomputing, it adds its dependents to the heap.

5. The program continues with the previous step until the heap is empty.

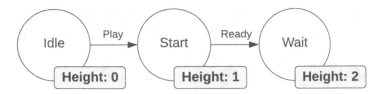

Figure 10-6. *Topological sort applied to a portion of the reaction game state diagram*

Figure 10-6 denotes a potential application of topological sort to a portion of our reaction time state diagram. Here, we have the Idle state at depth zero, and as we proceed to start and wait, we go to different levels of the graph, which will require recomputation if we go to a previous state. For simplicity of understanding, we only include the three states here.

Topological sorting answers the questions posed earlier in the following way:

1. What nodes should the program update if an input changes?

   a. Only those it has added to the heap

2. In what order should the program update them?

   a. It should recompute nodes with a smaller height before those with a large height, ensuring that it recomputes a node's inputs before the node itself.

Interaction with Mutable State

During iOS application development, we must deal with mutable state from network calls and potential peripherals through various iOS developer kits. This creates a slight incongruency with the runtime we have discussed since reactive languages typically assume that their expressions are purely functional, where a pure function is defined as a function where

1. The return values are identical for identical arguments.

2. The function has no side effects.[4]

Note   A side effect refers to the modification of the nonlocal environment.[5] Commonly, this occurs when a function (or procedure) modifies a global variable passed by reference; however, there are other ways to modify the nonlocal environment, including performing I/O.

To better understand pure functions, let us look at an example: a pure function that performs addition. Our add function always returns the same value for identical arguments and has no side effects.

```
func add(a: Int, b: Int) -> Int {
  return a+b
}
```

However, if we add an I/O interaction such as print, we have now introduced a side effect and no longer have a pure function.

```
func add(a: Int, b: Int) -> Int {
  print("adding")
  return a+b
}
```

---

[4] Brian Lonsdorf (2015). Professor Frisby's Mostly Adequate Guide to Functional Programming.

[5] Spuler, D.A., & Sajeev, A.S. (1994). Compiler Detection of Function Call Side Effects. *Informatica (Slovenia), 18.*

By enforcing pure functions, the update mechanism can perform updates while leaving the specific order unspecified (enabling optimizations). However, as mentioned in iOS development, we do not have a purely functional environment. In this situation, a reactive framework is embedded in a programming language with state, which requires a partial solution to enforce pure functions for the reactive runtime.

To accomplish this, a language might offer a notion of a mutable property. A mutable property is a way to encapsulate mutable state in a way that the reactive update system is aware of. By making the reactive system aware of the mutable properties and when changes to it occur, it enables the nonreactive part of the program to perform a data mutation while enabling the reactive library to be aware of and respond to this update.[6]

Another option is to encapsulate the notion of state. For instance, callbacks can be installed on the appropriate properties in the object-oriented library to notify the reactive update engine about state changes. Changes in the reactive component are then pushed to the object-oriented library via these callbacks.

Functional Reactive Programming

Functional reactive programming (FRP) is a programming paradigm that applies the building blocks of functional programming (e.g., map, reduce, filter) to reactive programming. FRP has been used extensively for programming graphical user interfaces. This is because utilizing stream processing and reactive programming tenets to display data provides a composable, declarative way to define UI interactions.

---

[6] Cooper, G. H., & Krishnamurthi, S. (2006). Embedding dynamic dataflow in a call-by-value language. Retrieved March 6, 2023, from https://cs.brown.edu/~sk/Publications/Papers/Published/ck-frtime/

FRP can be broken down into two primary abstractions:

1. Behaviors: Change continuously

2. Events: Happen at points in time

These two abstractions have simple semantics. A behavior is a function from time to value. Events are pairs of time and value. Because FRP is a functional paradigm, events and behaviors describe things that exist rather than actions that have happened or are to happen (i.e., what is, not what does). Semantically, a (reactive) behavior is just a function of time. At the same time, an event (sometimes called an "event source") is a list of time/ value pairs ("occurrences").[7]

Almost anything can be a behavior, including user input. Behaviors are captured asynchronously by defining a side-effecting operation that will execute when the behavior is sampled. The "listening" to the behavior is commonly called subscribing. Figure 10-7 represents a graphical view of a behavior where the x axis is time. Notice that behavior is defined at every point in time because it is a function.

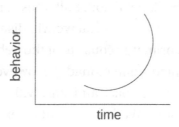

Figure 10-7. *Graphical representation of a behavior*

Compare our graph of a behavior to Figure 10-8, where we graphically represent an event. Notice how the graph of an event is discrete. Take a tap event, for example; each individual tap occurs instantly. But other than those exact moments on which the tap happens, there's no tap occurrence.

---

[7] Conal Elliott (2009). Push-pull functional reactive programming. In *Haskell Symposium*.

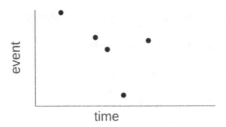

Figure 10-8. Graphical representation of an event

The concepts of behaviors and events mesh well with UI-heavy applications that rely on user input to transition between states.

Diving deeper into behaviors, the modern FRP interface has standardized around several classes representing different behaviors as

1. Monoids

2. Functors

3. Monads

More FRP classes are presented in the paper "Push-pull functional reactive programming" by Conal Elliott. Still, these are the most commonly applied to reactive frameworks and what we will discuss here since the Combine framework primarily consists of the behavior and event paradigm (along with functors and monads). However, to fully understand the system, it is essential to step back and start with category theory before moving into specific portions. While this is not an exhaustive definition (as this would require its own book), this section will provide a high-level reference for category theory and functional concepts that map to Combine behaviors in the following section.

Category Theory

Category theory is a branch of mathematics covering many key concepts in functional programming. A category is an algebraic structure that models objects and their relationships with each other. The connections between different categories are called morphisms (represented by arrows). Every arrow f can be defined as a pair of objects it connects [a,b]. We can define f: a → b for each object pair connected by a morphism.

A category can also be represented algebraically as an operation with arrows. For every f: a → b and g: b → c, their composition g ∘ f is also an arrow, which connects a and c (g ∘ f: a → c).

Figure 10-9 outlines a mathematical category with objects a, b, and c, as well as morphisms f, g, and f ∘ g. Additionally, Figure 10-9 maps this to a more concrete category representing typecasting a value between double, string, and integer.

Categories must also follow three rules, which will appear in several other aspects of functional programming:

1. Composition: The composition rule states that for every object a, b, and c and morphism f and g, the category must have a morphism from a to c (as shown in Figure 10-9). You represent this as g∘f between a and c.

2. Associativity: This means that if you do the composition of f, g, and h, it does not matter if you first compose f to g or g to h.

3. Identity: This means that for every f: a → b, the following is true: $i_b ∘ f = f = f ∘ i_a$. In other words, identities are neutral to composition, which is represented graphically by an identity arrow connecting to itself: a → a (the loop).

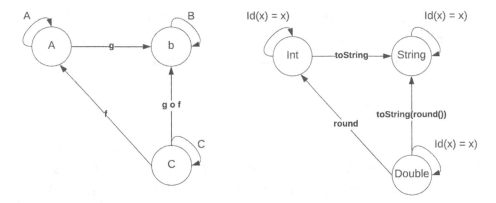

Figure 10-9. *Mathematical and concrete categories*

Functors

Following basic category theory, we can discuss functors. A functor f is a transformation between two categories, a and b. A functor can be expressed as f: a → b. F must map every object and arrow from a to b. In layman's terms, a functor is anything that can be mapped over (most commonly a list).

An example of a functor in code is the map function which in Swift applies to any generic data structure, and for collections such as a list, we can efficiently utilize the built-in map function.

```swift
let cast = ["Steve", "Alex", "Kim", "Chloe"]
let lowercaseNames = cast.map { $0.lowercased() }
// 'lowercaseNames' == ["steve", "alex", "kim", "chloe"]
let letterCounts = cast.map { $0.count }
// 'letterCounts' == [5, 4, 3, 5]
```

Monoid

In computer science, a monoid is a set, a binary operation, and an element of the set with the following rules:

1. Associativity of binary operations.

2. It is possible to define an identity element for the elements.

3. We must be able to combine values using the monoid.

The property of associative requires that the equation a op (b op c) = (a op b) op c always be true given the operation op and the elements a, b, and c.

An identity element is an element where the other elements in the set are unchanged if an operation is applied to it.

An example of a monoid in action is adding a set of numbers. In this situation:

1. The set consists of integer numbers.

2. The binary operation is addition.

3. The identity element is zero.

Addition is associative because a + (b + c) = (a + b) + c.

Monoids are important because, given a sequence of elements and a function (in our example, addition) of a type (integer), we can combine them with the function in any order (due to the associativity of the function). Therefore, we can apply higher-order functions to any monoid.

A common example of monoids in computer science is the map-reduce programming model. Given a data set, map-reduce consists of two operations:

1. Map: Mapping arbitrary data to elements of a specific monoid

2. Reduce: Folding those elements so that the final result is just one element

Monads

In terms of category theory, a monad is a monoid in the category of endofunctors,[8] where an endofunctor is a functor that maps a category back to that same category. This is a complex way of saying that a monad is essentially a wrapper around a value, such as a promise or a result type. In Swift, we have a built-in monadic type with optionals. However, it is also common for engineers to create their own type, such as a wrapped result type.

```
enum Result<WrappedType> {
    case something(WrappedType)
    case nothing // potentially an error
}
```

There is one caveat with this definition of a monad; it is not enough to simply wrap the type. We also need to know how to interact with the structure and compose functions that output values of the type of the monad. With these elements, we can compose a sequence of function calls (a "pipeline") with several operators chained together in an expression. Each function call transforms its input value and has a specific operator to handle the returned monadic value, which is fed into the next step in the sequence. One example of this is the compact map function in Swift. Compact map understands how to deal with the Swift optional type (a

---

[8] MacLane, S. (1971). Categories for the Working Mathematician. New York: Springer-Verlag.

monad), unlike the basic map function. In the following code sample, we see the output produces null values with the map function, but these are correctly filtered out when utilizing the compact map function.

```
let possibleNumbers = ["1", "2", "three", "//4//", "5"]

let mapped: [Int?] = possibleNumbers.map { str in Int(str) }
// [1, 2, nil, nil, 5]
let compactMapped: [Int] = possibleNumbers.compactMap { str in
Int(str) }
// [1, 2, 5]
```

With the overall structure of reactive and functional reactive programming defined, we can start to understand how Combine leverages FRP and how we can apply this to our iOS application data processing.

FRP and Combine

FRP is the model Combine implements to publish and subscribe to events. Additionally, Combine exposes different functional behaviors we can utilize to modify data in our pipeline. This section reviews how the Combine framework concepts map to FRP. It is not an exhaustive resource for all Combine-specific operations. For that, Apple documentation is the best source.

Publishers and Subscribers

In Combine, Publishers and Subscribers represent the events. The Combine Publisher protocol defines the requirements for a type's ability to transmit a sequence of values over time to one or more subscribers. Similarly, a Subscriber defines the requirements for a type to receive input from a publisher.

In Figure 10-10, we have modified our marble diagram from Figure 10-1 to reflect the publisher and subscriber model with Combine. Each marble here represents an event. Here, we have outlined the following:

1. The subscriber subscribes to the publisher.

2. The subscriber requests values.

3. The publisher sends values.

4. The subscriber performs a map operation on values.

5. The publisher sends a completion.

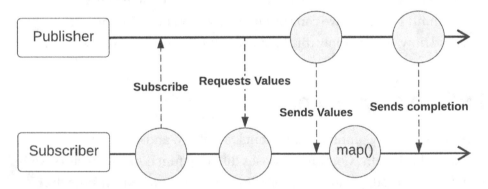

Figure 10-10. *Publisher and subscriber data flow diagram*

Combine Behaviors

The Combine framework provides many behaviors. The most commonly thought of when thinking in terms of FRP concepts we defined earlier are functors and monads.

Functor

Mapping and filtering are both examples of functors and are concepts we have used in previous architecture chapters as part of our Combine pipelines to structure data. Another example in the Combine framework utilized in our MVVM example is the remove duplicates function. Figure 10-11 outlines the remove duplicates function as a marble diagram.

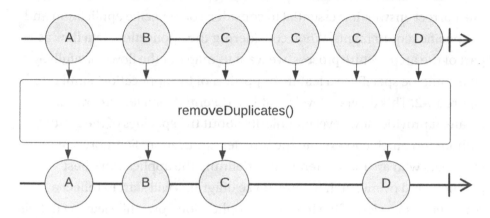

Figure 10-11. *Publisher and subscriber data flow diagram applied to removeDuplicates method*

Monad

In addition to utilizing functors, Combine uses monads via the Any publisher type system, as seen in our previous architecture examples where we define our publisher.

`AnyPublisher<[ModelProto], Error>`

Because Combine follows FRP, it is essential to understand these concepts. With this, the Combine framework provides a way to utilize FRP inside the Swift programming language. However, developing or using a different framework to offer similar results is possible. While the framework can change, the underlying tenets will not. As a result, when looking to architect an application utilizing the reactive programming

349

paradigm, the exact internals of the framework are less critical than the overall concepts. In the next section, we will review application architecture utilizing the tenets of reactive programming.

Application Architecture

Application architecture is an ever-evolving process, and there is never one correct answer. It is essential to consider your specific application and its specific requirements. When considering the application data flow as part of the architecture process, we want to map out the flows carefully. One could be specific to a feature or portion of the application, similar to Figure 10-2. This diagram level would be essential for a feature owner to create. It provides low-level granularity about the specifics of the feature without too much context into the broader application. For more senior engineers who are more interested in defining the application's best practices and overall architecture, these diagrams will start to reflect a comprehensive view of the high-level application flow while leaving details for other feature owners.

As an example, we will go through our Photo Stream application to provide a potential overall architecture diagram, including the reactive programming paradigm. We will start as if we are a lead architect architecting the design of the complete system and then break it down into what senior engineers may focus on specifically.

Application Overview

As the lead application architect, it is your goal to understand the entire application data flow end to end and be able to provide guidance on best practices as well as design a similar scope application. We need to understand the data flow at a high level to do this for our Photo Stream application.

Additionally, we will need to think through some of the more complex interactions of the system. First, let us define some system goals to ensure we are on the same page.

1. Reactions: We need the ability to react to photos in the Photo Stream.

2. Comments: We need the ability to comment on photos.

3. Get new photos: We need the ability to publish photos to the Web and get updates with new photos for the Photo Stream.

To support this performantly, we should implement incremental computing to provide faster updates. This is helpful when considering what the user will want to see. Do we want them to wait for a full update from the server before certain features such as the reaction count update? Or do we want to perform this update optimistically? We should prevent the delay and allow users to see their local updates immediately. Taking this a step further, we could define a local task handler so that if multiple updates are scheduled, we can take into the relative priority of events for execution. Figure 10-12 outlines a hypothetical state diagram to describe the abovementioned interactions.

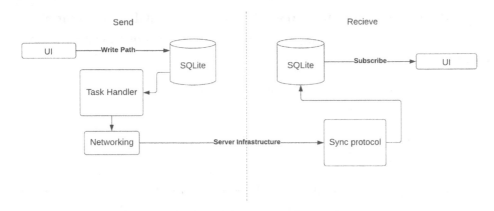

Figure 10-12. *Sample application architecture with the data flow*

Given a real application instead of our Photo Stream example, this diagram would take considerable effort to arrive at. We need to deeply understand the requirements for our application now and in the foreseeable future. Additionally, we may be taking an existing application and re-architecting it to scale, so it may be necessary to understand previous architecture decisions and how we can best fit it into the existing structure. Chapter 11 will cover in more detail the best practices for arriving at these decisions.

Given that we have decided to use a reactive model and serve optimistic updates, we still need to map out the different states and data models so that other engineers and teams understand how their features and areas interact with the overall system. We can define three distinct data models that require consideration:

1. Server data model: The data from the server that does not have optimistic state updates applied.

2. Optimistic state: Data generated on the client side represents the mutations that are not completed.

3. Combined data model: To render the most up-
   to-date and correct state, we must combine the
   optimistic state with the server data model to
   produce one unified experience. The combination
   of server and optimistic state can happen in our
   subscription pipeline so that the data presentation
   layer does not have to concern itself with
   understanding the correctness of the data.

As a system architect, it is also important to consider the trade-offs
of any approach, and utilizing an optimistic data model approach is not
without trade-offs.

1. The optimistic update model increases complexity
   since the overall system needs to know how to
   combine the data model and what data should have
   an optimistic state.

2. To ensure the data model is kept up to date, we need
   to ensure that local updates are correctly matched
   with server updates requiring an ID that can be used
   to sequence changes and mutations.

Given the scale of a large application, Figure 10-12 may even be too
broad of a view for one engineer. For example, say our Photo Stream had
both ads embedded in the organic posts and a complex onboarding flow
to capture new users. With this, we may even have a specific architect
for the data layer and separate engineers working on other areas of the
application where each area onboarding and ads may have their own
architects. Regardless, at some point, at least one engineer needs to think
through the overall application design, how the different design patterns
will interact, and how data will flow through the application.

Area Owner

The next level down from being responsible for designing the overall application is owning a specific area. While there are many areas to own, including the data presentation layer, which would consist of owning the significant UI interactions and understanding the application architecture of the UI. The data presentation layer could also further break down into portions. For example, owning the Photo Stream section and another engineer and team (potentially multiple teams) would own a different flow, like onboarding.

Utilizing what we have learned in this chapter about incremental computing, we will focus on another large area of the application, the task handler, instead of focusing on the UI. The task handler creates deltas based on updates that could include commenting on a photo, liking a photo, or adding a photo to the Photo Stream. These deltas are given to the task handler to process appropriately. The task handler, as defined in Figure 10-12, is responsible for coordinating optimistic state updates and network-backed state updates. Figure 10-13 outlines a potential architecture for such a task handler.

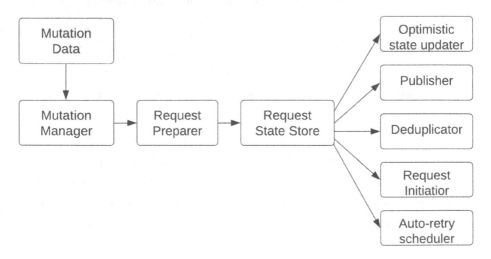

Figure 10-13. *Example task handler*

Because our hypothetical software architect provided the high-level guidance that we want to support an optimistic data flow and say how they want data to flow throughout the application, this empowers our area owner to develop their own components and delegate to their team or teams.

Breaking down our theoretical task handler, we have several components:

1. Mutation data: The data object the product layer creates and passes to the mutation manager for processing.

2. Mutation manager: Top-level object that provides the public API that higher-level abstractions interface with. Additionally, the mutation manager allows subscribing to updates for mutation results.

3. Request preparer: Prepares the request state based on the mutation data. This class ensures that expired or ineligible mutations restored from the disk are handled properly before proceeding.

4. Request state store: This object takes care of all the request state management and keeps the sources of all request states. Additionally, the request state store ensures that the subsequent ordering of state updates is executed correctly. These include the following:

   a. Optimistic state updater: This class updates the optimistic state, which in turn updates the UI for events that we want to reflect changes optimistically.

   b. Publisher: Publishes updates to the data layer.

    c. Request deduplicator: This class is responsible for deduplicating mutations. If a mutation on the same data is executed twice, the deduplicator is accountable for knowing the relative priority of the mutations and canceling the correct one.

    d. Request initiator: This class initiates the mutation process, and eligible mutations are executed, or scheduled for batch execution.

    e. Auto retry scheduler: When a mutation is queued execution attempted, the retry scheduler provides a mechanism to retry mutations if necessary and defines the configuration rules for retry attempts.

While the mutation manager is just one small area of the overall application, it in and of itself is a large complex area that could support multiple engineers. Another example of a portion of the application we have not even touched on is that different types of content or media could have different relative priorities. To implement priority ordering for execution, our task executor could implement different queues.

Feature Owner

Stepping down a level to a senior engineer, you are most likely a feature owner. The high-level principal engineer's diagrams and your area lead (sometimes a staff engineer) will help to guide your own feature development and architecture inside the broader system. More specific and targeted diagrams like the reaction diagram in Figure 10-2 are necessary. Figure 10-2 explains the specific game feature, which could fit into a broader application. In the context of our Photo Stream application, this could be that you own the Photo Stream layout or several more minor features like reactions and comments inside the view.

As a feature owner, you will be applying the tenets of the defined architecture (reactive programming here) but not necessarily defining new patterns. Your focus will be more on design patterns, as discussed in Chapter 6. It is equally important to understand the broader patterns of this:

1. Puts feature work into context and helps understand the best practices and why behind the decisions.

2. Establishes a clear path and strategy for career growth. By understanding the principles beyond your current scope, you have the technical understanding to progress and take on more responsibility, and suggest potential wider knowledge to suggest improvements.

Benefits of Reactive Programming and FRP

Many large applications perform data access synchronously at the infrastructure layer, and then the product (UI layer) accesses the data via an in-memory cache. The synchronous approach introduces a variety of issues, including the following:

1. Data readiness: All surfaces must be aware of infrastructure concepts like caching strategy and cache warming (early request to prepare the cache). Having the UI layer handle these infrastructure concerns leaves the product layer with too much knowledge of the underlying infrastructure and a wide surface area for potential bugs.

2. Data inconsistency: Each surface has to apply an optimistic state to the published data model to display up-to-date and accurate data. The UI layer must have an awareness of the data layer and how to merge changes to ensure the data is correct.

3. Missing data: Each call site is manually responsible for understanding what data exists and how to handle missing data – potentially fetching the data.

These three problems are more prevalent in large-scale applications where there are many different features and distinct product groups that may share the same underlying data. FRP and data streaming present an elegant way to write event-driven applications without resorting to traditional methods of updating, such as callbacks or the observer pattern (known to impact code quality and program comprehension negatively).

Instead, reactive programming provides a unified way for the UI layer (across product surfaces) to listen for updates in a data location-agnostic manner (whether this data is local or directly from the network) while improving code quality. The unification process raises the level of abstraction in your code base, allowing engineers to focus on building features without worrying about the underlying infrastructure.

The benefit is magnified in large-scale modern mobile applications due to the nature of large teams and the highly interactive nature of contemporary UIs. Applications have evolved to be more real-time, where modification of fields, adding comments, or adding reactions often automatically triggers a back-end request to save the data while optimistically updating the UI to reflect the new values on the user's device. The increasingly interactive nature of modern UIs means that even smaller-scale applications benefit from reactive programming. At the same time, reactive programming provides a rock-solid foundation that, if implemented well, will scale with the application. Overall, reactive programming offers a toolkit for us as engineers to manage the increased complexity required from modern application interactions and better manage large-scale data flows.

Reactive programming is not without some trade-offs though it:

1. Increases additional frameworks requiring knowledge and ramp-up time. Additionally, once a framework is integrated into the application, it can be difficult to migrate.

2. Complex debugging. Debugging inside of a reactive framework is complex and can require additional tooling.

3. Increased ramp-up time for new engineers. New engineers joining the team may not be familiar with reactive programming and will consequently require additional ramp-up time.

Summary

We have covered a lot of ground in this chapter, from defining the fundamentals of reactive programming to layering in functional concepts and reviewing how we can utilize these concepts to architect iOS applications. In the architecture review section, we broke down several portions of our Photo Stream application and put them in the context of different engineers by level and role.

Notice how we touched on Combine but did not focus on the actual Combine implementation and syntax because the syntax used can change with the framework. More important is understanding the ideas behind reactive programming, how to layer in functional concepts, and how to architect an entire application system regarding a reactive data flow. By understanding the concepts of FRP and reactive programming, you can apply them to architect a system for any number of applicable frameworks, not just Combine.

Three Key Takeaways from This Chapter

1. Your ability to architect and describe solutions will come down to understanding the application use case, and best practices, and your ability to clearly communicate this to other engineers via level-appropriate diagrams.

2. Reactive programming and FRP provide a conceptually straightforward and performant way to write event-driven applications declaratively.

3. We can apply FRP via the Combine framework. However, we are not limited to any specific framework. By understanding the overall tenets of reactive programming, we can apply them to existing frameworks like Combine or entirely new frameworks.

Further Learning

1. Reactive Imperative Programming with Dataflow Constraints: https://arxiv.org/pdf/1104.2293.pdf

2. Journey Through Incremental Computing: www.youtube.com/watch?v=DSuX-LIAU-I

3. Category Theory for Programmers: www.youtube.com/playlist?list=PLbgaMIhjbmEnaH_LTkxLI7FMa2HsnawM_

PART III

Approaching Application Design At Scale

CHAPTER 11

System Design Process

Overview

This chapter marks the beginning of Part 3. Thus far, we have reviewed the underlying iOS fundamentals (Part 1) and techniques to build scalable applications (Part 2). However, being able to write quality code and architect applications well is only a portion of what is necessary to deliver valuable software in a large company. In this environment, engineering and business teams can have competing priorities causing conflict and adding risk to project success. Additionally, engineering teams themselves can have competing priorities and conflicting launches. These added risk factors result in significant cross-functional communication requirements, resulting in additional planning and launch scheduling requirements.

To manage the added complexity in the planning and execution phases, we will define a framework (software development life cycle) and the critical soft skills necessary for the proper implementation of the framework. The rest of Part 3 will dig more into individual skills and competencies required for leading projects so that you can combine your technical skills with leadership and soft skills required for further success.

© Eric Vennaro 2023
E. Vennaro, *iOS Development at Scale*, https://doi.org/10.1007/978-1-4842-9456-7_11

This Chapter Includes

This chapter will focus mainly on the plan and design phases of the software development life cycle (SDLC) and the fundamental skills to plan and execute projects, including

1. Building necessary engineering documents

2. Aligning and communicating with key stakeholders on crucial project principles

3. Setting goals and milestones successfully

As an introduction, we will also provide an overview of all the steps in the SDLC. Subsequent chapters will focus on the SDLC test, deployment, and maintenance phases in more depth.

Software Development Life Cycle (SDLC)

The software development life cycle (SDLC) is a time-efficient process to design and build high-quality software products. SDLC aims to minimize project risks through proactive planning to ensure the software meets expectations after release. While there are different methodological approaches to SDLC, Figure 11-1 outlines a generic series of steps that divide the software development process.

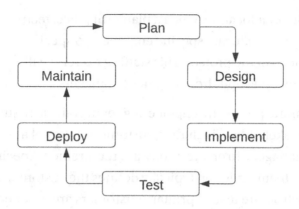

Figure 11-1. *Software development life cycle*

How SDLC Works

In this section, we will break down the different steps outlined in Figure 11-1. We keep these steps relatively general so that they can apply to some of the standard SDLC models used by teams. After defining the steps here, we will review some traditional models.

Plan

The planning phase includes tasks geared toward requirements gathering and staffing. Engineers need to assist in

1. Performing a cost-benefit analysis: Commonly referred to as goal setting and involves providing salient advice on the potential business upside and trade-off with engineer investment and infrastructure costs.

2. Engineering estimate: To support the cost-benefit analysis, engineers estimate the timeline and required effort to reach the end goal.

3. Engineer allocation: Once a plan is in place, tech leads must allocate specific engineers to specific portions of the project. This staffing exercise will also involve input from engineer managers.

In the planning phase, the engineering team collects requirements from product stakeholders, including customers, internal and external experts, and managers, to create a software requirement specification document. The team's mission typically defines the customers. For example, infrastructure teams' primary customers are other engineers looking to use their products to speed their own development (or provide a stable platform). For product teams, the customers are end users, so user research, design mocks, and product intuition will guide the planning phase.

The documents made in the planning phase set expectations and define common goals that aid in understanding project importance, gaining stakeholder alignment, and promoting a smooth project execution.

These documents will take several forms:

1. The strategy review document: A high-level business-focused document requiring engineer input and primarily driven by business stakeholders like product or project managers.

2. The long-range planning document: Not only planning for the short term but understanding the long-term vision for the project is a hallmark of a senior tech lead. The long-range planning document is more high level than the detailed road map. It includes information related to future project growth, areas of development that need staffing, and how the project can grow over time.

3. The short-term road map: A detailed document on the next few quarters or up to one year, including clear milestones, goals, and planning to achieve the short-term goals. At this point, the road map will be rough estimates as more design effort is needed. As timelines are updated and further fleshed out, it is necessary to communicate this to leadership.

Strategy Review

The strategy review can take different names. Regardless of the term, its creation is led by the business group, and its purpose is to communicate to leadership the cost-benefit analysis, upside potential, and project timeline. Engineer input is vital to understand the timeline and goals in the short term. Additionally, tech lead input is required to understand the broader engineering strategy long term and what engineering investments are needed to support the continued long-term project goals.

Long-Range Planning Document

The long-range planning document informs the overall technical direction for the project. This document feeds into the strategy review and short-term road map by defining the overall engineering vision. By outlining the engineering vision for the project, all team members and cross-functional partners understand the strategy and align their goals accordingly. The long-range strategy document also assists management in understanding the growth necessary for the team (hiring needs) and individual engineers' career paths. This document should outline infrastructure stability goals, future metric wins, and potential product ideas. Collaboration with data science resources may provide opportunity size estimates for future work when available.

The long-range planning document must

1. Contain an architecture diagram of the future state of the software system, including what we want to achieve and an explanation of why the engineering effort is necessary to drive additional business value.

2. Define key success metrics and any intermediate metrics that help us to measure how short-term gains lead to long-term success criteria.

3. Outline the steps necessary to get from where the team is now to the desired end state and the intermediate milestones. This timeline should stretch from two to five years and provide reasonable estimates and success criteria for each intermediate milestone.

Teams aligned around a core purpose and understanding are more productive and motivated. A long-range plan is one of the essential tools for inspiring the team based on the product's future success. An example of a long-range planning document is included in Chapter 17.

Note   Defining the long-term architecture creates shared direction so your team can autonomously make day-to-day decisions while building toward the broader vision.

Road Map

The road map is more detailed and immediate than the long-range planning document and defines short-term task-level items, and leads to an intermediate goal in the long-range planning document. The road map should have clear success criteria with metric-backed goals and a clear understanding of the software necessary to reach them.

Note Road maps connect strategic goals with potential features and engineering changes required to reach them.

The road map includes detailed task-based breakdowns and clearly defines success criteria for the specified SDLC period. The road map will also include goals for each quarter. Most road maps are one to two-quarters long. Typically any longer, and it becomes difficult to estimate work accurately. Depending on the feature developed, the road map and success criteria may be more tied to existing software or features being built or more linked to metrics such as increased user engagement.

To further structure our road map, we can divide our complex product decisions into clear themes with their associated goals. Each theme can have its success criteria and build into a complete project plan. In the road mapping template displayed in Figure 11-2, we can divide our project into themes based on different engagement levers and prioritize accordingly.

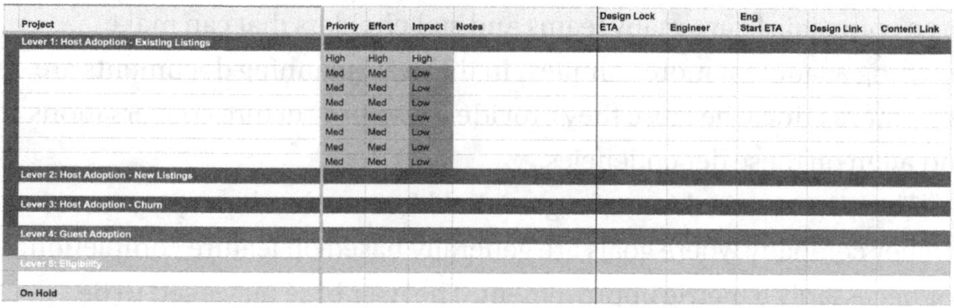

Project	Priority	Effort	Impact	Notes	Design Lock ETA	Engineer	Eng Start ETA	Design Link	Content Link
Lever 1: Host Adoption - Existing Listings									
	High	High	High						
	Med	Med	Low						
	Med	Med	Low						
	Med	Med	Low						
	Med	Med	Low						
	Med	Med	Low						
	Med	Med	Low						
	Med	Med	Low						
Lever 2: Host Adoption - New Listings									
Lever 3: Host Adoption - Churn									
Lever 4: Guest Adoption									
Lever 5: Eligibility									
On Hold									

Figure 11-2. *Sample road map with themes referred to as levers*[1]

Both road maps and long-range planning documents are essential, especially in large organizations, because they are powerful communication tools for aligning all stakeholders. They provide a single source of truth for anyone unfamiliar with the current project state, goals,

---

[1] `https://docs.google.com/spreadsheets/d/1zlx3RuidNOW4OZf7ghO7p2SqoR53Ungv9JFT-PhHwxI/edit#gid=184965050`

and product vision. Additionally, during their creation, they provide a forum for discussing the problem space so the team can align on the best approach and provide feedback before implementation.

Lastly, it is critical to keep planning documents up to date. Working with business partners to update the road map appropriately is vital as the project progresses. Depending on the company structure, engineers or business partners take different roles in writing the road map; however, it is always the engineers' responsibility to provide technical input on necessary software infrastructure and the feasibility of goals.

Differences in Planning at Small and Big Companies

At large companies, planning takes a long-range view with more focus on incremental metrics improvement. While large companies build new features (and sometimes new products), key metrics and product features are often already established, requiring a deep understanding of specific product areas and how to drive continuous improvements. Additionally, large companies have many teams and stakeholders that can make reaching alignment more complex. In this way, planning documents are even more critical because they provide a way to structure conversations and align on these dependencies.

There is increased room for greenfield feature development at a smaller company where goals are generally based on feature completion, not necessarily a metric improvement. The user base may need to be larger to perform A/B testing or other detailed performance assessment methods; thus, goals may come down to feature completion without any apparent bugs or crashes. Still, design documents are essential to define performance guardrails and a culture of best practices to support the application as it grows. Figure 11-3 outlines these differences.

	Small, Early Stage Company	Mature, Larger Company
Timeline	**Shorter** *Harder to predict the future, requiring roadmaps with shorter timelines.*	**Longer** *Planning reflects established goals and vision and can take longer to realize.*
Dependencies	**Minimal** *Smaller teams and less stakeholders present fewer dependencies and requirements allowing team to move faster*	**Complex** *Smaller teams and less stakeholders present fewer dependencies and requirements allowing team to move faster*
Goals	**Mid-Term** *Startups and smaller companies are focused on validating their business idea and goals typically reflect this.*	**Long-Term** *Roadmaps are focused on nuanced and built to focus on the long-term goals*

Figure 11-3. Differences in planning for early stage and more mature larger companies

Design

In the design phase, software developers review the engineering requirements and identify the best solutions to create the required software. Engineers will consider integrating preexisting modules and identifying libraries and frameworks that could speed the implementation process. They will look at how to best integrate the new software into the organization's infrastructure. In both the design and planning phases, it is essential for tech leads to reach alignment with other engineering stakeholders on the design's approach. Here is where architecture documents shine and where the knowledge from Part 2 of this book is best applied.

Additionally, the design phase should further inform the planning stage. As critical architecture decisions converge, engineer leaders must communicate any related timeline changes to the required stakeholders and appropriately update roadmapping and other planning documents.

At large companies working on massive applications, the design phase is critical. With so many dependent teams and extensive internal infrastructure, driving alignment between teams and choosing a solution that works well with internal tooling are vital. The implementation may only work correctly if the solution meshes with the internal infrastructure. Or if stakeholders are not aligned on the timeline, the underlying infrastructure may shift unbeknownst to the product team, causing delays or production bugs. Having a clear design document makes a team's plan easy to share and reference by others to gather feedback and avoid unplanned situations.

It is easier to gain alignment and context via casual conversations at smaller companies or on smaller applications with only a few engineers. The entire code base may be greppable by a single engineer, which entirely avoids some of the conflicts. As the application continues to scale, the ability to document design decisions helps inform future decisions and helps new team members ramp up and gain context on past choices.

Note   The plan and design phases are critical for a senior tech lead and are where the tech lead's domain expertise is most important. The tech lead sets the team up for success during the implementation phase by leading the planning and architecture design. As a tech lead, you cannot do the entire implementation alone. Still, by planning and designing well, you can give clear guidance to other team members, enabling them to execute against their priorities and deliver quality software during the implementation phase.

Implement

After agreeing on the planning, timeline, and goals, the time comes to implement the necessary engineering changes. During the implementation phase, if the team is well positioned for success, the tech lead can take a backseat role and focus on reviewing code, writing some code, and helping mentor the rest of the team to meet the objectives. By positioning the team well, the tech lead enables execution without requiring heavy involvement. During this extra time, the tech lead can focus on shoring up the launch path and thinking about future opportunities to drive the project ahead. The primary skills necessary to succeed in the implementation phase are related to Part 1 of this book, where we discuss core software engineering competencies. Here, we have already defined the design and need to write correct code leading to a high-quality implementation. The tech lead can help enforce this standard by holding a high standard in code reviews.

In the implementation phase, tracking progress toward goals and implementing incremental product testing are critical. By implementing incremental product testing, the team can avoid surprises during deployment. Depending on the team's implementation of the SDLC, there are different ways of tracking development progress. Typically there needs to be some way of analyzing the requirements to identify smaller coding tasks that add up to the final result and monitoring their completion against dates on the road map. Depending on the company, this may fall more on the product management team or the engineering tech lead. Either way, the tech lead must be involved in tracking progress and helping speed up the team's expertise.

Additionally, suppose the team starts to fall behind. In that case, it is the responsibility of the tech lead to identify the risk, raise it to relevant stakeholders, and present alternative engineering solutions to solve the problem. Ways to speed up the project include increased input from subject matter experts, more engineering resources, or cutting scope.

Test

The test phase should execute in parallel with the development phase. As engineers write new code and complete features, the individual developers are responsible for writing unit and integration tests. Upon feature completion, more holistic testing should occur. Depending on the company setup, this can include internal bug bashes and dogfooding sessions. Additionally, quality assurance testers can be leveraged to continuously check critical features for any bugs and ensure that the application meets specifications defined in the planning phase.

Continuous product testing on the eventual deployment infrastructure stack is critical to ensure all features work as expected for end users. To accomplish this, on iOS, teams can utilize tools like Visual Studio App Center and TestFlight to distribute builds. However, this goes beyond just the iOS application. The iOS application will most likely interact with the network, so the associated API and back-end teams must ensure they properly set up their code to support the new features. One way to do so is to use different developer flags controlled by configuration to turn the feature on for only a subset of testing users. To widen the number of users on the new feature set and gather more bug reports, some companies institute corporate dogfooding where all employees utilize internal builds of the product to test the latest features.

Note   An item should only be marked complete once deployed and tested on the production serving stack. By enforcing this, the team can reduce bugs and avoid communicating that a feature is finished to leadership only to find that it will not work in the production environment.

Deploy

Software deployment and feature release are another stage requiring much tech lead input. The release schedule, timing, and strategy may differ depending on the team's goals and specific projects. As a tech lead, you must define this with the relevant stakeholders. For example, suppose you are leading a large project migration. In that case, there may be set milestones based on necessary feature sets, or if you work on a metric-based team, specific measurement weeks may require project releases to align with them.

Teams should not wait to deploy changes – getting an early and continuous signal is critical to ensure regressions and bugs are found sooner rather than later. This way, aligning the deployment pipeline with the eventual release process via build configurations is vital. Additionally, this unblocks getting continuous feedback from the ongoing test and implementation workstreams.

Note   The implement, test, and deploy phases should all run in parallel to one another to avoid issues during the actual product rollout. By waiting until the very end to test and deploy on the production infra, you risk hidden bugs surfacing and delaying the release.

To execute the implement, test, and deploy phases in parallel, we can utilize an experimentation platform where different features can be independently enabled and disabled with metrics collected to validate the effects of changes. Experimentation platforms ensure changes can be monitored and, hopefully, seamlessly disabled if something is amiss. We will discuss experimentation in more detail in Chapter 14.

Maintain

In the maintenance phase, the team fixes bugs, resolves customer issues, and handles any subsequent software changes. In addition, the team monitors overall system performance via metric dashboards and logging. The team will monitor the user experience to identify new ways to improve the existing software for the next planning phase. It is helpful to buffer additional time during planning to ensure developers have time to address bugs found in the deployment or maintenance phase.

Given how the different phases interact, we can rewrite Figure 11-1 to represent this in Figure 11-4. Here, we draw additional lines representing the development cycles between the implementation, test, and deployment phases. We have highlighted with light gray the key steps tech leads should concern themselves with, and dotted lines represent links between the implementation, design, and plan phases as tech leads should continuously look to evaluate the planning and design phases.

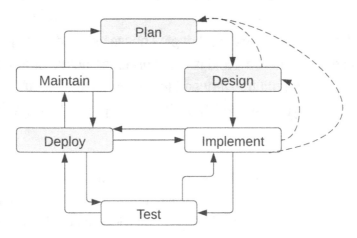

Figure 11-4. *Modified SDLC*

SDLC Models

In the previous section, we discussed the overall SDLC and mentioned that different models describe some implementation steps more specifically. While it is not necessary to follow the exact steps of one of these specific models, they do represent commonly used implementations. Most models are geared to optimize a part of the SDLC and are created to help organizations implement the SDLC.

Waterfall

The waterfall model organizes the SDLC phases sequentially, and each new step depends on the outcome of the previous stage. Conceptually, the SDLC steps flow from one to the next, like a waterfall. Figure 11-5 outlines the steps of the SDLC organized for the waterfall method.

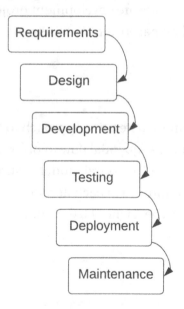

Figure 11-5. Waterfall method

Key Tenets

Three main principles guide the waterfall method:

1. Low stakeholder involvement by detailed planning

2. Strong documentation

3. A sequential structure

Pros and Cons

The waterfall model provides a disciplined approach to the SDLC and provides a tangible output at the end of each phase. However, given the sequential nature of the process, there is little room for requirements change once a step is complete, which can lead to engineers building software that does not address the business use case. Therefore, the model is most suitable for small software development projects, where tasks are easily arranged and managed, and requirements can be predefined accurately.

Spiral

The spiral model combines an iterative approach to the SDLC with the waterfall model's linear sequential flow to prioritize risk analysis and iteratively ship software. The spiral model ensures that software is gradually released and improved in each iteration. Each iteration also involves building a prototype. Figure 11-6 outlines a spiral model iteration applied to the SDLC.

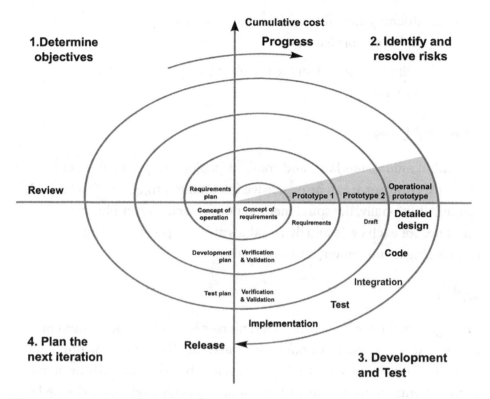

Figure 11-6. Spiral method[2]

Key Tenets

1. Consider the opinions and success criteria from all critical stakeholders.

2. Identify and consider alternative approaches for satisfying the stakeholder requirements.

---

[2] Boehm, B (July 2000). "Spiral Development: Experience, Principles, and Refinements." *Special Report*. Software Engineering Institute. CMU/SEI-2000-SR-008.

3. Identify and address risks that stem from the selected approaches.

4. Obtain approval on the cycle's strategy and success criteria.

Pros and Cons

The spiral model suits large and complex projects requiring frequent changes. However, it can be expensive for smaller projects with a limited scope. Additionally, the spiral method does not clearly emphasize timelines for each cycle and deliverables at those points, making it challenging to implement business goals.

Agile

The Agile method arranges the SDLC phases into several development cycles. The team iterates through the phases rapidly, delivering only small, incremental software changes in each cycle. They continuously evaluate requirements, plans, and results to respond quickly to change. The Agile model is iterative and incremental, making it more efficient than other process models. Figure 11-7 illustrates a cycle in the Agile model. The overall project will consist of many of these cycles.

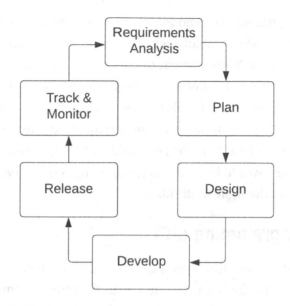

Figure 11-7. *Agile development cycle*

Key Tenets

1. Prioritize individuals and interactions over processes and tools.

2. Prioritize working software.

3. Customer collaboration is critical.

4. Flexibility in responding to changes.

Pros and Cons

Rapid development cycles help teams identify and address issues in complex projects early on and before they become significant problems. The Agile method also promotes engaging with customers and stakeholders to obtain feedback throughout the project life cycle – addressing an important issue with the waterfall method. However, overreliance on customer feedback can lead to excessive scope changes or end the project midway.

Additionally, the Agile methodology does not always scale well due to the communication overhead, lack of documentation, and complex process requirements. Without clear documentation, aligning with stakeholders in large environments where good documentation and design documents are critical tools in driving alignment is difficult.

Lastly, the Agile methodology defines many principles and practices that are rigid and difficult to follow, especially in a large company where many stakeholders would be necessary. This causes most teams only to adopt a portion of the Agile method.

Extreme Programming (XP)

XP is a form of Agile methodology with particular emphasis on software quality. XP advocates for frequent releases in short development cycles to improve productivity and introduce checkpoints for adopting new customer requirements. Like agile, XP dictates many vital principles and elements that are difficult to implement in a large-scale project due to their complexity and rigidity. These elements include

1. Pair programming

2. Extensive code review and unit testing of all code

3. Waiting to program features until they are needed

4. A flat management structure

The methodologies namesake is from the fact that XP takes the elements of traditional software engineering best practices to extreme levels. For example, pair programming is considered a beneficial practice; taken to the extreme in XP, all code is written in pairs. Figure 11-8 demonstrates an extreme programming project life cycle.

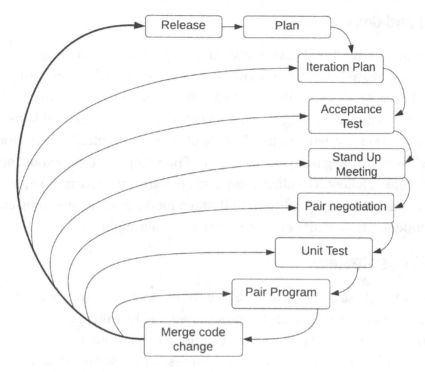

Figure 11-8. XP development cycle

Key Tenets

1. Extreme programming sees feedback as most useful if done frequently and promptly and that feedback is critical to learning and making changes. It stresses that minimizing the delay between an action and its feedback is important for its effectiveness.

2. Assuming simplicity and treating every problem as if its solution were straightforward. Other system development methods plan for the future and promote coding for reusability – extreme programming rejects these ideas.

3. Embrace change.

383

Pros and Cons

The practices in XP are heavily debated, with proponents claiming that the increased flexibility removes overhead and cuts development time. However, XP's flexibility and lack of future planning can lead to costly development redesigns and project scope creep. These problems compound at scale, where careful future planning is required to ensure all stakeholders are aligned. Due to the lack of planning, documentation, and strict steps to follow, XP suffers from many of the same cons as the Agile methodology and is typically not well suited for the intricate planning and dependency management required for large-scale applications.

Methods Review

Across all of these methods are a few key tenets that apply well to large applications at scale. Embodying these tenets and learning skills to address them allow you to lead projects successfully across any methodology. A tech lead plays a crucial role in project success and ensuring the team meets its goals. We can see some recurring themes across all of these approaches, namely:

1. A focus on documentation and planning helps projects succeed at massive companies.

2. Flexible iterations with iterative planned releases help teams ship software and detect bugs.

3. Communication across stakeholders is critical across all methodologies.

4. Testing is vital to hold a high bar for software quality.

Being able to lead across these areas is how a TL can build skills for success in different environments. Since testing is a separate stage in the SDLC, we will focus on skills related to effective planning and as the critical skills required in this chapter.

Crucial Role of the TL

While there are multiple views on executing a software project regardless of the exact methodology utilized as a tech lead, some key tenets need to be followed for continued success when leading a team in the long term. Leading a successful team goes beyond a single project or single release. At a software product company, the expectation is to lead and grow a team of engineers for years, which cannot be done simply by maintaining the existing project at its current scope. Developing a project requires synthesizing new ideas and actively growing the project, resulting in new software development life cycles for these subsequent endeavors. To do so, we need to take a more long-term and iterative approach to stay ahead of the active development phase and plan the long-term vision.

Because of this, the tech leadership role is most important at the start and end of the project. At the beginning of the project, the tech lead drives the planning, ensuring alignment with the long-term vision and addressing the significant technical challenges. In a business context, this also involves communicating the goals and timeline for broader tracking. This necessitates tech leads to understand the business context in addition to technical aspects and to align on goals and delivery schedules. Depending on the team's goals and methodology, setting them can differ, but alignment across stakeholders is critical to ensure that work is delivered on schedule and within the designed constraints.

Note   Some companies take a very top-down approach to goal setting and some of the project leadership responsibilities, but many Silicon Valley tech companies espouse bottom-up planning, meaning more focus is put on engineering ideas coming from the implementation team and placing the burden on both managers and tech leads to come up with ways to drive business value.

Large-scale projects are complex and can cross multiple teams, making organizing and leading product rollouts complicated. All experiences must meet the launch timeline and must function together. To this end, it is essential to have experienced tech lead input on the proper launch path.

By leading the beginning and end of the project in detail, the senior tech lead allows their team to grow and develop via mentorship in the execution phases. This also provides the tech lead time to think ahead on future product direction and ensure that the overall project stays on track.

The broad SDLC and understanding of the tech lead's pivotal role transcend any specific formal steps. Memorizing and following a particular design process strictly without truly understanding the value a strong tech lead provides is of little importance. Instead, the value is in knowing and developing the skills to communicate and lead a development team. The SDLC and methods such as Agile provide heuristics, similar to a software design pattern on how to best lead based on hundreds of years of combined developer experience. By being flexible and focusing on the skills necessary to lead, you can quickly adapt to any methodology. Here, we break these skills down into individual items. Later in Chapters 16 and 17, we combine these personal skills with broader leadership tenets for large teams and practical examples. By first breaking down leadership skills to the individual level, we are approaching people skills and leadership development like we did with technical concepts, where the individual skills serve as the building blocks to a more comprehensive team leadership.

A Skill-Focused View

Regardless of the methodology, the end goal is delivering the software and driving business value. As a senior tech lead, your job is explicitly to lead from a technical aspect and be able to

1. Navigate the technical problem space

2. Design and lead the technical solution

3. Communicate clearly

4. Set up appropriate time-bound goals (milestones)

Problem Navigation

Problem navigation involves demonstrating the ability to organize the problem space, constraints, and potential solutions in a systematic manner. To accomplish this, you must ask questions to reduce ambiguity and systematically target the most critical problems. To do so, it is essential to proactively minimize ambiguity by asking clarifying questions (e.g., how many friends can a user have? How big is the data set?). This information leads to exploration into the most critical problem areas and guides significant parts of the design process and solution requirements.

The initial questions should be helping you to better understand what engineering abstractions could be used and any potential pitfalls. In some cases, business partners may be unaware of the constraints from existing infrastructure or even privacy problems. It is essential to work with them when crafting a workable solution. Additionally, defining the requirements for quantitative analysis is integral to navigating the problem space for goal setting. With a quantitative framework, it is easier to create goals consistently.

Moreover, an awareness of the product from an end-user perspective is necessary to better understand the business perspective and holistically drive toward the shared business vision.

Solution Design

Once the problem space is clarified, it is necessary to design a working solution for the complete problem and outline essential portions of the overall design in detail. You must consider the broader context in the design and keep scale and multiple development teams in mind. For example, if your team is building the feature, other teams may be responsible for a shared web or infrastructure layer that you depend on for feature development. Involving them early and working to call out their portion of the solution are essential when driving toward a shared goal.

During solution design, the tech lead must create an effective working solution that addresses multiple critical aspects of the problem in an easy-to-understand manner. The design should consider the required scalability across large amounts of data and users (e.g., accounting for large-scale data in their design, such as syncing with error correction). The working solution should include a detailed rollout plan, including rollout stages, metric-based evaluation, and success criteria.

The tech leads must have experience developing products and the technical ability to architect complex solutions involving design patterns and architectural best practices. The level of technical expertise requires tech leads to articulate dependencies and trade-offs in the solution and identify challenging aspects of the problem, including foreseeing and mitigating potential failure points.

When expressing these technical challenges and foreseen points of failure, it is essential to articulate them as trade-offs, for example, understanding the weaknesses of a standard design or architectural patterns (e.g., scaling up engineers on the project, amount of code, or amount of users). Tech leads should be able to leverage various experiences to illustrate points of failure.

Beyond technical skills, it is also essential to understand how technical decisions impact product behavior for different end-user populations. By understanding the business constraints, you can work well with business partners to drive technical solutions that support business value. Without this connection, you risk having the technical solution diverge from the business requirements creating a gap. To have this connection, frequently connect with business partners to ensure UI and engineering designs are applicable, functional, and achievable in the required time frame and meet product requirements.

Communication

As a software engineer leader, having the skills to navigate difficult conversations is imperative. Sometimes, the business and engineering functions will disagree on technical decisions due to business constraints. Even within the technical space, disagreements commonly stem from divergent technical approaches. Navigating these conversations and driving decisions is a crucial skill for any tech lead. We can systematically manage complex and potentially contentious discussions by building a framework. Our framework will work toward four fundamental principles:

1. Understand everyone's point of view.

2. Guide the conversation and provide solution options addressing all concerns.

3. Communicate in a shared context to tell a convincing story and ensure everyone drives toward the same goals.

4. Proactively communicate risk. No one likes surprises.

Communication Framework

Understand Everyone's Point of View

Overall it is essential to address and align on the problems causing contention between you and the other person. Whether business related or technical, you can gain a more in-depth understanding by digging deeper to understand the details and driving factors behind the person's opinion. Understanding the other person's point of view is essential when structuring the rest of the framework. This understanding allows us to provide mutually beneficial solutions and align on the crucial data to further guide the conversation.

It is critical to ask questions necessary to gain understanding and listen attentively to the response to comprehend someone else's point of view. Here, the goal is not to argue or disagree; it is simply learning, which may require further clarifying questions until you fully understand their point of view. To confirm that you do comprehend their point of view, you should restate your perceived idea of their opinion back to them. By accurately responding to a person what was said, you show that you are listening, not just hearing, and that you genuinely understand the feelings and message they are trying to convey.

Note   Active listening is a method of listening and responding to another person that improves mutual understanding, defuses tense situations, and helps find solutions to complex problems.

For example, say you work on a team that prioritizes building new user engagement features to optimize for increased daily active users and session length. You also know from previous analysis that application startup performance positively impacts user session length. Your business partners want to quickly release a new feature to keep up with their competition. However, it requires building on a legacy module with a high application startup cost.

Additionally, the legacy module has limited user coverage and no documentation, making development difficult and error-prone. From an engineering perspective, refactoring the legacy component improves development, startup performance, and ease of future feature development; however, this will delay the release of the high-priority business feature.

Your business partner is very concerned and does not want to take on any risk to the project or delay the launch for any reason. Given the cross-cutting concerns, you must align with the business stakeholders on the best path forward. To do so, as outlined in our framework, we need to understand the business partner's point of view entirely. Start by asking clarifying questions to understand why they are so risk-averse to this feature and why the launch date is so important to hit. Maybe you will find out it is not critical. Or you may find out that the company needs this feature to compete with a competitor, and even if the feature is not perfect, reaching the launch date is critical for the company's success and future growth.

Overall, we must align on the relative risk of delaying the launch to address the technical debt against building the feature quickly and incurring further technical debt. To do so requires a complete understanding of the landscape.

Key Tenet   Active listening allows you to understand everyone's perspective without injecting your viewpoints and is a prerequisite for guiding the conversation toward a solution.

Guiding the Conversation

Once we understand the solution space, we can begin driving the conversation to a conclusion. Given a complete understanding of everyone's goals and objectives, we can craft a series of narratives to address these goals. When coming to a solution, it is essential to consider alternative options or ones that may be less optimal from an engineering perspective but more optimal from another perspective. For example, revisiting our previous scenario, while from an engineering perspective, it makes more sense first to address the technical debt and then build more features, from a business perspective, this is a critical launch that requires feature support, so even if we suffer a performance loss and suboptimal feature in the short term.

We can phrase this as two solutions: one from the business perspective and the other from the engineering perspective. By presenting both options, you can solicit feedback from all relevant stakeholders and drive the conclusion. When providing options, it is essential to select one as the recommended option; this further frames the conversation in a solution-oriented manner. For all solutions, it is vital to

1. List out the pros and cons of each so all parties can align on the relative risks.

2. Display all parties' points of view. It is important to list everyone's key concerns, which also checks that you genuinely understood their opinions in step one of the framework.

3. Document the recommended solution.

Sometimes, reaching a solution is complex, and not everyone will be aligned. Do not be afraid to escalate to others for help. Utilizing a trusted and neutral third party can help to drive a solution without causing further tension. For example, say you and another engineer disagree on the approach to a critical migration. If you cannot easily reach an agreement after listening to both methods, mapping the pros and cons, and further presenting solutions, then a trusted engineer whose opinion is respected can help serve as a tiebreaker.

To help prevent unresolvable conflict, aligning on a common language is also helpful so that everyone understands the solutions presented. Often, an agreement cannot be reached because involved parties do not feel any of the solutions (or the recommended solution) adequately understands and address their viewpoint. Without using a shared language and values framework, it is much easier to have these misalignments.

Lastly, while driving the conversation, tempers may flare. It is essential to stay calm and solution focused. Getting emotionally involved in a specific solution or taking feedback personally can cause reaching further alignment to be more complex and less business focused. By staying company focused, it is easier to drive alignment calmly. If you see tempers flare or the situation derails, try rescheduling the conversation for another time. Additionally, adding a trusted third party to the meeting who can serve as a mediator can help relieve tensions.

Key Tenet   Present multiple solution options with one recommended solution. When driving alignment, stay solution focused and avoid emotional attachment to a specific answer.

Using a Common Language and Value Framework

To better guide the conversation and set the tone for the solution space, utilizing a common language framework for all parties involved helps ensure everyone understands the solutions. Since both engineers and businesses use data, data-driven decisions can serve as a bridge between esoteric engineering concepts and business decisions. We should ground this data in metrics related to business outcomes, such as; like bug report rates, the average time to deliver a feature, developer satisfaction, and team goal metrics.

Revisiting our example from the previous section, we can strive to verify our hypothesis that the legacy module is impacting the user experience and developer speed. To understand the impact on user experience, we can assess the number of support issues and bug reports between that component and others. If available, review the module's specific performance metrics to understand if it takes materially longer to load. From the developer speed perspective, we can also check the number of critical tasks and bug reports to understand if engineers are spending materially more time maintaining this area of the code. We can even combine with step 1 of our framework and further format the data to tell a compelling story with a path to shared success.

If you cannot see the hypothesized difference after analyzing the available data, it may indicate that the problem is less critical than initially theorized. You must verify your hypothesis and convince yourself of the impact on the business to convince your business partners.

One great thing that can come from working on telling the story from the perspective of your business partner is that you may realize that the effort required to fix something is not worth it – the business value is not there. There are times when engineers do like to over-architect features; doing this analysis helps us gain confidence that the work is necessary or allows us to accept that we should probably take the slight tech debt and move on.

Additionally, to tell a more impactful story, you can tie the solutions back to specific company or team values – hopefully, your company or management structure helps to provide values. These values can be "move fast" or "focus on users." Ensuring your solutions align with these values and are expressed in your document helps create a shared context with overarching principles to guide the discussion.

Communicating Risk

Lastly, it is always important to communicate any risks to the project timeline. No one likes surprises, and by sharing any development risk earlier, you mitigate the potential for long-term unscheduled project delays. By flagging risks and presenting potential alternative paths, you also give your stakeholders options on how to proceed and help gain buy-in on the decisions made. Providing options improves stakeholder buy-in because giving them a choice makes them feel part of the decision-making process and the product's future success. Now that we have defined our communication framework, we can apply this to both technical and business communication.

Technical Communication

1. Technical communication requires articulating technical ideas, viewpoints, and vision. Technically solid communication necessitates the ability to reason in logical and structured ways as they relate to engineering. It is helpful to utilize a data-driven scientific approach.

2. Understanding the problem space.

3. Formulating a hypothesis.

4. Explaining this hypothesis in a logical manner backed by supporting metrics.

5. Considering and articulating technical ideas and the associated trade-offs. No solution is perfect.

The ability to engage on complex technical subjects and break them down in a focused, logical, and organized manner allows you, as a tech lead, to delegate the specific portions of the technical design to other engineers in an understandable way. To communicate well in a technical context requires a deep understanding of the underlying technical foundation, which, for iOS engineers, is defined as core iOS competencies, knowledge of concurrent systems, and design patterns for iOS applications.

Once a design is architected and documented, it is essential to review it with the team, and it is expected for everyone to have feedback on the technical proposal. The teams' feedback presents an excellent opportunity to address gaps in the design. In this way, we are following our framework:

1. Understanding everyone's points of view here centers on grasping the critical components of the technical solution.

2. Building an engineering document guides the
    conversation and presents our solution in a
    common language.

Some further nuanced steps for complex technical discussions are
when software designs have cross-cutting concerns with other tech
leads' areas of expertise. In these situations, their feedback requires
careful consideration. With cross-cutting concerns, it is necessary to
reach alignment with key stakeholders across the engineering teams
and push forward with a singular technical plan. Understanding critical
stakeholders' opinions and aligning with them are vital before presenting
the engineering plan in a large group meeting. This way, in a one-on-one
setting, you can understand their perspective and what feedback they
have, which will help drive the solution. You can garner further input and
understand their preferred solutions by aligning with key people before
more significant group discussions.

Sometimes, goals across organizations in companies can cause
complex technical issues that are difficult to resolve. For example, say your
team focuses on enabling ads in the Photo Stream to drive revenue, and
to further drive revenue, your team is allowing advertisements at the top
position on the feed. You draft the overall design for the project, including
the client and server portions, to enable ads to take the highest place. The
ranking team – a back-end machine learning–focused team in a different
org – is concerned with this proposal. The ranking team aims to optimize
ranking and block the project because their models cannot handle
position-one-ads. They require six months of technical work to update
their models; otherwise, they risk their topline metrics goal of driving
ad conversions due to model degradation. The fundamental problem is
that the goals are misaligned; you are trying to drive revenue, and they
are trying to have the best prediction model (which incidentally drives
revenue).

To resolve this, you can involve relevant stakeholders and align across company values. For example, by developing the feature now, the project is aligned with the value of "moving fast." However, they can counter and say you are not "putting the user experience first" by delivering subpar ads. Because of the fundamental misalignment, the conflict may not be resolvable at your team level; it may be necessary to escalate to a leadership role between the two organizations. Do not be afraid to raise these issues; delaying in this situation can cause further problems.

Communicating Business Needs

In addition to understanding the technical concepts, it is equally vital for senior tech leads to understand the business concerns and relevant business domain concepts. By better understanding the business constraints, engineers can communicate clearly and map the technical trade-offs in the context of business requirements. It is not enough to map the engineering trade-offs to business concerns. We must also be able to explain them in a business-driven context. Additionally, as mentioned in our framework, establishing a shared language for decision-making is critical. Without that, it is easy for context to be lost and decisions to get off track. Typically data is a common language across business and engineering, and by framing decisions in this context, we can drive the conversation.

Even while using a data-driven approach and understanding the business perspective, what makes business engineering concepts difficult is twofold:

1. Sometimes, what is best from an engineering perspective may not be the best for the business.

2. Business problems that seem simple to solve may have complex technical challenges or require underlying migrations lengthening the implementation timeline.

397

Business conflicts are complex and more often require escalation across non-engineering organizations. Hopefully, business and engineering are well aligned. In situations where engineering and business are not aligned and cannot come to a resolution at the team level, it is necessary to document both points of view and reasoning and escalate to the proper leadership person who can communicate across the organizations and drive a resolution that is aligned across the organizations. By only resolving such conflicts at lower levels, you risk missing essential context and causing further problems closer to the software release. Remember, increasing business value is critical for a company, and engineers help to accomplish this, meaning that business value is always essential when deciding what work is the highest priority.

Note   To ensure engineering-driven work gets the required attention, engineers must learn to communicate in business terms.

Setting Goals for Success

Setting realistic goals aligns the team and sets expectations with leadership. Determining feasible goals requires technical expertise to size the engineering complexity and uncover the hidden complexity. Goals also help keep track of progress and align external stakeholders. A helpful acronym when defining goals is "SMART"; we generally want our goals to be SMART, where SMART stands for specific, measurable, achievable, relevant, and time-bound.

S: Specific

An actionable goal requires specificity. A specific goal answers the following questions:

1. What needs to be accomplished?

2. Who is responsible for accomplishing the goal?

3. What steps need to be taken to achieve the goal?

For example, our specific goal can be to grow the number of monthly users of our mobile application by optimizing our onboarding flow and creating targeted social media campaigns.

M: Measurable

Part of a specific goal is its quantifiability. By aligning on success criteria measurably, teams can track progress and know when the work is complete. To make our preceding goal more measurable, we can redefine our goal to include increasing our mobile application monthly users by 1,000.

A: Achievable

For a realistic goal, we must ask ourselves: Is your objective something your team can reasonably accomplish?

On further inspection and data analysis, we may realize that increasing the number of monthly users of our mobile application by 1,000 is a 25% increase, which in one quarter is unreasonable. Instead, optimizing our conversion flow by 10% is more feasible.

Ensuring the achievability of your goal is much easier when you are the one setting it. However, that is not always the case. When goals are communicated top-down, it is necessary to communicate any restraints you may be working under that make the goal difficult or impossible to achieve. Even if you cannot change the end goal, at least you can make your position (and any potential blockers) known up front.

R: Relevant

Understanding the broader picture and business context is essential to ensure your goal is relevant. Here, we know our goal is appropriate because growing the number of monthly users helps us to increase our profitability since we will have more users to display advertisements to.

T: Time-Bound

To correctly measure success, we need to understand the time required to reach the goal and when we can start working to achieve the goal. Additionally time-bound goals allow everyone to track progress. Thus, to finalize our goal, we need to make it time-bound.

We will grow the number of monthly users of our mobile application by 10% within Q1 of 2022. This will be accomplished by optimizing our onboarding flow and creating targeted social media campaigns beginning in February of this year. Increasing our user base will increase our advertisement revenue, a key success metric for our business.

Note   Using the SMART framework helps you succeed in setting and attaining big and small goals.

Different companies have different approaches to goal setting, and it is essential to stay flexible and work within the established shared system, so everyone has context and understanding. Broadly speaking, it is helpful to know what is likely to be accomplished, that is, 80% likely, 50% likely to be completed, and what risks exist along with mitigation strategy and ask for help on how to address them. This allows a standard view of the problem space and sets expectations.

Understanding the cost of an engineering project in terms of engineering resources and the value the project will drive for the business is critical. These two principles combine with the ability to set goals and deliverables. To successfully set technical goals, tech leads must be product, team, and technical experts. Depending on the type of team and company policy, the exact nature of the goals and how they are developed is different. Regardless of how the goals are created, we must break them down into achievable intermediate milestones to track progress toward the broader goal. In this way, milestones are time-bound goals.

When developing our goals and milestones, we need to understand the type of team and goal structure. We can break this down into three areas:

1. Product teams that are geared toward creating new product experiences. Typically the user experiences being built are the main goals; however, understanding the user impact via metrics is essential. Typically important metrics can include performance-based and user engagement–based metrics.

2. Infrastructure teams are those developing the underlying infrastructure and whose clients are other teams. Typically the goal is similar to product teams where the software built is the goal. For infrastructure teams, more emphasis is put on service-level obligations and objectives to ensure that the infrastructure functions performantly and meets expectations.

3. Metric-driven teams. This category is broader and can encompass teams related to user growth, machine learning optimization, and performance optimization. Typically teams related to the optimization space have specific metric-driven goals they are responsible for, for example, reducing application startup or driving more new user signups via machine learning targeted campaigns and software optimizations. These teams typically spend more time in the analysis phase and less time coding.

Goal for Product and Infrastructure Teams

Since both the product and infrastructure teams' primary objective is to produce usable software, their goals are typically driven by new feature completion. Breaking down the required software infrastructure into smaller portions that can be completed iteratively as intermediate milestones is critical. This tracking of the overall progress is more manageable and provides opportunities for continuous testing and deployment as smaller portions of the broader features are completed. Even though the general goal is driven by feature completeness, it is still critical to define metric success criteria. Examples of this can include

1. Setting performance regression guardrail metrics for infrastructure migration

2. Arriving at service-level objectives for underlying infrastructure performance that triggers alerts if they are violated

3. Setting specific engagement guardrails for new product launches to ensure the success of new features

Goal for Metric-Driven Teams

Metric-driven teams focus more on driving specific goal metrics than engineering new features. Typically metric-driven teams

1. Spend less time and focus on engineering improvements

2. Require more time on careful data analysis for sizing
    based on past levers and intermediate metrics;
    that is, measuring session movement is complex
    and takes a long time; however, we can see that
    increased user engagement with content typically
    correlates to session gain so that we can measure
    success on user content engagement.

3. Careful analysis is required to avoid setting
    unrealistic expectations of engineers' ability to enact
    change in the system.

Why Is SDLC Important?

Software development can be challenging to manage due to changing
requirements, technology upgrades, and cross-functional collaboration
required to deliver a project. With only a handful of engineers working on a
project at a small firm, or a solo project, long-term planning is less important,
and it is much easier to drive alignment with only a few stakeholders.

As projects and teams grow, the importance of driving precise
alignment across stakeholders and communicating upward to leadership
and downward to subordinate leaders increases. Without this, it is easy
for projects to fall behind. The software development life cycle (SDLC)
methodology provides a systematic management framework with specific
deliverables at every stage of the software development process to facilitate
better tracking, communication, and deadline management.

Following the SDLC methodology promotes getting stakeholder
agreement on software development goals and having a plan to achieve
those goals. Regardless of the methods used to implement the SDLC,
following the overall steps establishes a clear framework tech leads can
utilize to deliver value and successfully lead large projects.

Here are some benefits of SDLC:

1. Increased visibility: The SDLC increases visibility across the planning and development process for all stakeholders.

2. Improved planning: Efficient estimation, planning, and scheduling.

3. Higher quality software: By systematically delivering software aligned across functions and well tested, we increase our chances of building the right software.

Some trade-offs of adopting SDLC

1. Time commitment: The SDLC increases the time and costs for project development via rigid planning and documentation, which may be detrimental for small or solo projects where this level of planning is unnecessary.

2. Increased complexity delaying releases: The SDLC forces testing and release cycle management. For large projects, thorough testing and release management should be requirements. However, simply releasing to the iOS App Store without beta testing or a complex experimentation framework may be desired for small or solo projects. Additionally, with low numbers of users, A/B testing a feature may not be possible, leading to diminished returns from this approach. Chapter 14 delves into more details on A/B testing.

Note   For most projects, following the SDLC process is an effective project-creating process to ship the best software over time efficiently.

Summary

We started this chapter by discussing the software development life cycle and the different stages. We then presented some standard methods of implementing these steps and keys to success. Zooming out, we saw a lot of overlap in these critical tenets and how, regardless of the exact methodology used, the skills required to take a project from ideation to production and continue to add value long term come down to

1. Navigate the technical problem space

2. Design and lead the technical solution

3. Communicate clearly

4. Set up appropriate goals

By doing these four things, we can succeed in any context and be flexible enough to adopt any methodology.

One aspect of leadership overlooked by the SDLC is the long-term strategy or vision for a technology area. Tech leads should look to get ahead of the SDLC by understanding the critical technical decisions and overall framework and software architecture needed to continue driving business value year after year. By focusing on the skills necessary:

1. Navigate the technical problem space

2. Design and lead the technical solution

3. Communicate clearly

4. Set up appropriate goals

Tech leads can design systems for long-term success.

Four Key Takeaways from This Chapter

1. Communication is critical. Even if you can develop the best technical solutions, you need to be able to communicate them in a way others can understand and support.

2. Business value is critical for overall company success. When thinking about technical solutions and growing a project over time, it is critical to align with business partners, understand their needs, and transform the needs into SMART goals to guide project planning.

3. The tech lead's role is essential in all aspects of the SDLC, but most important in the beginning and end. By driving the technical solution and then, in the future, establishing the launch path, you empower other engineers to grow and ensure the project aligns with the initial goals.

4. Project leadership for tech leads goes beyond the SDLC. It is essential to think several iterations ahead to form a long-term vision for the project's success.

Further Learning

1. The Mythical Man-Month: Engineering sizing and challenges

2. Extreme Ownership: Overall conflict resolution and active listening from a military leader

3. Start with Why: Simon Sinek TED talk. He keys in on a lot of principles of active listening

4. Agile Development: More information on Agile methodologies

5. A compendium of planning documents: `www.lennysnewsletter.com/p/my-favorite-templates-issue-37`

CHAPTER 12

Testability

Overview

Following the SDLC, we must begin testing after we start implementing the feature. Initial testing may involve unit tests specific to the logic built. As the feature develops and the launch date is closer, it is crucial to begin implementing more rigorous forms of testing. These should include integration tests and manual testing steps to ensure the feature development work and continue to work as more features are developed. Without comprehensive testing, building confidence in feature correctness is difficult, which poses a real risk to launching the feature.

This Chapter Includes

We will discuss the importance of testing in the SDLC and then break down different testing portions into

1. Unit testing: The minimum requirement to correctly demonstrate the logic in specific class functions.

2. UI testing: A method to verify user interface elements' layout on the screen stays consistent.

3. Integration testing: A method to show multiple components function correctly as subsystems.

© Eric Vennaro 2023
E. Vennaro, *iOS Development at Scale*, https://doi.org/10.1007/978-1-4842-9456-7_12

4. Contract testing: A type of integration testing specific to verify that the interface between two services meets the agreed-upon standards. For mobile, this is commonly the mobile client and the associated API gateway.

5. Manual testing: Beyond automated tests, we should have a physical step to verify features are working correctly. Manual testing also helps verify application interactions with the physical world work accurately.

6. Managing a giant test suite: At scale, there are too many tests to run all of them all the time. We must decide what frequency to run tests and which tests are most important.

Why Test

As software engineers, we aim to iterate on and complete features contributing to company goals as quickly as possible. To continuously deliver quality code, it is necessary to ensure the code is easy to understand and bug-free. Testing encourages both and promotes overall quality code. When testing best practices are applied across the code base, they promote

1. Fast feature development

2. Fewer bugs

3. Faster bug detection

These aspects are increasingly important at scale as the amount of legacy code and the number of engineers working concurrently on the application increase. With a smaller application, it is relatively easy to understand the different functionality and code paths; however, in a more extensive application, it is easier to run into code paths that have not been modified in years. In addition, at large-scale companies, there may be shared libraries where a small change could affect many application areas or other applications utilizing shared code. Since it is impossible to manually test all potential use cases, we need a combination of manual and automated tests.

Manual testing provides a way to test real-world feature interactions and validate scenarios end to end. Manual tests are especially important for user-facing features requiring interactions with the physical world. Even though many gestures and events are automatable, it is difficult or impossible for them to capture the overall user experience, including animation fluidity. Additionally, manual testing allows testers to explore new combinations of interactions, something that would otherwise require new testing scripts. Automated testing does; however, present a way to quickly test many different scenarios and provide quick feedback to verify software logic correctness.

Both manual and automated tests present unique challenges.

1. Testing UI code is complex. UI testing involves verifying the interface layout and animations are correct; this requires complex scripts that are difficult to update and/or actual manual testing.

2. Xcode is slow. Compiling and running an extensive suite of automated tests takes a long time, especially if they launch the iOS simulator.

3. Dependencies are challenging to test. UIKit and Foundation were built with a runtime whose techniques date back to the 1980s when modularity and testability were less critical than managing tight memory constraints.

4. Managing manual testing requires time and effort. Manually testing your features is relatively simple. However, constructing a coordinated effort to test critical flows for an entire application over time is more complex and requires a combined effort.

Unit Testing

Unit testing is the most basic testing type. Unit testing aims to test a specific unit of code (where a unit is loosely defined). For any feature developed, essential logic should have associated unit testing. Not all code should require unit tests. Unit tests should cover all possible code paths, not just the success path. Additionally, we only want our tests to fail when the class under test changes, not when any changes occur to underlying dependencies. We do not want our tests to fail when

1. Someone adds a bug to an unrelated class

2. The outside world (the file system, network, etc.) is unavailable

3. Persistent settings or other dependencies change underneath us

Unit tests are most critical for logically complex portions of code. Well-written unit tests express the different use cases of the classes and define success and failure criteria, which helps new engineers understand those code areas. If unit tests fail due to unseen dependencies, engineers will lose confidence in the testing system and start skipping tests and ignoring failures. We want to test a class WrappedUserSettings that parses some JSON, writes the results to UserDefaults, and updates an existing dictionary with new values.

```swift
class WrappedUserSettings {
  static func updateSettings(fromJSON json: String) {
    let parser = Parser.shared
    let defaults = UserDefaults.standard
    guard var newSettings = parser.parse(
      json: json) else { return }
    if let settings = defaults.object(
      forKey: "user_data") as? [String:String] {
        newSettings.merging(settings) {
          (new, _) in new
        }
    }
    defaults.set(newSettings, forKey: "user_data")
  }
}
```

In the playground, we define a test runner and test case.

```swift
import XCTest
class TestRunner: XCTestCase {
  func testUpdateSettings() {
    let json = "{\"name\": \"steve\"}"
    WrappedUserSettings.updateSettings(fromJSON:json)
    let expected = ["name": "steve"]
    XCTAssertEqual(
      expected,
      UserDefaults.standard.object(
        forKey: "user_data") as? [String : String],
      "User defaults should contain the updated name"
    )
  }
}

TestRunner.defaultTestSuite.run()
```

413

Now, our test passes and will detect when a bug is added to the
WrappedUserSettings class. However, it will fail at the wrong times if the
simulator starts modifying the UserDefaults dictionary or if our JSON
parser were to contain a bug. If our test was an integration test, we would
want it to detect bugs in the JSON parser, but this is a unit test, so we only
want to see failures in our WrappedUserSettings class. We can illustrate
this by adding an additional test. Here, we have a test that only passes since
UserDefaults continues to store the already-added value for the name.

```
// values from the old test
func testUpdateSettingsOldShouldFail() {
  let json = "{\"email\": \"echo@gmail.com\"}"
  WrappedUserSettings().updateSettings(fromJSON:json)
  let expected = "steve"
  XCTAssertEqual(
    expected,
    (UserDefaults.standard.object(
            forKey: "user_data"
    ) as? [String : String])?["name"],
    "User defaults should contain the updated name"
  )
}
```

The preceding example is a bit contrived because we could ensure
that UserDefaults is cleared out before starting each test; however, if our
code was more complex, it is possible another aspect of the code could
modify UserDefaults at test runtime. In general, by not mocking our
dependencies, we create a scenario where external factors could influence
our testing.

Anytime bugs in a class are detected by a different class's unit test;
we see incorrect behavior that could require complex debugging. So how
do we prevent this? We can utilize dependency injection to control all
dependent objects used by our class, allowing us fine-grained control

over all dependency behaviors. We could use a mocking library such as Mockingbird to support this behavior or create mock objects ourselves. If your code base does not have classes that conform to protocols, it may be easier to utilize a mocking library. A mocking library can also help mock classes like UserDefaults. The existing dependency injection setup will help guide your choices on mocking options. Here, we will create the mocks without using an external library by ensuring all objects conform to a specific protocol.

```
protocol ParserProto {
  func parse(json: String) -> [String: String]?
}
```

Of course, we must also adapt our WrappedUserSettingsUpdated to accept our dependencies via the initializer.

```
class WrappedUserSettingsUpdated {
  private let parser: ParserProto
  private let defaults: UserDefaults

  init(
    jsonParser: ParserProto,
    standard: UserDefaults
  ) {
    self.parser = jsonParser
    self.defaults = standard
  }

  func updateSettings(fromJSON json: String) {
    guard let newSettings = parser.parse(
      json: json) else { return }
    if var settings = defaults.object(
      forKey: "user_data") as? [String:String] {
        newSettings.merge(settings) {
```

415

```
        (new, _) in new
      }
    }
    defaults.set(newSettings, forKey: "user_data")
  }
}
```

We also need to mock the UserDefaults object. To do so, we first create a protocol with the UserDefaults values we utilize.

```
protocol UserDefaultsProto {
  func object(forKey defaultName: String) -> Any?
  func set(_ value: Any?, forKey defaultName: String)
}
```

Now we ensure UserDefaults conforms to our protocol.

```
extension UserDefaults: UserDefaultsProto {}
```

Lastly, we must update all our call sites to utilize our new protocol, such as

```
private let defaults: UserDefaultsProto
```

We can proceed with our tests now that we have updated our code. First, we will create the necessary mocks to ensure we have fine-grained control over our unit tests. First, the parser:

```
class MockParser: ParserProto {
  var parseResult: [String: String]?

  func parse(json: String) -> [String: String]? {
    return parseResult
  }
}
```

And now the UserDefaults mock:

```
class MockUserDefaults: UserDefaultsProto {
  var values: [String:Any]?

  func object(forKey defaultName: String) -> Any? {
    return values?[defaultName]
  }

  func set(_ value: Any?, forKey defaultName: String) {
    values?[defaultName] = value
  }
}
```

Finally, we can update our tests, including an additional test case showing that we no longer suffer from the carryover effect. Here, we also utilize the setUp method, which runs before each test case, ensuring that the tests start from a known, predictable state.

```
class TestRunner: XCTestCase {
  private var userDefaults: MockUserDefaults!
  private var userSettings: WrappedUserSettingsUpdated!
  private var mockParser: MockParser!

  // runs the setup methods once before each test
  // method starts
  override func setUp() {
    userDefaults = MockUserDefaults()
    userDefaults.values = [String:Any]()
    mockParser = MockParser()
    userSettings = WrappedUserSettingsUpdated(
      jsonParser: mockParser,
      standard: userDefaults)
    mockParser.parseResult = nil
  }
```

```swift
// Test's with the new setup, we are confident
// the only key in the dictionary is name
func testUpdateSettingsNew() {
  mockParser.parseResult = ["name": "jim"]
  let json = "{\"name\": \"jim\"}"
  userSettings.updateSettings(fromJSON:json)
  let expected = ["name": "jim"]
  XCTAssertEqual(
    expected,
    userDefaults.object(
      forKey: "user_data") as? [String : String],
    "User defaults should contain the updated name"
  )
}

func testUpdateSettingsFails() {
  let json = "{\"name\": \"steve\"}"
  mockParser.parseResult = ["name": "billy bob"]
  userSettings.updateSettings(fromJSON:json)
  let expected = ["name": "steve"]
  XCTAssertNotEqual(
    expected,
    userDefaults.object(
      forKey: "user_data") as? [String : String],
    "User defaults should contain the updated name"
  )
}

// we do not have a carry over effect anymore and
// the result is not equal
func testUpdateSettingsCarryoverEffect() {
  let json = "{\"name\": \"steve\"}"
```

```
      mockParser.parseResult = ["email": "billy bob"]
      userSettings.updateSettings(fromJSON:json)
      let expected = ["name": "steve"]
      XCTAssertNotEqual(
        expected,
        userDefaults.object(
          forKey: "user_data") as? [String : String],
        "User defaults should contain the updated name"
      )
    }
}
/** Test Output
Test Suite 'TestRunner' started at 2023-06-10 16:45:55.995
Test Case '-[__lldb_expr_1.TestRunner
testUpdateSettingsCarryoverEffect]' started.
Test Case '-[__lldb_expr_1.TestRunner
testUpdateSettingsCarryoverEffect]' passed (0.027 seconds).
Test Case '-[__lldb_expr_1.TestRunner testUpdateSettingsFails]'
started.
Test Case '-[__lldb_expr_1.TestRunner testUpdateSettingsFails]'
passed (0.011 seconds).
Test Case '-[__lldb_expr_1.TestRunner testUpdateSettingsNew]'
started.
Test Case '-[__lldb_expr_1.TestRunner testUpdateSettingsNew]'
passed (0.001 seconds).
Test Case '-[__lldb_expr_1.TestRunner testUpdateSettingsOld]'
started.
Test Case '-[__lldb_expr_1.TestRunner testUpdateSettingsOld]'
passed (0.003 seconds).
Test Case '-[__lldb_expr_1.TestRunner
testUpdateSettingsOldShouldFail]' started.
```

```
Test Case '-[__lldb_expr_1.TestRunner
testUpdateSettingsOldShouldFail]' passed (0.001 seconds).
Test Suite 'TestRunner' passed at 2023-06-10 16:45:56.040.
    Executed 5 tests, with 0 failures (0 unexpected) in 0.043
    (0.045) seconds
**/
```

Now we have a full array of unit tests with no external dependencies! The set of unit tests we produced has the added benefit of easily explaining the system to any new developer. A unit test suite should include every possible use case of the function or API. It is a living source of documentation.

Imagine you are working at a large tech company and trying to integrate with another team's underlying library for AR effects. Now the team may have written documentation, but documentation can quickly get out of date. Instead, you view their API unit tests. These tests include every API, every use case for the API, and clear success and failure criteria allowing you to easily understand how to use the API and integrate it into your code. While the tests do not provide a high-level overview of the library, they provide a low-level understanding of the internal implementation.

Writing Code That Stays Testable

When writing tests, we must consider long-term maintainability. Otherwise, we can end up with many flaky (a flaky test yields both passing and failing results even with no code, or test, changes) and broken tests that engineers ignore. We follow the Law of Demeter to ensure our code is consistently testable; loosely coupled, well-tested classes should only know their immediate dependencies.[1] Unit tests that rely on other classes make the code brittle and testing complex. To illustrate this, we have the following delegate method that creates a Photo Stream unit and adds the ability to react to a story. Here, we both instantiate the reaction object and execute the like method.

```
func didPressLike(
  with reactable: ReactablePhotoStreamStory
) {
  let reactionManager = ReactionManager(
    userId: currentUser
  )
  reactionManager.likeStory(reactable)
}
```

Instead, we can modify the method and surrounding class so that the method only does one thing.

```
init(reactionManager: ReactionManager) {
  self.reactionManager = reactionManager
}
```

```
func didPressLike(
  with reactable: ReactablePhotoStreamStory
) {
  reactionManager.likeStory(reactable)
}
```

Now we have a reusable and testable class in the ReactionManager. We can simplify the testing of both this and the initial classes since we are no longer concerned with external dependencies.

---

[1] K. J. Lieberherr and I. M. Holland, "Assuring good style for object-oriented programs," in *IEEE Software*, vol. 6, no. 5, pp. 38–48, Sept. 1989, doi: 10.1109/52.35588.

Setter Injection

In this book, we have used constructor injection throughout to inject our dependencies. Another option is setter injection; with setter injection, an object exposes setter methods to override parts of the object's behavior. We can change our class earlier to remove the initializer and utilize properties instead. Since the property is public, we can modify the dependency externally. Alternatively, one could create a public setter and private property.

```
class WrappedUserSettingsUpdated {
  var userDefaults: UserDefaultsProtocol = UserDefaults.
  standard
}
```

Setter injection does require that every test knows how to override all the behaviors of each dependency of the class under test. For example, a dependency may access a database today, and you can override the behavior in a test environment. Tomorrow, that same dependency may access the network to download information. This change may not cause the test to fail initially. Eventually, if run in an environment with no network access (or unreliable network access), the test may begin to fail. This behavior creates a brittle test environment prone to flaky tests.

The fragile test environment created by setter injection is magnified over time in large-scale applications as more functionality is added. For example, an engineer may modify an object to include network access and cause failures in unrelated parts of the code base requiring a complicated debugging effort in unfamiliar code. This is why we suggest using constructor injection.

Integration Testing

Unit testing is an excellent way to ensure that individual code units work and provide living documentation of the program's internals. However, it does not account for complex interactions between components. Unit tests have limited value in ensuring the overall application functions correctly. Ensuring flows work together is the job of integration testing. While more expensive to write, integration tests are excellent for ensuring application correctness.

The general purpose of integration testing is to test the code without mocking dependencies to test how different components interact and ensure they work together to deliver the end user the correct result. Typically, at some level, mocks still exist. For example, a basic integration test could involve purposely changing our earlier unit test to use the underlying UserDefaults implementation. By not mocking the UserDefaults, we can ensure that end to end our system functions.

Integration tests for iOS can go beyond testing iOS-level components like UserDefaults and expand to cover network or other peripheral interactions. An integration test could consume live data from the server and test the application interactions to ensure the UI is appropriately displayed. Some teams mock data at the application's data layer instead of receiving live data from the server. This can help prevent unintended changes and reduces third-order effects like a poor network connection. The level of mocking will largely depend on the setup of the application and build pipeline; there is no one answer for how to write integration tests. When considering whether to utilize live data or mocks, it is essential to consider a few trade-offs:

1. Speed: Mocked data is often faster to retrieve and utilize since it does not require network access. When tests execute quickly, it is considerably easier to run them frequently, creating a quicker feedback loop for engineers.

2. Reliability: Using live data introduces additional complexity and failure points because it requires network connectivity to a back-end service.

3. Data consistency: Detecting when the live data changes and updating the associated mocks are complex and create inconsistency in test setups.

4. Test data management: Having a large amount of mocked test data requires some system to manage them. Data can be kept in human-readable formats like JSON and an understandable file hierarchy, making modifying and adding new test data seamless.

5. Dynamic data: Complex application flows can require multiple steps and specific data interactions depending on how your team manages test data. This can become complex and requires additional test data for each step in the flow.

6. Testing edge cases: Using mock data makes it easy to control edge case scenarios and specifically test them. With live data, edge cases can be more challenging to capture.

In addition to more traditional integration tests, services exist to provide automated integration tests, including UI. They provide a way to perform application testing on a wide range of devices and configurations, to understand how it will react for a range of users. The remote device farm has the added benefit of running on real devices with actual configurations. Given the UI-focused iOS applications, accurate UI integration testing is critical. However, they are less performant and require extra work to execute in parallel performantly.

Companies have invested in AI-based solutions to create more intelligent UI-focused automated testers. One such automated solution is Sapienz. Sapienz is an AI-based integration testing tool developed by Facebook to lessen the burden of manual testing and provide a frictionless way to manage integration testing. Sapienz works by sampling the space of all possible tests using search-based software testing.[2] Search-based software testing uses a meta-heuristic optimizing search technique, such as a genetic algorithm, to automate or partially automate a testing task.[3] Sapienz searches the application via UI interactions, builds a model of the system under test, and remembers valuable test cases for future reuse.

Sapienz tests through UI interactions, which guarantee that all issues Sapienz reports to engineers are found through the UI. Sapienz runs as part of continuous integration at Facebook and automatically designs, runs, and reports the results of tens of thousands of test cases daily, assisting engineers in discovering bugs in near real-time.[4]

Instead of building an automated tool like Sapienz and integrating it into an automated testing infrastructure to support distributed testing at scale, many companies opt to use an existing third-party device farm. A device farm is a common name for an automated testing infrastructure that leverages real devices for testing. To avoid building a device lab with massive up-front and ongoing maintenance costs, companies utilize existing cloud-based providers such as Google's Firebase Test Lab or Microsoft's App Center Test to provide a more cost-effective alternative to developing an in-house tool like Sapienz.

---

[2] https://engineering.fb.com/2018/05/02/developer-tools/
sapienz-intelligent-automated-software-testing-at-scale/

[3] P. McMinn, "Search-Based Software Testing: Past, Present and Future," *2011 IEEE Fourth International Conference on Software Testing, Verification and Validation Workshops*, Berlin, Germany, 2011, pp. 153–163, doi: 10.1109/ICSTW.2011.100.

[4] https://engineering.fb.com/2018/05/02/developer-tools/
sapienz-intelligent-automated-software-testing-at-scale/

Contract Testing

A contract test is a style of integration testing that tests the boundary of an external service verifying that it meets the contract expected by a consuming service.[5] Since these tests are based on specific changes to the API contract between server and client, they do not necessarily need to be run at the same cadence as other tests, potentially only once per day or when specific contract changes are detected. Contract testing helps to answer the following questions:

1. Does the consumer code make the expected request?

2. Does the consumer correctly handle the desired response?

3. Does the provider handle the expected request?

4. Does the provider return the expected response?

However, contract tests will not answer the question: Does the provider do the right thing with the request? This is the responsibility of other functional integration tests.

A failure in a contract test should not necessarily break the build the same way a functional integration test would. It should, however, trigger a task to the appropriate owner to further triage the inconsistency and address the gap. Fixing a broken contract test may involve updating the tests and code to achieve a consistent result. It will likely also start a conversation between service owners to discuss the change and ensure a mutual understanding of the downstream effects of the change. If the contract test is run before landing changes, it should block land to guarantee that service owners discuss any breaking changes and address them before landing the code.

---

[5] https://martinfowler.com/bliki/ContractTest.html

One option for contract testing is via Pacts. Pacts are a consumer-driven contract testing strategy that reduces the chances of unexpected contract breaks. Consumer Pact tests assume that the provider returns the expected response for the request and attempts to answer the question: Does the consumer code correctly generate the request and handle the desired response? Figure 12-1 outlines the Pact testing flow.

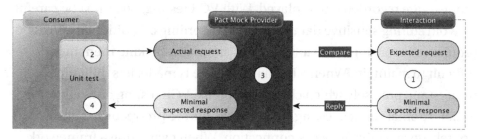

Figure 12-1. *Pact testing flow[6]*

1. The Pact DSL is used to define the expected request and response conditions that are registered with the mock service.

2. The consumer test code triggers a request to the mock provider created by the Pact framework.

3. The mock provider compares the actual request with the expected request. If the comparison is successful, it sends the expected response.

4. Lastly, the consumer test code verifies if the response was correctly understood.[7]

Many mobile applications now leverage GraphQL because GraphQL provides a type-safe, understandable, and easily modifiable domain-specific language for requesting data. If your application is leveraging

---

[6] https://docs.pact.io/getting_started/how_pact_works
[7] https://docs.pact.io/getting_started/how_pact_works

GraphQL, you can still utilize contract testing via Pacts. This is because GraphQL is just an abstraction over REST where requests are made via an HTTP POST and queries are formatted as stringified JSON within a query property of the request.[8]

An alternative to Pact testing's client-driven approach is to use VCRs. VCRs present a version of contract testing where the server-side HTTP requests are recorded and replayed. With VCR testing, one must be careful to avoid storing sensitive data in the VCR recordings. Additionally, VCRs require re-recording when any changes are made, making them more difficult to maintain. When a breaking change is made, it is difficult to understand precisely which clients will break. VCR testing does allow for easier external service testing since the results are pre-recorded and do not rely on an active network connection. When evaluating a framework, weighing the pros and cons of the different frameworks and choosing the one that best suits your application's needs are essential.

UI Testing

In iOS applications, the user interface and interactions are essential to the function of the application. Hence, testing the user interface and interactions is very important. Testing the application interface presents several challenges. It is difficult to keep UI tests current, and they can take longer to run, even when executed remotely. Running the tests remotely and prioritizing running them on the most critical flows are necessary to support UI testing at scale. In addition to UI integration tests discussed earlier, we can leverage snapshot tests to provide UI coverage.

---

[8] https://graphql.org/learn/queries/

Snapshot Testing

Snapshot testing takes a screenshot "snapshot" view of the user interface on different screens and compares them on a pixel regression basis. Snapshot tests verify the appearance of views and help identify visual regressions without tedious manual testing. Utilizing a distributed build system where every run instantiates all snapshot test cases helps support running many snapshot tests.

Manual Testing

While having a host of intelligent automated testing is essential, these tools only partially replace manual testing. Manual testing provides a gold standard for testing specific application flows and identifying errors. Additionally, this book includes dogfooding and early releases as manual testing. Dogfooding, having employees utilize beta applications before shipping, and shipping an early release to only a subset of consumers provide real-time manual testing feedback on the product before fully releasing. Dogfooding can be built and distributed as part of the iOS build system. At some intervals before submission for release to Apple, the build can be sent to all employees for usage if bugs are detected; they can be sent to team POCs for further triaging. Typically teams assign a rotating POC to handle such issues and refer to this as an oncall rotation (we will discuss the oncall pipeline and build system construction more in subsequent chapters).

It is not always practical to have the entire company dogfood the product. Your product may be geared toward construction companies, and the application itself is of limited usage to employees daily. In that case, organizing targeted dogfooding sessions before the feature release is more important. By scheduling a block of time for the entire team, not just engineers, to go through the project and explore the functionality, you can get early feedback on any issues and the overall feature design. You can receive holistic feedback from different perspectives by involving other business partners, such as product managers, designers, and others. To expedite and focus the dogfooding session, provide any login credentials for test accounts, dummy credit card numbers, or other necessary setup steps that other nontechnical team members may struggle with prior to the session. Additionally, by providing instructions on what feature is under test and critical success criteria, you can help further drive the discussion.

Having a quality assurance (QA) team is another way to add more manual application testing into the flow. QA testers receive clear, actionable test plans from engineers and will execute many different testing scenarios to understand and document bugs they find. Many QA teams will also perform exploratory testing beyond the initial cases and attempt to break the application, which is incredibly useful for building a robust product. Testers should provide detailed reports of how to reproduce the bug they find and a screen capture of what they viewed.

How much your company and application utilize automated tests vs. manual tests is up for debate and dramatically changes depending on the application and company culture. Automated testing provides a hands-off approach that avoids time-intensive and potentially expensive contracts with QA teams (or in-house staff). However, automated testing does not offer a real-world experience of using the application, and while tests should be fast and accurate, this is not always the case. Relying solely on automated tests may cause bugs to go unnoticed until right before or even right after release. Moreover, complex automated integration tests can become expensive to run due to device farm costs. By integrating manual testing into the feature development and release process and automated build pipeline, teams can take advantage of both automated testing and rigorous manual testing.

Manual testing is not without problems; detailed test plans must be maintained and updated; otherwise, QA resources spend time testing the wrong thing. Additionally, exploratory testing may yield a lot of low-value bugs – or experiences that are not bugs at all but just odd edge cases missing from the product specification delivered to the QA team. Triaging these bug reports takes time away from engineers who prefer to build features. By weighing the pros and cons, understanding the options available, and carefully considering the application's needs, you can make a suitable investment in both manual and automated testing.

To assist in this, running a cost-benefit analysis on when bugs are detected, by whom, how many bugs there are, and how much time engineers spend manually testing features helps evaluate where to put future testing investments. For example, if many bugs are found by engineers in dogfooding sessions days before a feature release, then integrating manual testing sooner is best. However, if many bugs are found in mostly older features due to changes introduced in newer features, then more automated integration and unit tests will help catch these. Of course, manual QA can also perform long-term testing of key flows to ensure they are always correct.

Managing Testing at Scale

When looking to manage a large suite of automated tests, engineers will inevitably run into the situation where Xcode is too slow to run all automated tests locally and even too slow in continuous integration prior to landing diffs. This is especially true for UI tests where the simulator is set up. Given that we want our automated tests to run quickly to provide real-time feedback to engineers, we need to prioritize specific test cases based on the following aspects:

1. Business impact

2. Critical features

3. Frequently used functionalities

4. Complex implementation

5. Buggy areas of the software

Test Case Prioritization

Given overall priority, we can run the most critical tests more often while minimizing the time and cost of running lower-value tests. To help understand how different features fit into the five aspects listed previously, we can first evaluate the application's main components to understand which ones are critical to the business. The features critical to the business should include anything related to the central business use case; common business-critical features include

1. Account management

2. Payments flow

3. Onboarding flow

Besides the main features, it is important to assess other utility features that are frequently used. For example, shared preferences and settings users change to include themes or language (localization) are also crucial for test coverage.

Despite prioritizing automated test cases, some application flows are not good candidates for automated integration tests. A flow involving third-party interactions, such as interacting with a payment gateway that is not easy to mock, presents a problematic situation for integration testing of different failure and success cases, or maybe situations requiring notification handling or interaction with the physical world. To handle these cases, we can prioritize manual testing.

After understanding how and what test cases need prioritizing, we can categorize them into test suites, where a test suite is a collection of similar test cases. For instance, we might have an application performance test suite or a critical flows test suite based on the test cases we prioritized earlier.

Categorizing Test Suites

By categorizing tests into suites (test bundles in Xcode), we can better understand when and how frequently they should be run. For instance, if we define a critical flows test suite, we can run this before any changes are landed to the main application. Or we can define a contract testing suite that only runs when API changes are detected. This way, we do not run the contract tests unnecessarily but do run them at critical times. Identifying necessary tests to run before landing specific diffs also creates a higher standard for code and allows teams to define tests whose failure should block code from landing.

By creating test suites, we also have finer-grained control over the runtime of specific test bundles. We can establish goals and ensure that test time does not exceed them, which forces us to prioritize which tests are run at which time. With Xcode, we also can define tests that require the simulator and those that do not. This information is then fed into the CI scripts set up to understand how to parallelize tests best. The parallel execution of tests is essential for UI tests because UI tests need to run on actual iOS devices or iOS simulators, resulting in longer execution times.

In addition to splitting tests into subsets and running each in a separate CI job, we can also use the Xcode parallel testing to achieve parallelism within one single CI job. However, parallel testing in the same bundle can constrain us to the runtime of the most extended test in the bundle.

Regardless of parallelization techniques, it is not possible at scale to run all tests before land. It is possible for a build to break the broader automated testing system that is not run at the time your change is being merged with the main application branch, creating a complex scenario where it is unclear what change broke the build. Quickly unblocking builds on failure is a tough challenge and often requires a unique oncall setup. The oncall will be notified whenever a build failure is detected and be responsible for debugging that changeset to revert the offending code.

Since we cannot fully cover the application with automated tests, we must also understand how to prioritize manual testing.

Prioritizing Manual Testing

Manual testing can suffer from similar issues to the automated testing problems outlined previously. Covering the application 100% via manual testing is inefficient and impractical. To avoid spending inordinate resources to cover the entire application, we can again prioritize the most important flows for continued coverage while dropping manual coverage for less critical components. The lower-priority areas can be covered by automated tests (potentially running less frequently).

When developing new features, we can ramp up manual testing to ensure that each iterative release is correct and our SDLC iterations lead up to a successful launch. Once the feature launches, we can scale back manual testing to a few critical flows or none at all, depending on the feature priority.

Managing Testing Over Time

Hopefully, we detect failures before merging our feature branch into the broader application branch; however, this does not always happen. Sometimes, failures are not detected until later via manual testing, dogfooding-reported bugs, or automated tests run on a less frequent cadence. Regardless of where the testing failure is reported, we need a universal way to detect and assign testing failures to the correct person for triage, prioritization, and distribution. Lastly, we must ensure that company-critical bugs are fixed before the build release. To accomplish this, we can set up a systematic continuous build system with release dates and checklists. We will discuss this in more detail in Chapter 16 as the last step in the SDLC.

What If I Have No Tests?

Inheriting a complex application with little to no tests is a difficult situation. First, justifying taking the necessary time to refactor the application and add tests can be difficult. Assuming you can prioritize this work by explaining the long-term value and developer happiness, you must consider how to execute the migration. If the code is built in a testable manner, it may be relatively easy to add tests. However, if the code is not, you must refactor the application to support better testing. In this situation, it may be best to start with unit tests that do not take external dependencies (where available) and, if possible, write integration tests (potentially using UI testing) to cover the key flows before refactoring the code in a more testable manner. The integration tests will provide a relative safety net to ensure that crucial application features are not broken during the migration.

Summary

Throughout this chapter, we covered testing in iOS applications. Testing should not be a static step in the SDLC; instead, it should be performed throughout as new features are developed and include testing on existing features to avoid regressions. Here, we broke down testing into automated testing and manual testing. To successfully test our application, we need both automated tests to provide fast, actionable feedback and a way to run many tests without huge human resource costs. However, they do not address all situations (even with wins in AI-based automated UI tests), and this is where manual testing shines.

Manual testing is critical for iOS applications because it allows them to test their interaction with physical world components such as the camera input (QR code recognition), document scanning, or augmented reality. While it is possible to automate many of the tests, manual testing is still required to fully understand the applications' performance.

Four Key Takeaways from This Chapter

1. Automated and manual tests are needed; balancing the two requires careful trade-off analysis and application understanding.

2. Managing testing goes beyond writing unit tests or just performing manual tests before release. It is a continuous process that needs to be connected with the release pipeline and proper oncall engineers for triaging and fixing.

3. Treat tests as first-class citizens in the software system. Quality testing contributes to overall code quality and is necessary to move fast at scale.

4. It is critical to involve manual testing via QA and automated tests as early as possible in the development process to ensure the application is tested continuously.

Further Learning

1. Hands-On Mobile App Testing: A Guide for Mobile Testers and Anyone Involved in the Mobile App Business by Daniel Knott

CHAPTER 13

Performance

Overview

Application performance does not fit neatly into the SDLC; some portion of performance via load testing could fit into the test phase. However, managing overall application performance over time does not have a designated step. Despite this, application performance is especially important in larger applications with many existing users and features.

Too often, when engineers discuss application performance, they only focus on application crashes and recommend using instruments to debug further. However, application performance is more than that. Application performance involves ensuring over the application's life span; it speedily renders the UI, handles poor network connectivity, and loads quickly at application start. Performance becomes increasingly complex as additional features are developed in large applications where overall performance can degrade slowly with no apparent root cause.

This Chapter Includes

We will discuss an overall view of application performance and why it is essential and requires prioritization through different stages of the SDLC. We will discuss the areas of application performance, techniques and strategies to address these, and some of the tools we, engineers, need to be familiar with to address performance problems at scale. Since

© Eric Vennaro 2023
E. Vennaro, *iOS Development at Scale*, https://doi.org/10.1007/978-1-4842-9456-7_13

most large companies utilize custom tools, we will focus on the classes of performance problems and understanding performance metrics with less focus on becoming a power user of a specific set of tools.

An additional aspect of performance is build performance. As an application scales, the overall application size can become quite large, and compiling the entire application for each run can become unmanageable. Compiler optimizations are available to speed up build times. Additionally, developers can make applications more modular so that they only need to build a subset of the application instead of waiting for the entire application to build. This chapter will only focus on end-user performance metrics, not build performance.

Why Performance Matters

Application performance is critical to providing a positive user experience. iOS users have high standards for their applications, and slow and unresponsive applications cause consumers to abandon them. Users expect modern applications to start instantly and always have responsive user interfaces. Even though modern iOS hardware can handle a range of sophisticated memory-intensive operations, it is still important to track performance. If the application looks and feels responsive, it is easier to keep users engaged.

With a larger-scale application, it is common for performance issues to creep in over time due to compounding effects of different features and legacy code impacting users' perception of the application and company brand. Even if the performance appears fast, developers must watch for battery consumption. No one likes using an application that drains their battery. Using a data-driven approach, we can evaluate application performance continuously and look to improve it.

iOS Factors to Consider

To build a data-driven approach to evaluating iOS performance, we need to

1. Identify key drivers of performance – our topline performance metrics.

2. Identify intermediate metrics that act as leading indicators for the performance metric defined in step 1. Good intermediate metrics are metrics whose movement is highly correlated with a similar trend in a topline metric.

3. Identify the second-order effects of improving our performance metrics. Typically second-order effects are observed in engagement and business metrics.

When evaluating performance metrics, it is vital to consider them and the associated business (engagement) metrics. One way to increase the priority of performance work and prioritize it for teams is by understanding and building a relationship between performance improvements and business impact. Performance improvements commonly correlate to increased user engagement, for example, if, through past launches, your team has linked a 5% reduction in startup time to a 1% increase in session. You can quickly scope future performance improvements related to session gain (assuming session gain is a crucial engagement metric).

Key Concepts

This chapter will discuss critical metrics (commonly referred to as topline metrics) to guide application performance tuning and measurement tools to help find and address performance issues. Before proceeding, we also need to clarify a few essential concepts that provide an overall methodology for evaluating application performance over time.

1. Topline metrics: Topline metrics are the company's critical metrics for decision-making. They may directly link to performance or indirectly through performance effect on business use cases. We will dive deep into performance metrics in the next section.

2. Intermediate metrics: Intermediate metrics are metrics whose movement links to a similar change in topline metrics. In most cases, intermediate metrics are more sensitive and provide a fast way to detect a potential shift in a topline metric.

3. Funnel logging: Funnel logging provides a detailed look into the intermediate metrics assisting in debugging and understanding. Intermediate metrics for funnel logging are specific metrics captured between the event's start and the end, where the end is the capture point of the topline metric.

4. Evaluating percentiles: By assessing performance using real-world application data formed into percentiles, we build an understanding of our application's performance and can uncover exciting areas of opportunity.

5. Monitoring: Monitoring includes building dashboards and alerts to track performance regressions. Monitoring allows engineers to track application performance over time and ensure new features do not cause unintended regressions.

Topline Metrics

These are the most critical metrics for the company. While sometimes requiring significant underlying changes to show movement, topline metrics are always essential for reporting and are the overall metrics relied upon the most for accurate reporting for investor and shareholder meetings. Topline metrics are typically related to revenue and user engagement. However, they can be related to whatever drives business growth and success.

Topline metrics also require diligent tracking and are the subject of scrutiny across the higher echelons of the company. For example, in our Photo Stream application, our main source of revenue is ads; for that, we need a high number of daily and monthly active users. We can then break down our topline metrics into revenue, CPMs (cost per mille, an advertiser term for cost per 1000 impressions), and impressions. These provide the company with an overall view of how effective ads are and the cost per ad.

In this way, ads teams and teams related to user engagement, such as what content is displayed in the feed, will have to track their respective metrics closely for communication with business partners. Additionally, if any fluctuation is detected in these metrics, high-priority incidents will be opened in partnership with business teams. From an engineering side, these investigations will be a high priority and high visibility requiring diligent investigations and retrospectives. These investigations must account for all factors, including market dynamics and yearly trends, including how holidays affect traffic. Many times these investigations will be internal to the company.

However, there are publicly available retrospective documents for many large public-facing incidents, such as GitHub's outage, where outdated information was served to consumers.[1] For GitHub, since

---

[1] https://github.blog/2018-10-30-oct21-post-incident-analysis/

their service is paid for, they must track reliability and uptime as topline metrics. Another example of this is from a company that prioritized reliability, Cloudflare. Cloudflare tracks all incidents-related reports[2] in a clear format so clients understand the behavior of their integrations. The reports include

1. Resolution status

2. Monitoring

3. Latest status update

4. How the issue was identified

5. Investigation steps[3]

Intermediate Metrics

Since topline metrics can be challenging to move and may require much more significant changes, having a series of leading indicators is helpful, or metrics that serve as a good indicator that a topline metric is also moving. Given this information, we can improve the intermediate metric reliably while assuming the topline metric will also show positive change. Because of the difficulty in moving certain topline metrics, certain teams will take company intermediate metrics as their topline metric. For example, a team may work on increasing sharing as sharing is linked to overall increased monthly active users. While the team cannot show meaningful change in user activity each quarter, they can increase sharing.

Additionally, only viewing topline metrics can hide failure situations that intermediate metrics reveal. Lastly, intermediate metrics allow for precise estimation of topline metric movement aiding in planning and estimation work for the next development cycle.

---

[2] www.cloudflarestatus.com/history
[3] www.cloudflarestatus.com/incidents/1z125rykf9zd

Funnel Logging

When considering performance metrics, we must also consider intermediate stages in the application. Unlike the preceding stand-alone intermediate metrics, the intermediate metrics here visualize the different stages of the performance measurement and provide a funnel-like view of the problem, allowing engineers to build a holistic picture of the performance bottleneck.

An example of this style of funnel logging is when evaluating end-to-end application latency. Our topline metric is end-to-end latency (assume you are on a performance team). However, assessing solely end-to-end latency does not provide enough information to succinctly debug problems because it does not help us uncover where in our application the bottleneck is. Is it network latency? Data processing in the application? We do not know. However, if we craft intermediate metrics logged at these steps, we can understand precisely how much time each scenario takes. For example, when measuring end-to-end response time for network requests, we would start the event on the network request sent and then measure when each of the following steps completes:

1. When the request was received

2. Cache availability status

3. Data processing

4. Image loading

5. Finally, view rendering

Apple provides the Signpost API, which allows for the measurement of tasks using the identical subsystems and categories used for logging. Xcode Instruments can display data recorded via the Signpost API to the timeline view. Additionally, Signposts can be used as part of custom instruments to represent the data.[4]

---

[4] https://developer.apple.com/documentation/os/ossignposter

---

Note   Funnel logging provides visibility into each step to tell the performance at each stage and more easily identify and fix bottlenecks.

Evaluating Percentiles

Once we implement logging and understand the topline metrics, we need to understand the data we receive. For performance metrics, we need to understand the typical value that users receive. We could evaluate the average (mean), but this is susceptive to being skewed by outliers. Instead, we can utilize the median in the form of a percentile.

First, we can focus on the P50 threshold, the value at which 50% of the values exceed the threshold. As a concrete example, we have the following latency values: 20, 37, 45, 62, 850, and 920. To compute P50, we remove the bottom 50% of the data points and look at the first remaining point: 62 ms. In addition to evaluating the median value to understand the average use case, assessing the long tail of potential values is essential to understand the worst-case scenario users see. To do so, we can start with the P90 latency, meaning that the latency is expected to be less than this value 90% of the time. By removing the bottom 90% of numbers from our sample data and looking at the first point, which remains, we get 920.

By aggregating data and evaluating the typical user experience, we can better understand the experience with our application and track potential regressions. Using percentiles for this has two advantages:

1.   Outliers don't skew percentiles like averages are.

2.   Unlike averages, every percentile data point is an actual user experience.

Analyzing the P90 and P99 values allows for a better understanding of why certain users have relatively worse experiences and can reveal areas of opportunity. It is easy to overlook the P99 latency as "well, only 1% of users will ever see this." However, there is a chance that within this data lies a trend. Perhaps this 1% of users are all the same users with a common attribute. In this situation, you can significantly improve these users' experience with the application.

Monitoring and Alerting

Ad hoc queries to evaluate the different percentile values for our performance metrics are insufficient to understand application performance and prevent regression. We need to create usable alerts and metric dashboards so that engineers can understand when problems are occurring and fix them. If we know that we only expect 10% of values to be above a certain threshold and see this spike to 50%, we know we have a problem that requires fixing. To evaluate these situations, we can create dashboards of our key topline and intermediate metrics updated in near real-time. For cases where we see considerable spikes, we can trigger alerts ensuring engineers promptly address the problem.

Note   Dashboards are a critical tool in monitoring as they allow engineers to get a holistic view of the system's performance without having to run ad hoc potentially time-consuming queries. When an alert triggers, engineers can use the dashboard's intermediate metrics to start investigating where in the system the problem is located.

Engineers can quickly check overall performance and understand potential regressions by combining our intermediate metrics, funnel logging, and percentile-based understanding of intermediate and topline metrics into succinct dashboards. The percentile-based thresholds can also be used to create alerts for critical scenarios, allowing engineers to address any company-critical issues rapidly.

Note   Monitoring and alerting provide the structure for baselining application performance and creating subsequent alerts when performance diverges from the baseline.

The Complete Performance Cycle

Knowing what metrics to evaluate is only half the battle. We also must understand how these metrics and the overall ability to address performance concerns fit into the application growth trajectory from small to large.

Know Your Tools

Regardless of application size, to prevent poor performance, it is necessary to understand how to write performant code. By writing performant code, we do not mean prematurely optimizing for nonexistent use cases but instead understanding how the system functions to support regular use. For example, using reuse identifiers (now enforced) is not a premature optimization, and neither is pushing network requests to a background queue to avoid blocking the main thread. Part 1 of this book explains best practices for the Swift language and iOS concurrency frameworks. Understanding and implementing these best practices are not premature optimizations and are on individual iOS engineers to learn and senior engineers to enforce as the standard.

Beyond writing quality code, it is essential to understand the iOS build system to optimize for performance. As applications grow, the importance of keeping the application modular also increases. We can control what modules are built to reduce compile time and build size.

Note   Knowing what needs to be executed on the main thread and what does not is critical. This way, we know exactly what work is deferrable to background threads and can improve our applications' responsiveness.

Lastly, it is critical to understand the performance monitoring tools available. Xcode provides a suite of tools:

1. Instruments: A developer tool provided as part of Xcode consisting of a rich set of tools for inspecting and profiling your application.

2. MetricKit: A framework to collect battery and performance metrics from users of the production application

3. Xcode Organizer: A tool that provides aggregate hang rate data for the publicly released application

4. XCTestMetric: A framework for performance testing

In addition to those tools, there are third-party solutions such as Firebase Performance, a powerful application performance monitoring library created by Google. Regardless of the performance tools available, it is vital to understand how to leverage them best to evaluate application performance.

Note   Always profile your application on an actual device. A device has the limitations of mobile hardware, whereas the iOS simulator has the power of your Mac. By running on a simulator, you may hide performance issues that present themselves when running on a device.

Application Growth

Depressingly, the performance of an application is expected to decrease over time. Every new release cycle adds more and more features that can reduce overall performance. Often the performance difference is unnoticed and is further hidden by hardware improvements that make it possible to hide the regression.

This is the "death by 1000 cuts" principle. Engineers will say they are only adding a minor feature, which will have no performance impact. When 50 other engineers, all working on the same application, make the same claim repeatedly for years, suddenly, the performance has significantly regressed.

Having a holistic approach to performance monitoring, essential logging in place, and guardrail metrics reviewed before launching new features can avoid some performance regressions. However, performance regressions still creep in, and many companies choose to spin up dedicated performance teams to keep application performance in check.

Debugging Performance Problems

Despite our best efforts, performance problems will creep in as our application grows. So how do we debug issues as they occur? First, we must understand the available tools to assist in debugging. Launching a tool such as App Launch in Instruments and viewing the overall performance are relatively easy. However, identifying the actual bottlenecks and how to fix them is considerably more difficult. Many times, the problem is open-ended. We may be broadly trying to understand how to improve performance without having a clear starting point.

In this situation, we first need to understand where our bottlenecks are and how we can address them. In an actual project, we must

1. Understand the available tooling

2. Utilize the available tooling to find the performance bottleneck

3. Understand the overall system and how it relates to the performance bottleneck

4. Understand how we can improve this

DoorDash has an excellent blog post discussing the process their team went through to address application start. First, they utilized Emerge Tools' Performance Analysis tool to profile their application for bottlenecks. Emerge Tools provides additional granularity and a richer overall feature set than Xcode Instruments.

The DoorDash team understood and utilized the available tooling to profile their application. While profiling the application, they found that it spent excessive time checking if a type conforms to a protocol (Swift protocol conformance), illustrated in Figure 13-1. After further investigation, they discovered that using String(describing:) to identify services came with a runtime performance penalty for checking if the type conforms to various protocols.

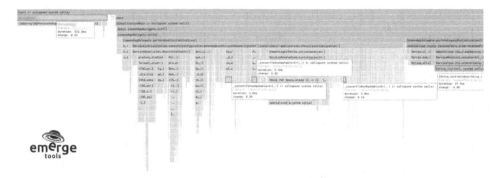

Figure 13-1. *Emerge Tools stack trace[5]*

Once the team identified the root cause, they could eliminate the string requirement and switch to identifying types using ObjectIdentifier (a pointer to the type), yielding 11% faster app startup times.[6] Figure 13-2 displays the detailed stack trace of the type checking to occur under the covers.

```
swift_conformsToProtocolMaybeInstantiateSuperclasses(swift::TargetMetadata<swift::InProcess> const*, swift::TargetPro_ptor<swift::InProcess>
swift_conformsToProtocolMaybeInstantiateSuperclasses(swift::TargetMetadata<swift::InProcess> const*, swift::TargetProtocolDescriptor<swift::I
swift_conformsToProtocolMaybeInstantiateSuperclasses(swift::TargetMetadata<swift::InProcess> const*, swift::TargetProtocolDescriptor<swift::I
swift_conformsToProtocol
swift::_conformsToProtocol(swift::OpaqueValue const*, swift::TargetMetadata<swift::InProcess> const*, _t::TargetProtocolDescriptorRef<swift::
tryCastToConstrainedOpaqueExistential(swift::OpaqueValue*, swift::TargetMetadata<swift::InProc_adata<swift::InProcess> const*6, swift::Target
tryCast(swift::OpaqueValue*, swift::TargetMetadata<swift::InProcess> const*, swift::OpaqueValu_adata<swift::InProcess> const*6, swift::Target
swift_dynamicCast
String.init<A>(describing:)
ServiceType.init<A>(describing:)                                 String.init<A>(describing:)
ServiceResolution.registerInstance<A>(_:)                        library: libswiftCore.dylib            Re_()
specialized static WebServiceMe_erService(resolver:webService:)  duration: 48.9ms                       Co_()
```

Figure 13-2. *Emerge Tools trace of String(describing:)[7]*

[5] https://doordash.engineering/2023/01/31/
how-we-reduced-our-ios-app-launch-time-by-60/

[6] https://doordash.engineering/2023/01/31/
how-we-reduced-our-ios-app-launch-time-by-60/

[7] https://doordash.engineering/2023/01/31/
how-we-reduced-our-ios-app-launch-time-by-60/

DoorDash's performance improvements are impressive. Generally, it is very optimistic to have wins of this size year over year. Instead, spending a significant amount of time finding tiny performance wins that, when stacked together, make a more substantial improvement is more common.

Apply Occam's Razor

Occam's razor is a philosophical and problem-solving principle that recommends utilizing the simplest solution constructed from the smallest possible set of elements. In the context of performance tuning and software engineers, we should take the most straightforward solution that optimizes for most use cases. We can apply Occam's razor throughout an application's life cycle to guide how we diagnose performance problems and how we consider optimizing for application performance.

When debugging and diagnosing performance problems, Occam's razor instructs us to first debug the most direct cause before focusing on more obscure reasons, such as issues with long existing code. Of course, obscure bugs do exist. We just do not want to jump to the unlikely case first.

Additionally, when writing new features, we should always look to optimize for the most common operations in an application. For example, DoorDash engineers improved the performance of their application by rethinking how they identified commands (tasks submitted for execution to a task processing engine) and generated their hash value. Initially, the hash value of a command was a combination of its associated members, which was decided as a way to maintain a flexible and powerful abstraction of commands. After adopting the new command pattern architecture, the wider team realized the design choice was premature and widely unused. By changing this requirement to a less flexible and more performant method, DoorDash followed Occam's razor and increased application start by 29%.[8]

---

[8] https://doordash.engineering/2023/01/31/
how-we-reduced-our-ios-app-launch-time-by-60/

Continuous Testing and Evaluation

Now, we know how to develop features with performance in mind (know your tools), debug problems when they occur, and optimize for the right scenarios (apply Occam's razor). The missing component is how to continuously ensure an application performs well through multiple feature development cycles. This requires performance testing and consistent evaluation. During development, it is necessary to test the effects of new features on overall application performance and the performance of the new feature being developed. Additionally, as features are released for beta testing and subsequent release, it is necessary to monitor the performance to collect real-world data beyond internal testing and profiling to evaluate regressions and overall performance.

Apple provides default tools at each stage for performance monitoring:

1. During development, Xcode Instruments provides a suite of tools for evaluating all aspects of performance, including performance testing, which is critical for essential flows. Performance testing provides an understanding of performance in an automated way to detect regressions.

2. During beta testing (including company dogfooding), Apple provides MetricKit, hang detection, and Xcode Organizer to detect performance issues.

3. Xcode provides MetricKit and Xcode Organizer to detect performance issues in production.

In addition to the provided tooling, many companies utilize custom-built solutions or third-party solutions such as Firebase and Emerge Tools. Regardless of the toolset used, the flow is similar. We will want to

1. Develop our feature with best practices and performance in mind

2. Test our feature on real devices to better detect performance issues

3. Run automated performance tests

4. Profile our application to catch any issues

5. Understand the problem in the context of our application's intended behavior

6. Make a proper fix

Note   Test early and often on older devices with minimum hardware requirements to ensure your application performs adequately across all devices.

Performance Metrics

Application Size

While application size does not affect in-app performance directly, it influences users looking to download the application. It places hard limits on users with low disk space and limited networking resources. If users run out of space on their devices, they will have to choose what applications to keep, and the largest applications are typically deleted first. No one wants their application deleted.

Beyond physical space, if your application is targeting a global reach, it is necessary to ensure that all potential users, even in rural and remote areas, can download it. Not all users have access to stable Wi-Fi or cellular data. In fact, 2022 ITU's Measuring digital development: Facts and Figures World Report reported only 89% of the world's rural population is covered by a 3G and above.[9] The report further states that

> *Nonetheless, lack of affordability continues to be a key barrier to Internet access particularly in low-income economies, even though this country group witnessed a nearly two-percentage-point drop in the income-adjusted price of mobile broadband services. A wide gap remains between high-income economies and the rest of the world. Compared to median prices that are paid in high-income economies, the [broadband] basket costs nearly 10 times as much in lower-middle-income economies and nearly 30 times as much as in low-income economies, after adjusting for differences in GNI per capita.[10]*

If you are working on an iOS application with a global reach, it is vital to account for the developing world. Given that a lot of the developing world is still unable to have the same kind of affordable access to data and the Internet, it is important to keep app size in mind to ensure all users have an opportunity to download and try the service.

Minimizing application size helps

1. Shrink the time it takes users to download the application

---

[9] www.itu.int/en/ITU-D/Statistics/Pages/facts/default.aspx
[10] www.itu.int/en/ITU-D/Statistics/Pages/facts/default.aspx

2. Allow users to download the application without a
    fast Internet connection

3. Minimize the hard drive space required to keep the
    application installed

Airbnb approached shrinking their application binary size by
compressing localization files that users are unlikely to use. This way, all
localized string files are compressed at build time and only decompressed
when needed at runtime. Secondly, Airbnb deduplicated strings by
removing those that do not translate. These optimizations helped Airbnb
reduce application size but required building a fully custom localization
system that requires maintenance and continued development work.[11,12]
With a small application, this type of optimization is not worth it; however,
as the application scales, the gains from reducing application size
outweigh the cons of maintaining a custom system.

Application Startup Time

Application startup is critical as it is the first experience the user sees when
opening your application. Application startup is so important that Apple
released official guidance in 2019 that developers should aim for rendering
the first application frame in 400 ms or less.[13]

The iOS system has three types of launches:

1. Cold start: A cold start is when the application is
    not in memory and no running process exists. This
    triggers a complete application reboot.

---

[11] https://medium.com/airbnb-engineering/
building-airbnbs-internationalization-platform-45cf0104b63c
[12] www.youtube.com/watch?v=UKqPqtvZtck
[13] https://developer.apple.com/videos/play/wwdc2019/423/

2. Warm start: A warm start is when the application
    was recently stopped and is still partially in memory
    (although no running process exists).

3. Resume: A resume is when the application is
    suspended. In the case of a resume, a running
    process exists, and the application is already entirely
    in memory.

We can think of the three different launch states as part of a spectrum.
For example, if we close and immediately re-enter the application, we will
likely trigger a resume. However, if we use a memory-intensive application,
switch to Messages to quickly reply to a message, and then re-enter the
initial application, the underlying iOS operating system may have evicted
the application from memory to allow the foreground application more
memory. This could trigger a warm start, or even a cold start. When testing
an application, we want to test under various conditions to match real-
world performance better.

Note   Do not confuse a resume with an application launch. With a
resume, the application is already launched and in memory.

We need to work within the existing iOS application startup cycle to
optimize application startup. Within the first 100 ms, iOS will perform the
necessary underlying system work to initialize the application leaving 300
ms for engineers to create the required views, load content, and establish
the first scene. The 300 ms overhead implies time is limited, and it is
critical to push work to a background queue or remove items from the
application start path. Figure 13-3 shows the application start timeline in
detail. In the first 100 ms, the system interface consisting of the runtime
linker (DYLD3), libSystemInit, and the runtime environment is initialized.

In the system interface phase, optimizations are minimal. We can, however, avoid linking unused frameworks (including third-party libraries) and hard link all dependencies to take advantage of underlying linker optimizations provided by Apple.

Following the system interface phase, the runtime init phase is where the language runtime is initialized, and all class static load methods are invoked. Here, framework optimizations can help to reduce static runtime initialization cost by reducing the impact of static initialization. This can be done by removing static initialization entirely or by moving code out of class load, which is invoked every time the application is loaded to class initialize, which is lazily invoked when the method is utilized.

Note   The Static Initializer Calls instrument measures the time your app spends running static initializers.

The second phase of the application startup (with a goal of 300 ms) contains UIKit, application, and first frame initialization. This phase represents the most prominent area for potential improvement. In the UIKit initialization phase, there is potential for optimization if the UIApplicationDelegate class is heavily utilized for code that is non-essential to startup. Again it is best practice to restrict code in the UIApplicationDelegate to only logic essential for application start. In application initialization, we want to identify work that can be deferred to background threads or entirely removed from the startup initialization. Lastly, for first frame rendering, we want to optimize the first frame by flattening the view hierarchy and lazily loading any views not shown during launch.

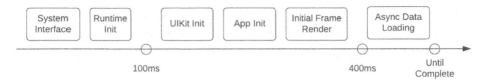

Figure 13-3. *Application startup path*

Now that we understand our goals and guardrails, we need to profile our application to understand how it measures up. To profile our application, we can utilize the App Launch template in Instruments. Some best practices for profiling startup time are as follows:

1. Reboot and let the system reach equilibrium to avoid variance.

2. Reduce network dependency by enabling airplane mode, mocking the network for a consistent connection, and removing the reliance on iCloud (or ensuring no iCloud data has changed).

3. Use a release build of the application to ensure the real compile-time optimizations are included.

4. Profile a warm start to help ensure system-side services are running in a consistent state and avoid the variance associated with a cold start.

5. Utilize the oldest supported devices since they are the least powerful.

The preceding steps help to create a consistent baseline for performance profiling. Sometimes, we may want to vary conditions, such as a warm vs. cold start, or simulate a bad network connection. Establishing a consistent baseline with the preceding steps is best before trying advanced situational testing.

Once the application is released, we can utilize metrics either from MetricKit or other third-party services to monitor application startup time for real-world use cases.

Application Responsiveness (Hangs)

An application that responds quickly to user interactions, including touches and gestures, makes users feel that they are directly manipulating the items on the screen. Applications that lag create frustration as the application appears uncontrollable. Application lag is commonly referred to as a hang. According to Apple, a delay of over one second will always look like a hang and a shorter delay may be perceived as one depending on the situation.[14] For example, a half-second delay while scrolling is jarring and may be received as a hang even though it will not if it takes half a second to load a view.

Additionally, a lack of responsiveness reduces user trust and signals that the application does not work well. Users are quite perceptive and notice small differences requiring applications to respond within a tenth of a second. Common areas susceptible to hangs include view loading, view updates, and scroll rate, making it critical to have performance testing and performance logging for these areas.

Common causes of application hangs are as follows:

1. Using the wrong API, such as using the CPU to perform expensive graphic manipulation

2. Incorrectly using the main thread, such as having the main thread of the application make network requests

---

[14] https://developer.apple.com/videos/play/wwdc2021/10258/

3. Performing synchronous updates on long-running
    processes, such as making asynchronous operations
    run synchronously via a concurrency primitive such
    as a semaphore

Engineers should reduce main thread usage by properly leveraging
concurrency tools and caching to avoid expensive recomputation.
Additionally, engineers should research APIs before implementation to
ensure the most performant ones are utilized. We should "know our tools."

In addition to "knowing our tools," we also need to profile and detect
hangs in our application. Xcode provides three helpful tools:

1. Time Profiler.

2. System Trace.

3. Xcode provides the Thread Performance Checker
    tool in the Diagnostics section of the scheme. To
    detect priority inversions and non-UI work on
    your application's main thread, enable the Thread
    Performance Checker tool from the Diagnostics
    section of the appropriate scheme (enabled in
    Figure 13-4).

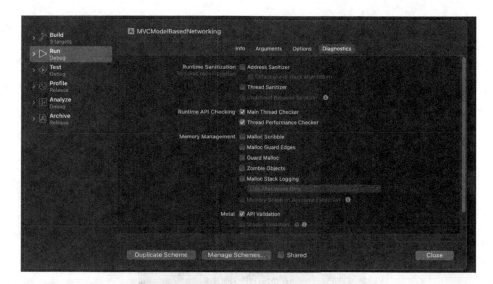

Figure 13-4. *Scheme with the Thread Performance Checker enabled*

Once the application ships, we can use our monitoring and alerting to detect hangs. We can use out-of-the-box Apple solutions on device hang detection, MetricKit, and Xcode Organizer.

1. MetricKit is the out-of-the-box solution provided by Apple. MetricKit supports collecting nonaggregated hang rate metrics and diagnostic reports from individual users on your beta or public release app.[15]

2. XCode Organizer provides an aggregate hang rate metric for users of the publicly released application.

---

[15] https://developer.apple.com/videos/play/wwdc2022/10082

3. On-device hang detection provides on-device notifications with feedback when hangs are detected in beta mode. On-device hang detection utilizes a low-priority queue in the background to avoid affecting the application's performance. By providing real-time hang detection, engineers can better test applications on devices in real-world low-network connectivity situations to ensure the application performs well. Figure 13-5 shows where to enable on-device hang rate detection.

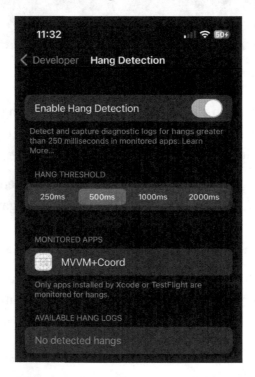

Figure 13-5. *Enabling on-device hang rate detection*

Battery Drain

Users prioritize applications that do not cause them to recharge constantly. In fact, users can even see which applications are draining their phone's battery the most. If your application uses a large percentage of battery power compared to other applications, users may stop using your application or uninstall the application entirely.

To further debug battery drain problems, we can review CPU usage closely related to battery drain. Clicking on the debug navigator allows you to view the energy gauge, which tracks the CPU usage of the application throughout a debugging session. Figure 13-6 shows the CPU report panel for our Photo Stream application. High CPU overhead is over 20%. Spikes are common during network requests and data processing; otherwise, CPU usage should be close to zero. If we see continuous CPU usage, this can represent a problem.

Figure 13-6. *CPU usage in the debug navigator*

Once the application is released, MetricKit allows developers to view aggregate data on battery drain and regressions collected from users. If not using MetricKit, other libraries also provide data on battery drain.

Application Crashes

Application crashes happen; however, as engineers, we must mitigate their frequency as much as possible. By adding logging and monitoring for application crashes to include stack traces, engineers can monitor the overall crash rate for the application and fix crashes based on the highest priority. Tracking crash rates in the beta testing phase before releasing a new feature to public users is critical. Overall crash rates should also be tracked via MetricKit or another third-party tool to monitor overall performance.

To debug a problem using a crash report, we can utilize the following best practices:

1. Retrieve the crash report.

2. Ensure the crash report is symbolicated or obtain a symbolicated crash report.

3. Examine the crash report for any clues on the issue and attempt to replicate it locally to determine the best fix. Additionally, check out identifying common causes of crashes for input.[16]

4. Based on the outcome of step 3, implement the fix and the associated test.

Note   Symbolicated crash reports provide the most insight about a crash and have function names on every frame of the backtrace (instead of hexadecimal memory addresses).[17]

---

[16] https://developer.apple.com/documentation/xcode/
identifying-the-cause-of-common-crashes

[17] https://developer.apple.com/documentation/xcode/
adding-identifiable-symbol-names-to-a-crash-report

What Is Symbolication?

When releasing an application, removing compilation steps that include debugging information from the final binary format is standard. Eliminating these steps obfuscates and minifies your source code by removing unnecessary characters, making the binary smaller and more difficult to reverse engineer. However, when an error is received, stack traces with obfuscated information make it impossible to track down the source of the crash.

Symbolication is the process of converting unreadable function names or hexadecimal memory addresses (in the case of iOS) into human-readable method names, file names, and line numbers. The crash report must be symbolicated to determine the exact reason behind the crash reliably.

Even with a symbolicated crash report, debugging based on a crash report can be complex and may require extra steps to replicate. If you cannot reproduce it, sometimes, relying on other engineers with different devices or requesting QA to replicate the bug can be helpful, especially in providing a symbolicated crash report. Otherwise, add additional logging to the build and review the logs to understand better what could cause the crash.

Network-Related Metrics

Networking is essential to any modern mobile application where network access is required to pull updated information and sync across devices. Given the ever presence of mobile devices, the chances of end users making requests in low network areas are high. Your application's ability to handle these situations provides a robust application solution for users. One factor to consider is all possible edge cases, such as what happens if a user goes through a tunnel. By thinking about these situations, holistic solutions can be developed with input from product managers.

Additionally, performing exploratory testing with the help of a QA team helps find and address low network connectivity situations before feature release.

To fully understand the impact of network connectivity on the performance of your application, it is necessary to evaluate

1. Network latency

2. Network load

3. Network errors

Latency

To properly understand network latency, we must track the API latency, intermediate points throughout the application, and the end-to-end response time for the overall network request time to the view rendering. Once we have proper logging to evaluate the latency at different portions of our application, we can group the network traffic into percentiles and evaluate the latency for other users. Armed with this information, we can assess the application's performance for most users (fiftieth percentile – P50) and outliers (ten percent – P90). Using P50 latency, we can set an average bar for application latency and hold a standard for the application. Using P90 latency, we can evaluate outliers to understand the worst-case scenario. The outlier data can reveal interesting trends and potential areas for improvement. For example, if we ascertain that almost all of our P90 end-to-end latency comes from cold starts on 3 or 4G, we know there is a specific scenario we can improve on.

In addition to evaluating the network latency, measuring the cache miss rate and retrieval time is also helpful in understanding the performance. There can also exist nuanced trade-offs between waiting longer for network content and quickly displaying content from the cache. For example, in our Photo Stream application, the fresh photos from the network have a more accurate ranking score (ML-backed story ranking). They are also more relevant (updated and recent) than photos stored on the on-device cache. However, waiting longer to load the first story negatively correlates with session length and users returning to the application. Here, it is unclear how long we should wait on a network request before showing content from the cache. We must balance the positive effects of fresher, more relevant network content with the negative impact of network latency. To arrive at the optimal solution, we can run an experiment with different timeout settings – the time we wait for the network request before showing content from the cache.

Load

In addition to network latency, we must consider network load, which refers to the number of network transactions or calls over a specific period. Application performance degrades under high network load. Even if this does not cause a noticeable UI lag for the user, it can cause a noticeable battery drain causing users to uninstall your application. By profiling the application in Xcode, we can evaluate the network load. For a more holistic understanding of the network load on users' devices, additional logging can be added to track the number of in-flight network requests.

Errors

Networking errors also contribute to an overall poor application experience and can degrade performance by requiring retries and contributing to crashes.

Engagement Metrics

Engagement metrics often track company-critical topline metrics and are typically geared toward tracking revenue generation and product growth either into different user segments or geographics. Some examples include

1. Monthly active users (MAU) and daily active users (DAU)

2. Device and operating system metrics

3. Geographic location

4. Session length

5. Retention rate (churn)

Engagement metrics are business-critical metrics that help guide engineers and determine high-priority work areas and impact. They guide judging the severity of an incident and required response prioritization.

While performance metrics may not directly influence engagement metrics, application performance can act as an intermediate metric for engagement. For example, say for our application a 10% performance improvement could lead to a 1% engagement improvement. Thus, by improving application performance, we may be able to improve business critical engagement metrics.

A Brief Practical Example

There is a potential hang in our application. Can you spot it? Even if we profile our application with the App Launch Instruments, we will not immediately spot a hang. Figure 13-7 shows an initial trace of the application. To generate the trace, we ran our MVVM application from Chapter 8 on a device using the App Launch Instruments tool. In Figure 13-7, everything running on a device appears to load quickly, and the application overall performs smoothly.

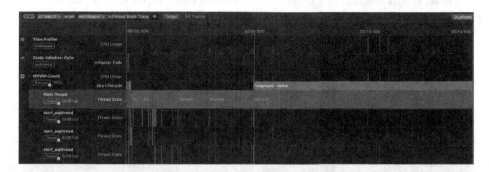

Figure 13-7. *Initial startup trace of our MVVM application*

However, we are dispatching to the main queue in the photo repository, which means work done in the repository sink block is done on the main thread due to the receive(on:) call.

// Repositories/PhotoRepository.swift

```
photoRepository.getAll().receive(on: DispatchQueue.main)
```

If we move this dispatch to the view-model, we can avoid performing data repository work on the main thread. We can add a sleep statement in the sink block to simulate a large complex block of work in the data layer.

// Repositories/PhotoRepository.swift
```
} receiveValue: { [weak self] photos in
            guard let sSelf = self else {
            return
        }
          sleep(4)
          sSelf.allPhotos = photos
          .compactMap{ $0 as? PhotoModel.Photo }
      }.store(in: &cancellables)
```

469

Now, when we run our trace, we can see a clear hang displayed in Figure 13-8 as the red block. With on-device hang detection, we also get a notification on the device regarding the hang.

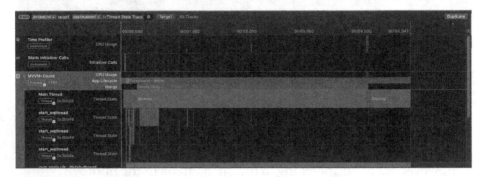

Figure 13-8. *System trace with hang from sleep*

So how can we fix this? We can move our Dispatch to the main thread logic to the view-model, freeing the main thread and removing the hang.

`// Scenes/PhotoStream/PhotoStreamViewModel.swift`

`photoModel.allPhotosPublished.receive(on:` **`DispatchQueue`**`.main).map`

Figure 13-9 documents the performance trace using the App Launch Instruments tool. Now when viewing the trace, it is clear the hang is gone. Even with the sleep statement blocking the completion of the data load, we have made the UI usable. Notice that on the device, you can switch tabs to the settings tab, whereas before, the UI was completely stuck.

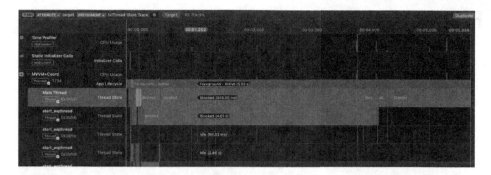

Figure 13-9. *Trace showing how to move the dispatch sync and remove the hang*

If this was a more complex example instead of a sleep statement, it could be complex logic in the data layer that takes time to load. In that situation, we would need to carefully consider when we dispatch to the main thread for UI manipulation; otherwise, we may block the main thread during critical loading times.

Summary

Performance is a critical component of application development. Degraded performance can cause increased battery drain, laggy user experience, crashes, and bloated binaries, all of which lead to lower user engagement. By integrating performance testing, establishing critical metrics for monitoring and alerting, and ensuring performance tooling is well understood, we can mitigate performance regressions and hold a high bar for overall application health. Debugging performance problems is a massive space deserving of its own book. Here, we have covered a framework for prioritizing, understanding, and addressing performance problems by tracking key metrics and understanding the principles of performance investigations.

Four Key Takeaways from This Chapter

1. Startup time is critical for application success. Minimize work on the startup path and, where possible, optimize what work we do.

2. Performance is critical in ensuring that users have a great experience with your application.

3. Performance is more than simply profiling the application in instruments. We must define metrics, create performance tests, and monitor real user data on application performance.

4. Application performance will slowly decay over time as features are continuously added. We must combat major regressions and "death by 1000 cuts" through automated performance testing, alerting, monitoring, and the best usage of available tooling.

Further Learning

1. How Apple optimized app size and runtime performance

   a. https://developer.apple.com/videos/play/wwdc2022/110363

2. Ultimate application performance survival guide

   a. https://developer.apple.com/videos/play/wwdc2021/10181/

3. Improving application performance

   a. `https://developer.apple.com/documentation/xcode/improving-your-app-s-performance`

4. Tracking application hangs

   a. `https://developer.apple.com/videos/play/wwdc2022/10082`

CHAPTER 14

Experimentation

As software engineers, we must diligently test any changes we make throughout all steps of the SDLC. Testing encompasses performance testing, correctness testing (automated tests), and production experimentation to validate the user's response to the changes. In scientific terminology, production testing is referred to as hypothesis testing. Typically we have a hypothesis that users will respond favorably to a new feature, change, or performance improvement. However, we must test and validate our idea before concluding the change is successful. To include hypothesis testing in the SDLC, we need a basic understanding of statistics and software experimentation infrastructure to support such testing.

This chapter assumes your application has the necessary software infrastructure for testing and instead focuses on the statistical knowledge needed to correctly set up experiments and analyze the results. While statistics may seem simple, it is not always intuitive, which can lead to drawing inaccurate conclusions.

This Chapter Includes

This chapter includes an overview of why experimentation is important and a powerful tool used by all major tech companies. To do so, we will first review a theoretical experimentation platform to ensure we are all on the same page. After we will review

© Eric Vennaro 2023
E. Vennaro, *iOS Development at Scale*, https://doi.org/10.1007/978-1-4842-9456-7_14

1. The scientific method and hypothesis testing

2. Designing an experiment and controlling for unintended side effects

3. Test statistics and results analysis

4. Common pitfalls including the network effect and experiment pollution

Why Experimentation Is Important

One accurate measurement is worth more than a thousand expert opinions.

—Admiral Grace Hopper

Controlled experimentation[1] is a powerful technique utilized in traditional sciences; however, it is not always applied to software engineering. Best guesses are often made, and changes are implemented based on perceived value; however, this does not allow measurement of the realized value. Formal experimentation makes it possible to ascertain the actual effects of the changes to our software. Commonly we refer to this style of testing as A/B testing. A/B testing is a randomized experiment involving two variants (test and control), although the concept can be extended to multiple variants of the same variable.

Note   A/B testing is an experimentation process where versions of an experience are compared against each other to determine which one performs best. To evaluate which variant performs the best, statistical analysis is used.

---

[1] A scientific statistics-based test done in a controlled environment as to manage external factors.

Statistical-based hypothesis testing allows software engineers to

1. Maximize the value of changes, whether that is to maximize profit, engagement, or something else entirely. For example, if we change our UI to shrink the gap between ads, we can work to maximize ads revenue. However, without statistics, we can only guess the user response and revenue change from our UI update. To fully maximize the value of our change, we need to experiment with different ad gaps and understand the effects.

2. Allow engineers to validate the effects of their changes on end-user behavior. Evaluating the effects of changes is also helpful for complex software migrations. For example, suppose our application is being migrated to a new database. In that case, no change to user behavior is expected, and executing an A/B test can confirm this or provide insight into a problem with the migration.

3. Evaluate ideas with near real-time analysis based on experimental data, which unblocks faster iterations on business goals.

4. Quantify the impact of changes which allows us to maximize the value of our changes and set appropriate goals.

Every software application has a goal, and experimentation allows us to scientifically validate our progress in reaching that vision.

Theoretical Experimentation Platform

Before diving into the details of experimentation, let us first build a shared understanding of the tooling and setup for experimentation and A/B testing. For those unfamiliar with the concept of A/B testing, this section provides a primer for different areas you may want to explore further. For those familiar with A/B testing platforms, this section presents an option on the setup and provides some context for the details discussed in subsequent sections. This section also includes a portion on network effects testing via clustering.

The overall goal of an experimentation platform is to

1. Allow engineers to allocate experiments in test and control groups. Behind the scenes, the platform will handle randomized user allocation, deallocation, and track exposure logging (which determines when to assign users to the test or control group based on engineer-specified criteria).

2. Allow engineers to analyze the results of experiments and view necessary data to ensure experiments are working correctly.

3. Allow for mutual exclusion of experiments for testing correctness.

To meet these requirements, we need constructs to represent

1. Units: What we are experimenting on. This will be users (represented explicitly by a user ID).

2. Experiment groups: Distinct experiences that users will see. Each group has its own experience.

3. Experiments: A collection of groups and the necessary parameters for each group. Most experiments will have two groups (test and control) split 50/50.

4. Targeting rules: Targeting rules allow us to determine which units (users) are eligible for the experiment.

5. Universes: A universe is a collection of experiments. A universe allows running multiple experiments simultaneously while guaranteeing that a unit (user) will not be involved in more than one experiment within a single universe at the same time (mutual exclusion).

Universes for Experimentation

In our example setup, a universe consists of all eligible users (statistically speaking, a universe is our population suitable for testing). We can have many universes that will exist orthogonally, containing the same users implying that universes are not mutually exclusive. A user can be in multiple experiments across universes at the same time.

Inside a universe, we allocate users to different experiments. We will utilize a hashing algorithm to assign users to a specific segment, which is then allocated inside an experiment.

Example segment hashing algorithm where we produce 1000 segments:

$$segment_{userID} = hash(userID + universeName) \, mod \, 1000$$

In this way, the same user can only be in one experiment in a universe, allowing experiments inside a universe to be mutually exclusive. Once an experiment is deallocated, those users return to the pool of users eligible for other experiments. Figure 14-1 outlines the universe setup and potential experimentation allocation strategy.

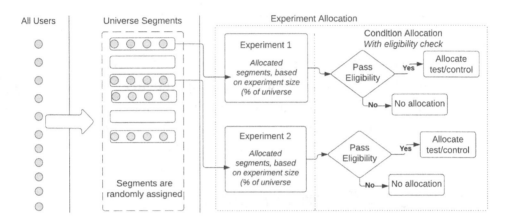

Figure 14-1. *Example experimentation allocation strategy, with universe segmentation and eligibility checks*

While Figure 14-1 outlines the allocation strategy, Figure 14-2 shows the potential UI an engineer using the experiment engine may see when creating a new experiment inside a universe. The figure is from the Darkly platform, a third-party experimentation framework. Note how we also select metrics we want to monitor; the importance of this will come into play later on in this chapter.

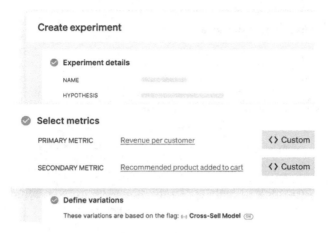

Figure 14-2. *Example experiment creation from the Darkly platform[2]*

Experiment Tooling

Inside an experiment, we want to control user allocation to the test and control group (or multiple test groups). For this type of setup, we need to consider the capabilities of our analysis platform carefully. While it is statistically possible to compare differently sized test and control groups, not all platforms support this type of analysis. Figure 14-3 outlines the allocation of three test groups all receiving 5% traffic in the Darkly platform.

---

[2]https://launchdarkly.com/features/experimentation/

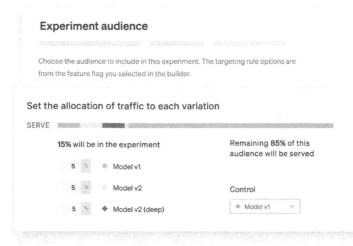

Figure 14-3. *Example allocating users to the test and control groups referred to as variations on the Darkly platform[3]*

Additionally, we want to support different overrides. These overrides allow us to quickly test our changes without exposing users to the production treatment. The overrides can also let us target users based on the application version (this prevents our test group from having ineligible users). Figure 14-4 shows an example of this targeting on the Darkly platform.

---

[3] https://launchdarkly.com/features/experimentation/

Figure 14-4. *Example targeting only specific users in Darkly and assigning them to different experiment groups (variations)*[4]

Lastly, we want to control exposure logging. Exposure logging refers to the point in time the user is exposed to the treatment. For example, if we show the user a new option in the application's settings page, we would want to expose the user on the settings page load. If we exposed the user automatically or on application startup, we could expose users who will have never seen the settings page and thus never seen the treatment we are testing. One caveat here is we may be interested in the overall ecosystem effect of the change. In this situation, if we utilize exposure logging, we will lose track of second-order effects on users not exposed, failing to capture the broader effect on the ecosystem.

---

[4] https://launchdarkly.com/features/experimentation/

Cluster Testing (The Network Effect)

In addition to setting up user-based experimentation, we may want the ability to track changes requiring user networks. For example, say we develop a two-player game for our messaging application. For users to play, they both need to be in the experiment. To ensure both users are in the experiment, we can utilize cluster testing to set up clusters of related users. Almost everything will work the same for our experimentation platform except at the user allocation level. Instead of allocating users, we will allocate groups of users clustered together based on some attribute (say, top five most commonly messaged). Figure 14-5 outlines a cluster allocation strategy similar to the user allocation strategy earlier. Here, we have allocated clusters based on our defined user behavior. Next, these clusters of experimental units are allocated to universe segments via a hashing algorithm. After that, the universe segments are assigned to experiments.

The experiment allocation strategy is similar in that universe segments are hashed and randomly split via a hash based on the experiment name into randomized segments. Depending on whether the segment was allocated to a unit or cluster experiment, these segments could be user or cluster based, allowing us to allocate for both user-based and cluster-based experiments.

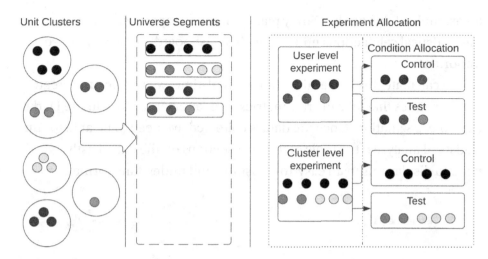

Figure 14-5. *Cluster experimentation allocation where user IDs are colored dots and circles represent clusters of user IDs*[5]

Metrics Evaluation Platform

In software engineering experiments, our metrics platform is our data collection method. We perform data collection with relative ease since all our metrics are easily harvested via logging and formatted for easy consumption via data pipelines. While the pipelines and storage requirements for the data are complex, the overall data collection is much simpler than for laboratory-based experiments or those conducted for drug trials where sample sizes are small and data must be manually collected at medical sites.

Specifically, for our metrics collection platform, we want to leverage our logging and the data collection pipelines to display relevant metrics in an easily consumable way. This way, engineers can reason about their experiments utilizing statistical best practices. Figure 14-6 outlines

---

[5] https://arxiv.org/pdf/2012.08591.pdf

an example of this on the Darkly platform. This chapter will dive into the statistical calculations underlying this dashboard and why they are important.

To calculate this in real-time or near real-time, we will need to create data pipelines that take the raw metrics such as error rates or, in the Darkly example, pagination. Once the data is collected, we need to be able to run statistical analyses (the topic of the next section) on the data. Lastly, we need to display this in an easy-to-consume and understand format.

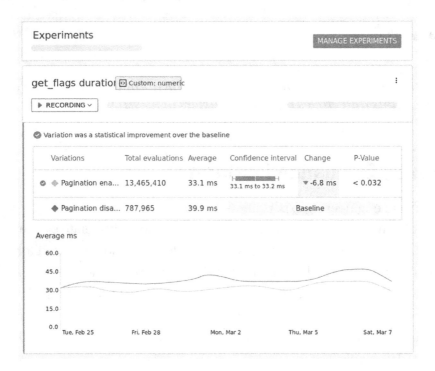

Figure 14-6. *A sample dashboard to evaluate metrics from the Darkly platform. Note the inclusion of the p-value and confidence interval[6]*

---

[6] https://launchdarkly.com/features/experimentation/

The Scientific Method and Hypothesis Testing

Now that we have defined our theoretical experiment setup, let us dive into how to test our work. Whenever we build new features or fix bugs, we do so to improve the experience for our end users. However, to ensure we improve the experience, we must validate the effects on our users. To do this, we use the scientific method and hypothesis testing. The scientific method is outlined in Figure 14-7 and refers to the overall thought process for understanding the effects of changes we want to make. It starts with the question or problem we want to solve and ends with analysis and results sharing. Hypothesis testing refers explicitly to the three steps of the scientific method (research the topic area, formulate a hypothesis, and test with an experiment), where we apply statistical techniques to experimental data to determine if a given hypothesis is true. We utilize statistics because statistics represent mathematical techniques to evaluate the uncertainty of inductive inferences and provide us a level of certainty that our changes are effective.

Note   Inductive inference is generalizing from a finite set of past observations or extending an observed pattern to future instances or instances occurring elsewhere.

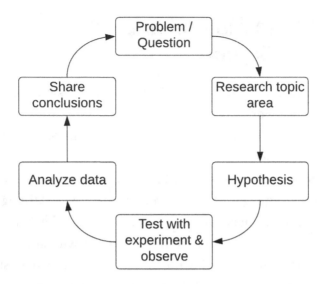

Figure 14-7. *The scientific method*

Applying the Scientific Method to Our Photo Stream Example

Imagine you are on the team scaling the new Discover feature for the Photo Stream application. Previously, users could only see content for connected users, but with the new Discover surface, users can now find content from unconnected users. To access the Discover surface, users must navigate through the options menu (more options ➤ discover). Currently, overall traffic to the Discover surface is low. Your team believes the Discover surface is an important lever to improve application growth and is interested in quickly increasing traffic to the surface. As a first step, the team conducts a brainstorming session to develop new ideas for addressing the low traffic.

After brainstorming, you have several ideas on how to increase traffic to the surface and settle on the most promising one: instead of having to first click on the more options menu, the Discover surface will have a top-level tab bar icon, allowing easy access to the Discover surface.

Now that your team has decided on what idea to try, you design how to implement the feature. As part of the feature design, you also design an experiment to test the feature. For this, you will use an A/B test where you have one set of users who are excluded from seeing the Discover tab bar icon (the control – a) and a group who will see the new experience (the test group – b).

After one month (the time necessary for metric stability), you will use your company's experimentation framework to observe key metrics related to your initial hypothesis (around overall traffic to the Discover tab and any performance regressions). Then you will consider how the outcome of these data points relates to the original hypothesis and if we can disprove the null hypothesis. Lastly, you will share the findings with the broader team.

Note   Metric stability is important. Some metrics need time to stabilize and produce accurate results. You risk reading inaccurate results and reaching an incorrect conclusion by not waiting for the metric to become readable.

Given our scientific method framework, we can break down the previous steps into the following:

1.   Question/problem: Our Discover surface has low traffic (problem). How to increase traffic to the Discover surface (question)?

2.   Research topic area: Brainstorming potential solutions.

3.   Hypothesis: By adding a top-level tab bar icon for the Discover surface, we can drive more traffic by increasing the visibility of our feature.

4. Experiment design and test: Design an experiment to evaluate the Discover tab feature on a subset of user traffic (the population), collect data and information (observation), and apply an A/B test for the hypothesis. If the experiment regresses user experience severely, it may need to be stopped prematurely.

5. Analyze: Once the experiment has been observed for long enough, we analyze the results to conclude the experiment's success.

6. Share conclusions: After completing the experiment analysis, we must share the results with the broader team to understand the potential for launch, share knowledge, and further collaboration.

In the rest of this chapter, we will dive into the hypothesis definition, experimental design, and results analysis steps for our example. We will skip over data collection because data collection is typically automated via data pipelines, and metrics are pre-computed for software engineers with data engineers or separate teams of software engineers handling the pipeline creation and maintenance themselves. Creating a data ingestion system and subsequent metrics computation pipelines is a complex topic worthy of its own book.

Experiment Design and Implementation

First, we must define our hypotheses:

1. Null hypothesis: Moving the Discover tab entry point to the tab bar does not impact the number of visits to the Discover surface.

2. Alternative hypothesis: Moving the Discover tab
    entry point to the tab bar positively impacts the
    number of visits to the Discover surface.

While seemingly simple, hypothesis definition can become complex
and suffer from scope creep as people may push for testing multiple
things. An example of scope creep is bundling the Discover tab entry point
and Discover surface latency improvements together. By combining these
two changes into one test variant, we lose the ability to see what is actually
causing the results seen in the experiment. It is essential to limit this and
clearly define the hypothesis under test. After defining our hypothesis, we
need to define our experiment. Defining the experiment includes

1. Choosing the test statistics

2. Assessing sample size and distribution

3. Implementing the necessary engineering work to
    run the experiment

By the end of the experiment design and implementation phase, we
will understand what statistics we will use to assess the hypothesis, how
large of a sample size we need to get statistically significant results, what
users we will target, and what engineering work is needed to implement
the experiment.

Choosing Test Statistics

When choosing test statistics, we want to look for statistics that will help
us assess whether the alternative hypothesis is true. In our Discover
tab example, we can use the number of daily visits. After running the
experiment, we can look at the number of daily visits in both our test and
control groups and compute a p-value and/or confidence interval (we
assume the hypothetical experimentation platform does this). If we get the

effect we hoped for, we can accept the alternative hypothesis and launch the feature or fail to reject the null hypothesis and go back to synthesize a new hypothesis.

P-value   In null-hypothesis significance testing, the **_p_-value** is the probability of obtaining test results at least as extreme as a result observed, under the assumption that the null hypothesis is correct. A very small _p_-value means such an extreme observed outcome would be improbable under the null hypothesis.[7]

Confidence Interval   A range of estimates for an unknown parameter. A confidence interval is computed at a designated _confidence level_; the 95% confidence level is the most common, but other levels, such as 90% or 99%, are sometimes used.[8,9] The **confidence level** represents the long-run proportion of corresponding CIs that contains the parameter's actual value. For example, out of all intervals computed at the 95% level, 95% of them should contain the parameter's true value.[10]

In addition to goal metrics for analysis, it is helpful to include counter metrics or guardrail metrics. For example, say we want to drive more traffic to the Discover tab but not at the cost of the main feed engagement. In this

---

[7] Muff, S., Nilsen, E. B., O'Hara, R. B., & Nater, C. R. (2022). Rewriting results sections in the language of evidence. _Trends in ecology & evolution, 37_(3), 203–210. https://doi.org/10.1016/j.tree.2021.10.009

[8] Zar, Jerrold H. (1999). _Biostatistical Analysis_ (4th ed.). Upper Saddle River, N.J.: Prentice Hall.

[9] Dekking, Frederik Michel; Kraaikamp, Cornelis; Lopuhaä, Hendrik Paul; Meester, Ludolf Erwin (2005). "A Modern Introduction to Probability and Statistics."

[10] Illowsky, Barbara; Dean, Susan L. (1945-). _Introductory statistics_, OpenStax College. Houston, Texas.

situation, we may include a counter metric for overall visits to the main feed. If we negatively impact this, it may hurt our chances of launching. Additionally, we should monitor application and server performance to understand any additional performance cost from the Discover tab change (a guardrail metric).

Assess Sample Size and Distribution

When assessing sample size and distribution, we want to understand the following:

1. Required sample size to reason about our test statistics in a statistically significant manner (we define statistical significance later in this chapter)

2. Factors that could affect user eligibility and how this can impact our required sample size and distribution (homogenous vs. heterogeneous groups)

Required Sample Size and Effects on Analysis

A larger sample size shrinks our confidence interval and provides a better understanding of the true effect of our experiment. For example, say for our experiment, we have a sample of 1000 users, and we record the impact on visitation. Now, let us run this same experiment with a million users. With the larger sample size, we will observe an effect that more closely models the true effect, shown by the distribution of estimates clustering more closely around the true effect (the mean).

To illustrate this effect on a small scale, we can create a normal data distribution and artificially shrink the confidence interval to mirror a larger sample size. Due to its wealth of statistical libraries, we will use Python for coding samples in this chapter.

```
# pip3 install to install dependencies
# run via command line: python3 example1.py 20 5
# to mirror a larger sample size rerun with: python3
# example1.py 20 3
import numpy as np

# Set seed for the random number generator, so we get the same
random numbers each time
np.random.seed(20210710)

# Create fake data
mean = 100
sample_size =  int(sys.argv[1]) if len(sys.argv) > 1 else 20
standard_deviation = int(sys.argv[2]) if len(sys.argv) >
2 else 5
x = np.random.normal(mean, standard_deviation, sample_size)

print([f'{x:.1f}' for x in sorted(x)])

## ['88.6', '89.9', '91.6', '94.4', '95.7', '97.4', '97.6',
'98.1', '98.2', '99.4', '99.8', '100.0', '101.7', '101.8',
'102.2', '104.3', '105.4', '106.7', '107.0', '109.5']
```

Now we can view our distributions with our "small" and "large" sample sizes in Figures 14-8 and 14-9. In Figure 14-8, the distribution of the values is larger; thus, the 95% confidence interval is larger, and a wider range of values would be deemed acceptable.

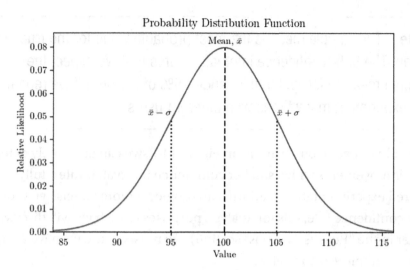

Figure 14-8. *Probability distribution with "small data set"*

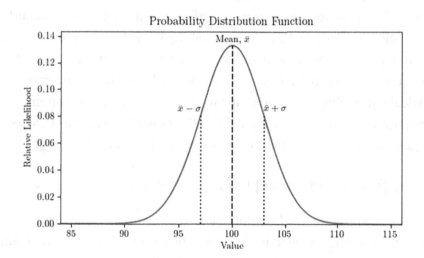

Figure 14-9. *Probability distribution with "large data set"*

Note   The sample mean is the most probable value for the true mean. The 95% confidence interval denotes that we expect the sample mean to fall within this range 95% of the time if we repeat the experiment many times with different users.

As illustrated in our example in Figure 14-9, we can accurately detect smaller movements with a smaller confidence interval. While a fully featured experimentation platform can provide a more concise view of these confidence intervals for analysis purposes (which we will discuss further in the "Results Analysis" section), we must ensure we have a large enough sample size to analyze.

There is a limit to how large a sample size we should have though. Using too large of an experiment increases treatment exposure (we may not want to expose too many users to extreme testing experiences) and limits available space in the universe, making it harder to run orthogonal tests (different test in the same universe as to maintain mutual exclusion among tests). As a general rule, tests should be large enough to gather statistically meaningful data and no larger. To guide this assessment, we can utilize the minimum detectable effect discussed in the "Results Analysis" section as a means to estimate the size of experiments.

Factors That Could Impact User Eligibility

Now that we know we need a sufficiently large sample size to detect metrics movement, we need to assess any blockers. In our case, we want to ensure that a reasonably large number of users are eligible to see and interact with the Discover tab. For instance, if the Discover tab was only available in Japan, but 90% of our user base was in Peru, this could present an issue in our ability to analyze the data.

Results Analysis

Let us jump forward in time and say we have let our experiment on the Discover tab run for one month, which, given our number of users, is long enough to gather significant results. Understanding this time frame is important for adequately evaluating results and is the result of many factors, including experimentation power, which we will calculate later in this section. To properly analyze experiment results, we must

1.   Understand the types of errors we may encounter

2.   Understand how to holistically interpret our results using effect size, power, and the p-value

Types of Errors

Understanding the potential for erroneous results and how to address them is a big part of results analysis. We refer to these errors as Type I and Type II errors. Type I and II errors are essential to understand because our experiments are on a sample of users and not the entire population, which introduces a degree of randomness in our metrics that can sway our results, making it difficult or impossible to draw conclusions from them (commonly referred to as noise). By understanding these error types, we can better understand how to diagnose, interpret, and avoid them.

A Type I error represents the false-positive rate, the likelihood that we will reject the null hypothesis when it is true. Regarding our Discover tab entry point experiment, a Type I error represents concluding that our feature has an impact on visitation and launch even though it does not have an actual effect on visitation.

A Type II error represents the false-negative rate, the likelihood that we will fail to reject the null hypothesis when it is false. Regarding our experiment, a Type II error means that we will conclude that our entry point has no impact on Discover surface visitation and fails to launch even though it does impact visitation. Figure 14-10 illustrates the aforementioned in tabular format and includes the probability notation that these errors map to.

	Our feature has no effect on visitation	Our feature increases visitation
Launch our feature	Type I Error Probability = α	Correct Probability = 1-β
Do not launch our feature	Correct Probability = 1-α	Type II Error Probability = β

Figure 14-10. *Overview of error types and their meaning*

The Type I error is commonly referenced as the alpha (α) and represents the significance level. We choose the significance level before the experiment starts depending on the risk of making a Type I error. We can choose to decrease the alpha from 5% to 1% if the risk presented by a Type I error is high and more confidence is needed that the decision is correct. This effect is illustrated in Figure 14-11.

Sampling Distribution of Null Hypothesis

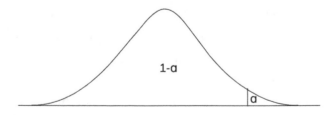

Figure 14-11. *Sample normal distribution of the null hypothesis assuming our feature does not affect visitations*

The Type II error, known as the beta (β), is set by the significance level of the experiment. The Type II error rate is not set before starting the experiment and instead depends on the significance level, size of the delta, sample size, and data variance and is illustrated in Figure 14-12. The inverse of beta is statistical power (shown in Figure 14-14).

Statistical power represents the probability of detecting an effect when there is an actual effect. Power helps us to understand if we can reasonably detect the effect we expect from the experiment. Statistical power is the area under the alternative hypothesis distribution and outside the null hypothesis's confidence interval.

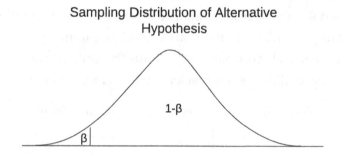

Figure 14-12. *Sample normal distribution of the alternative hypothesis assuming our feature impacts visitation*

Understanding Statistical Significance

Throughout this chapter, we have used the term "statistical significance," but we have yet to define it mathematically. Statistical significance occurs when it is very unlikely that the null hypothesis is true. For a result to be statistically significant, it must have a minimal Type I error rate (false-positive rate). This is why we set the alpha (Type I error rate) at the beginning of our experiment.

During the experiments runtime, we use p-values to measure the actual Type I error, which is defined as the probability of observing a delta at least as extreme as the observed delta if the null hypothesis is true (our new entry point does not affect visitation). If the p-value is less than 5%, there is little chance we would observe our new entry point affecting visitation by chance. We can then confidently report that we have a statistically significant result.

Note   Saying we are confident in launching a new product or feature means we are statistically confident, implying we have seen statistically significant results.

In addition to the p-value, we can also use the confidence interval to understand whether a result is statistically significant. Figure 14-13 outlines a sample confidence interval overlaid on sample data distribution. The confidence level is equivalent to 1 minus the alpha, implying that the p-value and the confidence interval lead to the same conclusion.

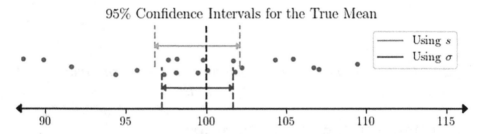

Figure 14-13. *Generated confidence interval with both standard error and standard deviation*

Calculating the P-Value

In order to calculate the p-value, we must first determine the likelihood of obtaining our results if the null hypothesis were true. When it comes to hypothesis testing in software engineering, we can utilize a binomial distribution to model our data. This type of distribution allows us to determine the probability of observing a certain number of successes in a series of trials, with the probability of success on a single trial denoted as p.

The binomial distribution assumes that p remains consistent throughout all trials,[11] which is often the case in software engineering scenarios involving user visitation and click-through rates. To be more specific, we can mathematically model a binomial distribution to determine the probability of achieving a certain number of successes in a series of independent Bernoulli trials, given a specific probability p.

$$P(k;n,p) = P(X = k) = p^k \left(1 - p^k\right)^{n-k}$$

We can easily model this in Python utilizing the SciPy kit where num_converted is k successes we see in our experiment (e.g., conversions or visitations), the total is the n independent trials, and the probability base conversion rate, bcr, is the base conversion rate of our control (the expected rate).

```python
import scipy.stats as scs

def p_val(num_converted, total, bcr):
    """Returns the p-value for an A/B test"""
    return scs.binomtest(
        num_converted-1,
        total,
        bcr,
        'two-sided').pvalue
```

Here, we have utilized a two-sided test designed to tell if the sample mean is significantly greater than or less than the control group's mean.

---

[11] www.itl.nist.gov/div898/handbook/eda/section3/eda366i.htm

Two- vs. One-Sided Tests

A two-sided, or two-tailed, test denotes that we wish to test statistical significance on both sides of the normal distribution. If the significance level (the alpha) is 0.05 for a two-tailed test, then half the alpha is applied in each direction, so .025 in each side (tail) of the distribution of your test statistic. For example, given a sample mean and value y, a two-tailed test allows us to compare whether the mean is significantly greater than y or less than y. Given that our alpha is .025, the mean is significantly different from our value y if the test statistic is in the top 2.5% or bottom 2.5% of the probability distribution (resulting in a p-value less than .05).

In contrast, a one-tailed test only tests for statistical significance in one direction, which means that the .05 is in one tail of the distribution of your test statistic. Revisiting our previous example with value y, we must choose to test either if the mean is significantly greater than or less than y. The result is statistically significant if it is in the top (or bottom) 5% of its probability distribution instead of 2.5 (still resulting in a p-value of less than .05).

The one-tailed test provides more power to detect an effect in one direction; however, we do not account for unexpected changes by not testing in both directions. For instance, if we only assess our UI change for if it improves user engagement via a one-sided test, we would miss out on the potential for our UI change to hurt user engagement.

Returning to our example, let us say we flipped a coin 100 times and received heads 70 times. In this situation, our null hypothesis is that we have a fair coin and will see 50% heads and 50% tails. So what is the probability of seeing results at least as extreme as the observed result? Do we have a biased coin?

```
import scipy.stats as scs
def p_val(num_converted, total, bcr):
    """Returns the p-value for an A/B test"""
```

```
return scs.binomtest(
    num_converted-1,
    total,
    bcr,
    'two-sided').pvalue
# $ python3 example3.py
print(p_val(70, 100, .5))
# 7.85013964559367e-05
```

After running our code, we can see the p-value is 7.85013964559367e-05, which is very, very small, indicating that we can reject our null hypothesis and do have a biased coin.

The p-value is our main lever to detect if our results are statistically significant. It is also essential to address our sample size. For example, if we had only run ten trials and had seven heads, would we be nearly as confident that the coin is biased? Or that we are seeing a false negative (Type II error)? To do so, we should also look at statistical power.

Statistical Power and the Minimum Detectable Effect (MDE)

As discussed earlier, the Type II error and power vary with the chosen significance level, delta size, sample size, and variance in the data.

1. Significance level: As α decreases, β increases, and power decreases, meaning that a smaller α or false-positive rate comes at the cost of a higher false-negative rate and lower statistical power.

2. Delta size: As the magnitude of the delta increases, beta decreases, and power increases. Thus, it is easier to detect larger changes in a metric.

3.   Sample size: As the sample size of an experiment
     increases, the variance/width of the sample
     distribution decreases, the beta decreases, and the
     power increases.

4.   Variance in the data: As the variance in the data
     increases, the width of the distribution increases,
     decreasing the power.

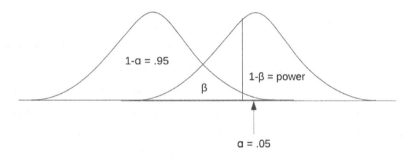

Figure 14-14.   *Relationship between Type I and Type II errors with an*
illustration of power. Alpha is .05 representing a one-sided test

Among the factors influencing power at the start of the experiment,
we can control the sample size and the α. To ensure our experiments
have the best chance of getting statistically significant results, we should
analyze the required sample size for our given alpha, detectable effect, and
power level. The detectable effect is the minimum effect we can expect
to detect with our experiment setup (called the MDE). Before starting an
experiment, it is important to evaluate the minimum expected metric
movement so we know what the MDE should be. Understanding the MDE
requires having an idea of the anticipated movement before starting the
experiment. To do so, we can look at other similar experiments that may
require an in-depth offline analysis (or, in the worst case, guess and test).
When evaluating experiments, it is good practice to question the sample
size and metric movement the experiment owner expects to see to ensure
they have worked through the calculation.

Even after the experiment concludes, it is helpful to look back at the minimum detectable effect to understand how likely we are to see statistically significant results. The MDE helps us know how repeatable our results are in future experiments.

Additionally, suppose your metrics are reading neutral. In that case, you may need to consult the MDE for the experiment to understand if there is enough power to detect the actual effect of the neutral metric. If the MDE for an important metric is higher, then you will likely be unable to draw statistically significant conclusions about that metric from your current experiment. It is helpful to consider previous comparable experiments to understand the MDE and subsequently required experiment size.

Ideally, your experimentation framework will support viewing the minimum detectable effect from past experiments. We can calculate the required sample size for a similar experiment. Here, we demonstrate such a calculation mathematically and then implement it using Python.[12]

$$n = 2(\underline{p})(1-\underline{p})\left(Z_\beta + Z_{\frac{a}{2}}\right)^2 / (p_\beta - p_A)2$$

n: sample size per group

Z_β: z-score that corresponds to the power

$Z_{a/2}$: z-score that corresponds to the level of significance or confidence interval. Typically 95%

$\underline{p}$: average of p_a and p_b

p_a: the success rate of the control group

p_b: the success rate of the test group

$p_\beta - p_A$: is equivalent to the effect size. Or theorized minimum detectable effect (the minimum effect we want to be able to detect)

---

[12] https://web.stanford.edu/~kcobb/hrp259/lecture11.ppt

In Python, this would translate to

```
# min_sample_size.py
import scipy.stats as scs
from plots import *
import math

def min_sample_size(
  base_rate,
  mde,
  power,
  sig_level
):
  # standard normal distribution to determine z-values
  standard_norm = scs.norm(0, 1)

  # find Z_beta from desired power
  z_beta = standard_norm.ppf(power)

  # find Z_alpha
  z_alpha = standard_norm.ppf(1-sig_level/2)

  # average of probabilities from both groups
  pooled_prob = (base_rate + base_rate+mde) / 2

  min_sample_size = (2 * pooled_prob *
    (1 - pooled_prob) * (z_beta + z_alpha)**2
        / mde**2)

  return math.ceil(min_sample_size)
```

Now we can reliably detect our minimum required sample size before running an experiment!

```
min_sample_size(.1, .02, .8, .05)
# Min sample size per test group: 3843
```

Holistic Results Analysis

So far, we have discussed evaluating the p-value to ensure our results are statistically significant and how Type I and Type II errors express themselves. However, when assessing our results, we also need to look at the overall magnitude of the change. Is our sample size so large that we can detect minimal but meaningless changes (such as improving the click-through rate by .00002%)? Lastly, we need to consider statistical power to understand if we can easily replicate our results or if, while statistically significant, they may not be replicable in future experiments (Type II error).

Evaluating the experiment results holistically and not solely judging experiment success based on p-value is very important since a larger sample size can easily produce small statistically significant changes of immaterial impact. Recently, the American Statistical Association (ASA) published a journal article discussing that statistically significant p-values do not necessarily imply the presence of larger or more important effects, and larger p-values do not imply a lack of importance or even lack of effect.[13]

Instead, the ASA suggests that researchers recognize the limitations of evaluating a p-value without further context and consider a holistic study design and analysis, including an overall understanding of the results, which should include the power, sample size, and realized effect. For software engineering, we can leverage our experimentation platform to calculate these values; however, it is up to us as engineers to properly utilize the platform and ensure

---

[13] Ronald L. Wasserstein & Nicole A. Lazar (2016). The ASA Statement on p-Values: Context, Process, and Purpose, The American Statistician, 70:2, 129–133, doi: 10.1080/00031305.2016.1154108.

1. Our results are repeatable

2. Our p-value meets significance standards

3. Our effect size is large enough to represent a meaningful change in the population

Practical Example for Holistically Interpreting Results

This section will build on the Discover surface tab bar entry point experiment referenced early in the chapter. We will review some of the underlying statistical calculations for confidence intervals, experimental power, and stat-sig movement on a sample data set to build confidence in our results analysis skills. Ideally, your experimentation framework will calculate these values, so you do not have to do these calculations by hand. To better understand experiment results analysis will walk through some of these calculations in Python using generated data. We will gloss over some of the details of the Python internals and instead focus on the high-level impact to experiment reading for our theoretical Discover tab entry point experiment from earlier.

Continuing with our Discover tab example from earlier in the chapter, recall our null and alternative hypotheses:

- The null hypothesis is adding the Discover tab entry point on the tab bar results in no change in the visitation rate.

- The alternative hypothesis states that adding the Discover tab entry point on the tab bar changes the visitation rate.

We can mathematically define our null and alternative hypotheses where we also define $\hat{d}$ ($\hat{}$ symbol denotes an estimated probability) as the difference in probability between the null and alternative hypotheses:

$$\hat{d} = \widehat{p_b} - \widehat{p_a}$$

$$H0 : \hat{d} = 0$$

$$H1 : \hat{d} \neq 0$$

To simulate data for our test, we will utilize pre-generated data with a sample size of 2000 (1000 in each test and control group) with a theorized rate of improvement of .02 between the test and control groups. To ensure results match, the sample data set is included in the source code as sample_data.csv.

```python
import pandas as pd

ab_data = pd.read_csv('sample_data.csv')
# skip formatting code...
"""
        converted  total      rate
group
A              94    985  0.095431
B             125   1015  0.122167
"""
```

Now we can inspect the raw visitation data and rates. Between the test and control, the rate of change is about 0.03, which is close to the lift we initially theorized of 0.02. Now, this provides an understanding of the overall rate of change and that this is a decent improvement between the test and control groups. However, we have not assessed the statistical magnitude of the change, and thus, we don't have enough evidence to say the change was truly effective.

First, let us format our sample data so we can reason about the total members in our trial, the total that saw the discover tab (labeled as converted users in code), and the rate for these groups.

```
# example3.py
# Conversion Data
a_group = ab_data[ab_data['group'] == 'A']
b_group = ab_data[ab_data['group'] == 'B']

a_converted = a_group['visited'].sum()
b_converted = b_group['visited'].sum()
a_total = len(a_group)
b_total = len(b_group)

p_a = a_converted / a_total
p_b = b_converted / b_total

# base conversion rate
bcr = p_a
# difference
d_hat = p_b - p_a
```

Now we can utilize our previous calculation to determine if our change is statistically significant.

```
p_value = p_val(b_converted, N_B, bcr)
# .006
```

Great! Now we know we have a statistically significant change. .006 is less than our alpha value of .025 (two-sided test). However, we still need to understand our experimental power, which helps us to reason about our results fully.

To build confidence, we can look at the distributions in terms of their probability of success. To do so, we can plot them as binomial distributions and compare them to see the difference in Figure 14-15.

```python
# example3.py
# Raw distribution

fig, ax = plt.subplots(figsize=(12,6))
xA = np.linspace(
    a_converted - 49,
    a_converted + 50,
    100,
)
yA = scs.binom(a_total, p_a).pmf(xA)
ax.bar(xA, yA, alpha=0.5, color='red')
xB = np.linspace(
    b_converted - 49,
    b_converted + 50,
    100,
)
yB = scs.binom(b_total, p_b).pmf(xB)
ax.bar(xB, yB, alpha=0.5, color='blue')
plt.xlabel('visited')
plt.ylabel('probability')
# display plot
plt.show()
```

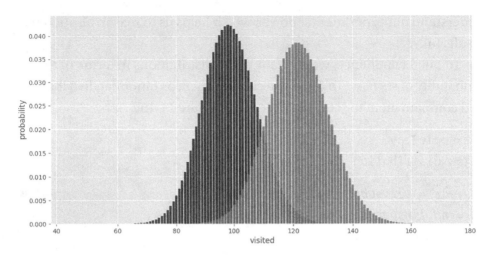

Figure 14-15. *Binomial distributions; red is the control group, and blue is the test group*

We can see that the blue test group had more visitations than the red control group. The peak of the test group is also lower than the control group, meaning the number of samples is different. Our sample means are different and so do our sample size and standard deviations. To more accurately compare our test and control groups, we must calculate the probability of success for both the test and control groups.

To do so, we need to standardize the data for the differences in population size and then compare the probability of success. First, we can normalize our individual test and control distributions. For this, we need to calculate the standard error for each group. By evaluating the standard error, we can understand the variation in our sample data and see how closely our sample values cluster around the mean.

To do so, we must define the mean and variance (standard deviation). We can do so as follows where P is the success (visitation of the Discovery tab) probability:

$$E(X) = p$$

$$Var(X) = p(1-p)$$

$$\sigma = \sqrt{p(1-p)}$$

Next, we can leverage the central limit theorem to calculate the standard error. The central limit theorem states that the means of a random sample of size, n, from a population with mean, μ, and variance, σ^2, are normally distributed with mean, μ, and variance.[14] Practically this means that by calculating many sample means, we can approximate the true mean and that the standard deviation will equal the standard error of the mean even if the original variables are not normally distributed.

Given that, we can define the standard error from our success probability.

$$\sigma_x = \frac{s}{\sqrt{n}} = \sqrt{\frac{p(1-p)}{\sqrt{n}}}$$

And utilizing the central limit theorem, we can define our distribution as normal as follows:

$$\hat{p} \sim Normal\left(\mu = p, \sigma = \sqrt{\frac{p(1-p)}{\sqrt{n}}}\right)$$

In Python, we can then model our standard error and create a new plot of our distributions in Figure 14-16.

```python
import numpy as np
import matplotlib.pyplot as plt
import scipy.stats as scs
```

---

[14] Kwak, S. G., & Kim, J. H. (2017). Central limit theorem: the cornerstone of modern statistics. Korean Journal of Anesthesiology, 70(2), 144–156. https://doi.org/10.4097/kjae.2017.70.2.144

```
# example3.py
# standard error of the mean for both groups
se_a = np.sqrt(p_a * (1-p_a)) / np.sqrt(a_total)
se_b = np.sqrt(p_b * (1-p_b)) / np.sqrt(b_total)

"""
Standard error control: 0.009558794818157494
Standard error test: 0.010199971022850756
"""

# plot the null and alternative hypothesis
fig, ax = plt.subplots(figsize=(12,6))
x = np.linspace(0, .2, 1000)
yA = scs.norm(p_a, se_a).pdf(x)
ax.plot(xA, yA)
ax.axvline(x=p_a, c='red', alpha=0.5, linestyle='--')
yB = scs.norm(p_b, se_b).pdf(x)
ax.plot(xB, yB)
ax.axvline(x=p_b, c='blue', alpha=0.5, linestyle='--')
plt.xlabel('Converted Proportion')
plt.ylabel('Probability Density')
```

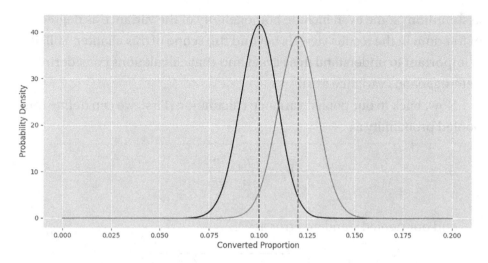

Figure 14-16. *Normal distribution for control (red) or test (blue) with mean conversion rate represented by dashed lines*

The distance between the red and blue dashed lines (denoting the mean conversion rate) equals $\hat{d}$. We had previously defined $\hat{d}$ as

$$\hat{d} = \widehat{p_b} - \widehat{p_a}$$

By plotting our normalized distribution with standard error, we can reason about our data in a standardized way. However, both our distributions still have different standard errors. To fully standardize our results and account for this difference, we must create a pooled standard error. The pooled standard error allows us to collect the standard error for the entire system; up until now, we have collected this for the test and control groups separately.

One problem with utilizing the pooled variance calculation is that it assumes that the variance between test groups is homogenous. If this assumption is false, and our variance between samples is not homogenous, our analysis will be ineffective (low power to detect effects). A detailed understanding of how modern statistical platforms avoid this assumption (some even include homogeneity of the variance as degrees of freedom in the results view) is beyond the scope of this chapter. Still, it is important to understand this caveat and that calculations considering heterogeneous variance exist.

Now, back to our pooled variance calculation. First, we can define our pooled probability as

$$\hat{p}_{pool} = \frac{p_a + p_b}{n_a + n_b}$$

and our pooled standard error as[15]

$$SE_{pool} = \sqrt{\hat{p}_{pool} * \left(1 - \hat{p}_{pool}\right) * \left(\frac{1}{n_a} + \frac{1}{n_b}\right)}$$

n_a is the sample size of the first sample (control).
n_b is the sample size of the second sample (test).
p_a is the probability of success of the first sample (control).
p_b is the probability of success of the second sample (test).

Note   When the null hypothesis suggests the proportions in the test and control groups are equal, we use the pooled proportion estimate $(\hat{p})$ to estimate the standard error.

---

[15] Cote, Linda R.; Gordon, Rupa; Randell, Chrislyn E.; Schmitt, Judy; and Marvin, Helena, "Introduction to Statistics in the Psychological Sciences" (2021). *Open Educational Resources Collection*. 25.
   Available at https://irl.umsl.edu/oer/25

Once we have our pooled standard error, we can re-plot our data in a normalized fashion and make an apples-to-apples comparison between our test and control groups. To better visualize this relationship, we can use some advanced plotting in Python to display the p-value, power, alpha, and beta. Figure 14-17 illustrates this calculation, which implements our previous calculations.

```
# plot with stats
plot.abplot(
    a_total,
    b_total,
    p_a,
    d_hat,
    b_converted,
    show_power=True,
    show_beta=True,
    show_alpha=True,
    show_p_value=True
)
```

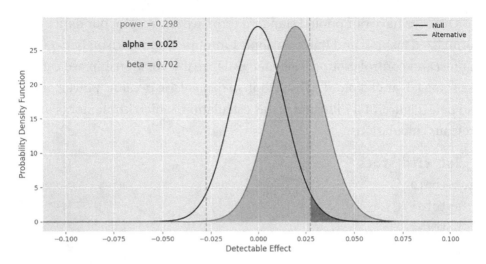

Figure 14-17. *Normal distribution for control (red) or test (blue) with dashed lines representing the confidence intervals*

Now reviewing our results, we can see that our statistical power is low. While we see a change in the conversion rate of .03 and p-value of .006 (less than our alpha of .025), the low statistical power points to a potential Type II error. If we launch our change globally after our experiment, we may not realize our gains. One way we can improve the power is by increasing the sample size. Before launching, we may call this out as a risk and rerun the experiment with a larger sample size to validate our results.

Utilizing our min_sample_size calculator from earlier in this chapter, we can re-plot our data with a sample size large enough to generate 80% power, as shown in Figure 14-18.

```
# utilizing our min_sample_size calculator
min_sample_size = m.min_sample_size(.1,.02)
# Min sample size per test group: 3843
# plot power
plot.abplot(
    min_sample_size,
    min_sample_size,
```

```
  p_a,
  d_hat,
  b_converted,
  show_power=True
)
```

Now we can see a situation where our results are statistically significant. The statistical power is equal to .8, and as a result, the curves for the null and alternative hypotheses are narrower, and the confidence interval is smaller.

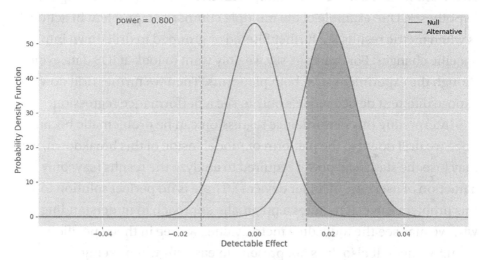

Figure 14-18. *Normal distribution for control (red) or test (blue)*

Normally you will have an experimentation framework and established metrics calculations, so you do not have to re-create these plots and statistics in an ad hoc manner. However, the core principles still apply. We must be able to reason about our data in a statistically sound manner to ensure we have adequate statistical power, sample size, and overall understanding of the results. Otherwise, we risk incorrectly accepting or rejecting the null hypothesis.

Common Pitfalls

Now that we have gone over hypothesis testing and the scientific method applied for software engineers, let us discuss some common experimentation pitfalls to avoid.

Multiple Comparison Problem

Each alternative hypothesis focuses on a single metric. If we want to check our feature's impact on multiple metrics, this requires multiple hypotheses. One example of the multiple comparison problem in action is when metric results are further filtered or grouped to drill down into specific changes. For example, say we only want to look at iOS data even though the experiment is on both platforms. Then we further drill down to expose different device models only to see a performance regression.

Interpreting this performance regression can be problematic because once we drill down to the platform or model inside of this breakdown, we may lose the statistical power required to analyze the results (say, only a fraction of users are on older devices). There is no perfect solution to this problem since. It requires a pragmatic approach to understanding why we may see the individual metric values we see in their specific circumstances. It also does not present an easy out when seeing statistically significant metric regressions (assuming the regression is bad). It may be that we see an actual regression. Still, it requires careful analysis to understand if we have significant experimentation power to detect the change we are seeing.

Experiment Pollution

Experiment pollution can occur when two experiments test a similar change in a nonmutually exclusive way. Say one experiment adds an additional tab entry point for the discover page while another change adds a banner deep link to the discover page. Suppose there is a significant overlap between the users in both experiment populations. In that case, it is impossible to tell which change has the statistically significant effect or if it is a combination of the two.

When designing experiments and working with other teams, it is essential to set up the universe in a way that allows for mutually exclusive experiments. Additionally, it is important to have a process to review experiments and detect potential pollution before starting.

Claiming Not Statistically Significant Results are Neutral

If the confidence interval for your experiment includes zero, that does not mean that the actual change is equal to zero. It means that given the observed data, a change of zero cannot be ruled out. To be confident that you are not substantially changing a metric, it is not enough to have a confidence interval that includes zero. The lower bound of the confidence interval must also be more significant than moderate or small negative values.

Running Experiments That Are Too Small (Underpowered)

The larger the sample size for the experiment, the smaller changes you can detect. If you run an experiment that is too small, the results can be largely unhelpful and consist of noisy data with large confidence intervals. It is important to ensure your experiment is large enough to have a chance of finding statistically significant results given an estimate of what the magnitude of the true delta likely is. This is the basis of the power calculation we discussed earlier.

P-Hacking

P-hacking is when engineers search through different filters and time ranges (subpopulation selection) to identify a specific pattern that matches their success criteria. P-hacking is common when there is business pressure on an experiment to produce specific results, and the experiment turns out to be neutral. A common p-hacking strategy is to modify the population selection criteria, such as particular dates or device type filters that cause the results to read as statistically significant even though the overall aggregate is neutral. By doing this, the 95% confidence intervals are not representative of the actual population (i.e., not guaranteed to contain the truth 95% of the time).

Additionally, p-hacking results make it challenging to replicate your experiment, given the initial assumptions. Engineering leaders should review all experiments to ensure engineers are not p-hacking results to produce the desired outcome.

Filtering on Posttreatment Variables

Looking at experiment effects in a subpopulation of users can give biased results if the treatment itself can affect who ends up in that subpopulation. For example, suppose we do not have an exact metric to determine who a teen is and instead make an inference based on several factors, including user's discover tab view habits, to define teen status. If, for our experiment, we are interested in the effect the Discover tab entry point has on visitation rates, we should then assess the visitation rate metric in our metrics platform. However, if we filter based on teens as the subpopulation in our metrics platform to evaluate teen visitation data to the Discover tab, we introduce a confounding result and potentially create a feedback loop since we may be changing who is defined as a teen by our treatment behavior. Given the confounding result and potential feedback loop, we cannot interpret the experimental results correctly.

Dilution

Even if we do a proper power analysis and determine our MDE, we can still run afoul. For example, if we expose 100% of users in our test group on application startup, but we actually have only 40% of users who see the treatment reducing our sample size by more than half. Especially if we do not notice that this occurred, we may not realize we have seriously changed our ability to detect changes.

Not Waiting for Results to Stabilize

Some changes, especially UI related, can have a novelty effect, where users react differently at first than they do over time. They may see a new tab bar button and, out of curiosity, explore it, but that may not carry over to long-term engagement. We may drastically alter our results by utilizing the first few days of data for newly exposed users.

Additionally, suppose we were to query a specific time range, potentially very early on in our experiment. In that case, we may only have a small subset of users who will have seen the treatment, and these users may only represent "power users" (the most frequent users). Then our results will be skewed toward the power users and have limited power (depending on how exposure logging is done). It is best to wait long enough for data to stabilize so that the deltas reflect the long-term effects we are interested in and users represent all users on our platform.

Nonrepresentative Test Experiences and Populations

The previous problem also closely relates to this one. Previously we mentioned that only focusing on a specific subset of power users is not representative of the broader population. However, there are other reasons we may end up in this situation, such as if we cannot test in different geographic locales due to regulatory constraints or if only iOS is ready (not waiting for Android). However, if we launch without including these excluded users, our launch results may differ significantly from our test data.

Moreover, suppose we split our experiment into several iterations, improve the Discover tab performance substantially, and separately test the addition of the Discover tab entry point. In that case, we do not have a clear view of how these changes interact. The performance change may be innocuous; however, if we were instead testing separate UI changes, we may end up in a situation where experiences clash, and users do not like them. Without testing all our changes together, we will not discover these situations until after launch.

Ignoring the Network Effect

Certain experiments may rely on several users interacting jointly. For example, suppose we were to roll out sharing discoverable content via a messaging feature for users' friends. In that case, it may be very difficult to test this change on users since both the sender and receiver need to be part of the experiment. Suppose a user's top ten friends (other users they engage with) are not in the experiment with them, even if they have access to shareable content via messaging. In that case, they may not use the sharing feature since no one they typically talk to is eligible to receive the message. To combat this, we can utilize a network-based test. In this setup, we will use the cluster-based universe allocation to cluster users into the test and control groups with their close friends. This way, we know that the user can use the feature in the way we intend to make our test more closely mirror the production environment.

Pre-AA Bias

Pre-AA bias occurs when one or both of the segments utilized for testing have a previous bias affecting the current experimental results. Most experimentation platforms will randomize users for experiment selection; however, for some treatments that require careful measurement and can have confounding factors, such as improving session loss, pre-AA bias can still exist and negatively impact results. For other experiments, such as latency measurement, AA bias may not matter. Work with your team to understand the specific nuances of experimentation. In some situations, it is necessary to start multiple simultaneous experiments or specific AA variants to assess the effects of AA bias.

Additionally, some experimentation platforms can take away some of the effects of pre-AA bias by calculating a seven-day average of the required metrics before the experiment's start date. This allows for a normalization of the starting level when calculating different test statistics later during the results analysis phase.

Additional Validation Steps

After reading this chapter, you are well equipped to conduct successful experiments and review others' experiments for correctness. However, even if we follow all the best practices presented here and have a battle-tested analytics and experimentation framework, we may run into unexpected or unexplained behavior. There are three ways we can work to combat these challenges:

1. Validating results via a backtest: Even after launch, we should create a group consisting of a small percentage of users who will not see our experience (commonly called a holdout). This way, even when

we launch, we can evaluate the change against our holdout users. If we see unexpected metrics changes, we can detect them in the holdout.

2.   If possible, before launching, we can run our launch candidate in a separate experiment in another universe to better guarantee a more randomized "new" group of users. This will help us better understand the reproducibility of our results.

3.   If potential AA bias is expected, look at assessing the key metrics values prior to the experiment start and potentially starting multiple iterations of the same experiment to lesson the risk.

Summary

Experimentation via A/B tests is a critical tool for software engineers that allows us to validate and measure the effects of our changes. As engineering leaders, we must think critically about how we design our experiments and how we analyze the results to ensure we are reaching the correct conclusions and shipping the most effective changes. To analyze experiment results, you will likely rely on an experiment platform, not custom Python code. However, understanding why we experiment the way we do and what statistics underlie the methodology is important when reviewing experiments for correctness and understanding potential edge cases.

Key Takeaways

1. Ensure the experimentation process follows the scientific method. By doing this, you are applying a standard battle-tested decision-making process.

2. Ensure your experiment, or those of engineers you review, is appropriately set up and avoids common pitfalls. By properly reviewing experiments on your team, you can ensure experimentation is done right the first time and build confidence in the results.

3. Type I error rates relate to the alpha, and Type II error rates relate to the power. To avoid Type I error rates, we need to set the alpha for our experiment at a suitable level. To avoid Type II error rates, we must ensure our experiment has enough power to reliably detect the effect we want.

4. When evaluating results, it is important to look holistically at the data available to understand the overall effect size, the statistical significance (p-value), and experimental power.

Further Learning

1. Statistical Power Analysis for the Behavioral Sciences (2nd Edition)

2. Heterogeneity tolerance testing via the Satterthwaite approximation www.ncbi.nlm.nih.gov/pmc/ articles/PMC3783032/

3. Using Effect Size—or Why the *P* Value Is Not Enough www.ncbi.nlm.nih.gov/pmc/articles/PMC3444174/

4. Manipulatable power tool https://rpsychologist.com/d3/nhst/

CHAPTER 15

Application Release and Maintenance

In our journey through the SDLC, we have worked through planning and developing testable features via experimentation and automated tests. Now it is time to release the completed feature or project. After release, we need to ensure our feature is maintained correctly. While launching and maintaining a small feature is relatively simple, releasing a large project is more complex. Properly releasing and maintaining a large project at scale takes time, coordination, and a mature build system and requires careful planning to ensure proper monitoring for release. Figure 15-1 outlines the SDLC's maintenance and deployment (release) sections that we will discuss in this chapter.

© Eric Vennaro 2023
E. Vennaro, *iOS Development at Scale*, https://doi.org/10.1007/978-1-4842-9456-7_15

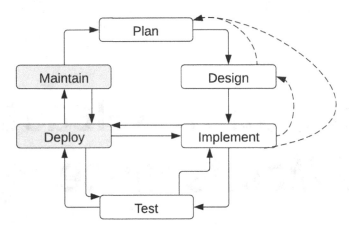

Figure 15-1. *SDLC highlighting the maintenance and deployment steps*

This Chapter Includes

This chapter includes a detailed look at the engineering challenges associated with continuous integration and continuous delivery (CI/CD), a system to deliver ongoing monitoring throughout the life cycle of the application, including testing, beta releases for manual testing, and eventual release. In the first section of this chapter, we will dive deep into the role CI/CD systems play in supporting the release and maintenance of large projects. Next, we will discuss the necessary steps to ensure a smooth release, including some of the more process-oriented steps tech leads must ensure happen. Lastly, we will discuss some of the critical alerting and monitoring steps required to maintain previously launched features.

Managing Continuous Integration and Delivery: The Build Process

To successfully release a large project, it's essential to quickly and efficiently release builds with unfinished features that are disabled for production users. This means carefully gating new features and having a system in place to disable them (using feature flags, which are part of the experimentation platform). Feature flags allow for continuous testing and feedback on the project throughout the SDLC iterations and before launching the feature or project.

Say we want to build the Discover surface for the Photo Stream application, as mentioned in Chapter 14. If it takes three months to fully build the feature, we can decompose it into three one-month cycles (we could even have more granular cycles):

1. Building the module, experimentation infrastructure to hide the feature, API consumption, and entry point to the surface. The cycle ends with the application skeleton merged[1] into the master branch and hidden from production users.

2. Building the UI components to display and interact with Discover tab surface elements. The cycle ends with the components merged into the master branch and hidden behind a feature flag.

---

[1] In this chapter, we use merge to generally mean combining changes from a feature branch into the main (master) branch. Depending on version control utilized, the specific terms may vary.

531

3. Connecting the surface end to end, including deep link notification support and sharing to other surfaces. The cycle ends with the completed feature hidden behind a feature flag and awaiting production release.

Note A feature flag is a common term for a gating mechanism allowing engineers to remotely and dynamically, at runtime, toggle a feature's visibility (or functionality if the feature is not user-facing) on and off without requiring an infrastructure change or deployment.

Each of these cycles represents one or more SDLCs, and at a minimum, in each step, we will want to have tests implemented for the completed work. Additionally, throughout each cycle, the existing application functionality must remain intact. Cycles two and three should also involve some aspects of manual testing. Figure 15-2 outlines how these three cycles may lead to a launch. We need competent build and release pipelines called continuous integration and continuous delivery (CI/CD) to support large-scale automated testing and build distribution for manual testing. While many large companies make custom-release solutions, common tools like Fastlane and third-party services such as CircleCI and Travis CI help support CI and CD. This section will outline some essential features and aspects of managing an extensive release system while leaving the tooling agnostic.

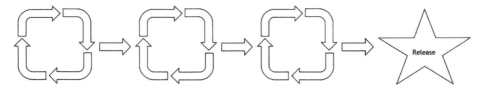

Figure 15-2. *Three SDLCs followed by 100% production release*

Much like the SDLC, the overall CI/CD pipeline can be broken down into smaller steps that unblock the successful release process starting at the individual pull request level and advance to a full production release.

At each level, we want the ability to have rapid high-signal continuous feedback about the effects of developers' code changes while efficiently using the company's compute resources (servers are not free after all). A high signal-to-noise ratio is critical so that engineers do not waste time tracking down failures unrelated to their changes. For instance, if every time an engineer submits a pull request, several of the automated tests run fail consistently, the engineer will not take those tests seriously. Their failures will be bypassed, and changes will land anyway. If this behavior continues, the tests will not provide a useful signal and will instead be classified as noisy. Without proper testing, potential production problems are more likely to occur. Rapid and frequent, highly accurate (high-signal) feedback is crucial so engineers can fix bugs in their code quickly and not attempt to bypass or ignore tests to save time (potentially due to business pressures or unreliable tests).

To meet the time pressures and reliability constraints to deliver high-fidelity results while maintaining a low server compute load, we must run different builds and test suites at different times based on

1. Coverage: Do not build and test it unless the change may actually have broken it.

2. Speed: Faster builds and tests consume fewer resources

3. Flakiness: Flaky builds and tests are unreliable and disruptive. A flaky test is a common term for a test that passes and fails irrespective of code changes, making it an unreliable estimate of code correctness.

4. Correlation: If builds always succeed or fail together, build only one on every diff.

We follow a continuous delivery and integration process that focuses on specific constraints. This process starts at the individual pull request level and continues until the application is submitted to Apple for review and released on the App Store.

When we submit a pull request for review,[2] we run a series of automated tests to ensure that the code changes do not have any unintended consequences. This involves analyzing the code changes using a CI server and running the required tests, which are typically small, fast snapshots containing the most relevant tests. This process is outlined in Figure 15-3 and is typically the entire process for small projects. After the pull request (PR) has passed tests and is approved, it is immediately rebased or merged onto the main working branch (typically referred to as the master branch) for commit. However, this strategy does not scale well. This is because the rebasing and merging processes require integrating the changes from the pull request into the main working branch. When hundreds of engineers are working on a single project, the working branch can quickly change, resulting in merge conflicts or changes that interact badly with each other, causing failure. In my own experience on large monorepo iOS applications, there can be upwards of 100 pull requests landed per hour, meaning the main working branch changes really fast!

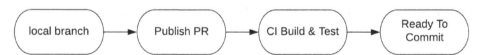

Figure 15-3. *Life cycle of a pull request. Ready to commit represents that the PR is ready for the merge or rebase operation, allowing the code to be added to the master branch.*

To mitigate this problem once a pull request is approved and scheduled for inclusion in the master branch, we can rebase the pull request changeset onto the master branch and run additional tests. This

[2] Here, for simplicity, we are focused on Git version control terminology; however, the process is applicable to any flavor of version control.

helps alleviate the concern of running too many tests on each iteration of the pull request (utilizing valuable compute resources and causing additional lag time for engineers) and helps to prevent failures due to merge conflicts. Lastly, once the commit is merged into the master branch, we can run additional tests to ensure that the master branch is stable. Checking the master branch adds an additional layer of protection against merge conflicts and changes that, while independently passing all automated tests, interact badly together, causing failures.

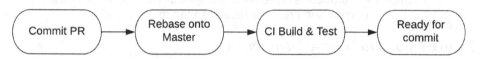

Figure 15-4. *Landing (merging or rebasing) a PR onto the master branch*

Figure 15-5 combines these different flows into a holistic approach to managing continuous integration at scale. Here, we have hundreds of engineers working on various features and merging their code directly into the master branch, commonly called the trunk. This style of version control is often called trunk-based development. Utilizing short-lived developer branches is preferred to long-running developer branches at scale because it avoids complex merge conflicts resulting from long-running developer branches that become stale and out of sync with the latest changes on the master branch. Merge conflicts with long-running developer branches are extremely problematic when large numbers of engineers are working on the same project.

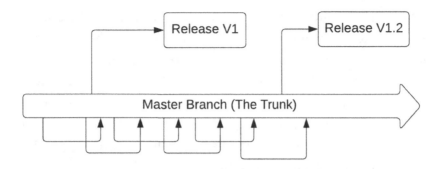

Short-lived branches representing engineer work done by one
person and once approved landed to the trunk

Figure 15-5. *Trunk-based development*

Independent of code merging to the master branch, a series of tests
are continuously run at a lower frequency across a broader range of
functionality to assist in detecting additional failures. These tests help
increase overall coverage while minimally impacting server capacity.
Table 15-1 outlines the different testing phases we have reviewed, their
frequency and effect on server capacity. It's important to note that
providing quicker feedback requires more server computation, which
can be costly. When many developers make changes simultaneously,
the number of test runs increases exponentially, leading to significant
consumption of computing resources.

Additionally, given the scale of development, we must run additional
tests when the pull request is updated to master for merge (column 3)
and after the commit is landed to master (column 4) to ensure the overall
monorepo remains stable. This additional testing produces additional
server overhead but ensures the main branch remains stable.

Continuous testing, on the other hand, only requires a constant
number of test runs per day and scales better. To balance the need for
engineers to receive prompt, actionable feedback with the available
computing resources, it's essential to carefully select which tests to run
during each phase.

Table 15-1. *Mapping test phases to feedback timing and capacity requirements*

	Pull Request Submitted	Merge Pull Request	After Commit	Continuous
Frequency	For each pull request	At merge time	At commit time	At a predefined time
Feedback timing	Very early	Early	Delayed	Very delayed
Required capacity	Very high	High	High	Low

Keeping Master Stable

Despite our best efforts with automated testing, sometimes, breaking changes can land to the master branch, causing instability. Master branch instability can result from merge conflicts (despite utilizing trunk-based development) and the direct landing of breaking changes that were not caught during testing. To help keep the master branch stable and avoid inevitable breakages, we can create a special oncall rotation where engineers monitor master branch tests to ensure they pass. If tests fail on the master branch, the oncall engineer must debug based on the commits merged during that time period and revert the offending code. This can be quite complex given that hundreds of changes can land each hour.[3]

---

[3] https://engineering.fb.com/2017/08/31/web/rapid-release-at-massive-scale/

Note   An oncall rotation is a common name for a group of engineers who rotate, taking responsibility for a specific (usually time-consuming) task, such as keeping the master branch stable. By rotating, engineers share the workload and also the knowledge, avoiding burnout and single points of failure.[4]

Managing Build Times

To speed up the automated testing process and reduce the time it takes for engineers to receive results based on their changes, it is recommended to assess the application's build time. One way to achieve this is by breaking down the application into modules and using an advanced build system tool like Buck or Bazel. With this approach, the system can cache unchanged modules, resulting in faster build times for CI. For instance, Airbnb witnessed 50% faster CI builds after switching to Buck.[5]

Uber also switched to using Buck as they scaled the number of modules in their application from 5 to over 40. They were using CocoaPods before, which slowed down automated testing since it required every application and module to build for every code change submitted for review.

Note   Buck is a build tool built for monolithic repositories (monorepo) that can build code, run unit tests, and distribute build artifacts across machines so that other developers can spend less time compiling *old* code and more time writing *new* code.[6]

---

[4] https://developers.soundcloud.com/blog/building-a-healthy-on-call-culture

[5] https://medium.com/airbnb-engineering/building-mixed-language-ios-project-with-buck-8a903b0e3e56

[6] https://buck.build/

538

Advanced build system tools like Buck are made for monorepos (a monorepo is a version-controlled code repository that holds many projects). Advanced build systems are a common way to manage large iOS applications because they reduce tooling maintenance and standardize the development process across related areas of code. A well-designed monorepo consists of small, reusable modules, and Buck leverages this to intelligently analyze the changes made and build only what is needed. Buck specifically provides caching and takes advantage of multicore CPUs so that multiple modules can be built simultaneously, including unit tests.

Uber leveraged Buck's distributed caching feature as part of their build system optimizations so that when a target is built, it is not recompiled until the code in that target (or one of the targets it depends on) changes. That means you can set up a repository where the tooling will intelligently determine what needs to be rebuilt and retested while caching everything else. Engineers at Uber saved time using the artifacts compiled remotely on CI servers locally for their builds.[7]

Continuous Delivery

We can establish a release cadence now that we have a stable build system and optimized build time. For our internal release cadence, we can utilize our build system to deliver updated builds based on the stable master branch consistently. For this process, we can integrate with a tool like Fastlane[8] that helps automate the code signing and release process, saving engineers from manually making these changes. With these capabilities, we can deliver nightly builds to QA teams and enable company-wide dogfooding on stable master branch builds. These builds can be delivered

---

[7] www.uber.com/blog/ios-monorepo/
[8] https://fastlane.tools/

using an in-house solution or TestFlight (a tool provided by Apple for build distribution and beta testing),[9] which would mirror a beta testing environment.

Dogfooding is an older term first defined in the 1990s as "eating your own dog food" and initially used by advertisers.[10] Software companies have since co-opted the term to mean employees utilizing their own products. Dogfooding helps to provide a customer's point of view on the product and assists in teams building better product intuition. It also helps to reveal bugs early on in the software process.

Company-wide dogfooding of changes allows engineers to receive early feedback and help catch regressions sooner. It is essential to combine the continuous delivery setup with our experimentation platform and the concept of feature flags to avoid showing changes that are not ready for release to our users. We can enable features for employees, QA, or some subset of the two via the experimentation framework to allow for targeted dogfooding.

The Release Infrastructure

From an infrastructure perspective, each step thus far leads to a successful release, and while there is a lot more that goes into a successful launch (which we will discuss in the next section), currently, we are assured that we have

1. A stable development environment that continuously delivers early builds of the application to QA and developers for testing

---

[9] https://developer.apple.com/testflight/

[10] W. Harrison, "Eating Your Own Dog Food" in IEEE Software, vol. 23, no. 03, pp. 5–7, 2006, doi: 10.1109/MS.2006.72

2. Ability to leverage the infrastructure to get
    continuous feedback from automated tests and daily
    input from manual tests and dogfooding to discover
    bugs early in the development process

At this point, we can build, test, and dogfood our feature on internal builds, but we have yet to release (or deploy) it to end users. The release stage has its own engineering challenges. At a high level in the release stage, we must ensure the following:

1. All work is done on a short-lived development
    branch and merged into the master branch first
    (assuming tests pass).

2. On a weekly cadence, say, Monday at 4 am,
    branches are cut and merged into the release
    branch. Figure 15-3 shows a release branch being
    cut from the trunk.

3. The following week is spent fixing potentially
    launch-blocking bugs and ensuring the branch
    is stable.

4. End of the day Monday (approximately one week
    after the branch cut), we submit the code on the
    branch to Apple for review.

5. The application should then be reviewed by Apple
    and released live Thursday (if the review goes
    smoothly).

Table 15-2 outlines the process outlined previously in a calendar format.

Table 15-2. *Three SDLCs followed by 100% production release*

MON	TUES	WED	THUR	FRI		SAT	SUN
Branch cut V1	Only merge launch blockers					Only merge company-critical blockers	
Submit v1 Branch cut v2	V2 only merges launch blockers		Release v1	V2 only merges launch blockers		Company-critical blockers	

In an ideal world, we catch potential launch blockers prior to the release cycle date reserved for the product launch. If the project is set to launch on May 1, having all changes set for inclusion by April 15 provides an additional week to find and fix any problems without bumping up against the release cycle timeline and constraints outlined in Table 15-2 (it is always best to get changes in early to leave time for additional QA and last minute bugfixes).

The release cycle puts added pressure on when code changes included in the release can be landed. Since the week before the release, only changes that meet the bar as a launch blocker are able to be included. This is because there is limited time to test late-stage changes, and new additions present a risk of creating bugs at the last minute. We must provide clear guidance to empower engineers to decide whether launch-blocking criteria are met or if company-critical blocking criteria are met. By giving clear criteria, we can confidently delegate to engineers so that they can decide what can be merged in what stages of the week. To define the process formally, we can institute a release oncall where an oncall represents a group of engineers who will take turns serving as the point of contact for any release-related concerns (a similar process to how we keep the trunk stable).

The following are some sample criteria for launch blockers and company-critical launch blockers that can be defined for the release oncall:

1. Launch blockers

    a. A new feature you want to launch has a bug that will delay the launch unless fixed. You can, however, disable the feature with a feature flag.

2. Company-critical blockers

    a. A new code change has broken an existing feature inside of the application causing an instant crash.

    b. A new code change introduced a critical regression to the application startup time.

Release Oncall

To handle the release process, teams often establish a rotation of engineers responsible for releasing the application, known as the release oncall (sometimes referred to as "captain"). This helps distribute the burden of release responsibility among team members, reducing the pressure and cognitive load associated with managing application release and avoiding a single point of failure associated with having the same engineer always release the application.

During their week of service, the release engineer should focus on resolving any launch-blocking issues and ensuring that all automated tests for the build are passing. They should also monitor key metrics during the weekly push. Depending on the application's scope and scale, multiple release oncall engineers may be required. To reduce the preparation time and help onboard team members faster to the release oncall, we should do the following:

1. To ensure consistency in oncall processes, it is essential to establish a single source of truth for documentation. Ample documentation assists new engineers in learning the processes, common pitfalls, and solutions to typical issues faced by oncalls. This documentation, also known as a runbook, should codify best practices in a formal and centralized way. This will result in faster onboarding for new team members and better distribution of knowledge to the entire team.

2. Outline the release oncall schedule months in advance on the engineer's work calendar to provide time to prepare and time to swap slots based on engineer availability. Allowing engineers to change oncall weeks alleviates some of the pressure around oncall and reduces the impact on engineers' work-life balance. No one wants to cancel paid time off to manage an application release.

3. Automate, automate, automate. The more of the release process we can automate via tools like Fastlane, the less work is required for individual engineers. In addition to automating the CI/CD portion, automating the necessary sign-offs and approvals, communicating status updates, and queuing launch-blocking tasks can help reduce the workload. Even if these tasks cannot be automated entirely, even partial automation and well-documented processes can help reduce cognitive load and result in less human error.

How to Measure System Success

As we have discussed measuring performance and experimentation success, we also want to ensure our build system meets the objective and continuously delivers on its promises. Our objective is the ability to unblock engineers to merge code reliably and quickly while safeguarding our application and release from failures. To do so, we can define three topline metrics:

1. Reliability: How consistently are engineers landing high-quality code?

2. Correctness: How frequently are pull requests breaking master?

3. Time to signal: How long do engineers need to wait for automated tests to complete?

By tracking these metrics, we can ensure that our CI/CD system is effectively meeting the needs of engineers.

Can We Move Faster?

Releasing the application now takes about one to one and a half weeks to fully roll out new changes, which starkly contrasts with current web development continuous release cadences where changes can land in production in mere hours. There are good reasons for requiring a slower release cadence for mobile applications because once the application is shipped, it takes time to fix any problems, meaning it is difficult to fix problems once they reach production. We cannot simply roll changes back like we can on the Web. Succinctly the constraints on mobile are as follows:

1. We need to be extra careful about changes launched because we cannot easily take them back. That level of detail requires extra debugging time to ensure the final release is high quality.

2. We must allot time for App Store Review. We cannot meaningfully change the amount of time Apple requires for review and instead must work with Apple and the provided constraints.

3. It is difficult to continuously have a beta program covering all devices, meaning that additional time is needed internally to stabilize and test across a wide range of devices.

Releasing a Large Project

Now that we have a CI/CD system built that can support our continuous testing and delivery of features, we need to leverage it correctly to streamline releasing large projects. Regardless of the type of project we are looking to launch, there are some best practices to follow during building our feature and leading up to the release. These best practices correspond to different phases of feature development:

1. When building the feature

2. When internally dogfooding the application

3. Meeting the launch standards

4. During a limited release

5. During the production release (deploying to all eligible users)

When Building Our Feature

We cannot wait until we are about to release to consider the necessary steps for release. During feature development, we must think critically about the release and the specific product requirements for release. These requirements can include

1. Performance constraints

2. Privacy standards

3. Security standards

4. Business or engagement metric movement

5. UI standards

6. Dependency on other engineering teams

During development and individual SDLCs leading up to a project release, we must ensure we are correctly testing our features and constantly coordinating with business partners to update them on feature capabilities and critical metric readings.

Some of these constraints such as privacy and security standards may not be completely related to the code. This may require a more nuanced understanding of the product landscape and business commitments to end users. For example:

1. Suppose we are working on end-to-end encrypting our Photo Stream application. In that case, we need to ensure that the application is fully migrated to the end-to-end encryption stack and has no legacy endpoint access that presents a risk if discovered.

2.   We may need to protect a specific cohort of users, such as teens, or users by geographical region (the European Union – EU). We must ensure the code aligns with product standards and that the selected user cohorts do not see the feature.

3.   In the case of end-to-end encryption, we, as engineers, know the code base best and must ensure that the principles are upheld. For example, if we inspect the text after it is unencrypted on a device, we may violate the spirit of end-to-end encryption. Or, more egregious, if we log that data for debugging purposes, we are definitely breaking end-to-end encryption.

As engineers, it is our duty to identify potential issues before they reach the users. Since we are familiar with the code base, we should notify the product team of any problems that may arise. For instance, if we aim to implement a specific feature in the product specification, we should consider the possibility of limited Wi-Fi connectivity and suggest solutions to the product team.

When working on a project that relies on metrics, it's important to ensure that our launch candidate has the potential to meet the goals. Throughout development, the team should track long-term trends to understand what may happen after the launch. This will allow the team to have a frame of reference for debugging issues if the post-launch results differ from pre-launch.

Note   Before launching, what questions would I ask if I was reviewing a launch? Or what questions does my leadership ask? And make sure to have the answers ready.

If you are working on infrastructure-related changes or a broader infrastructure migration, your goal might not be to move metrics but rather to keep them stable. It's essential to have a baseline understanding of potential metric movement during the build phase to build confidence toward release. If you detect regressions early on, you can work to improve them or raise the issue to leadership to better understand the trade-off between negative metric movement and the benefits of launch. For example, suppose launching is critical for privacy constraints or compliance with EU regulations. In that case, it might be necessary to launch despite the regression and make a thoughtful trade-off for future metric improvement.

It's important that we do not wait until the last minute, or even worse, after launching, to address any concerns that may arise. To avoid this, we should consider launch requirements from the beginning and keep them in mind as we experiment and release. If we are migrating infrastructure that requires other teams to make changes, we need to keep those teams updated in a timely manner. By involving teams early on, we can work together to create a migration timeline that considers their abilities to comply and avoid any unintentional feature breaks upon launch.

Who Are These Concerned Business Partners?

We have discussed frequently throughout this book that we may need to understand business partners' perspectives and consider their input. Essentially, a business partner could be anyone you work with or rely on to help define guidelines or product standards. This could include

1. Legal and policy advisers.

2. Marketing and communications teams.

3. Privacy specialists.

4.   Product specialists, including user researchers, product managers, and internationalization specialists.

5.   Sales teams.

6.   Other engineers. Other engineers may be your primary client and business partners if you work on an underlying infrastructure project.

When aligning for a major launch, we must work closely with all business partners to meet all business requirements. Additionally, there may be required external communications and other policy changes that will influence the launch timeline. For example, if the marketing team needs to release a series of global communication posts before the engineering launch, then from an engineering side, we must make sure not to launch until the marketing is also aligned.

Meeting Launch Standards

Before launching, it is critical to ensure all external stakeholders are aligned. For infrastructure or data migrations, this can involve more business partners but is typically more engineering minded. It is key to ensure that all relevant engineer partner teams are aware of the migration, adoption path, and timeline. Additionally, we must have an understanding of any regressions. For product-related feature launches or infrastructure changes that modify the product experience (such as a UI redesign to new components), there can be more involvement from different business stakeholders whose input is required.

While it is not necessarily your job as an engineer to manage the overall process and reach alignment with each stakeholder, it is your job to hold the bar for the overall release and ensure the engineering rollout goes smoothly. A smooth rollout requires business alignment. If you notice or perceive any gaps, you must raise the issue and push for a fix. For example, suppose you know that a privacy review must be completed before launching, and you have not seen or done a privacy review to avoid missing a critical step. In that case, you must raise the issue with the appropriate business stakeholders to push for a resolution.

In addition to business concerns that could block a launch for metric-driven teams, it is critical to position the launch at the right time for metric readings. Some teams will have specific metric reading weeks to ensure stability. Or for ads, holiday seasons are typically avoided due to massive ad pricing shifts. It is not possible to be aware of every nuanced requirement, such as ad pricing shifts. Still, it is critical to assess the situation and discuss it with relevant stakeholders with experience to ensure the launch is timed correctly.

Dogfooding and Limited Release

Once we have an eligible launch candidate capable of meeting the launch standards, we must test it on real users in a limited fashion to limit any hurt caused by bugs. For some products, dogfooding may be relatively easy (having internal employees regularly utilize the feature) to gather feedback before release. However, this may be harder for some applications due to the nature of the user base. To counteract this, engineers can structure internal dogfooding sessions where the project team members try out the new feature. Internal dogfooding sessions can still add value in finding bugs, even with employee dogfooding.

Additionally, teams can utilize a limited release where the product is released to a small set of users who have opted into testing new features. If the product is business to business, these businesses potentially have an arrangement to test early features. Either way, it is essential to gather both user-based and metric-based feedback to ensure the new project launch does not regress performance and user experience and meets the project's original intent.

The main difference between a limited release and dogfooding is that dogfooding can occur more continuously as builds are pushed to the master branch; they can be distributed weekly for employees as part of the testing cycle, while limiting testing is a more formal process typically only done when required for significant new product releases, such as an entirely new application, or when large-scale internal dogfooding is impossible.

Release

Once a project can pass the limited release stage without any regressions, it is finally ready for release. At this point, all changes should be included in the production application and disabled via a feature flag (part of the experimentation framework). By releasing behind a feature flag, we can control the rollout speed and closely monitor the effects on users.

During the release process, the team must identify a good time for the release. For example, releasing on a Friday is a bad idea since no one is available to monitor the release on Saturday and Sunday. Once a sensible release date is picked (perhaps Tuesday since Tuesday aligns well with our hypothetical release cycle listed earlier), we must also create a plan to manage any problems with the release. We need a clear point of contact in case something goes wrong and a clear set of metrics to monitor to ascertain if something is going wrong.

After release, we should start a backtest. A backtest is when we hold out our feature from a small number of users to monitor the continued effects using our experimentation framework. We should see consistency between the pre-test experiment readings and the backtest readings. If we do not see consistent readings, this may indicate an underlying issue with the production feature.

Alerting and Monitoring

Alerting and monitoring are critical components of feature development and launch. While not the most exciting part of software engineering, alerting and monitoring provide insights into how our products perform and a vehicle to detect and debug potentially nuanced, complex issues only found in production.

Logging

Effective alerting and monitoring require proper logging. It is essential to add logging at crucial stages during feature development to collect the necessary data to monitor the project. Engineers should ensure that the logging added allows them to prove that their feature is working correctly at a granular level. For instance, if the project requires delivering ads with a gap of two photos between them, logging is crucial to show the ad and photo's ordering and delivery on both the server and client. To avoid missing logging, it is recommended to add a specific section for logging in to the project planning document and the task tracker. This way, the team can review the logging and provide input if they feel more or less is required and progress is trackable. Additionally, creating a specific logging-related section explicitly mentions any changes in data collection, which can trigger privacy reviews.

Once we have logging in place, the data we collect is referred to as metrics. Metrics can represent anything from performance-related concerns we discussed earlier, including crash rates, user engagement, entry rates, and anything else critical for your application or project. Metrics recorded from logging are the base values utilized to correlate diverse factors, understand historical trends, and measure changes in your consumption, performance, or error rates.

Monitoring

Metrics refer to the data in your system, while monitoring involves collecting, aggregating, and analyzing these values to gain a better understanding of your components' characteristics and behavior. Creating a dashboard to visualize these metrics using company tooling is also important. In the monitoring phase, it is crucial to aggregate the raw metric data and present it in a way that allows other engineers to comprehend the significant parts of the system's behavior.

Converting raw metric data into usable aggregations can be a time-consuming process. To effectively present the data and visualize alert thresholds, assessing specific conditions and identifying deviations from expectations are essential. For instance, for daily visitation metrics, we may need to create trend-based graphs or use slow drift detection to track gradual changes over time. On the other hand, for crash rates or timeouts, percentile checks (like the performance section) can help us understand the typical user experience (P50) and outliers (P90, P99) so we can set appropriate static thresholds. For example, if we notice a spike in average application latency that exceeds what we believe to be the P99 case, it could indicate an apparent issue with the system.

To enable effective data aggregation, the monitoring system should retain the data and track the metrics over time. This allows us to leverage the data trends to understand the expected and desired behavior and define actionable alerts based on divergence from historical trends.

Alerting

Alerting is a crucial component of a monitoring system that takes action based on changes in metric values. Alerts are made up of two properties:

1. A metrics-based condition. This could be a predefined static threshold.

2. An action to perform when the values fall outside of
    the acceptable conditions. This could be in the form
    of calling an engineer's primary device to notify
    them of a problem.

With proper alerts, engineers do not have to constantly check
dashboards to understand system performance. Alerts allow for passive
software system management by defining situations that make sense to
actively manage and notifying engineers when these situations occur.

To effectively handle alerts, we need to differentiate between their
levels of severity. This enables us to notify teams in a manner that
suits the magnitude of the problem. Additionally, this approach helps
avoid alert fatigue caused by excessive "high-priority" notifications for
minor problems. Alert fatigue can cause real high-priority issues to be
overlooked. For instance, for a minor crash, engineers may get notified via
an internal task system or an email, while for a major crash that impedes
a launch, they would receive a direct call or notification on their primary
phone.[11]

Logging to Alerting Example

Using our end-to-end encryption migration mentioned in the previous
section, if we know we want to protect specific user cohorts during the
migration specifically in the EU – say specifically from seeing sharing since
it is not encrypted – we can set up specific logging for sharing sends and
receives, cross-reference it by country, and create a critical alert if a sharing
spike is detected for users in the EU.

---

[11] www.pagerduty.com/, a commonly used alerting service.

Maintenance

Once the release is successful, the team will move on to new work, and the release-related extra attention will diminish, leaving the regular teams oncall to handle issues. And because we have instituted proper alerting and monitoring, we are prepared to detect any unexpected problems. A typical team will institute oncall rotations to receive alerts for any production issues.

If the team is working on projects that heavily rely on metrics, they may need to frequently report the backtest numbers to ensure that they are on track to meet their goals. For instance, if the team has committed to increasing the revenue by 2% within a year, then the revenue number in the backtest should steadily approach a 2% gain as more projects are launched. Any fluctuations or reductions in revenue could pose a significant challenge for the team.

Summary

This chapter completes our tour of the SDLC. We have now discussed planning, building, testing, and releasing critical projects. With proper planning, we set ourselves up for smooth project execution, and by considering early release constraints, we can position the team for a smooth release process. First, we must have the proper CI/CD system set up to manage large-scale project maintenance and release. Next, we must lead the critical components of the project release.

1. Ensure all internal stakeholders agree on the release date and have signed off on necessary privacy or other commitments.

2. Ensure the launch candidate is stable and passes all testing stages.

3.   Ensure a launch plan is established, including the following:

    a. An experiment is set up to support the launch.

    b. A launch oncall rotation.

    c. Proper alerting and monitoring.

    d. Plan to establish a backtest post-launch.

During the feature development phase of the project, we can ensure that we meet quality standards and have a viable launch candidate through early dogfooding of available builds and experimentation with earlier versions of the feature. Without the ability to continuously deliver builds and an experimentation framework to test, we would be blind to the effects of our changes. Lastly, once released, we must continue to monitor to ensure the feature and change set are successful – this is especially important for metric-driven wins where metric movement must be sustained for the entirety of the half. Figure 15-6 combines the CI/CD system for iOS build distribution with our release process.

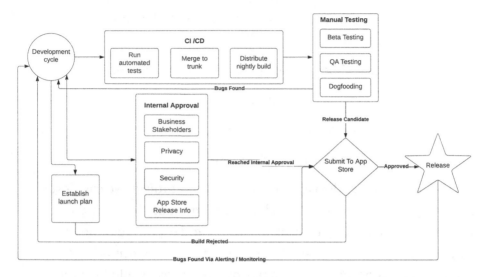

Figure 15-6. *Release process with related concern and build distribution/test setup*

At each stage in the SDLC, we have reviewed engineering and people-related challenges. Especially during the lead-up to a project launch, a lot of communication is required to align all stakeholders. In the final part of this book, we will discuss the people skills necessary to help successfully complete the SDLC and release a large project.

Key Takeaways

1. Plan early and revise often. During the software building phase, it is critical to continuously ensure that the project is on track (or trending toward) meeting the launch criteria.

2. Have alerting, monitoring, and a proper backtest in place to ensure that once released, the project is continuously evaluated for correctness.

3. Launching a project is not all about technical challenges, while infrastructure and software correctness are required, it is equally important to navigate the people challenges and business constraints to ensure the software built meets expectations.

4. Continuous integration is different at scale. We must run tests at additional stages in the landing process and carefully monitor the master branch for failures to ensure that all engineers can work effectively and continuously merge high-quality changes.

Further Learning

1. Trunk-based development

   b. `https://trunkbaseddevelopment.com/`

2. Uber optimizing CI build time (this is in Go, but similarly applicable for iOS)

   a. `www.uber.com/blog/how-we-halved-go-monorepo-ci-build-time/`

PART IV

Leading At Scale

CHAPTER 16

Leading Multiple Teams

We have made it through quite a journey thus far. Now, we must discuss how to put together the different portions of this book (iOS fundamentals, software architecture, SDLC skills, and project leadership best practices) in the context of expectations and soft skills necessary for success. At engineering levels past senior, it takes more than just engineering chops to prioritize and execute projects especially over long periods where building up junior engineers and cultivating good relationships across the broader organization are essential.

At the point in your career that you start to lead multiple teams and own broader product direction, most tech companies split into two parallel tracks: management and senior IC (individual contributor). The senior IC levels typically map to staff and principal. At staff and principal levels, engineers need not only the technical skills acquired in the first two parts of this book but also the leadership and soft skills to successfully lead large teams.

One method to model the technical skills required to reach these super-senior levels is the t-shaped model. Figure 16-1 outlines the *t-shaped model* where the depth of experience comes from the first two parts heavy on iOS fundamentals and architecture. Meanwhile, the breadth of knowledge comes from the chapters centered around leading projects, experimentation best practices, CI/CD best practices (dev-ops), and

© Eric Vennaro 2023
E. Vennaro, *iOS Development at Scale*, https://doi.org/10.1007/978-1-4842-9456-7_16

back-end engineering (not something we discussed, but good to know). In addition to the technical depth and breadth covered by the t-shaped model, communication and soft skills become increasingly critical as more of your time is spent on planning and resolving conflicts or other issues. Your goal is to set the direction to unblock your engineers so they can make progress on more technical tasks without worrying about product direction.

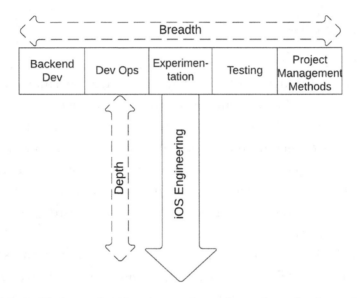

Figure 16-1. *T-shaped software engineer based on the learnings thus far*

This Chapter Includes

This chapter will contextualize the t-shaped developer model based on different levels and senior engineer archetypes. At more senior levels, you will no longer be responsible for one team of engineers. In fact, you will be responsible for leading multiple teams executing independent projects that must all align and mesh together for a common goal and combined launch – a focus of this chapter. You will truly partner with management to achieve team goals and set technical direction. Additionally, we will discuss mentorship. Success is not defined merely by executing one project but by being able to mentor, develop, and grow a team for years to achieve multiple successful projects. By merging our soft skills with our technical abilities, we can achieve this level of success and grow with our team.

Engineer Archetypes

A senior engineer must have sufficient scope, breadth, and depth of knowledge. All three increase at each increasing level of seniority, and ignoring any one of them will not help. Here, we will define the following engineer archetypes:

1. Fixer

2. Tech lead

3. Architect

4. Executive assistant

Regardless of your archetype, you will still need to retain technical skills and depth of knowledge; otherwise, you will not be able to provide actionable advice or provide technical direction. Additionally, you will need advanced communication and leadership skills (soft skills) to navigate difficult decisions and thorny conflicts.

Fixer

Fixers can dig deep into complex problems and drive solutions where others cannot. An iOS-focused example of a fixer could be an engineer who understands the entire application architecture and can drive performance improvements by fixing esoteric bugs or improving overall application architecture patterns. This fixer can operate across the whole application, both product and underlying infrastructure layers. A fixer can also identify a problem and, instead of fixing it on their own, lead a team to address the issue.

Tech Lead

The tech lead is the most common engineering archetype and partners closely with managers to drive progress and lead projects to success. An iOS-focused example of a tech lead could be a senior engineer leading the onboarding flow team. This engineer is the primary point of contact for all new features and oversees technical architecture, scoping, and goal setting for the onboarding flow of the application. As tech leads become increasingly senior, their scope increases, and they will lead multiple teams with subordinate tech leads.

Architect

The architect is typically a role reserved for higher-level engineers working at or beyond an organization level. They are primarily responsible for a critical area's direction, quality, and approach. Architects rely on in-depth knowledge of technical constraints, user needs, and organization-level leadership to execute successfully. An iOS-focused example of an architect would be the individual who designed the overall architecture flow of the application. For instance, the architect of a messaging application will need to handle client-side caching, message receiving, message sending, notification handling, and overall metadata storage (among other things). They work with other back-end architects to mesh the front end into the holistic software system.

Executive Assistant

The executive assistant role is rare and typically involves close partnership with organization leaders to provide engineering perspective to leadership and commonly works on helping to staff critical but unknown projects across an organization. In general, they provide additional leadership bandwidth in large-scale organizations. An example of an executive assistant could be an engineer who works closely with senior management to identify unstaffed but critical projects and then reaches out across the organization to find senior engineers with the bandwidth to take on the projects. The executive assistant will then help track project progress and provide technical guidance and mentorship if required.

Given the variety of roles and overall flexibility, there is no one true definition. For instance, the Staff Engineer blog by Will Larson describes these senior engineer archetypes slightly differently.[1] Moreover, the exact job role will also differ depending on the level of seniority and company expectations. Regardless, each archetype must mentor and lead other engineers. Thus, irrespective of the exact senior archetype, soft skills (interpersonal skills that characterize a person's relationships with others) are critical for long-term success and growing your career beyond individual contributors.

Throughout this chapter, we will refer to the senior engineer as the tech lead; however, most information applies to any senior leadership archetype. Some portions may apply less if you are an executive assistant or fixer since these tracks rely on slightly different skill set (with the fixer leaning more technical and the executive assistant leaning toward more breadth and managerial skills). Regardless, for most senior engineers, it is critical to be able to lead and deliver successful projects.

---

[1] https://staffeng.com/guides/staff-archetypes/

Requirements of Senior Engineer

You must have sufficient breadth, depth, and scope to operate as a senior engineer. These three components define the different aspects of software complexities.

1. Breadth is the ability to understand concepts outside your core domain necessary for project success – for example, knowledge of statistics and experimentation.

2. Depth is the ability to understand in great detail your core competencies.

3. Scope defines the size of the project. With a large-scale project, the coordination overhead increases, and project leadership and communication skills become increasingly important.

Breadth

Senior engineers need to have expertise in both breadth and depth, which they can apply to both existing systems and the creation of new ones. They should have a thorough understanding of the system, enabling them to break it down into smaller parts and delegate tasks to subteams or individual engineers.

Depth

Depth in software development refers to the capacity to design or implement a highly complex segment of the system, which only a few individuals can accomplish. It indicates that you thoroughly comprehend your strengths and can effectively apply them to real-world issues.

We can think of breadth and depth in the context of a t-shaped developer. As software engineers, we need both; however, focusing too much on breadth will make it challenging to lead more complex projects and grow further on the senior engineer track.

We can also break this down into the different parts of this book. In the first two parts, we discussed iOS architecture and language fundamentals. Both focus on depth of experience. Next, we focused on the breadth of expertise through understanding experimentation, performance, and the release process.

Scope

In some rare cases, you may be a specialist solving exceedingly complex technical problems in a very specialized narrow domain, but this is not the norm. In most situations, the expectation is for senior engineers to have sufficient scope for their current level. Here, we classify our levels as follows:

1. Level six – senior principal: Wide cross-pillar or organization scope.

2. Level five – principal: Cross-cutting scope spanning a specific organization or pillar.

3. Level four – staff: The engineer still has sizable scope but is constrained to one organization or pillar.

4. Level three – senior: The engineer has medium scope and consists of one or two teams delivering projects in an organization or pillar.

Project scope is often attributed to cross-functional collaboration but also to engineering-focused projects. Some examples matching scope to our levels:

1. Depth of knowledge in iOS, specifically in a specialty such as on-device machine learning or graphics processing.

2. Drive a mentorship initiative across multiple teams.

3. Scale the mentorship initiative to include multiple directions, such as involving the product management organization to help software engineers improve their project management, prioritization, and communication skills.

4. Find bottlenecks in development practices and fix them.

5. Design holistic solutions for multiple projects across the underlying system infrastructure.

Note   This chapter is about soft skills and leadership practices, not about how to get promoted in your specific organization or company. Standards between companies differ, and the best approach is to ask your manager *what the different levels look like for your team*.

Applying Depth, Breadth, and Scope

Level Three: Senior Engineer

Senior engineers can run projects for a small team and take care of the most challenging tasks in the project. At this level, your project will consist of tasks that can be completed by yourself or more junior members of the team, depending on bandwidth constraints. Figure 16-2 outlines what a small project would look like with multiple tasks and where the senior engineer is completing the most complex portion.

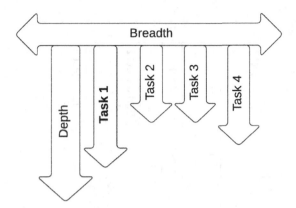

Figure 16-2. *Small project consisting of multiple tasks*

Level Four: Staff Engineer

Your team is now larger, and so are the projects. At this level, the expectation is that you can take a vague project, break it into manageable tasks and subprojects of level three scope, and ensure that all the projects connect with each other (this is breadth). For your role in the project, you can pick some complex tasks at the heart of the project, or you may have to finish one of the defined subprojects due to a shortage of engineers on the team. Figure 16-3 outlines a staff-level project consisting of multiple subprojects and a complex task or portion taken by the staff engineer.

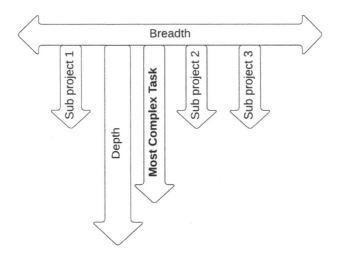

Figure 16-3. *A medium-sized project consisting of small subprojects and some complex tasks*

Level Five and Beyond: Principal Engineer and Above

Projects at this level and beyond are usually quite vague and scoped by directors, VPs, or the C-suite. They typically require input from cross-functional partners, including legal and privacy. These level projects can be subdivided into level three and four-scoped projects. Principal engineers oversee these projects to ensure the individual teams are actively collaborating and looking to address any gaps. Figure 16-4 visualizes a principal engineer project with multiple more complex subprojects that require delegating to staff or senior engineers.

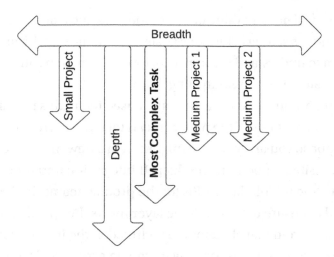

Figure 16-4. *Large project consisting of small and medium projects*

Connecting the Overall System

In addition to taking some of the more complex portions of the project as the senior engineer, it is your job to ensure the overall project is successful. When leading multiple complex subprojects, it is critical to ensure that work is not duplicated and that all vital pieces of the project work together and have no gaps. Connecting the entire system requires expert knowledge and the ability to provide clear guidance to subteams.

As the leader of a metric-based team, it is vital to make sure that each subteam working on their specific part of the project is contributing to the overall project goal by achieving metric wins that combine well together. For instance, if you are in charge of the onboarding team that focuses on new user acquisition, your team may be working on performance improvements, UI changes in the onboarding process, and machine learning–based campaigns. As the tech lead, you are responsible for ensuring that every part of the project complements one another. If the performance improvements cater to low-value region users, but the machine learning team only targets high-value regions the new user acquisition from the performance

573

improvements will not add value on top of the machine learning team's work. This requires setting achievable goals or working with the machine learning team to understand the impact of low-value regions and how the models can evaluate new user targeting there.

For a more product and infrastructure-based team, this may involve ensuring that all portions of the project mesh together correctly. For example, suppose you are leading a migration to a new infrastructure stack and are responsible for both the product UI integration and product infra team to create the middle-layer APIs for the product teams. In that case, you will need to ensure that the middle layer meets the specifications of the product team and that all items are included. If the intermediate layer does not correctly account for syncing metadata across devices and this is not discovered until later testing, the entire rollout may be delayed.

In both situations, the tech lead is also responsible for laying out the overall path for launch. This will consist of a series of experiments on the leading launch candidate to ensure the team is confident in a successful launch. As discussed in past chapters, this may involve heavy usage of the experimentation framework to monitor critical metrics. Here, communication is also vital. The tech lead must establish what test versions are required and the goal for each test. The tech lead must also communicate with all involved parties to understand the launch timeline and ensure critical cross-functional pieces are in place.

Brief Aside for Metric-Driven Teams

For product or infrastructure teams where the deliverable is mainly code based, metric-driven teams can require a more complex lever combination geared toward driving their metric of choice (in the following example, the team is driving revenue through ads placement). Because this is not always straightforward or well understood, here is an example of a combination and strategic methodology for calculating relative metric gain where different teams may work on other aspects of the project.

Establish the Goal

Example goal – show ads at the top of our Photo Stream application, with minimal engagement loss expressed as a ratio of revenue to session loss of 90 or above. We cannot launch with a ratio of less than 90.

Through Iterative Experimentation, Establish Leading Levers

Each lever here would be worked on and optimized by a different team of engineers, with the tech lead responsible for how to best combine them for a final launch.

1. Establish a baseline: We gain 6% revenue (6% given 100% revenue is the baseline) but have a .6% session loss, leaving us with an efficiency of ten, which is not very good.

$$6\% / .6\% = 10$$

2. Lever 1: User-based personalization via machine learning techniques produces a range of revenue to session loss data based on the percentage of users covered. This is based on the area under the curve (AUC) the model produces, where revenue and session loss are graphed on the x and y axis. The curve shows the relative efficiency for different values of user coverage and the most efficient point. Without getting too in depth here, we can assume that the modeling team uses this data to produce a chart with key operational points for us. Each operational point includes the revenue, session loss, and associated user coverage. For sample usage later, assume we have two points on the curve:

    a. At 60% revenue, we incur a 30% session loss while targeting 40% of users.

    b. At 90% revenue, we incur a 50% session loss and target 80% of users.

3. Lever 2: Triggering ads only at specific intervals (once per two hours). Yields 60% of the base revenue gain but only incurs 20% session loss.

4. Lever 3: Ensuring only high-quality ads are placed in the top position via filtering based on the perceived ad value. Here, we have a relative efficiency curve depending on the percentage of ads we filter. For simplicity, we assume that the curve is linear and cutting 50% of low-quality ads retains 75% of the relative revenue and 50% of the session loss.

Relative revenue is the percentage difference between the upper bound (baseline) revenue gain, so 75% relative revenue would mean an absolute gain of 4.5% (with 6% as the absolute gain).

Understand Additive Combinations for the Launch Candidate

First, we must find the most efficient lever, and we can set this as the baseline since it is the most effective. In our example, triggering (lever 2) is the most efficient given its revenue-to-session trade-off. This leaves us with a revenue upper bound of 60% of the total opportunity size (perhaps that 40% is an opportunity for the next launch). Next, we have two levers that are malleable based on the specific values: the number of users exposed for personalization and the number of ads filtered for ad quality. Here, we can evaluate multiple points based on the remaining efficiency lift we need to reach our goal. Our thought process is as follows:

1. Assume the starting point is triggering since it
    has the best efficiency lift compared to any other
    lever. Triggering gives us an efficiency ratio of
    60% revenue and 20% of the starting session loss
    providing an efficiency metric of 36. Much improved
    over our starting point, but not enough!

$$(6\%*60\%)/(.6\%*20\%)=36$$

2. Evaluate the remaining levers. Our remaining levers
    show that personalization is more effective as it can
    yield 90% revenue at the same session loss. Plugging
    in the addition of personalization to our formula we
    now have an efficiency metric of 64. Much better,
    but we still need more!

$$(6\%*60\%*90\%)/(.6\%*20\%*50*)=64$$

3. Since we need more lift, we can evaluate adding
    in our third most effective lever – ad quality. If we
    target retaining 75% of the revenue we have an
    efficiency metric of 97. Now this achieves our goal!

$$(6\%*60\%*90\%*75\%)/(.6\%*20\%*50\%*50\%)=97$$

We can create a tabular format for this in Table 16-1.

Table 16-1. *Tabular format of additive levers and effects*

Lever Name	Revenue Retention	Remaining Revenue	Session Lever Reduction	Remaining Session Loss	Efficiency
Baseline	N/A baseline	6.00%	N/A baseline	0.50%	12.00
Triggering	60%	4%	20.00%	0.10%	36.00
Personalization	90%	3%	50.00%	0.05%	64.80
Ad quality	75.00%	2%	50%	0.03%	97.20

The tech lead's role here is more nuanced than necessarily leading and code-based project. They must think through and ensure the key experiments are run to establish leading performance levers and that the launch candidate can be reasoned about and adequately formed.

Balancing Each Dimension

Regardless of engineering level (four, five, or six), depth is still essential. You must be able to lead the project's technical vision and guide the engineers below you. If you do not complete any technical parts of the project or do not have the technical depth needed, you will not be able to provide this guidance and cannot easily guarantee project success. As the levels progress, the cross-functional communication aspect and project management aspects become more intense – you will need an increased breadth of experience and rock-solid communication skills to lead projects of increasing complexity.

A senior engineer's work aims to ensure that the project your team is working on is delivered on time. If you were to do it alone, it would take a very long time. No one around you would grow, hence the need to focus on delegating the tasks that the people around you can do and concentrate on the things that most require your attention – for example, designing and presenting the overall project architecture, designing and implementing the most complex portion of the project, or serving as the de facto point of contact to represent your team in meetings, allowing the rest of the development team to write software meeting-free (if your team is very meeting heavy).

Becoming a Well-Rounded Senior Engineer

We have discussed the requirements of a senior engineer and the necessity of technical competence at different levels of scope, breadth, and depth. Now the question is, how do you get there? What skills are required? Well, we have already discussed the technical breadth and depth aspects but not the necessary soft skills.

These skills involve the following:

1. Learn more about the product and its implications on engineering.

2. Understand the broader company strategy and the role your team plays.

3. Assume the best intentions and be nice.

4. Mentor and help those around you grow.

5. Become an expert communicator.

Brief Aside on Understanding Technical Concepts

It is not enough to understand base iOS application design and architecture. Tech leads must also understand the details of the application architecture they work in. As projects scale, it is more important to understand the broader company architecture pattern, not just for the iOS application but also for the front and back end. This counts toward technical depth and ensures you can develop large-scale projects that fit the existing system architecture.

Why Are Soft Skills Needed?

1. As you take care of larger and larger projects, you will need to cover more breadth of knowledge across internal systems.

2. The larger the projects, the better you have to be at communication and project management. Specific activities you can do with a five-person project will not work with a fifty-person project.

3. To complete work on time or further scale a project, it is important to delegate tasks to others. Helping your team grow is key to achieving success.

4. Larger projects with increased ambiguity require more meetings with many people. First impressions matter, and it may take time and a lot of effort to change a negative first impression into a lasting positive impression. Being nice can help avoid this situation entirely. Making a good impression and cultivating a reputation as a hard-working individual who can complete complex projects are essential to potential growth.

Situational Leadership Model

If less qualified team members can handle something, delegate it, freeing you up to work on the most critical portions of the system while allowing those beneath you to grow. We can apply the situational leadership model to understand better when and what to delegate. The situational leadership model provides a framework for how to grow and develop those around you.

The situational leadership model is based on the principle that there is no one-size-fits-all approach to leadership. The most effective leaders can adapt their leadership style to the specific situations they encounter, considering the readiness and willingness of the individuals or groups they lead. Effective leadership depends on the people being influenced and the particular task or function that needs to be accomplished.[2]

The situational leadership model has two fundamental concepts:

1. Leadership style

2. The individual or group's performance readiness level (also referred to as maturity level or development level)

Leadership Styles

Hersey and Blanchard coined the situational leadership model to characterize leadership styles based on the degree of task and relationship behaviors that leaders provide to their followers. They classified all leadership styles into four behavior styles denoted as S1 to S4. However, the names of these styles vary depending on the version of the model used.

Here, we will define them as follows:

---

[2] Hersey, P. and Blanchard, K. H. (1977). *Management of Organizational Behavior 3rd Edition – Utilizing Human Resources*. New Jersey/Prentice Hall.

1. S4 Delegating: Leaders delegate responsibilities to the group and monitor progress but are less involved in the execution and decision-making process. In S4, the employee makes most decisions regarding what, how, and when. The role of the leader is to value the individual's contributions and support their growth.

2. S3 Supporting: Leaders work closely with the team and provide more help in decision-making than when delegating. In S3, the leader and employee make decisions together, and the role of the leader is to facilitate, listen, draw out, encourage, and support.

3. S2 Coaching: Leaders provide direction and direct feedback to gain support for their approach and assist in concluding. Here, the leader explains why, solicits suggestions, and encourages task accomplishment attempting to motivate the individual.

4. S1 Directing: When directing, leaders tell individuals exactly how and what to do while closely monitoring the process. In S1, the leader closely tracks performance and goals to provide consistent feedback.

Across all four styles, the leader is responsible for the following:

1. Active listening: Effective coaches listen actively to their team members, asking questions and seeking to understand their perspectives.

2. Goal setting: Leaders work with team members to set clear goals and objectives that are achievable and aligned with organizational objectives.

3. Providing feedback: Leaders offer constructive feedback on team members' performance, focusing on specific areas for improvement and providing actionable suggestions for improvement.

4. Modeling behaviors: Leaders lead by example, modeling the behaviors and values they expect from their team members.

5. Encouragement and support: Leaders encourage and support their team members, celebrating successes and offering help when needed. Celebrating wins and showing appreciation for hard work can motivate and inspire team members to continue to strive for excellence.

6. Continuous learning: Effective leaders are committed to constant learning and development, staying up to date with industry trends and best practices, and sharing this knowledge with their team members.

While there is no optimal style for leaders to use in all situations, influential leaders must be flexible and adapt according to the problem. Additionally, to successfully lead a large-scale project (level four or five), it is impossible to direct or even coach every individual; one must balance their efforts across all four levels and think critically about the approach for a given individual. For example, we cannot delegate a large portion of a level five project to a new college graduate – that would set them and us up for failure. We can utilize the development level to understand which operating model to use.

Development Levels

Development levels are also task specific even within software engineering and determined by the commitment to solving the task and competency to do so:

1. D4 Very High: Individuals are willing and able to take responsibility for complex tasks and complete them independently. These individuals are autonomous and commonly recognized as an expert. They are also self-assured and confident.

2. D3 High: Individuals with a high skill level to complete complex tasks need more confidence or willingness. They are a capable but cautious contributor with moderate to increased confidence.

3. D2 Medium: The individual is willing to complete tasks but lacks the necessary skills to do so successfully. This level is categorized by *disillusioned learners*, which can lead to frustration and demotivation. D2-level individuals are also, at times, afraid to make mistakes and overly cautious, preventing their growth to D3. Lastly, a properly progressing D2-level individual may be advancing from D1 and eagerly charging ahead; this person may have variable performance and require additional guidance before moving to D3.

4. D1 Low: Individuals are unwilling to take on independent tasks and lack both the skills and confidence to do so successfully. At this level, tech leads are looking for individuals eager to learn.

A person might be generally skilled, confident, and motivated in their job (D3) but would still have a development level D1 if asked to perform a task outside their skill set – such as requesting an iOS engineer to build a Ruby on Rails back end. This individual is most likely to progress quickly back to their previous development level with some coaching in the specific areas they are unfamiliar with. In the example of the iOS engineer asked to work on Ruby on Rails, they may need support in learning the Ruby best practices or Rails framework, but after some initial coaching, they should move back to a D3 plus level. When combining the necessary leadership style changes with the development levels, our example engineer went from a D3, probably someone you could rely on to delegate tasks to (S3 or S4) to an S2. However, with proper coaching (mentorship), they can progress quickly to S3 or S4 and back to D3 or D4 in the new tech stack.

As a leader, it is critical to understand these situations and apply the proper guidance for the individual and their unique circumstances. To achieve this, we can split the situational leadership model to divide engineers into quadrants and better understand what level of work we can give them. Depending on their level of maturity, we can also provide targeted mentorship to help guide them to the next level.

Figure 16-5 shows the model as a unit, with each development level mapping to a leadership style and with directive behavior on the x axis and supportive behavior on the y axis. In directive behavior, the leader provides frequent feedback and one-way communication. This is more taxing for the leader. In supportive behavior, the leader offers constructive feedback, practices active listening, and helps subordinates become involved in decision-making. Both dimensions go from low to high.

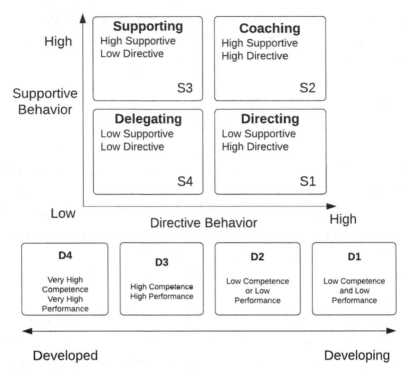

Figure 16-5. *Situational leadership model with the development levels*

The situational leadership model leads to four ideal situations:

1. D1: Low competence and high commitment where the leader must use S1 to provide high directive behavior and help the employee achieve competencies for the job. Here, the employee is highly committed and only requires a little motivation. The expectation is for the employee to progress quickly to the next level. D1 typically represents new graduates higher at entry level.

2. D2: Requires high directive and supportive behavior. The leader must train the employee to solve the task and motivate the employee to solve the task. This is the most complex development level but is a critical stage for progressing to D3.

3. D3: Requires S3 level. The leader knows the employee can solve the task, but the employee has reservations. The leader knows this and supports the employee to solve the task.

4. D4: Employee can solve the task and is keen to solve it; both leader and employee know this. Therefore, the employee can have a lot of autonomy on this. An employee can be D4 at a specific task regarding technical ability and engineering project level.[3]

Common Pitfalls

Oversupervision: Micromanaging

Micromanaging is a leadership style in which a manager or supervisor closely oversees and controls every aspect of their team members' work. This can include monitoring their every move, giving excessive feedback, and taking on tasks that should be the responsibility of team members. Micromanaging can be detrimental to team members' morale, motivation, and autonomy, leading to reduced productivity and burnout.

To avoid micromanaging, leaders can take several steps:

1. Set clear expectations: Communicate each project or task's goals, expectations, and deadlines. This will help team members understand what is expected of them and reduce the need for constant monitoring.

---

[3] Blanchard, Kenneth H. (2003). The one minute manager. [New York]: Morrow, an imprint of HarperCollins Publishers.

2.   Delegate tasks: Assign tasks to team members and give them the freedom to complete them in their own way. This will help build trust and confidence in team members' abilities.

3.   Provide support: Offer guidance and support to team members as needed, but allow them to take ownership of their work.

4.   Encourage open communication: Create an environment where team members feel comfortable asking questions, sharing concerns, and offering feedback.

5.   Focus on results: Instead of focusing on the process, focus on the results. This will help shift the focus from micromanaging to empowering team members to achieve their goals.

Undersupervision

Undersupervision occurs when a manager or supervisor fails to provide adequate support and guidance to their team members. This can lead to confusion, frustration, and a lack of direction, which can ultimately impact team members' performance and job satisfaction.

To avoid under supervision, leaders can take several steps:

1.   Establish clear expectations: Same as with how to avoid micromanaging.

2.   Provide regular feedback: Offer constructive feedback on team members' performance, focusing on specific areas for improvement and providing actionable suggestions for growth.

3. Be available and approachable: Be available to answer questions, provide guidance, and offer support to team members as needed. Encourage open communication and make it clear that you are there to help and support them.

4. Develop a coaching mindset: Adopt a coaching mindset and work with team members to develop their skills and achieve their goals. This involves providing guidance, support, and feedback on an ongoing basis.

5. Foster a culture of learning: Encourage team members to learn and grow by providing access to training, mentorship, and coaching opportunities. Celebrate successes and recognize team members' achievements to inspire continued growth and development.

By avoiding under- and oversupervision, leaders can ensure that their team members receive the support and guidance they need to perform at their best. Remember that effective leadership involves finding the right balance between providing advice and support and empowering team members to take ownership of their work.

Note   Effective leadership requires matching the specific individual need for leadership style with the goal of moving toward D3 and D4 and S3 and S4.

Applied to Leading Multiple Teams

Since the optimal number of direct reports for a leader is usually between five and ten people, as you lead more significant projects, the expectation is that they will also lead teams, and you will lead through them. This allows the leader to communicate effectively, provide support and guidance, and establish personal relationships with each team member.

When leaders have too many direct reports, they may struggle to give each individual the attention and support they need, resulting in confusion, frustration, and a lack of direction. Additionally, as the number of direct reports increases, the leader may spend more time managing administrative tasks and less time on strategic planning and coaching.

To support these large-scale projects, we can scale the situational leadership model. Instead of focusing on directly delegating a specific portion of work to an individual, now the individual being empowered will be responsible for a more significant part of the project and potentially delegating to others. This subtle shift requires tracking changes over a wider surface area (increased breadth) while maintaining a similar depth of knowledge. If anything goes wrong, you are expected to be able to help debug and provide expert support. Or if the area is outside your wheelhouse (i.e., part of your breadth), you are expected to find the correct person to help or raise this issue to management for proper support.

Note   The goal is to create autonomous self-organizing teams capable of executing against objectives within a specified time frame. To do so, we must provide clear goals (remember, good goals are SMART) so that people understand the purpose behind coaching and direction and respond positively.

Practical Example

As we have done throughout the book, we will provide a practical example of using situational leadership in practice. Here you are, a senior leader and your team has just hired Jon.

Jon has just graduated college and is pleased to get a job. He is highly motivated and feels he can quickly acquire the skills for the job (representing D1, S1). As the tech lead, you provide Jon with direction on completing simple development tasks and check in frequently.

After a while, you notice Jon is getting frustrated that it is taking him longer to understand the build system and process for landing high-quality code than he initially thought. After talking with him, he shared that initially, the slow build times and his unfamiliarities with coding led to many iterations with long lag times. However, now that he understands the system a bit better, he is becoming more efficient with fewer cycles but is becoming frustrated with the particular build cycle time and blames the build system for slow feature development. Jon has reached D2 and is at risk of becoming unmotivated by these headwinds.

To counter this, you switch to S2, explain why this is happening, redirect, and re-teach him the importance of preventing bugs before running time-consuming tests. You also provide some tips on how to leverage Buck to compile a smaller, more focused changeset faster. Over time you follow the employee closely and see his continued progress. He is becoming more and more independent and completing tasks more quickly. Now you become more responsive and supportive of their choices and help to build confidence as Jon moves toward D3.

Fast-forward three years, and you see Jon no longer consults you for feedback and makes impressive independent choices. You recognize his expertise and leverage him for complex tasks that challenge him, including giving Jon a level four project, whereas previously, Jon was completing tasks at a level three. As Jon grows to take on more level four projects, he may slide back to S2 or S3. This is fine and even expected as you provide more guidance on how he can grow to take on additional complexity.

Notice how in our practical example the level of scope Jon takes grows from three to four as he cycles forward and then back in situational leadership levels. This mirrors the promotion path of engineers, and while promotions are the job of managers, senior engineers' mentorship and guidance play a critical role in the promotion and growth process.

Trade-Offs

The situational leadership model does not consider working toward multiple tasks and goals at one time and does not explicitly consider this when reviewing levels. Additionally, the model does not consider how employees express their lack of ability or motivation. Some are overconfident, and some will hide their true intent out of fear of reprisal or losing their job.

To combat these problems, the practitioner of situational leadership is required to be a capable leader. The leader must understand the different leadership requirements and have competency across those tenets, which can require additional self-learning and experience. In this book, we have reviewed those competencies. Additionally, as a tech leader, you are not alone. You should partner with your manager to better understand individual needs, concerns, and pressing goals to prioritize the correct level of leadership involvement.

Relationship Between Senior Engineers and Managers

Senior engineers and managers have some overlap in their roles, as seen through progressing engineers through levels in the situational leadership model – both senior engineers and managers

1. Mentor people

2. Work on project planning and roadmapping

3. Deal with business partners and other cross-functional partners to drive solutions and clarify ambiguity

However, there are some significant differences too:

1.   Senior engineers persuade managers to staff and prioritize projects. The final staffing call is left to management.

2.   Senior engineers do not generally deal with people issues or performance ratings. However, senior engineers may play a key role in mentoring engineers to reach performance goals.

As you become more senior in your career, you will work more closely with your manager, almost as a partner, both striving to solve the same problems, just from different angles, with you spending more time on solving the technical challenges and your manager spending more time on people, resourcing, and sometimes building cross-functional relationships.

Mentorship: Scaling Oneself

To successfully use the situational leadership model, we must mentor those around us to go from D1 to D4 and S1 to S4. As a senior engineer, it is very rare to jump into a fully built team and deliver high-priority projects at level four and beyond. Often, senior engineers are instrumental in growing the team and potentially starting with only a few junior members and growing to support more complex scoped projects requiring more senior leadership from those once junior engineers. Without a defined mentorship setup and growth trajectory, this is essentially impossible.

Effective mentorship can be a powerful tool for career development and personal growth. It involves building a positive and supportive relationship between a more experienced mentor and a less experienced mentee. Through mentorship, mentees can gain valuable insights and guidance on navigating their career paths and achieving their goals, while mentors can cultivate their leadership skills and give back to the community.

To be an effective mentor, it is essential to establish clear expectations and goals from the beginning of the relationship. This includes defining the mentee's objectives, identifying their strengths and areas for improvement, and setting clear milestones for progress. The mentor should also be open to feedback and willing to adjust their approach to meet the mentee's needs. Communication is vital in mentorship, and mentors should be accessible and approachable and actively listen to their mentee's concerns and questions.

Mentors should also provide opportunities for learning and development, such as sharing their knowledge and experience, offering constructive feedback, and recommending training and networking opportunities. They should encourage their mentee to take ownership of their development and explore new challenges and opportunities. Finally, a successful mentorship relationship should be built on trust and mutual respect. Mentors should model ethical behavior, respect the mentee's confidentiality, and always maintain professionalism.

Building Relationships

In addition to mentorship, senior engineers must be experts in building relationships. To develop good relationships with those around us in both technical and nontechnical capacities, we help ensure that people will want to work with us. In fact, they will enjoy working with us and want to provide feedback because they believe in you and the projects you lead and are thus bought-in to the success of the project.

There are multiple models to approach building relationships; three that we will present here work well together for building good relationships with coworkers regarding difficult technical work-related conversations, broader social situations, and team building.

1. Be nice. A short moniker to think about and apply: remember, always be nice! And if you do not have anything nice to say, do not say anything at all. Be nice is a good phrase to remember to always assume the best intent and help when phrasing your responses.

2. Build trust. A framework from Robin Dreeke's book *The Code Of Trust* defines a set of principles for building relationships and trust between teams. This is incredibly useful when thinking about how to approach conversations and team building.

3. Influence people. A framework from Dale Carnegie's book *How to Win Friends and Influence People*. While incredibly dated, this book sets the gold standard for principles of how to influence others and build relationships through time-honored practices like remembering their birthday and kids' names. Small details make a difference and can augment how we approach conversations in the first two frameworks.

How to Be Nice

Being nice can be divided into three parts. The first is in technical conversations and decision-making. In a technical context, we want to be nice and make sure others feel their opinions are valid and heard. However, we also want to be firm with what we think the right decision is. By supporting others instead of dismissing ideas, you facilitate an open environment where everyone's feedback is valued, and they feel comfortable sharing.

The second form that being nice takes is in everyday interactions and meetings. This applies to first impressions and overall getting to know your coworkers. Learn about your coworkers, not just their in-office work, but a little about themselves outside of work. By forming personal connections, you help build positive relationships with your coworkers, improving trust and communication. Trust and communication are critical components of a healthy team.

To build this connection, you can strive to understand what their hobbies are, do they have children (if so, how old?), and when are their birthdays. You should not pry into their lives, but these conversations can come up organically through simple questions like "How was your weekend?" When they mention something like, "Oh, this weekend I went to my kid's soccer game," now you can ask, "How long have they been playing soccer?" Or "How old are they?" Now you have had a very typical conversation, and it is on you to remember the details so you can ask about their kid's soccer progress in the future. The idea is to have regular everyday conversations but ask for pertinent details (active listening) and then do whatever you must to remember relevant information. You can take notes or add birthdays to a particular calendar.

The last part of being nice is providing clear, actionable feedback with concrete examples. This is nice because it is the expectation of a good leader; you are doing those around you a favor by being honest and up-front with them. By providing concrete examples, you make the feedback as actionable as possible.

How to Build Trust

In the Code of Trust, former FBI agent Robin Dreeke develops principles to help people build trust in their personal and professional relationships. The code consists of five main principles:

1. Suspend your ego: This means letting go of the need to be correct and instead focusing on the other person's perspective and feelings.

2. Be nonjudgmental: Avoid making assumptions or passing judgments about the other person, and instead approach them with an open mind.

3. Establish rapport: Find common ground with the other person and build a connection based on shared interests and experiences.

4. Validate the other person: Show empathy and understanding toward the other person's thoughts and feelings, and acknowledge their point of view.

5. Ask strategic questions that help you understand the other person's needs and motivations and allow them to share their perspective.[4]

By following these principles, anyone can develop the skills to build trust with others and establish strong relationships. We can apply these principles to our technical and nontechnical communication.

How to Influence People

How to Win Friends and Influence People is a self-help book by Dale Carnegie, initially published in 1936. The book provides practical advice on how to build strong relationships with people and gain their trust and respect. Based on this framework, we can work to influence those around us and make strong connections with them.[5]

---

[4] Dreeke, R., & Stauth, C. (2017). *The code of trust: an American counterintelligence expert's five rules to lead and succeed.* First edition. New York, St. Martin's Press.
[5] Walsh, B. (December 1, 2014). How to Win Friends and Influence People. Director, 68(4), 32.

1. Show genuine interest in other people: Listen actively and show empathy toward others.

2. Smile: A simple smile can make people feel at ease and more comfortable.

3. Remember people's names: Using someone's name in conversation helps create a connection.

4. Be a good listener: Let others talk about themselves and their interests.

5. Avoid criticism: Instead, offer constructive feedback and praise.

6. Build relationships based on common interests: Find common ground to establish a connection.

7. Show appreciation: People respond well to being appreciated and valued.

8. Encourage others to talk: Ask questions to show interest and encourage others to open up.

9. Talk in terms of others' interests: Understand what motivates others and use that to establish a connection.

10. Give honest and sincere appreciation: Show genuine gratitude and praise for others.

Combining the Frameworks

These principles can help you build strong relationships with others and become an expert communicator through active listening and the ability to provide honest feedback. This will also allow you to effortlessly gain the trust and respect of those around you, building your influence with them. Influencing other people expands across technical and nontechnical decisions you make and factors into how you build relationships and be nice since your friends are naturally more inclined to agree with you. Building good relationships with your team and across the broader business organization can make your work environment happier and more productive for everyone.

Summary

In this chapter, we reviewed the different senior engineer archetypes, which have a lot of overlap in responsibilities. That is, you must consistently lead large-scale projects while supporting the growth and development of other junior engineers. We can help these engineers by applying the situational leadership model. At this point, you can synergize your skills as a t-shaped developer across both breadth and depth and leverage different communication patterns via being nice, influencing others, and building trust to get things done in a complex operating environment.

In the book's next and final chapter, we will discuss a theoretical example of putting together different projects at each level for a mythical company to fully understand how projects are broken down and scoped and the unique challenges and expectations faced at each level.

Key Takeaways

1. If you choose to stay as an IC as your career progresses, you will reach a parallel track with management as a staff or senior engineer. To find success at this level of seniority, in addition to technical skills, it is paramount that you

    a. Learn more about the product and its implications on engineering

    b. Understand the broader company strategy and the role your team plays

    c. Learn more about the broader company technology architecture, both front end and back end, to understand how they work enough to design with them in mind

    d. Mentor and help those around you grow, which helps you also to scale up to lead larger teams

2. At any level of your career, you should assume the best intentions and be nice! By doing this, others will want to work with you, which will open doors later on for you and your career.

3. As a staff or principal engineer, it is critical not to lose your technical depth or breadth. Your technical skills are the key differentiating factor between you and your peers.

Further Learning

1. Robin Dreeke

    a. Discusses building relationships and forming a solid team

2. Right the Ship

    a. Discusses a similar leadership framework built to empower individuals on their ship

CHAPTER 17

Practical Example

This chapter is a culmination of the different parts in this book. We will outline the role of engineers at various levels to show their day-to-day activities and how they utilize specific skills to accomplish their jobs. We will see how very senior engineers (staff and principal) rely on communication, software architecture, and breadth of knowledge, while ground-team senior engineers rely more heavily on technical depth. In all cases, a certain amount of technical depth is required to ensure projects adhere to project goals, timelines, and budget constraints.

To illustrate these situations and interactions between engineers, we will review a narrative sample of a top-down project MVP iteration. We have included a sample project plan at the end of this chapter.

Top-Down vs. Bottom-Up

The top-down approach to software project management involves starting with an overall project plan and then breaking it down into smaller tasks and activities. With the top-down approach, project creation happens at higher echelons of management. Then the involved ground team creates comprehensive project plans that define their portion of the project's goals, scope, and major deliverables.

Top-down project management is effective for large migrations and project initiatives that require a lot of careful cross-organization communication since the approach helps to provide a clear nexus of

© Eric Vennaro 2023
E. Vennaro, *iOS Development at Scale*, https://doi.org/10.1007/978-1-4842-9456-7_17

command and control. By starting with a high-level plan, the top-down approach helps allocate resources effectively and ensures that critical tasks are identified and prioritized early in the project.

However, the top-down approach lacks individual team autonomy, with decisions cascading down from higher-level management. This leads to ground teams becoming discouraged, especially if they feel there is a better approach to solve the problem or there is a misalignment between the team's actual capabilities and the goals given to them. The lack of team involvement can also lead to miscommunications as it is difficult for the senior management decision-makers to have the required information for decision-making (and information much travel through multiple hierarchical layers).

The bottom-up approach to software project management takes a different perspective. It involves starting with a goal provided by higher management and then leaves how to reach it open-ended. In this situation, the ground-team members identify and define the individual projects that aid them in reaching border organization-level goals. Bottom-up project management helps to encourage innovation and creative solutions to problems by involving all members of the teams in all phases of planning and project creation.

While increasing morale and efficiency, as teams do not have to wait on higher-level management for all decisions, bottom-up planning does introduce risk where teams have trouble aligning toward a shared goal. Additionally, with increased autonomy, team members have the freedom to add additional requirements to projects leading to scope creep and loss of focus on the company priorities.

Both approaches require detailed task decomposition into smaller tasks and milestones. The choice of a bottom-up or top-down approach depends on factors such as the project's complexity, team dynamics, and organizational preferences. In practice, a combination of top-down and bottom-up approaches can be used, where top-down directives help iterate toward a broader shared goal faster and the bottom-up approach is useful for innovation working toward clear goals with open-ended ways of accomplishing them.

Setting the Scene

To start our practical example, we will follow the project synthesis for our tech company Mango. Mango is a giant tech conglomerate with many applications. Mango usually practices strictly bottom-up planning. However, for this project, the CEO, Steve, is practicing a hybrid approach since migrating to end-to-end encryption (E2EE) is a company priority.

The cast of characters:

1. *Erica: Chief technical architect for the Photo Stream application.*

2. *Blaine: Tech lead on the thread-view iOS product team who is currently working hard for a promotion to staff.*

3. *Sally: Senior engineer with the executive assistant archetype. Sally is responsible for helping investigate and staff projects.*

4. *Mike: Erica's manager who partners with her for mentorship.*

5. *Tom: Back-end infrastructure tech lead supporting the back-end server infrastructure work for the project.*

6. *Kelly: Web front-end tech lead supporting the web front-end portion of the project.*

7. *Garrick: A fixer who moves around to different areas of the iOS and mobile application, addressing problems in the code base.*

In response to the recent privacy trend, Mango CEO Steve and the rest of the C-suite are discussing a significant upgrade to the security infrastructure, moving the Photo Stream application to utilize end-to-end encryption (E2EE). This is a complicated endeavor because the Photo Stream application consists of a Connected feed showing content from connected users (users who have agreed to connect and share content with each other), a direct message feature for directly sending and sharing photos or videos (including support for group messaging), and a Discover feed that shows unconnected content primarily from influencers. Both the feed experiences show advertisements that are also the company's primary means of revenue generation.

To assist in scoping the changes necessary for E2EE, the company CTO, who focuses more on business strategy for the entire family of applications, suggests working with Principal Engineer Erica, the chief architect of the Photo Stream product group, who has a deep and comprehensive understanding of the application as a whole, including the current security model and the client-server architecture.

Erica meets with the CTO, Photo Stream VP of product, VP of design, VP of Photo Stream data and analytics, and her manager, Matt (a director in the Photo Stream project group), to discuss the switch to end-to-end encryption and align on the overall project direction. They agree to start small with a minimum feature set where only the direct message feature is E2EE and only for 1:1 chat messages.

Jumping into Erica's Day...

Erica sits at her desk after meeting with her manager to discuss moving the Photo Stream application to end-to-end encryption. She briefly checks her email to catch up on outstanding high-priority items for her twenty-percent time project[1] (improving the organization's experimentation best practices). Next, Erica begins writing a five-year plan based on the directional alignment reached with her manager and other key business

---

[1] A common term for a part time project taken in addition to one's main project.

partners. Erica reflects on the main product surfaces for the Photo Stream application, including the iOS, Android, and web applications. Erica incorporates these with the necessary underlying infrastructure components and forms a rough draft of a five-year plan to first migrate the infrastructure to E2EE, support base product requirements, and iteratively launch, starting with the minimally viable project.

Throughout her week, she meets one on one (1:1) with key stakeholders across the mobile, client, infra, back-end infra, and web teams to drive the overall architecture further and build a comprehensive plan. Erica is coaching and driving all stakeholders to align on utilizing the existing infrastructure where possible. Additionally, Erica supports using the signal protocol for E2EE, drastically reducing the engineering implementation overhead and allowing support for iOS, Android, and web clients.[2]

After formulating a rough draft, Erica meets with her manager Matt to discuss the engineer selection (see the chapter appendix for the complete project plan).

"Hi Erica, this proposal looks great. We should also sequence the rollout with the infrastructure teams more. We must ensure they have the availability to meet these requirements."

"Thanks," Erica replied, continuing, "I also wanted to discuss staffing. We need at least one senior representative from each area in more detail and delegate the different portions."

Mike nods and responds: "Yes, I've already talked to the wider org managers. We will have Mike (Android product), Steph (mobile infrastructure), Tom (back-end infra), Kelly (web front end), and Blaine (iOS product). For Blaine, I'm working on developing him to be the team TL at the principal level. This project is good for him to show his technical breadth. I'd like you to help mentor him to ensure he understands the increased responsibilities."

---

[2] https://signal.org/docs/

"Sure, I think Blaine will also need additional help with the technical breadth here. He has mostly worked in the optimization space and has less knowledge of the thread-view stack," Erica responds. She then heads back to her desk to schedule a meeting for the five of them to discuss kicking off the project and some technical details necessary to finalize the five-year plan. Erica also includes her manager as optional for context. She organizes the meeting for one week away, and after she has her regularly scheduled one-on-one sessions with Mike, Steph, Tom, Kelly, and Blaine. This way, she can gather input from the first and build alignment on the proposal before a larger meeting.

Erica starts to lead the meeting with the chosen engineer leads across the mobile, web, mobile infra, and back-end infra areas. "Hi, everyone," Erica begins, "I hope you have all had a chance to review the preliminary engineering plan, milestones, and architecture diagram. Today I would like to review the tentative milestones and overall system architecture diagram for how we want to approach migrating to E2EE."

Erica proceeds to the architecture diagram of the current system state. "First, let's look at the client-server contract. We will utilize the existing infrastructure wherever possible and add support inside the messaging services for E2EE traffic."

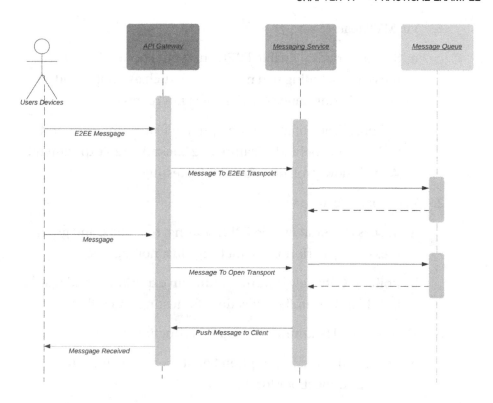

Erica continues, "Next, for our mobile clients, we will follow existing conventions and utilize our cross-platform C libraries with the signal protocol for E2EE. This will allow us to guarantee consistency across mobile clients and will integrate well with our existing C wrapper for SQLite database access. This has the added benefit of reducing the binary size and working with our existing push-based approach for messaging content."

Erica further defines the feature set and follows milestones for the group.

1. V0: MVP feature set

   a. Success criteria: Enable E2EE encrypted option for a direct message including rich media types such as photos and videos. Performance metrics must not regress.

   b. Rollout: Usage of E2EE is an optional feature for users and will be gated behind a feature flag backed by an experiment. We will slowly roll out after careful testing.

2. V1: Expand feature set

   a. Success criteria: Enable E2EE sharing, reactions, and group messaging. Performance metrics must not regress.

   b. Rollout: Gate new features behind an experiment and feature flag. Follow a similar procedure for testing and rollout.

3. V2: Advanced feature set to match production

   a. Advanced shared encryption keys for encrypted content among connections for the feed.

   b. Rollout: Gate new features behind an experiment and feature flag. Follow a similar procedure for testing and rollout.

4. V3: Cutover and final stabilization

   a. Success criteria: Support switching all supported modes to E2E encryption by default with little to no performance impact.

   b. Rollout: Gate changes behind an experiment and feature flag to roll out to 100% of the public.

"Does anyone have any questions on the milestones?" Erica says as she opens the floor for questions. Blaine asks, "Regarding the careful metric evaluation – What overall metric collections should we monitor? Are there any ones we need specifically for E2EE?"

"That's a good question," Erica replies, "I have a follow-up meeting scheduled with the Data Analytics and other key stakeholders. We still need to follow up on the timeline for having a unified understanding of application performance as it applies to this project."

"Also, have we discussed with the UI/UX team when the design mockups will be ready? Otherwise, I am not sure we can start on the majority of this work?" Blaine continues.

"Yes, we expect one month for UI mockups, given the small changes. From my previous conversations with the design team, they will start on the mockups for the MVP now and then work on the mockups for V1 immediately to ensure they unblock development work," Erica replies. After a brief pause, she proceeds, "ok any other questions we are almost at the end of the meeting."

"For the existing client logging framework, will we need to make any changes to support the move to E2EE? I'm concerned if we meet all the privacy requirements here," Steph from the client infra team chimes in.

"We still need to reach alignment with the privacy team to understand what changes are required. Luckily the logging framework already supports policy-based filtering, so the overall effort should be low." Erica answers.

"Ok, looks like we are out of time for this meeting, and another team wants the meeting room. In two weeks, we will sync on individual portions of the architecture pattern as follow-up items. I will also follow up with the Data Analytics team to align on critical metric collections for launch. After the meeting ends, I will publish the meeting notes to the group, including the aforementioned action items. Take care, everyone. We will meet again in two weeks to finalize the individual teams' milestones."

Based on feedback from the tech leadership meeting and her thoughts, Erica schedules a follow-up meeting with several essential partner teams and jots down a brief agenda of key questions.

1. *Data Analytics*

   a. *What support model do we have for understanding what key org metrics engineers need to monitor as part of broader rollouts?*

   b. *What if any additional metrics pipelines are required? Or what changes to existing pipelines are needed to support end-to-end encryption?*

2. *Privacy Foundation*

   a. *What steps are required for compliance with E2EE?*

3. *Core Infrastructure*

   a. *Do the necessary server infrastructure changes present problems for server capacity?*

4. *Design (UI/UX)*

   a. *When can we expect mockups for the MVP feature set?*

5. *Marketing*

   a. *What is the go-to-market (GTM) strategy for E2EE? What is the plan to build momentum for switching to E2EE? And does this timeline affect our ability to launch?*

6. *QA*

   a. *We want to involve QA early to prioritize manual test plans across the different teams and help build alignment for subteam leads. Who are the right POCs (points of contact) for our subteams?*

While everyone is busy working on their project plans, Erica ensures she has scheduled weekly one-on-one check-ins with each TL to discuss complexities and the project plans further. Erica brings up her existing project plan in her next meeting with Blaine (the iOS product tech lead).

"I'm glad you brought up the project plan," Blaine replies. "I need to know who to talk to on the client infrastructure team for API endpoints specification."

"You should use Steph as your main point of contact. She is leading the overall client infrastructure migration across iOS and Android. For next week's meeting, please ensure you have finalized the API contract with her for iOS," Erica replies. "Reviewing your project plan, I'm curious how you plan to monitor your changes in production?" Erica asks.

"Oh, I assumed we would use the existing logging framework with a flag for E2EE traffic. However, we may need to add additional logging at the product level to understand specific traffic to the E2EE surfaces," Blaine comments.

"That's good, but I feel there is some hidden complexity in how we will handle this change, and it will be good for everyone on the team to understand how you will handle this. Especially for a large-scale migration, we must ensure that we have solid intermediate metrics for the experience. This will help us verify the user experience," Erica states. Before ending the meeting, she advises Blaine to work with the Data Analytics team to review metrics collection for potential experiment sizing.

With the direction provided by Erica, Blaine started to break down the iOS product level into subprojects for engineers on his team. During a meeting with his manager, Blaine explains his plan. "So I've broken down the project into three sections. I will work directly with Samantha for the thread-view and provide her with well-scoped tasks. I think the notification handling portion will be a bit more complex and a good senior engineer–scoped project we can give to Dale. Lastly, I've broken down the UI-related changes into loosely scoped tasks for Evan and Kelly; they should have enough coding-heavy tasks for the next quarter."

"This looks great," Blaine's manager replies, "I think the large UI tasks will be perfect for Evan and Kelly. One concern I have is regarding Anthony's work for the next half. He will need a large-scoped, more ambiguous project."

"Yes, I've been thinking about this too," Blaine says, "I don't see enough scope here for him, but I know group messaging is very important for the next milestone. I want Anthony to focus on the group's theme work. I know it isn't encryption related, but it is relevant product knowledge for the next milestone, and having Anthony build that context is super valuable for the team."

"Ok, I will talk to Anthony and see how he feels about the project. I want to make sure he is good with the decision," Blaine's manager replies. "Otherwise, I think this looks good. I like how you have divided up the work for the team."

Meanwhile, based on input from different team POCs, Erica creates the overall timeline, including more detailed milestones for the V0 portion, and reviews the work with her PM. With the finalized project plan, Erica is ready to brief the VP-level leads she reports to and the CTO on the overall strategy, success criteria, and milestones.

V0 Timeline:

1. Infra (in parallel)

   a. Client infrastructure support for E2EE and new API endpoints for six months. With the first draft available by April

   b. Server infrastructure to support E2EE

2. UI design E2EE changes will be complete by early February.

3. Four months for client work to support new write paths and UI controls.

4. By July first, update data pipelines, and the Data Analytics team will compile essential metric collections for analysis, including a unified view of application performance.

5. In early September, we will begin the experimentation and testing process for rollout.

Notes on the Planning/Scoping Phase

We have reached the end of our theoretical project's scoping/planning phase. Some highlights from our planning phase are as follows:

1. Erica utilizes a well-thought-out project plan that follows the company's templates and recommended process. By following the company's templates, Erica ensures her project plan is easily understood by everyone. She then leverages the plan to drive discussions throughout the planning process. Throughout the process, she builds relationships through one-on-one (1:1) meetings and seeks feedback from individual stakeholders before presenting the final ideas. This way, she avoids surprises or dissenting opinions and creates a comprehensive design.

2. Set up 1:1 meetings and a weekly group cadence. 1:1 meetings are an important tool for getting feedback, developing personal relationships, and giving advice – which is difficult in group meetings. By scheduling 1:1's, Erica is ensuring she is building long-lasting relationships with her team and giving herself opportunities to provide mentorship to them.

3. Erica lays out time-bound goals for her subordinate leaders. This helps her to delegate successfully since she has built-in points in time to check in and ensure that team members are not falling behind.

4. Blaine is working to build his team by scheduling Anthony to work on themes. While this is a smaller project, he is helping build Anthony's knowledge in an essential area of the stack, preparing him to take on more scope in the future and allowing Blaine to take on more scope as the TL.

5. We can see across the levels that the TLs are very busy planning and scoping work for the team. Erica and Blaine play vital roles in unblocking the teams they are working with. While Erica purely focuses on the project at hand as a team tech lead, Blaine also works closely with his manager to ensure that all engineers on his team have sufficient scope and growth opportunities.

Jumping Back into Our Story...

Now that the overall goals of the project have been defined, the project is put in context of the long-term technical road map/architecture, team members are assigned, and the plan is outlined. The teams move into execution mode. To support the execution, Erica schedules weekly 1:1 meetings with each tech lead (TL) and biweekly sync meetings with crucial engineering and cross-functional partners to sync on progress, identify blockers, and ensure the project is on track.

For this, Blaine has worked closely with his manager and product manager to define a scheduled meeting cadence and high-priority work items, and his two senior engineers have broken down their smaller portions of the project into associated tasks and continue to oversee the work items for his team, review diffs, and help to unblock engineers.

Engineering development goes smoothly along with the underlying client infrastructure, allowing for a set of endpoints for Blaine's team to be exposed. During development, Blaine reviews a large amount of code for the teams and takes a complex portion of the project concerning rewriting the thread-view for the direct messaging component, and aligns with his team internally on connecting the new UI components with the underlying APIs.

At the next status meeting, Blaine provides his update: "Progress is on schedule; for iOS, we are ramping up end-to-end testing and ensuring that the features are tested on real data. We are also starting a task board to triage P0 or launch blocking bugs. So far, we haven't gotten any, but we still have to onboard more features for testing."

"That is good to hear," Erica replies, "for my update, I'm continuing to work with the Data Analytics and privacy teams to gain alignment for launch. We still need a list of company-critical metrics, and the privacy review is in the final stages with legal. Lastly, we need to push the launch date back one day to align with the marketing team's timeline. They want to run a few campaigns first and have a scheduled interview with a news outlet in the EU. If there are no other updates, I will let you all go. Thanks, everyone."

After the meeting, Blaine returns to his desk and sees a message from his PM. *Hey, did you see the recent manual testing results? It looks like QA is surfacing as a potential launch blocker.* Reviewing the task board, Blaine responds, "Oh, *interesting, there is a significant delay for users with many messages and contacts. This could definitely pose an issue to launch. I will have the team start to investigate the root cause."*

After replying to his PM, Blaine starts a group chat with Erica and the client infrastructure POC to inform them of the results.

Given the circumstances, Blaine raises this as a risk at the next weekly sync with Erica. "Further investigation shows that bootstrapping the underlying mailbox with E2EE is slow. From a product level, we have ascertained that the regression is not happening at our level. We believe this is infrastructure related; however, they are too busy to look into the internal sync protocol for the inbox loading."

"I see," Erica replies, "this is concerning since it may affect the rollout. After this meeting, I will follow up so we can get some more eyes on the problem." Immediately after, Erica finds her manager and Sally at their desk area: "Hi Sally, something concerning came up today. We may have a sizable regression at the client infra level. I think we need to get some engineers to look into this more. I'm curious if you can help us to review the problem with Blaine and find appropriate staffing."

"Yes, I can help with this. Let me connect with Blaine and then circle back with you later today."

Later that day, Sally comes back over to discuss.

"So this is definitely a big problem. I think we can have Garrick look into this. I spoke with him and his manager; he has the bandwidth and is interested in this type of work. He also has experience across infrastructure and product-level features and is a senior engineer with a proven track record of delivering high-value projects. I specifically mentioned that we will need to handle the improvements to the sync protocol and add additional logging so that the team can better monitor the regression in production."

"Awesome, glad this was easily staffable. In the meantime, I will continue working with the performance team to understand how they typically handle features that can regress performance. We must understand their framework for trading off startup regression for other metric wins."

Erica and her manager Matt, who is helping to drive the discussion, discovered that, unfortunately, the benefits of E2EE do not neatly fit into the increased engagement that the performance team typically uses as their trade-off measurement. Because of this, Erica does not feel she can resolve this on her own and raises these concerns to leadership so they can discuss how to measure this type of trade-off for E2EE, which is not seen as an engagement win, but a necessary product change. Meanwhile, Garrick continues to look into mitigating the problem.

While Erica continued to discuss the trade-offs around E2EE messaging performance regression with leadership and why it may not be possible to completely eliminate the regressions since we are essentially loading two inboxes for messaging Garrick was able to mitigate the issue. He found a way to mitigate the issue by loading fewer messages in the inbox and thread-view. This creates a product trade-off since more refreshes are required for clients with many threads and large thread histories. However, after discussing with Erica and Sally, they agree that this trade-off is worth it since the eventual plan is to cut over fully to E2EE.

With client performance regression for large inboxes mitigated, the teams proceed toward launch. Erica communicates this with the leadership team and begins to set up a joint experiment with the proper parameters to enable the different teams' required features for E2EE.

Additionally, Erica has pulled in members from the Data Analytics team to help ensure the team is checking the correct post-launch metrics. During these conversations, Erica and the Data Analytics team realized they could improve the experience by utilizing cluster testing. Cluster testing will help ensure that people who commonly message each other will all be included in the test so that they have people to message. Erica further defines the launch path feature flag and experiment setup as follows:

Version	Size	iOS	Android	Web	Infra
V0	10%	Default	Default	Default	Default
V1	10%	enable_e2ee	enable_e2ee	enable_e2ee	enable_e2ee read/write paths

Notes on the Execution/Testing Phase

1. During the execution and testing phase, the ground teams take center stage, and the leadership team, including Erica, takes a back seat.

2. As a ground-team TL, Blaine is implementing key features and leading the development of a small team.

3. Erica's role is still critical. She works behind the scenes to finalize the launch path, remove blockers, and resolve ambiguity.

4. Not just Erica but even ground-team TLs are focused on future portions of the SDLC. Here, we see Blaine is helping to ensure they properly test the features before release by scheduling employee dogfooding sessions.

5. Here, we introduce a new character, Sally. In our example, Sally is an executive assistant archetype who works with broader leadership to staff previously unsolved projects. Sally is critical in finding Garrick to work on the logging portion.

6. Garrick represents a fixer. He can dive deep into different areas of the stack and drive solutions to complex problems. This is one example of a fixer. A fixer can also lead a team for a specific project. For example, any TLs like Kelly or Steph could be a fixer archetype. Or they could be like Blaine, who is a team TL.

Jumping Back into Our Story...

For the product rollout, Erica defines an oncall schedule for engineers, sets up a dashboard for critical metric monitoring, and works to schedule internal communications as a heads-up in case anyone internally sees issues; they can direct them to Erica. Additionally, Erica monitors the experiment setup and uses the biweekly meeting with TLs to review launch metrics and track regressions.

In the following weekly meeting after the launch, Erica reviews the metrics with the team. "The intermediate metrics look good – I don't see any red flags either. I am concerned with the overall level of traffic. Fewer people are switching threads to utilize E2EE than expected. Is anyone on the Data Analytics team here? Will we be able to gather enough signal from this test?"

"Yes, I'm here; we have concerns as well. Given the low traffic, we do not have a large enough sample size to understand performance regressions across all devices. We can attempt to increase the experiment size; however, this will not fully mitigate the issue."

"Ok, let's boost traffic for now, and we can sync up offline on improving this for future iterations," Erica replies. After the meeting, Erica approaches Sally at their desk area.

"Hi Sally, do you have a minute to talk?" As Sally nods, Erica continues, "The traffic for the latest E2EE experiment is very low, and I do not think we will have adequate data across device types and geographic regions. Especially for geographic regions, we see most adoption coming from US/EU countries, with almost no adoption from LATAM. We will need to boost traffic more uniformly before cutting over to E2EE fully; otherwise, we will not have confidence in performance."

"This makes sense. Perhaps we can leverage the same dual write strategy we used before?" Sally says.

"Precisely my thoughts," Erica replies, "I think we will need to scope in the engineering effort for this as a hard dependency for cutover."

"This sounds great, but we still need to work on how to staff this project and further scoping on the timeline. I hope this does not delay the launch," Erica's manager Matt chimes in. "Sally, can you work with the other senior managers in the org to find an engineer with bandwidth and help set them up for this project?"

"Definitely, we will have plenty of time, given that most organizations are in the planning phase now. It should not be hard to help get this prioritized, especially given the project's importance," Sally replies.

Notes on the Deployment/Maintenance Phase

Erica's role as chief architect becomes increasingly important again in the deployment and maintenance phases. She helps to plan and monitor the overall rollout for success. Additionally, you can see how her work in previous phases comes to fruition. We see how she helps to handle and mitigate the potential for startup regressions and collaborates with other organizational leaders to stay one step ahead. Erica also demonstrates this in her conversations with Sally, where she discusses adding dual write testing to the road map for the next half.

While the example does not detail sub-TLs such as Blaine's role, they will serve a similar position to Erica's for their team, mainly ensuring that the launch goes smoothly via monitoring metrics, setting up alerting chains, and clearing any blockers to success. A good TL will catch configuration issues and other problems early on or before launch, speeding up the process long term.

Notes on the Case Study Roles and Archetypes

Archetypes

Chief Architect

We saw Erica, the chief architect, as she outlined the overall timeline and rollout plan to include coordination across all portions to ensure the launch goes smoothly. She works closely with her principal engineers to ensure that all project parts are accurately scoped and possess individual rollout timelines and metrics.

Erica embodies three critical behaviors for success as a senior engineer leader:

1. Owns the most complex part: At this level, coordinating all moving pieces and deciding the overall architecture flow.

2. Delegates to subordinates: Erica delegates to subordinate leaders. She also works with her manager to understand what level of mentorship to provide (helping to coach Blaine).

3. She balances the short-term needs of the project with the need for a cohesive long-term vision.

Regardless of her archetype, these three behaviors are critical for long-term success.

Tech Lead

We saw Blaine as a team TL delegate the different features and components to team members while finding additional scope with help from Sally for a senior engineer on the team (classified as a fixer). Blaine also plans for future work by giving Anthony (a senior engineer on his team) the themes project. Blaine knows Anthony's experience on this project will tie in to their future work.

Executive Assistant

As an executive assistant archetype, we saw Sally assisting in investigating and staffing the project. Sally works closely with the management/ leadership team on understanding progress and "hotspots" areas of scope that come up throughout the migration that are understaffed.

Fixer

The last major engineering archetype is a fixer. Garrick represented this role as he could work deeply in the stack without necessarily owning a team. While in this case Garrick acted alone, a fixer could also drive a small team on a new product or cross-cutting infrastructure feature.

Overall Notes

We also saw the team collaboratively owned the problem space. Erica has included spots in the project plan for others to contribute, including design for creating UI mockups, POCs to add links to their specific design docs, and a spot for the cryptography expert to add their portion (see the project plan in the appendix). Everyone contributed to driving the solution in planning and had specific scope to own during execution.

While the ownership was collaborative, there were still some disputes. Realistically no project is without conflict. In our example, the central conflict to resolve was around the startup regressions. Navigating the conversation of potentially regressing another team's critical metrics is a challenging conversation to have. Luckily in our example, the situation was easily resolved by pushing a fix; however, this could have escalated and needed more senior leadership to broker a contract. Senior leadership is required in these circumstances because both parties need to share a common goal, and that is more difficult further down the chain where parties will care more about individual goals such as shipping the launch or avoiding a regression.

Another source of conflict here could have been over the logging changes. Luckily in our example, the framework was flexible, and the client infra team could easily control the logs via access permissions. However, this could have become a much larger project if the access permission framework did not exist or the client infra team was unaware of it. This could have involved a lengthy back-and-forth with the privacy team and potentially delayed the launch.

Summary

Throughout our practical example, we see some senior engineer archetypes: tech lead (Blaine), architect (Erica), fixer (Garrick), and executive assistant (Sally). While roles sometimes overlap, we see how everyone, especially at higher levels, needs a deep understanding of technical concepts and people skills to resolve thorny conflicts and provide actionable mentorship to others. Some, such as Garrick, require more deep technical knowledge, while Sally leans into her people and organizational skills more but still must rely on her technical skills to guide projects. We can categorize these as their superpowers. Each has one, and each is unique. For Erica, it is her overall technical depth and breadth of knowledge in the stack. For Garrick, it is his deep technical knowledge and ability to fix problems others cannot. When you reach staff and principal levels, you will also need to find your superpower.

We also see how Erica fluidly moves through the SDLC steps, staying ahead of the team to ensure that the rollout and future planning items go well. This helps and provides subordinate leaders time to make their own plans. It also requires enough technical expertise to move quickly and stay ahead of subordinate leaders without working double the hours.

Irrespective of your archetype, mastering the art of integrating soft skills with engineering core competencies is pivotal in propelling both yourself and your career toward spearheading larger and more impactful projects like Erica. To develop these essential skills, you can effectively utilize all four parts of this book. First, enhance your technical expertise, and then broaden your knowledge base and refine your soft skills.

Completed Five-Year Plan

Migrate to E2EE
  Migrate the Photo Stream application to E2EE
  Team: Photo Stream Application
  Status: **Draft**
  Last Updated: Thursday, May 21, 2023

Problem Alignment

Due to broader industry trends and the continued push toward privacy-first experiences, we would like to move as much of the Photo Stream application as possible to utilize E2EE.

High-Level Approach

To facilitate the move to E2EE, we will start with a small feature set and move toward broader sections of the application. At each stage, we will include testing. Once we have reached parity with non-E2EE features, we will perform a hard cutover where all new experiences will use E2EE by default. For nonmessaging surfaces, we will transition the feed tab to show only fully connected users' content via E2EE shared keys and keep the Discover tab non-encrypted to support ease of open content sharing.

E. Vennaro, *iOS Development at Scale*, https://doi.org/10.1007/978-1-4842-9456-7

Goals

Milestone	Success Criteria	Rollout Plan
MVP – MVP feature set	Enable E2EE for 1:1 direct messages, including photos with minimal to no performance regressions	Usage is optional, so the experience will be gated behind a feature flag backed by an experiment and slowly rolled out to users after internal testing
V1 – expanded feature set	Enable E2EE features for groups and content sharing. Minimal to no performance regressions are required	Usage is optional, so the experience will be gated behind a feature flag backed by an experiment and slowly rolled out to users after internal testing
V2 – advanced E2EE features	Enable a tree-based system of asymmetric encryption keys to create an encrypted connected feed experience. Minimal to no performance regressions are required	Usage is optional, so the experience will be gated behind a feature flag backed by an experiment and slowly rolled out to users after internal testing
V3 – cutover and stabilization	Entirely switch all encryption-enabled modes to the default experience for users. Minimal to no performance regressions are required	Usage is no longer optional. Changes are gated behind a feature flag and experiment. Once the rollout is complete, 100% of the public on eligible application versions will use E2EE features

Review Problem Alignment

Reviewer	Team/Role	Status
Alex	Leadership team	Aligned
Corinne	VP product	Aligned
Carson	VP design	Aligned
Dale	VP data analytics	Aligned
Matt	Director Photo Stream	Aligned

Solution Alignment

Overall we will utilize the existing infrastructure for the migration, namely:

1. Utilize the current push-based messaging model.

2. Existing messaging infrastructure on mobile, including underlying shared C libraries.

3. Extend server-side infrastructure to support E2EE read/write paths and notifications.

4. Extend the client website to support E2EE.

5. Extend server-side infrastructure to support the necessary metadata, including themes.

In addition, we will need to extend and write new components at the product layer to support E2EE. In the following diagram, new components are labeled green, and components required for extension are in yellow.

For encryption, we will utilize the signal protocol, which provides the following:

1. The protocol provides confidentiality, integrity, authentication, participant consistency, destination validation, forward secrecy, postcompromise security (future secrecy), causality preservation, message unlinkability, message repudiation, participation repudiation, and asynchronicity.

2. Group message support includes speaker consistency, out-of-order resilience, dropped message resilience, computational equality, trust equality, subgroup messaging, and contractible and expandable membership.[1]

However, it does not provide

1. Anonymity preservation

2. Servers to relay messages and store public key material in addition to the properties provided by the one-to-one protocol

3. Handling of reactions, typing indicators, and other features associated with a rich messaging experience

We will build these items.

---

[1] N. Unger et al., "SoK: Secure Messaging," *2015 IEEE Symposium on Security and Privacy*, San Jose, CA, USA, 2015, pp. 232–249, doi: 10.1109/SP.2015.22.

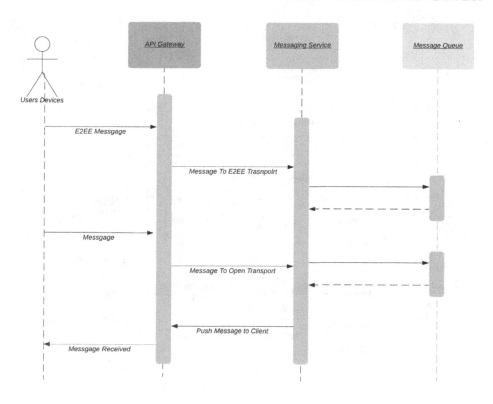

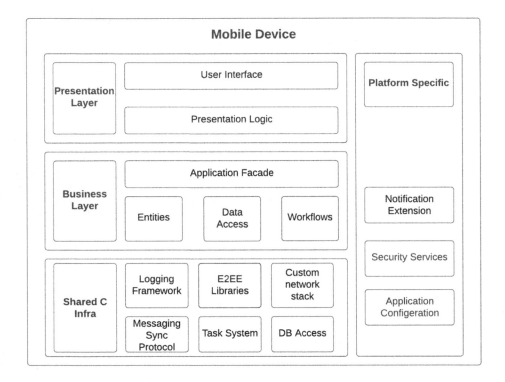

Key Scoping Documents for MVP Feature Set

POC	Role	Scoping Document
Blaine	iOS product	
Mike	Android product	
Steph	Mobile infra	
Kelly	Web product	
Tom	Back-end infra	

Future considerations:

1. Extend support for group messages.

2. Extend server support for tree-based nested encryption keys for multiple users and support for encrypted feed content.

3. Note: Ads will not be encrypted.

Key Flows

TODO: Insert mock to designs once ready from UI/UX design team.

Key Logic

Client

1. Extend underlying shared infrastructure library to include low-level Signal libraries to support cross-platform E2EE.

2. Support unified API to read and write to encrypted and open protocols seamlessly.

3. Support new product UI for E2EE experiences to ensure that the experience meets product standards.

4. Audit logging to ensure that no logging breaks the E2EE guarantee or any privacy/legal policies associated with E2EE.

5. Support notification flow for E2EE with E2EE encryption-approved notification text.

Server

1. Support storage read and write for E2EE data. Once a message is delivered, it must be deleted from the server.

2. Use the existing message queue system to deliver messages to all connected devices.

3. Use existing server infrastructure to store associated metadata.

Additionally for the server, we must cryptographically handle content for a connected feed. To do so, we will follow the following principle of indirection: to be authored by our back-end POC and cryptography expert.

Reviewer	Team/Role	Status
Matt	Manager	Approved
Arvin	CTO	Approved
Talia	Data analytics lead	Approved

Launch Plan

Date Column	Milestone	Success Criteria	Rollout Plan
2023-11-14	MVP – MVP feature set	Enable E2EE for 1:1 direct messages, including photos with minimal to no performance regressions	Usage is optional, so the experience will be gated behind a feature flag backed by an experiment and slowly rolled out to users after internal testing

(*continued*)

Date Column	Milestone	Success Criteria	Rollout Plan
2024-11-14	V1 – expanded feature set	Enable E2EE features for groups and content sharing. Minimal to no performance regressions are required	Usage is optional, so the experience will be gated behind a feature flag backed by an experiment and slowly rolled out to users after internal testing
2025-11-14	V2 – advanced E2EE features	Enable a tree-based asymmetric system of encryption keys to create an encrypted connected feed experience. Minimal to no performance regressions are required	Usage is optional, so the experience will be gated behind a feature flag backed by an experiment and slowly rolled out to users after internal testing
2026-11-14	V3 – cutover and stabilization	Fully switch all encryption-enabled modes to the default experience for users. Minimal to no performance regressions are required	Usage is no longer optional. Changes are gated behind a feature flag and experiment; once the rollout is complete, 100% of the public on eligible application versions will use E2EE features

Key Milestones

Target Date	Milestone	Description	Exit Criteria
2023-01-31	Begin execution	Wrap up project planning and enter execution mode	All teams have project plans submitted and approved by Erica
2023-02-28	UI mockups complete	Necessary to have UI mockups complete to provide the product teams enough time for implementation	Mockups for all critical flows completed by design teams and approved by both design and eng. leadership
2023-04-15	First draft API endpoints	The first draft of the server to client API endpoints must be finished by this time to allow for client team testing	Have available APIs for the product engineering teams to utilize for testing
2023-07-15	Data analytics pipelines updates	All pipelines are updated for specific E2EE metrics. And all privacy specifications are met	We have the ability to properly evaluate online experiments for E2EE without violating any privacy or legal commitments
2023-09-14	Internal org dogfooding	Internal testing within the org	No P0 bugs on a rolling seven-day basis
2023-10-14	Internal company dogfooding	Internal testing with the company	No P0 or P1 bugs on a rolling seven-day basis

(continued)

Target Date	Milestone	Description	Exit Criteria
2023-11-01	Begin experiment rollout	Begin MVP feature set rollout	Measure and monitor, only increase the rollout if no P0 bugs or regressions in key metrics are detected
2023-11-14	Launch MVP feature set	Rollout experiment to 100% public users	Measure and monitor
2024-11-14	V1 launch	TBD	TBD
2025-11-14	V2 launch	TBD	TBD
2026-11-14	V3 launch	TBD	TBD

Operational Checklist

Team	Requirements for Launch	Complete Y/N
Data analytics	1. Additional metric collections for E2EE 2. Holistic view of application performance	N
Marketing	1. Pre-launch publications 2. GTM plan	N
Design	1. Design mockups for new workflows	N
Privacy	1. Additional privacy requirements for E2EE 2. Ensure engineering solutions meet the privacy bar for launch	N
Legal	1. Understand the legal implications of E2EE and the risks that exist	N

Changelog

Date	Description
Jan 15, 2023	Updated architecture diagram to include the fact that the logging module will have to change

Open Questions

Index

A

A/B tests, 526
Access control lists (ACLs), 64
Access permission framework, 622
Actor model, 132, 152
Agile development cycle, 381
Agile method, 380
AI-based integration testing tool, 425
allPhoto's property, 248
American Statistical Association
    (ASA), 507
Apple ecosystem, 3, 25
Application architecture patterns,
    176, 180, 274, 566
Application design patterns,
    274, 276, 321
Application performance
    application growth, 448
    continuous testing/evaluation,
        452, 453
    data-driven approach, 439
    debugging problems, 448,
        449, 451
    engineers, 437
    funnel logging, 443
    intermediate metrics, 442
    monitoring/alerting, 445
    Occam's razor, 451, 452

    percentiles, 444, 445
    techniques, 437
    tools, 446, 447
    topline metrics, 439–442
    user experience, 438
Application release/maintenance
    large project, 529
    SDLC, 530
Application-wide architecture
        patterns, 179, 241
Archetypes, 623
    chief architect, 620, 621
    executive assistant, 621
    fixer, 622
    TL, 621
Architect (Erica), 623
Asynchronous function
        annotations, 131
Asynchronous programming, 111
Atomic, Consistent, Isolated, and
        Durable (ACID), 76
Automated integration testing, 173
Automatic reference counting (ARC)
    bugs, 44
    definition, 36
    developers, 36
    memory deallocation, 37, 38
    memory management, 37

© Eric Vennaro 2023
E. Vennaro, *iOS Development at Scale*, https://doi.org/10.1007/978-1-4842-9456-7

Printed in the United States
by Baker & Taylor Publisher Services